The Old Testament in the
Life of God's People

Elmer A. Martens

The Old Testament in the Life of God's People

Essays in Honor of
Elmer A. Martens

Edited by
JON ISAAK

Winona Lake, Indiana
EISENBRAUNS
2009

www.eisenbrauns.com

Library of Congress Cataloging-in-Publication Data

The Old Testament in the life of God's people : essays in honor of Elmer A.
  Martens / edited by Jon Isaak.
      p.   cm.
  Includes bibliographical references and indexes.
  ISBN 978-1-57506-158-0 (hardcover : alk. paper)
    1. Bible. O.T.—Criticism, interpretation, etc.   2. Bible. O.T.—Use.
  3. Bible. N.T.—Relation to the Old Testament.   4. Justice—Biblical teaching.
  5. Nature in the Bible.   6. Nature—Religious aspects.   7. Earth in the Bible.
  I. Isaak, Jon M., 1960–   II. Martens, E. A.
    BS1171.3.O44   2009
    221.6—dc22
                                                                    2008046543

Contents

Part 1

Christian Use of the Old Testament

Part 2

Aligning God's People with God's Call for Justice

Part 3

Addressing the Issue of Land in the Life of God's People

Preface

This book celebrates the contribution to OT theology by Prof. Elmer A. Martens, OT Professor Emeritus and President Emeritus of Mennonite Brethren Biblical Seminary, Fresno, California. It includes three essays written by Elmer himself, as well as fifteen others written by his former students, his colleagues, his friends, and even one of his professors! The essays are clustered around three topics—Christian use of the OT, aligning God's people with God's call for justice, and addressing the issue of land in the life of God's people—each of which is one of Elmer's particular interests. A biographical sketch and a list of the honoree's varied publications are included.

Elmer has had a productive career as teacher, author, and preacher—a career spanning almost six decades and five continents! Yet all talk of Elmer's numerous achievements must include the contribution of his wife, Phyllis. Phyll, as he likes to call her, has been a valued collaborator in all of his projects—as proofreader, dialogue partner, and soul mate.

After forty years of seminary teaching, Elmer is known to many as professor. He taught his signature class, OT theology, from 1968 to 2004 at MB Biblical Seminary, shaping an entire generation of preachers and Bible teachers. His OT theology textbook, *God's Design*, now in its third edition, continues to be used at the seminary as well as in translation in numerous other schools around the world.

Elmer's persona as mentor, advocate, and unwavering cheerleader is well attested. He consistently challenges practioners of biblical theology to attend to the "form and function" of the biblical text in the meaning-making enterprise of interpretation. His critique of the exegetical work of others is constructive—sometimes very direct, but always fair. He exudes enthusiastic support for former students in church and denominational ministries in both North America and elsewhere—regularly lecturing in places far from California, places where former students now serve.

Those of us who had him as our teacher remember how excited he could become over one of our ideas: often seeing the potential long before we did, ready with suggestions for turning a paper into a publication. Elmer began his professional life as a public school teacher and, even as a graduate school professor, retains his keen commitment to good pedagogy, good formation, and good mentoring.

For many, negotiating the gap between academy and church proves to be a challenge. Not so for Elmer. He models a happy relationship between scholarship and pulpit ministry. While producing publications for the academy, he also writes popular pieces for church periodicals. An avid columnist with prose that sparkles with clarity, elegance, and well-chosen words, he presents a bibliography that is impressive in scope. Known as an exceptional preacher (someone who preaches without notes), he is deeply appreciated for his service to the church, both locally and globally. Elmer is comfortable in the pulpit and in the classroom, and his love for the church and God's mission anchors all his endeavors.

As a scholar, Elmer exhibits all the characteristics of the professional academician: careful attention to detail, mastery of the field, unwavering focus, uncanny insight, great productivity, and rhetorically persuasive speech. In addition to these scholarly attributes, Elmer's energetic personality gives him a competitive edge. Whether it is to argue a theological point, to secure a better financial arrangement, or to make a game-winning move, Elmer loves the "cut and thrust" of debate. This sort of sparring is the "stuff of life" for Elmer, and life would be "oh-so-boring" without it. All of us who have come to cherish him (and still to disagree with him at points!) have found his rigor to be both stimulating and exemplary.

And so, Elmer, we offer this book to you as our attempt to recognize your love for the church, your impact on our lives, and your significant contribution to OT theology. Thank you. We salute you as scholar, mentor, and churchman.

—Jon Isaak, Festschrift editor
Associate Professor of New Testament
Mennonite Brethren Biblical Seminary
Fresno, California

Elmer A. Martens:
A Biographical Sketch

PHYLLIS MARTENS

My husband would be considered a high-energy person. From the time he was born on a farm in Main Centre, Saskatchewan, on August 12, 1930, he has been on the move. By the age of eleven, he was harrowing a field with a team of horses.

After grade school in a one-room country school, and high school, where he competed successfully in oratorical contests, he went off to Bethany Bible School in Hepburn, Saskatchewan. It was there that he decided to give himself over to God for what would probably be a life of Christian ministry of some sort. Elmer was one of the first in his farming community to go on to university. He received his Bachelor of Arts from the University of Saskatchewan in Saskatoon, with majors in history and English. With energy to spare, he took summer classes at the University of Manitoba to earn a Bachelor of Education degree in 1956. His first job was finishing someone's teaching year in a one-room country school near Stewart Valley, Saskatchewan. The next year he taught social studies to grades 7–12 in a four-room school.

Meanwhile, I was busy growing up in India, daughter of missionaries J. N. C. and Anna Hiebert, going to high school in Reedley, California, and then to Tabor College in Hillsboro, Kansas, and the University of Kansas for a degree in English.

We met when Elmer came to California to attend the Mennonite Brethren Biblical Seminary the year it opened, 1955, in Fresno. I was teaching English at Pacific Bible Institute. Because for that one year both schools met in the same building, and because we both enrolled in a seminary class taught by Dr. G. W. Peters, we came to know each other. Incidentally, Dr. Peters was the one who encouraged Elmer to leave a lucrative job of teaching to study at the seminary: "God is no man's debtor," he told Elmer. Dr. Peters was an extremely good, often highly provocative teacher.

We were married in 1956. Two years later Elmer graduated from the seminary and accepted the pastorate at the Butler Avenue Mennonite Brethren

Church in Fresno, California. He was a young but very energetic pastor. One of his sermons earned him a free trip to Israel because he had placed first in a national sermon-writing contest sponsored by the National Association of Evangelicals. The church grew quickly beyond the original nucleus; and so did our family. We had four children in those eight years, in the order boy-girl-boy-girl—a boy and a girl with blue eyes, a boy and a girl with brown eyes. Talk about organization!

Doctoral studies at Claremont Graduate School took the family to southern California. Elmer bicycled to school every day in spite of a leg still weak from an unexpected but successful surgery for melanoma. He enrolled in the Department of Philosophical Theology with Dr. John Cobb. Repeated visits from Dr. J. B. Toews, then president of the Mennonite Brethren Biblical Seminary in Fresno, led him to change his major to Old Testament studies. At the time (and now in retrospect), he saw this move as responding to God's purposes for him. The most influential faculty member at Claremont was, he says, Dr. Rolf Knierim, a forceful, inspiring, and very demanding professor recently arrived from Germany. His doctoral dissertation, under the direction of Dr. William Brownlee, a man he much admired, was on the topic "Motivations for the Promise of Israel's Restoration to the Land in Jeremiah and Ezekiel."

We moved back to Fresno in 1970 so that Elmer could begin teaching at the seminary. Little did we know that he would teach there for more than 35 years.

His important contribution to the seminary was to move it toward biblical theology, more compatible with Anabaptism than systematic theology. He tested the manuscript of his first book, *God's Design,* on a succession of students. This book, as well as a commentary on Jeremiah, was completed while he served as president of the school from 1977 to 1986. During this time he maintained a teaching schedule of two courses per semester and was frequently a speaker at Bible conferences in the supporting churches in Canada and the U.S.A.

On a two-year leave of absence from the school (1986–88), Elmer taught at Fuller Seminary in Pasadena, California, and at Trinity Evangelical Divinity School in Deerfield, Illinois. We spent roughly six months abroad during each of those years: at Union Biblical Seminary, India, and Nairobi Evangelical Graduate School, Kenya. These experiences ignited a passion for teaching the OT outside the U.S.A. Even before retirement in 1996, and certainly thereafter, he alone or the two of us together have been involved in teaching stints, short and long—seminary courses and doctoral programs in India, Japan, Korea, China, Russia, Kenya, Congo, Brazil, and Paraguay.

Elmer has especially enjoyed his 20-year association with the editorial council of the Believers Church Bible Commentary, which appointed him OT editor of the commentary series, published by Herald Press. His volume on Jeremiah not only was the first to appear, but it became the template for the series. He does not see himself as a front-running scholar but more as a scholar–broker, sharing with the church constituency the biblical scholarly work of others. My part in his writing career has been to edit his books and articles, using my experience from teaching grammar and writing.

For several years Elmer was program chair for the annual meetings of the Institute for Biblical Research. Apart from strong involvements in the local church (our denomination is Mennonite Brethren) and in the global church, Elmer has made his contribution as a member of numerous boards, including the international board of mission (1985–96) and the committee that produced the *Worship Hymnal* (1971).

Elmer has supported me in my professional pursuits as a creator of teaching games for learning English as a second language. Following our retirement, our interest in international students led to our providing housing for students from the nearby university. Other community involvements include mediation in the Victor Offender Reconciliation Program (VORP) and neighborhood Bible studies. Outdoor camping has been a stable recreational activity through the years.

Elmer's energy these days goes into writing and activities with grandkids. We celebrated our 50th wedding anniversary in August 2006, and humbly acknowledge God's abundant grace toward us and our family.

Abbreviations

General

AAR	American Academy of Religion
ANE	ancient Near East(ern)
JPSV	Jewish Publication Society Version
KJV	King James Version
LXX	Septuagint
MB	Mennonite Brethren
MT	Masoretic Text
NASB	New American Standard Bible
NEB	New English Bible
NIV	New International Version
NT	New Testament
NJPSV	Tanakh: The Holy Scriptures. The New JPS Translation according to the Traditional Hebrew Text
NRSV	New Revised Standard Version
OT	Old Testament
RSV	Revised Standard Version
SBL	Society of Biblical Literature
TNIV	Today's New International Version
TNK/TaNaK	Tanakh: The Jewish Publication Society Bible
WCC	World Council of Churches

Reference Works

AB	Anchor Bible
ABD	*Anchor Bible Dictionary.* Edited by David N. Freedman. 6 vols. New York: Doubleday, 1992
ABR	*Australian Biblical Review*
ACCS	Ancient Christian Commentary on Scripture
ANET	*Ancient Near Eastern Texts Relating to the Old Testament.* Edited by J. B. Prichard. 3rd ed. Princeton: Princeton University Press, 1969
ATD	Das Alte Testament Deutsch
AThR	*Anglican Theological Review*
AUSS	*Andrews University Seminary Studies*
BA	*Biblical Archaeologist*
BASOR	*Bulletin of the American Schools of Oriental Research*
BBR	*Bulletin of Biblical Research*

xiii

BBRSup	Bulletin of Biblical Research Supplement
BDB	Brown, F., S. R. Driver, and C. A. Briggs. *A Hebrew and English Lexicon of the Old Testament*. Oxford: Oxford University Press, 1907
BETL	Bibliotheca ephemeridum theologicarum lovaniensium
BHT	Beiträge zur historischen Theologie
BibInt	*Biblical Interpretation*
BIS	Biblical Interpretation Series
BJRL	*Bulletin of the John Rylands University Library of Manchester*
BSac	*Bibliotheca sacra*
BTB	*Biblical Theology Bulletin*
BWA(N)T	Beiträge zur Wissenschaft vom Alten (und Neuen) Testament
BZ	*Biblische Zeitschrift*
CBQ	*Catholic Biblical Quarterly*
CurTM	*Currents in Theology and Mission*
DCH	*Dictionary of Classical Hebrew*. Edited by D. J. A. Clines, P. R. Davies, and J. W. Rogerson. 5 vols. Sheffield: Sheffield Academic Press, 1993–2001
DNWSI	Hoftijzer, J., and K. Jongeling. *Dictionary of the North-West Semitic Inscriptions*. 2 vols. Leiden: Brill, 1995
DSD	*Dead Sea Discoveries*
EvQ	*Evangelical Quarterly*
EvT	*Evangelische Theologie*
ExpTim	*Expository Times*
HALOT	Koehler, L., W. Baumgartner, and J. J. Stamm. *The Hebrew and Aramaic Lexicon of the Old Testament*. Translated and edited under the supervision of M. E. J. Richardson. 5 vols. Leiden: Brill, 1994–2000
HAT	Handbuch zum Alten Testament
HSM	Harvard Semitic Monographs
HTR	*Harvard Theological Review*
HUCA	*Hebrew Union College Annual*
ICC	International Critical Commentary
IEJ	*Israel Exploration Journal*
Int	*Interpretation*
ISBE	*International Standard Bible Encyclopedia*. Edited by G. W. Bromiley. 4 vols. Grand Rapids: Eerdmans, 1979–88
JBL	*Journal of Biblical Literature*
JETS	*Journal of the Evangelical Theological Society*
JJS	*Journal of Jewish Studies*
JQR	*Jewish Quarterly Review*
JR	*Journal of Religion*
JSNT	*Journal for the Study of the New Testament*
JSNTSup	Journal for the Study of the New Testament: Supplement Series
JSOT	*Journal for the Study of the Old Testament*
JSOTSup	Journal for the Study of the Old Testament: Supplement Series
JSPSup	Journal for the Study of the Pseudepigrapha: Supplement Series
NAC	New American Commentary

NCB	New Century Bible
NIB	*The New Interpreter's Bible.* Edited by Leander Keck et al. 12 vols. Nashville: Abingdon, 1994
NIDNTT	*New International Dictionary of New Testament Theology.* Edited by Colin Brown. 4 vols. Grand Rapids: Zondervan, 1975–85
NICNT	New International Commentary on the New Testament
NICOT	New International Commentary on the Old Testament
NIDB	*The New Interpreter's Dictionary of the Bible.* Edited by Katharine Doob Sakenfeld et al. 5 vols. Nashville: Abingdon, 2006–
NIDOTTE	*New International Dictionary of Old Testament Theology and Exegesis.* Edited by Willem A. VanGemeren. 5 vols. Grand Rapids: Zondervan, 1997
NJBC	*The New Jerome Biblical Commentary.* Edited by R. E. Brown et al. Englewood Cliffs, NJ: Prentice Hall, 1990
NovT	*Novum Testamentum*
NSBT	New Studies in Biblical Theology
NTS	*New Testament Studies*
OBO	Orbis biblicus et orientalis
OBT	Overtures to Biblical Theology
OTL	Old Testament Library
SemeiaSt	Semeia Studies
SJOT	*Scandinavian Journal of the Old Testament*
SJT	*Scottish Journal of Theology*
STDJ	Studies on the Texts of the Desert of Judah
TDNT	*Theological Dictionary of the New Testament.* Edited by G. Kittel and G. Friedrich. Translated by G. W. Bromiley. 10 vols. Grand Rapids: Eerdmans, 1964–76
TDOT	*Theological Dictionary of the Old Testament.* Edited by G. J. Botterweck and H. Ringgren. Translated by J. T. Willis, G. W. Bromiley, and D. E. Green. Grand Rapids, Eerdmans, 1974–
ThTo	*Theology Today*
TLOT	*Theological Lexicon of the Old Testament.* Edited by E. Jenni, with assistance from C. Westermann. Translated by M. E. Biddle. 3 vols. Peabody, MA: Hendrickson, 1997
TRE	*Theologische Realenzyklopädie.* Edited by G. Krause and G. Müller. Berlin: de Gruyter, 1977–2007
TRu	*Theologische Rundschau*
TS	*Theological Studies*
TWOT	*Theological Wordbook of the Old Testament.* Edited by R. Laird Harris, Gleason L. Archer, and Bruce Waltke. 2 vols. Chicago: Moody, 1981
VT	*Vetus Testamentum*
VTSup	Supplements to Vetus Testamentum
WBC	Word Biblical Commentary
WMANT	Wissenschaftliche Monographien zum Alten und Neuen Testament
WTJ	*Westminster Theological Journal*
ZAW	*Zeitschrift für die alttestamentliche Wissenschaft*

Publications by Elmer A. Martens

Books, Edited Volumes, and Dissertations

Emil Brunner's Concept of the Bible. B.Div. Thesis. Mennonite Brethren Biblical Seminary, Fresno, CA, 1958.

Motivations for the Promise of Israel's Restoration to the Land in Jeremiah and Ezekiel. Ph.D. Dissertation. Claremont Graduate School, Claremont, CA, 1972.

God's Design: A Theology of the Old Testament. Grand Rapids: Baker, 1981 = *Plot and Purpose in Old Testament*. Leicester: InterVarsity, 1981. 2nd edition, 1994. 3rd edition, N. Richland Hills, TX: Bibal, 1998. Korean Translation, 1987. Russian Translation, 1995.

Jeremiah. Believers Church Bible Commentary. Scottdale, PA: Herald, 1986.

The Flowering of Old Testament Theology: A Reader in Twentieth-Century Old Testament Theology, 1930–1990. Edited with B. C. Ollenburger and G. F. Hasel. Sources for Biblical and Theological Study 1. Winona Lake, IN: Eisenbrauns, 1992.

Old Testament Theology. Institute of Biblical Research Bibliographies 13. Grand Rapids: Baker, 1997.

War in the Bible and Terrorism in the Twenty-First Century. BBRSup 2. Edited with Richard S. Hess. Winona Lake, IN: Eisenbrauns, 2008.

Chapters in Books

"Facing the Mission of the Church at Home." Pages 178–204 in *The Church in Mission*. Edited by A. J. Klassen. Fresno, CA: Board of Christian Literature, 1967.

"Realizing the Vision through Biblical Theology." Pages 35–40 in *The Seminary Story: Twenty Years of Education in Ministry*. Edited by A. J. Klassen. Fresno, CA: Mennonite Brethren Biblical Seminary, 1975.

"Wisdom Teachers and Priests in the Old Testament and Now." Pages 3–20 in *Called To Teach*. Edited by David Ewert. Perspectives on Mennonite Life and Thought 3. Fresno, CA: Center for Mennonite Brethren Studies, 1980.

"Immanuel Kant." Pages 161–64 in *The Cloud of Witnesses: Profiles of Church Leaders*. Edited by J. C. Wenger. Harrisonburg, VA: Eastern Mennonite Seminary, 1981.

"God's Goal Is Shalom" and "The Lord Is a Warrior." Pages 25–34 and 35–44 in *The Power of the Lamb*. Edited by John E. Toews and Gordon Nickel. Winnipeg, MB: Kindred, 1986.

"Narrative Parallelism and Message in Jeremiah 34–38." Pages 33–49 in *Early Jewish and Christian Exegesis*. Edited by Craig Evans and William F. Stinespring. Atlanta: Scholars Press, 1987.

"From Text to Sermon [Isaiah 40]." Pages 11–27 in *The Bible and the Church: Essays in Honour of Dr. David Ewert*. Edited by A. J. Dueck, H. J. Giesbrecht, and V. G. Shillington. Winnipeg, MB: Kindred, 1987.

"Jeremiah's 'Lord of Hosts' and a Theology of Mission." Pages 83–97 in *Reflection and Projection: Missiology at the Threshold of 2001*. Edited by Hans Kasdorf and Klaus Müller. Bad Liebenzell: Liebenzeller Mission, 1988.

"Jeremiah" and "Lamentations." Pages 515–50 and 551–58 in *Evangelical Commentary on the Bible*. Edited by Walter A. Elwell. Grand Rapids: Baker, 1989. Repr. in *Baker Commentary on the Bible*, 2001.

"Biblical Theology and Normativity." Pages 19–35 in *So Wide a Sea: Essays on Biblical and Systematic Theology*. Edited by B. C. Ollenburger. Text-Reader Series 4. Elkhart, IN: Institute of Mennonite Studies, 1991.

"The Multicolored Landscape of Old Testament Theology." Pages 43–57 in *The Flowering of Old Testament Theology: A Reader in Twentieth-Century Old Testament Theology, 1930–1990*. Edited by B. C. Ollenburger, Elmer A. Martens, and Gerhard F. Hasel. Winona Lake, IN: Eisenbrauns, 1992.

"Land and Lifestyle." Pages 298–320 in *The Flowering of Old Testament Theology: A Reader in Twentieth-Century Old Testament Theology, 1930–1990*. Edited by B. C. Ollenburger, Elmer A. Martens, and Gerhard F. Hasel. Winona Lake, IN: Eisenbrauns, 1992. Reprinted as pages 222–41 in *Old Testament Theology: Flowering and Future*. Edited by Ben C. Ollenburger. Winona Lake, IN: Eisenbrauns, 2004.

"Adam Named Her Eve." Pages 31–45 in *Your Daughters Shall Prophecy: Women in Ministry in the Church*. Edited by John E. Toews, Valerie Rempel, and Katie Funk Wiebe. Winnipeg, MB: Kindred, 1992.

"The Oscillating Fortunes of 'History' within Old Testament Theology." Pages 313–40 in *Faith, Tradition, and History: Old Testament Historiography in Its Near Eastern Context*. Edited by A. R. Millard, James K. Hoffmeier, and David W. Baker. Winona Lake, IN: Eisenbrauns, 1994.

"Yahweh's Ecotheology." Pages 234–48 in *Problems in Biblical Theology: Essays in Honor of Rolf Knierim*. Edited by H. T. C. Sun and K. L. Eades, with James M. Robinson and Garth I. Moller. Grand Rapids: Eerdmans, 1996.

"The Flowering and Floundering of Old Testament Theology." Pages 172–84 in vol. 1 of *NIDOTTE*. Edited by Willem A. VanGemeren. 5 vols. Grand Rapids:

Zondervan, 1997. Reprinted in *Direction* 16/2 (1997) 61–79. Reprinted, pages 169–81 in *A Guide to Old Testament Theology and Exegesis*. Edited by Willem A. VanGemeren. Grand Rapids: Zondervan, 1999.

"Numbers, Theology of." Pages 985–91 in vol. 4 of *NIDOTTE*. Edited by Willem A. VanGemeren. 5 vols. Grand Rapids: Zondervan, 1997. Reprinted in *Direction* 29/1 (2000) 54–63.

"Ezekiel's Contribution to a Biblical Theology of Mission." Pages 46–57 in *Die Mission der Theologie: Festschrift für Hans Kasdorf zum 70 Geburtstag*. Edited by S. Holthaus and Klaus Müller. Bonn: Verlag für Kultur und Wissenschaft, 1998. Reprinted in *Direction* 28/1 (1999) 75–84.

"God, Justice and Religious Pluralism." Pages 46–63 in *Confident Witness in Our Pluralistic World*. Edited by David W. Shenk and Linford Stutzman. Scottdale, PA: Herald, 1999.

"Nahum, Habakkuk, Zephaniah." Pages 448–518 in *The Old Testament Study Bible: Daniel–Malachi*. Springfield, MO: World Library Press, 1999.

"The Way of Wisdom: Conflict Resolution in Biblical Narrative." Pages 75–90 in *The Way of Wisdom*. Edited by J. I. Packer and Sven K. Soderlund. Grand Rapids: Zondervan, 2000.

"Reaching for a Biblical Theology of the Whole Bible." Pages 83–101 in *Reclaiming the Old Testament: Essays in Honour of Waldemar Janzen*. Edited by Gordon Zerbe. Winnipeg, MB: Canadian Mennonite Bible College Publications, 2001.

"The History of Religion, Biblical Theology and Exegesis." Pages 177–99 in *Interpreting the Old Testament: A Guide for Exegesis*. Edited by Craig C. Broyles. Grand Rapids: Baker, 2001.

"Jeremiah and Lamentations." Pages 295–593 in vol. 8 of *Cornerstone Biblical Commentary*. Wheaton, IL: Tyndale, 2005.

"The People of God." Pages 225–53 in *Central Themes in Biblical Theology: Mapping Unity in Diversity*. Edited by Scott J. Hafemann and Paul R. House. Grand Rapids: Baker, 2007.

"Toward Shalom: Absorbing the Violence." Pages 33–58 in *War in the Bible and Terrorism in the Twenty-First Century*. BBRSup 2. Winona Lake, IN: Eisenbrauns, 2008.

Articles in Periodicals

"Tribute to D. Edmond Hiebert." *Direction* 4/1 (1975) 265.

"The Promise of the Land to Israel." *Direction* 5/2 (1976) 8–13.

"The Problem of Old Testament Ethics." *Direction* 6/2 (1977) 23–25.

"Tackling Old Testament Theology." *JETS* 20 (1977) 123–32.

"Interpreting the Parables: A Case Study." *Direction* 10/2 (198l) 26–28.

"Preaching from the Old Testament: A Bibliographic Essay." *Direction* 11/2 (1982) 30–39.

"Psalm 73: A Corrective to a Modern Misunderstanding." *Direction* 12/4 (1983) 15–26.

"Jeremiah: Relevant for the Eighties." *Direction* 15/1 (1986) 3–13.

"The Pink Slip and the DMV [Case Study]." *Direction* 18/1 (1989) 3–4.

"Spirituality and Environment in Hosea." *ACTS Theological Journal* 4 (1991) 317–39.

"Embracing the Law: A Biblical Theological Perspective." *BBR* 2 (1992) 1–28.

"Forward to the Garden." *Direction* 21/2 (1992) 27–36.

"Tribute to Gerhard Hasel." *Journal of the Adventist Theological Society* 6/1 (1995) 93–94.

"Accessing the Theological Readings of a Biblical Book." *AUSS* 34 (1996) 233–49.

"The Shape of an OT Theology for a Post Modern Culture." *Direction* 25/2 (1996) 5–15.

"Publications by Elmer A. Martens." *Direction* 25/2 (1996) 73–85.

"How is the Christian to Construe Old Testament Law?" *BBR* 12 (2002) 199–216.

"Moving from Scripture to Doctrine." *BBR* 15 (2005) 77–103.

"Allen Guenther, the Scholar." *Direction* 35/1 (2006) 91–94.

"Impulses to Global Mission in Isaiah." *Direction* 35/1 (2006) 59–69.

"Impulses to Mission in Isaiah: An Intertextual Exploration." *BBR* 17 (2007) 215–39.

"Old Testament Theology since Walter C. Kaiser, Jr." *JETS* 50 (2007) 673–91.

Contributions to Dictionaries, Handbooks, and Encyclopedias

Word Studies on *bhl* 'disturb', *bhm* 'beast', *bô'* 'enter', *bûz* 'despise', *bûs* 'trample down', *bāmâ* 'ridge, high place', *bēn* 'son', *bqr* 'seek, cattle', *ṣrʿ* 'be diseased of skin', and eight shorter entries. *TWOT.*

Articles on "Accept," "Ablutions," "Alms," "Anoint," "Appeal," "Clean," "Freedom," "Hospitality," "Jubilee," "Justice," "Justice of God," "Poor," "Slave," "Suffering," and "Unclean" in *Nelson's Illustrated Bible Dictionary: An Authoritative One-Volume Reference Work on the Bible, with Full Color Illustrations.* Edited by Herbert Lockyer. Nashville: Thomas Nelson, 1986.

"Biblical Theology." Pages 83–84 in vol. 5 of *Mennonite Encyclopedia.* Scottdale, PA: Herald, 1990.

"God, Names of," "Day of the Lord, God, Christ, The," "Jeremiah, Theology of," "Lamentations, Theology of," "Praise," "Remnant," in *Evangelical Dictionary of Biblical Theology.* Edited by Walter A. Elwell. Grand Rapids, MI: Baker, 1996.

Word Studies on *'pq* 'gain composure', *bĕrîaḥ* 'bars', *dgl* 'lift the banner', *degel* 'banner', *ḥsm* 'muzzle', *ḥśk* 'refrain', *ṭbl* 'immerse', *ʿmd* 'stand', *tʿh* 'roam', *kwn* 'stand firm', *kbs* 'pound, beat', *mnʿ* 'withhold', *ndd* 'retreat', *nēs* 'banner', *nṣb* 'stand', *swr* 'turn aside', *ṣl* 'hesitate', *peh* 'mouth', *pnh* 'turn around', *plh* 'be treated differently', *rḥṣ* 'wash', *rĕmîyyâ* 'slackness', *śwb* 'repent, turn', *tʿh* 'wander off', and twenty-eight shorter entries. *NIDOTTE.* Edited by Willem A. VanGemeren. 5 vols. Grand Rapids: Zondervan, 1997.

"Jeremiah," "Baruch," "Gedaliah," and "Numbers, Theology of." *NIDOTTE.* Edited by Willem A. VanGemeren. 5 vols. Grand Rapids: Zondervan, 1997.

"Eichrodt, Walther (1890–1978)." Pages 482–87 in *Historical Handbook of Major Biblical Interpreters.* Edited by Donald K. McKim. Downers Grove, IL: InterVarsity, 1998. Reprinted, pages 404–9 in *Dictionary of Major Biblical Interpreters.* Edited by Donald K. McKim. Downers Grove, IL: InterVarsity, 2007.

"Sin, Guilt." Pages 764–78 in *Dictionary of the Old Testament: Pentateuch.* Edited by T. Desmond Alexander and David W. Baker. Downers Grove, IL: InterVarsity, 2003.

"Biblical Theology." Pages 109–11 in *Global Dictionary of Theology*. Edited by William A. Dyrness and Veli-Matti Kärkkäinen. Downers Grove, IL: InterVarsity, 2008.
"Community." Pages 189–91 in *Global Dictionary of Theology*. Edited by William A. Dyrness and Veli-Matti Kärkkäinen. Downers Grove, IL: InterVarsity, 2008.

Book Reviews

Biblical Theology I by C. Lehman. *Direction* 2/3 (1973) 88–89.

Understanding the Old Testament by O. J. Lace, ed., and *The Making of the Old Testament* by E. B. Mellor, ed. *Christian Scholar's Review* 3 (1974) 291–93.

No Place to Stop Killing by N. Wingert. *Christian Leader* (April 30, 1974) 24.

A Commentary on Genesis by H. G. Stigers. *Christian Leader* (January 4, 1977) 16.

Qumran and the History of the Biblical Text by F. M. Cross and S. Talmon, eds. *Christian Scholar's Review* 8 (1977) 258–60.

The Prophets and the Powerless by J. Limburg. *Theological Students Fellowship News and Reviews* (January 1979) 17.

Inerrancy and Common Sense by R. Nicole and J. R. Michaels, eds. *Christian Leader* (August 12, 1980) 12–13.

Opening the Old Testament by H. R. Cowles. *Mennonite Brethren Herald* (October 9, 1981) 26.

Grace and Faith in the Old Testament by R. M. Hals. *JBL* 101 (1982) 144.

The Land by Walter Brueggemann. *Direction* 11/4 (1982) 38–40.

Essays on the Patriarchal Narratives by A. R. Millard and D. J. Wiseman, eds. *JETS* 25 (1982) 240–41.

Old Testament Survey: The Message, Form and Background of the Old Testament by W. S. LaSor, D. A. Hubbard, and F. W. Bush. *Theological Students Fellowship Bulletin* 6/5 (1983) 19–20.

Schoepfer des Himmels und der Erde: Ein Beitrag zur Theologie des Jeremiabuches by Helga Weippert. *JBL* 102 (1983) 471–72.

The Authoritative Word by D. McKim, ed. *Mennonite Brethren Herald* (February 10, 1984) 34.

Ezekiel 1–20: A New Translation with Introduction and Commentary by M. Greenberg. *Christian Scholar's Review* 14 (1984) 63–64.

The Use of the Old Testament in the New by W. C. Kaiser, Jr. *Theological Students Fellowship Bulletin* 10/1 (1987) 34–35.

Understanding the Atonement for the Mission of the Church by John Driver. *Festival Quarterly* (Winter 1987) 38.

New Testament Ethics by Dale Goldsmith. *Mission Focus* 18/2 (1990) 28.

The Canon of Scripture by F. F. Bruce. *Christian Scholar's Review* 20 (1990) 191–93.

Introducing the Old Testament by Richard Coggins. *Int* 46 (1992) 86.

Upon the Types of the Old Testament by Edward Taylor. *Christian Scholar's Review* 22 (1992) 103–4.

Old Testament Theology: Essays on Structure, Theme, Text by Walter Brueggemann. *Int* 48 (1994) 191.

Studies in Old Testament Theology by R. L. Hubbard, R. K. Johnston, and R. P. Meye, eds. *Themelios* 20/3 (1995) 22.

Covenant: God's Purpose; God's Plan by John H. Walton. *JETS* 39 (1996) 635.

The Task of Old Testament Theology: Substance, Method and Cases by Rolf Knierim. *JETS* 41 (1998) 331–33.

Old Testament Theology (2 vols.) by Horst Dietrich Preuss. *JETS* 42 (1999) 704–6.

Theology of the Old Testament: Testimony, Dispute, Advocacy by Walter Brueggemann. *JETS* 42 (1999) 707–9.

The Old Testament and the Significance of Jesus: Embracing Change, Maintaining Christian Identity by Fredrick C. Holmgren. *Themelios* 25/2 (2000) 66–67.

Symbol and Rhetoric in Ecclesiastes: The Place of HEBEL *in Qohelet's Work* by Douglas Miller. *Direction* 33/1 (2004) 110–11.

What Have They Done to the Bible? A History of Modern Biblical Interpretation by J. Sandys-Wunsch. *JETS* 49 (2006) 582–84.

Encountering the Old Testament: A Christian Survey by Bill T. Arnold and Bryan E. Beyer. *Review of Biblical Literature* (2008) [http://www.bookreviews.org/].

Bible Translation Committees

New American Standard Bible (translation team), 1971.

New King James Version (Habakkuk), 1979.

International Children's Bible (Jeremiah), 1986.

New Living Translation (Jeremiah), 1996.

Editorial Work

Worship Hymnal (with hymnal committee). Winnipeg, MB: General Conference of the Mennonite Brethren Churches, 1966–71.

Editor (Old Testament). Believers Church Bible Commentary. Scottdale, PA: Herald, 1981–2005.

Editor. *Direction*, 1989–1995.

Editor (with Peter Klassen). *Knowing and Living Your Faith: A Study of the Confession of Faith* (International Community of Mennonite Brethren). Winnipeg, MB: Kindred, 2008.

Case Studies (available from the Case Study Institute)

"The Mennonites and Capital Punishment," 1977.

"The Circle Church and the Threatened Teachers Strike," 1977.

"Getting It Biblically Straight about the Middle East," 1977.

"The Prophet's Letter [Jeremiah 27–29]," 1977.

"Zerubbabel: To Build or Not to Build the Temple," 1977.

"The Aberdeen Heresy: Professor Smith and the Pentateuchal Problem," 1978.

"Parable Interpretation: Western or Eastern Style," 1980.

Column *"Window on the Bible,"* **Christian Leader, 1975–82**

"New Year's in April." *Christian Leader* (February 4, 1975) 15.

"Those Deceptive Patriarchs." *Christian Leader* (February 18, 1975) 17.

"The Bible and Flying Saucers." *Christian Leader* (March 4, 1975) 17.

"The Canaanites and Playboy Philosophy." *Christian Leader* (March 18, 1975) 17.

"Loyalty and Ancient Political Treaties." *Christian Leader* (April 1, 1975) 17.

"Ark Fever." *Christian Leader* (April 15, 1975) 17.

"A Remarkable Archaeological Find." *Christian Leader* (April 12, 1977) 17.

"Handmaid, a Meal and a Deal." *Christian Leader* (April 26, 1977) 17.

"Canaanite Songs, Gods and Goddesses." *Christian Leader* (May 10, 1977) 11.

"Hezekiah's Tunnel." *Christian Leader* (May 24, 1977) 17.

"The Oldest Hebrew Letters." *Christian Leader* (June 7, 1977) 17.

"A Divorce Settlement at Elephantine." *Christian Leader* (July 5, 1977) 23.

"Some Messianic Surprises." *Christian Leader* (December 5, 1978) 18.

"The Messiah in the Old Testament." *Christian Leader* (December 19, 1978) 17.

"Covenant? Yes! Contract? No!" *Christian Leader* (July 31, 1979) 15.

"Spotlight on Nations." *Christian Leader* (April 22, 1980) 20.

"The Traveler's Psalm." *Christian Leader* (August 14, 1980) 17.

"From Dan to Beersheba." *Christian Leader* (September 8, 1981) 17.

"Answering a Costa Rican [Exod 4:24–25]." *Christian Leader* (June 29, 1982) 15.

Guest Columnist, **Fresno Bee** *(Fresno, CA) Section B, p. 7*

"Justice in Which Victims Count." (May 3, 1992).

"It's OK to Talk about God." (June 7, 1992).

"Yearning for Grandchildren." (July 12, 1992).

"Hospitality to Foreign Students." (August 16, 1992).

"Wanted: A Church in Grubbies." (September 20, 1992).

"When We Are Shading the Truth." (October 25, 1992).

Articles in Church Periodicals

"Centennial Inventory." *Christian Leader* (February 23, 1960) 3, 18.

"Awake! Read! Live!" First award in National Association of Evangelicals sermon writing contest, "The Bible in National Life." *United Evangelical Action* (July 1962) 8–10. Also in *Seminary Journal* 1 (May 1962) 5–12.

"How Can Christian Community Be Established in the City?" (Symposium). *Mennonite Life* (January 1964) 18–20, 24–25.

"Be a Sharp Investor." *Christian Leader* (January 19, 1965) 4–5.

"What Is Involved in Community Outreach?" *Christian Leader* (August 16, 1966) 4–5.

"Church Outreach: What Is involved?" (Pamphlet). Fresno, CA: Office of Evangelism and Christian Education.

"Inspiring Funerals." *Christian Leader* (August 29, 1966) 19.

"A Missing Dimension." *Christian Leader* (November 7, 1967) 3–4.

"Situation Ethics." *Mennonite Brethren Herald* (January 26, 1968) 4–5. Also in *Christian Leader* (January 30, 1968) 4–5.

"Israel: The Miracle Country." *Christian Leader* (November 5, 1968) 4–5. Also in *Mennonite Brethren Herald* (November 15, 1968) 4–5.

"Israel Diary." *Christian Leader* (December 17, 1968) 18–19.

"Archaeology in Israel." *Christian Leader* (October 22, 1968) 4–5, 11. Also in *Mennonite Brethren Herald* (November 15, 1968) 6–7.

"About Those Christian Clubs on Campus." *With* 1/3 (September 1968) 5–8.

"Habakkuk's Hang-Ups." *Mennonite Brethren Herald* (April 4, 1969) 9, 18.

"The Kitteans Are Coming!" *Mennonite Brethren Herald* (April 18, 1969) 8, 25.

"The Dragnet." *Mennonite Brethren Herald* (May 2, 1969) 7, 22.

"God's Billboard." *Mennonite Brethren Herald* (May 16, 1969) 7, 21.

"Tell It like It Really Is." *Mennonite Brethren Herald* (May 30, 1969) 10–11.

"A Happening." *Mennonite Brethren Herald* (June 13, 1969) 9, 17.

"What If There Is No Money in the Bank?" *Mennonite Brethren Herald* (June 27, 1969) 8–9.

"Mennonite Brethren: Does the Shoe Fit?" (with Phyllis Martens). *Christian Living* 17/9 (September 1970) 2–9.

"Worship Aids in the New Hymnal" (with Eugene Gerbrandt). *Mennonite Brethren Herald* (October 22, 1971) 5.

"Retirement Can Be Exciting [Bill and Viola Will]" (with Phyllis Martens). *Christian Leader* (April 20, 1971) 15.

"Joseph Tells the Christmas Story." *Christian Leader* (December 14, 1971) 2–3.

"Impressions about Christian Work in Brazil." *Christian Leader* (September 5, 1972) 9.

"Attendance Exceeds Expectation at Curitiba." *Mennonite Brethren Herald* (August 10, 1972) 2–3.

"Which Bible Translation for Church Use? A Suggestion." *Christian Leader* (April 18, 1972) 2–5.

"Opportunities in Times of Moral Decline." *Christian Leader* (December 11, 1973) 2–4.

"A Look at Key 73 from the Old Testament." *Christian Leader* (April 3, 1973) 2–5.

"What about Biblical Genealogies?" *Christian Leader* (December 25, 1973) 18.

"Issues at Early Mennonite Brethren Conferences." *Christian Leader* (August 20, 1974) 6–8.

"The Use of the Old Testament in the Church." *Christian Leader* (October 15, 1974) 2–7, 14.

"Isaiah." *Mennonite Brethren Adult Quarterly* 41/1 (1974) 1–49.

"The Earth Is the Lord's . . . What the Bible Says about the Soil." *Christian Leader* (July 20, 1976). Also in *Gospel Herald* (July 27, 1976) 576–78; *Mennonite Brethren Herald* (August 6, 1976) 4–6; and *The Mennonite* (August 17, 1976) 489–90.

"Making the Old Testament Come Alive" (with John Fast). *Youth Worker* 25/1 (1977) 9–14. Also in *Youth Leader* (June 1978).

"The Old Testament: Its Stories. A Picture of God at Work." *Christian Leader* (August 16, 1977) 2.

"Ezekiel." *Mennonite Brethren Adult Quarterly* 43/4 (1977) 1–40.

"What Is Ministry All About?" *Mennonite Brethren Herald* (October 13, 1978) 4–5. Also in *Christian Leader* (October 10, 1978) 4–6.

"Psalm 23." *Christian Leader* (May 9, 1978) 2–3.

"The Marks of Christian Ministry." *Christian Leader* (October 10, 1978) 4–6.

"Unser Gott is unvergleichbar." *Gemeinde Unterwegs* 8 (August 1979).

"Taking God's Name in Vain." *The Mennonite* (June 26, 1979) 436–37.

"Keep the Sabbath Day Holy." *The Mennonite* (July 10, 1979) 452.

"The Challenge to Church Structure: Finding New Wineskins." *Christian Leader* (February 26, 1980) 8–9. Also in *Mennonite Brethren Herald* (March 14, 1980) 2–3.

"A Summons to Servant Leadership." *Mennonite Brethren Herald* (February 1, 1980) 32. Also in *Christian Leader* (October 21, 1980) 8–9.

"Family Worship: A Way of Meeting God and One Another" (with Phyllis Martens). *Mennonite Brethren Herald* (February 29, 1980) 5–7.

"The Energizing Spirit." *Christian Leader* (June 2, 1981) 2–3.

"A Little Chat with God." *Christian Leader* (May 5, 1981) 4.

"Old Testament Biblewalk: Genesis to Malachi." *Mennonite Brethren Adult Quarterly* 47/4 (1981) 1–41.

"Help Your Preacher Preach." *Mennonite Brethren Herald* (March 12, 1982) 4–5.

"The Future of the Mennonite Brethren Conference in Solidifying Its Calling." A Paper distributed by the Conference Minister, Winnipeg, MB (August 1983).

"Take Heed How You Lead." *Seminary Lecture Series* 6/3 (June 1984) 1–12.

"Are There Pastors Coming?" *Mennonite Brethren Herald* (May 18, 1984) 32. Also in *Christian Leader* (May 15, 1984) 11.

"Jeremiah's Burning Word." *Christian Leader* (December 25, 1984) 2–3.

"Christian Leadership: A Call to Serve." *Christian Leader* (January 22, 1985) 18.

"Fighting the Call to Ministry." *Christian Leader* (April 30, 1985) 4–5. Also in *Mennonite Brethren Herald* (July 5, 1985) 2–3.

"No Wiggle Room for Jeremiah." Mennonite Brethren Biblical Seminary Pamphlet, 1985.

"Letter to a Baffled Teen." *Christian Leader* (August 20, 1985) 4–5.

"Response to 'No Lifeguard at the Deep End'." *Perspectives* (Fall 1985) 8–9.

"In Grateful Remembrance [B. J. Braun]." *Christian Leader* (October 1, 1985) 5.

"If Life Is a Bowl of Cherries, Why Am I in the Pits?" *Seminary Lecture Series* (1985–86) 1–11.

"Perspectives on Creation." *Mennonite Brethren Herald* (August 15, 1986) 2–5.

"Sorting Out a Position on Capital Punishment." *Mennonite Brethren Herald* (April 17, 1987) 2–3.

"Huge Task of Reaching India." *Christian Leader* (August 14, 1987) 3–4. Also in *Mennonite Brethren Herald* (October 16, 1987) 16–17; and *Pulse* (August 14, 1987) 3–5.

"Shocking Prices, but Solid Churches." *Christian Leader* (October 27, 1987) 19.

"An Easter Experience." *Christian Leader* (October 27, 1987) 18–19. Also in *Mennonite Brethren Herald* (October 16, 1987) 16–17.

"I'd Rather Be in Japan in May." *Mennonite Brethren Herald* (September 18, 1987) 14–15.

"Capital Punishment and the Christian." Pages 19–31 in *On Capital Punishment* [a pamphlet] by Elmer A. Martens and John Redekop. Winnipeg, MB: Kindred, 1987.

"Finding Ways to Reach Urban Poor." *Christian Leader* (February 2, 1988) 16–17.

"The Lord Loves India." *Mennonite Brethren Herald* (March 4, 1988) 15–16.

"Building an Old Testament Library: The Minor Prophets." *Catalyst* 14/4 (April 1988) 2–3.

"Conscious of God's Grace." *Christian Leader* (July 19, 1988) 15.

"The 'Underside' of Mission Work in Zaire." *Christian Leader* (August 30, 1988) 16–17.

"Christian Mission and Government Policies." *Christian Leader* (September 2, 1988) 11.

"Praise and Petition for Policies." *Christian Leader* (November 22, 1988) 15.

"Africa and the Old Testament: The Mouth Is Medicine." *Mennonite Brethren Herald* (January 20, 1989) 10–11.

"Africa and the Old Testament—Wanted: Eight Children." *Mennonite Brethren Herald* (February 3, 1989) 12–13.

"Africa and the Old Testament: Can the Ethiopian Change His Skin?" *Mennonite Brethren Herald* (February 17, 1989) 16–17.

"Tribute to G. W. Peters." *Mennonite Brethren Herald* (February 17, 1989) 26.

"Africa and the Old Testament: Woe to the Women Who Hunt Souls!" *Mennonite Brethren Herald* (March 3, 1989) 10–11.

"Using the Bible to Make Ethical Decisions: Principles or Patterns." *Christian Leader* (March 28, 1989) 7–9.

"Making Ethical Decisions, Part I." *Mennonite Brethren Herald* (October 27, 1989) 10–11; "Making Ethical Decisions, Part II." *Mennonite Brethren Herald* (November 10, 1989) 10–11.

"The Squirrel Walks in the Dew." *The Mennonite* 104 (December 26, 1989) 599.

"Echoes of Aaron's Benediction in Pss. 67 and 121." *El-Shaddai* (January–February 1990) 3–7.

"Women in Ministry: The Dialogue Continues (with Frances Hiebert)." *Christian Leader* (April 24, 1989) 3–9.

"Why Preach?" *Suvarthamani* (March–April 1991) 28–30.

"Dealing with Life's Irritations." *Suvarthamani* (May 1991) 30–32.

"Comments about Preaching." *Suvarthamani* (June 1991) 21–23.

"Come Bless the Lord." *Suvarthamani* (June 1991) 23–25.

"India Responds to War." *Christian Leader* (April 23, 1991) 13.

"Of Colleges, VCRs and Professionals." *Mennonite Brethren Herald* (July 19, 1991) 22–23.

"Sampling Church Life in Korea, Part I." *Mennonite Brethren Herald* (June 28, 1991) 21; "Sampling Church Life in Korea, Part II." *Mennonite Brethren Herald* (July 19, 1991) 21.

"Korea: Mega-Churches; Few Mennonites." *Christian Leader* (July 16, 1991) 12.

"Fortschritt in Indien." *Mennonitische Rundschau* 67/8 (September 11, 1991) 18.

"Comments on the Sermon (Jeremiah 15)." *Suvarthamani* (August 1991) 23–29.

"Why Must the Mighty Fall? (with Fran Hiebert). *Christian Leader* (October 8, 1991) 3–5; "How Are the Mighty Fallen—Again!" *Mennonite Brethren Herald* (November 8, 1991) 6–7.

"Making Our Moves: A View from Inside Board of Missions." *Mennonite Brethren Herald* (November 22, 1991) 21. Also in *Christian Leader* (October 22, 1991) 12–13.

"What Does God Want Us to Do?" *Christian Leader* (October 11, 1991) 12–13.

"Kids Accept Responsibility for Broken Window and Learn Good Citizenship." *Victim Offender Reconciliation Program News* (November 1992).

"Jesus/Messiah." *Christian Leader* (February 25, 1992) 25.

"Leviticus, Numbers, Deuteronomy." *Mennonite Brethren Bible Study Guide* 58/4 (1992) 1–53.

"Psalms 42–43; Psalm 44; Psalm 45; Psalms 46–48." *Mennonite Brethren Bible Study Guide* 59/3 (1993) 38–53.

"History Is Repeating Itself." *Mennonite Brethren Herald* (August 26, 1994) 23–24.

"Loss of a Giant [D. Edmond Hiebert]." *Christian Leader* (April, 1995) 14–15.

"The Foundation beneath Our Name." *In-Touch* [Mennonite Brethren Biblical Seminary] (Winter 1995) 1, 4.

"Coming to Faith in Russia." *Witness* (January-February 1995) 1–2, 4.

Jeremiah and Lamentations. Mennonite Brethren Bible Study Guide 65/1 (1998) 1–56.

"Paraguay MBs Debate Political Involvement." *Mennonite Weekly Review* (March 10, 2003) 1–2.

"Paraguayans Make Impact beyond Numbers." *Mennonite Weekly Review* (March 10, 2003) 2.

"A Church of Prisoners." *Mennonite Weekly Review* (March 10, 2003) 2.

"Participating in Politics a Hot Issue among Paraguayan MBs." *Mennonite Brethren Herald* (April 11, 2003) 16–17.

"Leaving the Door Open: Paraguayan MBs Pass Guidelines for Possible Political Participation." *Christian Leader* (April 2003) 26–27.

"MBs and Mennonites in Paraguay." *Christian Leader* (April 2003) 27–28.

"I Am" . . . The Presence and the Glory: Studies in the Book of Exodus [Outliner]. Word Wise Series. Winnipeg, MB: Kindred, 2003.

"Taking the Yawn out of Reading Scripture." *Christian Leader* (November 2004) 21.

"A Personal Tour [Mennonite Brethren Biblical Seminary]." *Christian Leader* (September 2005) 13–15.

"Experiencing a Changing China." *Mennonite Brethren Herald* (July 1, 2005) 16.

"Walking on Holy Ground." *Mennonite Brethren Herald* (September 2, 2005) 4–5.

"China Thawing: Signs of God at Work." *Christian Leader* (October 2005) 28.

"The Gifts a Seminary Gives." *Evangelical Biblical Seminary* [Japan], *Fiftieth Anniversary Bulletin, 1957–2007* (October 2007) 15–16.

"Easter Meditation: The Resurrection Song." *Christian Leader* (March 2008) 8–9.

PART 1

———

Christian Use of the Old Testament

Embracing the Law:
A Biblical Theological Perspective

ELMER A. MARTENS

President and Professor of Old Testament, Emeritus
Mennonite Brethren Biblical Seminary
Fresno, California

The subject of 'law' (*tôrâ, nomos*) is tantalizing, partly because of the large place given to it in Scripture, partly because of the ambiguity of its definition and role, partly because of the way an assessment of law affects the relationship between contemporary Judaism and the Christian Church, partly because of the unceasing debate that surrounds it, and certainly because of the guidance that the law affords or does not afford for Christian behavior. So large is the arena of debate, even for one facet of the subject, such as Paul and Torah, that an attempt at a synthetic view of the subject covering both testaments is like entering a minefield.[1]

The purpose of this essay is to explore the subject of 'law' (*tôrâ, nomos*) from a biblical theology perspective. In defense of this attempt, one can offer the rationale that, beyond the debate of exegetical detail, Scripture is to be viewed wholistically. Theologians of either testament often proceed exclusively on their individual turfs, and they need to be called, whatever their specialization, to work toward synthesis. A look at the forest, rather than a microscopic examination of a twig, has its own rewards. Current discussion on the canonical approach to biblical interpretation is only one more incentive to pursue a less-than-atomized approach. Some fresh proposals on NT texts on law are altering

---

Author's note: The substance of this essay was presented as the annual lecture at the meeting of the Institute of Biblical Literature, New Orleans, November 16, 1990. It was published as "Embracing the Law: A Biblical Theological Perspective" (*BBR* 2 [1992] 1–28) and is reproduced here with permission from the publisher.

1. "The topic 'law' is an unresolved fundamental problem for a biblical theology that connects the Old and New Testaments" (P. Stuhlmacher, "The Law as a Topic of Biblical Theology," in *Reconciliation, Law and Righteousness: Essays in Biblical Theology* [Philadelphia: Fortress, 1986] 130).

the older theological landscape.[2] While these proposals are contested, they nevertheless invite additional probes in order to move toward a new synthesis. For all who see the Bible as Scripture, there is the deep-seated conviction that the two testaments belong together, that Christians deal with one entity when they deal with Scripture, and that, while our work may take us into specialization, the projected outcome is a statement broadly based on the entire Scripture.[3]

Both Hartmut Gese and Peter Stuhlmacher have attempted wholistic statements of this sort with respect to law.[4] Both follow a history-of-traditions approach, with Stuhlmacher building on Gese's work. Gese proposes two kinds of Torah: a Sinai Torah and a Zion Torah. The first, the more prominent, associated in the tradition with Moses, finds its locus in Deuteronomy and is characterized by details about worship, holiness, family, the larger society, and neighbor—the finest example of which is the Decalogue. Basically it is given to one people. The Zion Torah, by contrast, is for all people and is eschatological in orientation. The locus for discussion is the prophets (Isa 2:2–4; Mic 4:1–4; Isa 25:7–9; Jer 31:31).[5] Stuhlmacher traces these sets of distinctions into the NT more explicitly than Gese does, concluding with a taxonomy in which Matthew and James are in the lineage of the Sinai Torah. Paul and the book of Hebrews operate out of a Zion Torah.[6]

There is no evidence, however, it has been said in critique, that Paul was influenced by any generally held belief in an eschatological Zion Torah.[7] The Gese-Stuhlmacher differentiation is problematic also because of the sharpness by which Zion law is set over against the Sinai law. Moreover, it is flawed by the speculative nature of the tradition process on which the whole schema is built. At the end of the day, the law-gospel polarity remains.

The thesis argued here is that, with respect to law in the two testaments, there is a greater coherence and consistency, though along different lines, than

---

2. See, for example, E. P. Sanders, *Paul and Palestine Judaism: A Comparison of Patterns of Religion* (London: SCM, 1977); idem, *Paul, the Law and the Jewish People* (Philadelphia: Fortress, 1983); and J. D. G. Dunn, "The New Perspective on Paul," *BJRL* 65 (1983) 95–122 = *Jesus, Paul and the Law* (Louisville: Westminster/John Knox, 1990) 183–206.

3. Moves in the direction of a biblical theology are illustrated, for example, by the appearance, beginning in 1986, of the *Jahrbuch für Biblische Theologie*. See H. Gese, *Essays in Biblical Theology* (Minneapolis: Augsburg, 1981); and E. A. Martens, "Biblical Theology and Normativity," in *So Wide a Sea: Essays on Biblical and Systematic Theology* (ed. Ben C. Ollenburger; Elkhart, IN: Institute of Mennonite Studies, 1991) 19–35.

4. Gese, *Essays*; Stuhlmacher, "Law."

5. Gese, *Essays*, 60–92.

6. Stuhlmacher, "Law," 122–24, 126ff.

7. A. J. M. Wedderburn, "Paul and the Law," *SJT* 38 (1985) 619.

has been allowed by the Gese-Stuhlmacher approach. The law-gospel polarity must be transcended. The alternate model presented here is OT-friendly and is sensitive to law as gift, as boundary marker, and as life infusing. First, I will summarize the status of law as offered by OT theologians. Alongside this summary I will place recent NT exegetical proposals, because, due to a current paradigm shift, these have not yet been incorporated into NT theologies. Out of this process and this juxtaposition, a coherent biblical theology of law emerges.[8]

One fruitful route into our subject is to ask: What have OT theologians surmised about law? Since it is one of the functions of a biblical theologian to summarize the results of exegetical work, a short overview follows.

The Old Testament Assessment of Law

A survey of selected OT theologians shows that the theology of law follows three major strands. That is, law takes on slightly different color hues when viewed against different realities. Set against God, the author of law, law is good. Set in the context of covenant, law defines the people of God. Set over against the question of life, law is life infusing.

Law as a Good Gift

Theologians of the OT commonly give a positive assessment to law. Because the Torah is God's gift, it is good. The nature of this "good," however, can be variously described.

---

8. A working definition of law is "that body of statutes and commandments (the *ḥuqqîm* and the *mišpāṭîm*) associated with the covenant." R. E. Clements, building on Deut 4:44–45 says, "Torah is the comprehensive list of instructions and stipulations by which Israel's covenant with God is controlled" (*Old Testament Theology: A Fresh Approach* [Atlanta: John Knox, 1978] 110); see an additional definition on p. 118. See also Gese, *Essays*, 61. W. D. Davies offers four meanings: commandments; prophets, wisdom, and history; a cosmic function in connection with wisdom; the entire revealed will of God ("Paul and the Law: Reflections on Pitfalls in Interpretation," in *Paul and Paulinism: Essays in Honour of C. K. Barrett* [ed. M. D. Hooker and S. G. Wilson; London: SPCK, 1982] 4–16). For Knox Chamblin, law "denotes the rule of life which God gives to his people, that way in which they are to walk, those commandments which they are to obey" (K. Chamblin, "The Law of Moses and the Law of Christ," in *Continuity and Discontinuity* [ed. John S. Feinberg; Westchester, IL: Crossway, 1988] 181). A further discussion of definition is found in Dale Patrick, *Old Testament Law* (Atlanta: John Knox, 1985) 4.

Nomos is the Greek equivalent of the Hebrew word *tôrâ*. S. Westerholm has shown that 'norms' is an appropriate rendering for *tôrâ* and that, when Paul uses *nomos* to sum up Israel's obligations, he is "fully in line with the Hebrew usage of torah" (*Israel's Law and the Church's Faith* [Grand Rapids: Eerdmans, 1988] 106). See also J. D. G. Dunn, *Romans* (WBC; Dallas: Word, 1988) lxvii; and L. Gaston, *Paul and the Torah* (Vancouver: University of British Columbia Press, 1987) 10–11.

W. Eichrodt underlined that *Torah* was to be understood as disclosing the divine will. He observed that, with the giving of Torah, God outlines what is expected. The God of Israel, unlike the gods of surrounding peoples, is not capricious. With such a God as Yahweh, Israel may know exactly where it stands. Eichrodt states, "The fear that constantly haunts the pagan world, the fear of arbitrariness and caprice in the Godhead, is excluded."[9] Compared with the ancient Near East, Israel's secular law can be identified by several distinctive features, ~~according to Eichrodt~~ ısis on God throughout; moral precepts nest ~~~~ er value placed on human life; and a rejectic ~~~~ the administration of justice.[10] This disclosu ~~~~ es on disparate areas of human existence, tak ~~~~ devotion. This function of law is not destruc ~~~~ in Israel's life, is a large asset.

Brevard C ~~~~ with the will of God. God as depicted in E ~~~~ communicates. To know God is not a proce ~~~~ the fullest and most direct expression of w ~~~~ ai can be correctly understood within the car ~~~~ onomy, which addresses a new situation and s ~~~~ tion may approach and appropriate the law. "The Law of God was a gift of God which was instituted for the joy and edification of the covenant people. It was not given as a burden, but as a highest treasure and clear sign of divine favour."[12] Both W. Eichrodt and B. S. Childs delineate the contours of law vis-à-vis God. By the law, Israel deciphered something critical about its God. God is not arbitrary or capricious; God is accessible. Law is good.

---

9. W. Eichrodt, *Theology of the Old Testament* (2 vols.; Philadelphia: Westminster, 1961–67) 1.38. Since Eichrodt's writings in the 1930s, attention to the place of stipulation in ancient Near Eastern treaties has only reinforced a favorable assessment of law. These treaties show that the suzerain expected loyalty from his vassal. In God's covenant with Israel, these expectations of loyalty are not left ambiguous but are given a measure of concreteness. One knows with reasonable precision what loyalty entails.

10. Ibid., 1.74. See also M. Lind, who highlights the motive clause in Israelite law, a distinguishing mark from the ancient Near Eastern law. Lind stresses that in Israel laws were never oriented to the political office of kingship, as in the ancient Near East, but to Yahweh's word (Millard C. Lind, "Law in the Old Testament," in *Monotheism, Power, Justice: Collected Old Testament Essays* [Elkhart, IN: Institute of Mennonite Studies, 1990] 61–81).

11. B. S. Childs, *Old Testament Theology in a Canonical Context* (Philadelphia: Fortress, 1985) 53.

12. Ibid., 57. See also Paul Hanson, "Commands and prohibitions were not presented to the community as harsh and onerous impositions, but as loving protections safeguarding this space for fellowship with God" (*The People Called: The Growth of Community in the Bible* [San Francisco: Harper & Row, 1986] 53).

To quote the OT text itself: "And the LORD commanded us to do all these statutes . . . for our good always" (Deut 6:24). In Psalm 119, where God's Torah is the reason for praise, David writes, "Your laws [*mišpāṭîm*] are good" (Ps 119:39; see also v. 97). "The law [*tôrâ*]of the LORD is perfect [*tāmîm*], reviving the soul" (Ps 19:8[7]).

The first color hue, refracted through the prism of God the deity, is that law is the revelation of the divine will. Torah is an expression of God's intent. This revelation is a gift, a gift that is for Israel's and humanity's good.

Law and Covenant Community

Refracted through the prism of covenant, law displays another hue of color. The Torah is essential to the definition of a covenant people. The importance of this aspect of "law" is delineated by Ronald Clements, who centers his "fresh approach" to OT theology largely in *law* and *promise*.

The theology of the OT must be a theology of law, for law not only is more prominent than history but gives unity to the OT.[13] The importance of law derives from its primary connection to covenant. Here is a bond between God and Israel, based on election, that is unlike anything elsewhere. But the importance of law derives also from its connection with canon, since, according to Clements, it was with the book of Deuteronomy—a book dominated by law—that the canonical process began. Covenant, law, and canon mark off this people called Israel.

That the Torah gave definition to the people of Yahweh is clear from the following. (1) An elect people was marked by covenant which in turn included Torah. Clements notes, "It is as a consequence of belonging to the elect people of Yahweh that the Israelite finds himself committed in advance to obedience to *torah*."[14] Moses asked: "And what other nation is so great as to have such righteous decrees and laws as this body of laws I am setting before you today?" (Deut 4:8). (2) Disregard of the Torah brought punitive measures, one of the severest of which was exile from the land, the geographical identity marker of Israel's election status.[15] (3) The preaching of the prophets, in pointing to the offenses against Torah, alerted Israel to the covenant relationship that was being jeopardized.[16] In short, law was constitutive of covenant, and covenant, as spelled out in the canon, was the supreme mark of Yahweh's elect people.

Paul Hanson's work in OT theology is taken up with tracing the growth of community in the Bible. In this growth process, law plays an important role by

---

13. Clements, *OT Theology*, 130.
14. Ibid., 109.
15. Ibid.
16. Ibid., 125.

giving definition to the people of God. Hanson's discussion of law is nuanced differently from Clements's. Clements situates law next to election and covenant in shaping the community. For Hanson the Torah is a response to God's compassionate act, his initiative and deliverance in the Exodus. Hanson says, "Israel's legal structures . . . can be understood properly only when seen as aspects of its ongoing effort to describe the nature of a people owing its existence to God's gracious act of deliverance."[17] Hanson holds that the community is characterized by a triadic notion, one of which is righteousness (law). Two others are worship and compassion.

The Torah aims at structuring and regulating the community. Its emergence is in response to Yahweh, but its function is to demarcate a community. Hanson states, "The Decalogue is thus the culmination of a centuries-long process of a community's identifying itself in response to the creative, redemptive, sustaining and sanctifying acts of God."[18] Identification, more precisely, comes through the Covenant Code, the Cultic Decalogue (Exodus 34), and the Holiness Code. These codes encompass a broad sphere of behaviors— social, cultic, moral—which were to characterize the community of faith. Much in these codes is highly specific, such as when instruction is given not to afflict the widow or orphan (Exod 22:21–23). Other laws deal with diet and festivals. But in any case, whatever the laws, they are to be understood as characterizing a community.

Hanson rightly invokes the story of Ezra to show how law functions in consolidating a community. Commenting on Ezra 7:25–26, which spells out Ezra's assignment as teaching those who do not know the law of God, Hanson states, "The Torah (*dāt*) in Ezra's hand is here defined as the constitutional document of the Jewish community. By acceptance or rejection of the Torah, individuals define themselves as either inside or outside of that community."[19] Similarly, Nehemiah's covenant-renewing ceremony was intended to give the community solidarity and character (Neh 9:38–10:39).

In sum, both Clements and Hanson have the community sharply in focus when they discuss law. Clements's language is one of election, covenant, and law within covenant, whereby the community gains its identity. Hanson stresses the response nature of the legal provisions, a response designed to shape and characterize a community. Whereas for Eichrodt and Childs Torah is associated with the disclosure of the divine will, for Clements and Hanson the community has moved much more to center stage; Torah gives contour and definition to this community of faith.

---

17. Hanson, *People Called,* 51.
18. Ibid., 54.
19. Ibid., 293.

Law and Life

Still another color hue of law emerges when law is set alongside the broad reality of "life." Two theologians who are representative of linking law and life are G. von Rad and W. Kaiser.

In W. Kaiser's book on OT theology, law is discussed primarily in the chapter "People of the Promise: Mosaic Era."[20] Preceding a detailed discussion of "The Law of God," more particularly the moral, ceremonial and civil law, Kaiser provides a perspective on law, largely through Lev 18:1–5 and the expression "You shall keep my statues and my ordinances; by doing so one shall live: I am the LORD" (NRSV). Kaiser's question is whether, given the promissory covenants of the patriarchs, there is here a step down to a conditional covenant. His answer is essentially "No." There is not here, as other commentators suggest, a hypothetical offer of acceptance with God for any who might keep the laws perfectly. Kaiser stresses that the Sinaitic covenant is initiated by grace, and the statement "I am Yahweh" brackets the Leviticus passage and nuances that passage in the direction of sanctification rather than salvation. The passage highlights the necessity of obedience for "those who have claimed to have experienced the grace of God's deliverance."[21] Whether or not one agrees with Kaiser's interpretation, his point of departure for a discussion of law is significant. He rightly takes into account an impressive number of statements that link law with life.

G. von Rad precedes his discussion of specific commandments with the section "The Significance of the Commandments." Although quite wide ranging in his comments, he nevertheless notes, "The Decalogue raises one of the most important of all the questions in the theology of the Old Testament— how is this will for Israel to be understood theologically?"[22] He answers that

---

20. W. Kaiser, *Toward an Old Testament Theology* (Grand Rapids: Zondervan, 1978) 111–21.

21. Ibid., 113. Compare his elaborations in "Leviticus 18:5 and Paul: 'Do This and You Shall Live' (Eternally?)," *JETS* 14 (1971) 19–28; and in "God's Promise Plan and His Gracious Law," *JETS* 33 (1990) 289–302. Kaiser shies away from interpreting Lev 18:5 as dealing with "eternal" life. Granted that the expression is anachronistic for the OT, it is hard not to see "life" in Lev 18:5 as anything other than what the NT terms "eternal life," since it is the highest benefit the OT offers. Moreover, Paul's use of the Leviticus text in Rom 10:5 is, according to the interpretation defended below, supportive of the notion that the law, appropriated by faith, results in "life." To take Lev 18:5 at face value is not suggesting an alternate way of salvation. Salvation is not thereby gained by merit but remains the gift of God through grace in response to faith. The faith response consists of an embrace of the law comparable in NT terms to the embrace of Christ. A flawless, perfectionist keeping of the law is not in question. Besides, embracing the law includes offering sacrifice for infringing the law. A key to the interpretation is to understand the term "keep," which, as explained below, incorporates the English term "embrace."

22. G. von Rad, *Old Testament Theology* (2 vols.; San Francisco: Harper & Row, 1962–65) 1.192.

the revelation of the commandments is understood as a "saving event of the first rank."[23] The saving gift is the gift of life. Von Rad cites the *paraenesis* in Deuteronomy, which weaves together command and the promise of life (e.g., 5:33; 8:1; 16:20; 22:7). "The proclamation of the commandments and the promise of life were obviously closely connected in the liturgy from a very early time."[24] One example, also noted by von Rad, is Ezek 18:5–9.

The connection between law and life is explicated in Ezekiel 18, where the prophet presents three case studies: a righteous person, his unrighteous son, and the righteous son of the unrighteous man. The prophetic proposition is that the righteous person in observing the law shall live. Thirteen Torah stipulations in two similar but not identical lists do not exhaust, but are representative of, God's instructions to which this person adheres: for example, not to defile the neighbor's wife, not to oppress anyone, to give bread to the hungry, and to cover the naked with clothing (18:6–7). Ezekiel summarizes: "He follows my decrees and faithfully keeps my laws. That man is righteous; he will surely live" (18:9).

The critical question, given our agenda, is to understand the expression "he shall surely live." The expression must be seen against its opposite, "The person who sins shall die" (Ezek 18:20). Since the life of all terminates sooner or later, something other that the mere extension of existence, length of days, is meant by the phrase "he shall surely live." Both G. von Rad and W. Zimmerli have addressed the meaning of "life" in this context. Zimmerli lists and refutes several proposals: by "life" is meant the survival by the pious of the destruction of Jerusalem; "to live" refers to the glories beyond the final judgment; and "to live" is to return to the land.[25]

G. von Rad, examining the meaning of "life" in conjunction with the Psalms, concluded that "to live" was to be granted access to the sanctuary and so to be granted all that is incorporated by what it means to be in the presence of God; or, to put it differently, to be the beneficiaries of the promise "God will be with you."[26] These benefits, which included a satisfying experience physically, were not limited to the material, for as the psalmist declared, "and afterward you will take me into glory" (Ps 73:24). Indeed there is a mystical note in Ps 36:9, "For with you is the fountain of life; in your light we see light." Zimmerli also reaches for the Psalms in seeking an answer to the meaning intended by "life" and concludes, "In all these troubles, the appeal is

---

23. Ibid., 1.193.

24. Ibid., 1.194.

25. W. Zimmerli, *Ezekiel I* (Philadelphia: Fortress, 1979) 381.

26. G. von Rad, "'Righteousness' and 'Life' in the Cultic Language of the Psalms," in *The Problem of the Hexateuch and Other Essays* (New York: McGraw-Hill, 1966) 253.

always that Yahweh would turn his gracious countenance to the Psalmist. It is in this that life consists."[27] Ezekiel prompts us to understand life as that superlative quality of life which is more than existence but which partakes of the divine character. "To live," then, is to enjoy life with God, a reality that the NT will call "abundant life" and "eternal life."

Leviticus 18:1–5, a fulcrum text for W. Kaiser, and Ezek 18:5–9, to which von Rad and Zimmerli frequently return, operate on a similar theological platform with similar vocabulary. Leviticus speaks of *ḥuqqōt* 'decrees' and *mišpāṭîm* 'laws' (18:4–5) and so does Ezek 18:9: "He walks in my decrees [*ḥuqqōt*] and faithfully keeps my laws [*mišpāṭîm*]"(18:9). Moreover, in both Leviticus and Ezekiel the verbs are 'walk' (*hālak*) and 'keep' (*šāmar*). The parallelism of "walk" and "keep" may be captured by the English word "embrace." Both the Leviticus and Ezekiel text link the embracing of the law with life.

The term "embrace" is helpful; it is a corrective to the word "keep," which connotes immaculate performance of every legal detail, a kind of perfectionism. G. von Rad observes that for the preacher in Deuteronomy the threat does not come from failure to fulfill the law but from the "possible refusal to do so."[28] The OT view is that it is within reach to "keep" the law in the sense of embracing the law. That phrase, "embrace the law," signals a whole-hearted commitment to the law but does not imply a frantic attempt to measure up to each stipulation. To embrace the law is to seize it as one's orientation, to be guided by it and, yes, to obey it and so to keep it but not to be victimized by its jot and tittle. To embrace the law is to lock oneself to the Torah as the large entity that it is—a gift from Yahweh—so that in embracing the law one embraces God.[29]

When Israel is presented with the Book of the Covenant, the people respond, "We will do everything the LORD has said; we will obey" (Exod 24:7). To this sort of intention God responds, "Everything they said was good. O

---

27. W. Zimmerli, *OT and the World* (Atlanta: John Knox, 1976) 118.

28. Von Rad, *OT Theology*, 2.393.

29. That such a meaning, supplied by our English word "embrace," is appropriate follows from several considerations. Lexically, the sense of "embrace" is required in such expressions as *šōmēr napšô*, rendered 'guarding his life' (see Prov 13:3; 16:7; 22:5) with the sense of cherishing one's life. The root *šmr* occurs in the phrase *šāmĕrû derek* Y HWH (Gen 18:19). At issue in Gen 18:19, where Abraham's descendants are to be directed to "keep the way of the LORD" is a specific orientation—namely, giving oneself to a walk with God. Better sense is made of the expression by rendering 'embrace the way of the LORD'. So also in Ezek 18:9, "in my statutes he walks" is a matter of general orientation, or even attachment, which is followed by the parallel and more specific line, "and he keeps my laws." Here walking and keeping are parallel with the sense of "embrace" (see Zech 3:7). The term "embrace" is inclusive of the double element "obey God's voice and walk in his law" (Jer 32:23).

that their hearts would be inclined to fear me and keep all my commands always so that it might go well with them and their children forever" (Deut 5:28–29). Ahead of doing the commands is a decision to fear God. That this is the sense of "keeping the commandments" is clarified in Deut 17 when its opposite is depicted: "But if your heart turns away and you are not obedient, and if you are drawn away to bow down to other gods . . ." (Deut 30:17). The prophets, especially Jeremiah, frequently conclude indictment lists with the telling phrase "they forsook me [Yahweh]" (Jer 2:13, 17, 19; 5:7, 19; 16:11; 17:13). The opposite would be to cling to Yahweh, and this would entail embracing the law. It is because to embrace the law is to embrace Yahweh that Ezekiel can declare of such a person: "He is righteous; he will surely live" (Ezek 18:9).

With this dictum, that embrace of law means righteousness and hence life, other Scriptures cohere. "I will never forget thy precepts, for by them thou hast given me life" (Ps 119:93).[30] "See, I have set before you today life and prosperity, death and destruction. For I command you today to love the LORD your God, to walk in his ways, and to keep his commands [*miṣwôt*], decrees [*ḥuqqōt*] and laws [*mišpāṭîm*]; then you will live and increase" (Deut 30:15–16). "They [all the words of this law] are not just idle words for you—they are your life" (Deut 32:47). Attention to law results in life. Life is understood in a double way. Life signifies life in the promised land of Canaan, because of the focus in these verses; for example, "and the LORD your God will bless you in the land you are entering to possess" (Deut 30:16). The opposite of life is to be destroyed: "you will not live long in the land you are crossing the Jordan to enter and possess" (Deut 30:18). But more is at stake than existence in the land, for when the writer urges the choice of life, the explanation is "For he, namely Yahweh, is your life" (Deut 30:20). The "living" to which law-observance entitles us is a Yahweh-linked life. And so we are back to von Rad's understanding of life as the form of existence that is characterized by the immediacy of the eternal God. The promise for those who wholeheartedly embrace the law is life with God.[31]

In sum, theologians of the OT see the law as one might a rainbow with several hues of dominant color. First, understood in terms of its source, law is good. It derives from God, who by means of it discloses his will. Second, understood in terms of its recipient, law shapes, orders, and demarcates a community. The Torah is an identity marker specifying what it means to be a holy

---

30. The translation is by Childs, *OT Theology*, 52.

31. This "quality of life" is described in part in Psalm 119 with words such as "delight," "joy," and "freedom."

OT - Dderives from God & receipients, order a community - What it means to be holy 3 - Purpose embrace laws

people. Third, understood in terms of its pu[...] mount to embrace of Yahweh and results in [...]

The New Testament Asses[...]

If one moves from the OT, with its positive [...] is not a little surprised at some harsh things s[...] is Paul's strident word, "All who rely on the observance of the law are under a curse" (Gal 3:10). One readily agrees with Ronald Clements, "In a great many ways the New Testament reveals a markedly fresh and radical approach to the problems of the theology of law."[32] To begin with, however, would one not do well, especially when coming from the OT, to be open to the possibility that in some way the theologies of the two testaments on the subject of law cohere? In the absence of syntheses within NT theologies that incorporate the newer paradigm shift (discussed below), we shall now need to proceed more exegetically. As we shall see, some of the strands in law identified under the old covenant cohere with NT strands. One of these is the belief in Torah as a gift.

Law: A Good Gift

Like the OT, both the writer of John's Gospel and Paul—at least on occasion—affirm the law as good. In John one reads, "From the fullness of his grace we have all received one blessing after another. For the law was given through Moses; grace and truth came through Jesus Christ" (John 1:16–17, NIV). The assessment of the "law given through Moses" in this context depends on the solution to the meaning of the preposition *anti*, a hapax legomenon in the Gospel. The Authorized Version implicitly reads *anti* as antithetical, "And of his fulness have all we received, and grace for [*anti*] grace" (John 1:16). Then, building on the idea of contrast and inserting an unwarranted "but," v. 17 is made to read: "For the law was given by Moses, but grace and truth came by Jesus Christ" (John 1:17). In this way the translation "clarified" (or rather grossly misrepresented) the relationship between the law and the gospel as opposites.[33]

Ruth Edwards documents the views of scholars—an impressive list—favoring *anti* as 'upon'.[34] More-recent translations so render the text, "From his

---

32. Clements, *OT Theology*, 129.

33. An unfortunate rendering is given in The Living Bible: "For Moses gave us only the Law with its rigid demands and merciless justice, while Jesus Christ brought us loving forgiveness as well."

34. R. Edwards, "'*Charin anti Charitos*' (John 1:16): Grace and the Law in the Johannine Prologue," *JSNT* 32 (1988) 3–5.

fullness we have all received, grace upon [*anti*] grace" (RSV; NRSV; NEB; NASB)
and thereby give the impression of a cornucopia of bounty. She argues, however, that this translation is flawed because nowhere in Greek literature is there
an example in which *anti* means 'upon'. Indeed, the Greek preposition for
'upon' is *epi*. She proposes that *anti* be understood as 'instead of' with the sense
of 'replacement'. That is, one thing is superseded by another.[35] The leading
Fathers of the Greek Church so understood it. One grace-gift, namely the law,
has been superseded by another grace-gift, Jesus Christ. Yet, modern scholars,
injecting the supposed Pauline notion that law and gospel are opposed, have
resisted this interpretation, she says, apparently on the grounds that law would
not be designated a *charis* (gracious gift). Thus W. Zimmerli, for example, by
appealing to v. 17 as setting law and gospel in contradistinction, comments,
"Paul's antithesis of grace and law is adopted."[36] Consequently, even though
epi would by itself allow an interpretation favorable to the law, v. 17 is tilted to
give a negative interpretation of law.

A negative view of law assumes that in v. 17 there is antithetic parallelism.
The two halves, "for the law was given through Moses" and "grace and truth
came through Jesus Christ" are grammatically neatly balanced. The parallelism, as J. Jeremias and others have suggested, is progressive rather than antithetical.[37] Barnabas Lindars has proposed for v. 17 the sense "Just as the law
was given through Moses, so grace and truth came through Jesus Christ."[38]
The verse would then be an explication of v. 16, with the sense that, while the
new grace is clearly superior, the law, while an older grace, was nevertheless
clearly a grace.[39]

To this affirmative statement of the law by John we may add that of Paul:
"So then the law is holy and the commandment is holy, righteous and good"
(Rom 7:12; see also 1 Cor 3:7–15). It is because Paul shares with the OT the
understanding that in the law is the revealed will of God that his paranetic
sections so readily echo the law (e.g., Rom 13:8–10; Gal 5:13–6:10). Paul
counsels "those who are in" (to use Sanders's distinction of "getting in" and

---

35. Ibid., 6–9.

36. Ibid., 7 (citing *TDNT* 9.399).

37. Ibid., 8.

38. Ibid., 8 (citing B. Lindars, *The Gospel of John*, 98).

39. Edwards helpfully traces other references to law in John to show that John so understood
"law" ("*Charin anti Charitos,*" 8–10). The law is viewed positively even though now superseded
by Christ, just as, say, John the Baptist, who was a shining light, has been superseded by the true
light, Jesus Christ. Clearly, Jesus is a gift of grace, but so also is the law. W. J. Dumbrell, taking
into account the entire first chapter of John as context and comparing it with Exodus, makes
helpful observations but is still primarily concerned with explicating the contrast ("Law and
Grace: The Nature of the Contrast in John 1:17," *EvQ* 58 [1986] 25–37). But according to
Edwards, one should read John 1:16–17 not as contrast but as progression.

"staying in") to be observers of the law.[40] By no means is the law set aside as unimportant. It may be interpreted or prioritized, but it is certainly not dismissed, nor is it abrogated, but it is instead affirmed.[41] Paul's assessment of "law," as also Jesus' and John's, is positive. In this positive assessment, the NT is at one with the OT, as the summaries from W. Eichrodt and B. S. Childs have shown.

Law and Community

While Paul and Jesus affirm the law, the problem is (as has long been observed) that from both come statements that are negative about the law. This discordance has evoked a great many recent studies.[42] Douglas Moo opens an

---

40. Sanders, *Paul, the Law, and the Jewish People*, 6.

41. J. A. Ziesler observes that Paul does not often appeal to the law, but there is an "implicit attitude to the continuing validity of the Law for all Christians" (*Paul's Letter to the Romans* [London: SCM, 1989] 49). Similarly, Knox Chamblin writes a sustained argument on continuity but with greater attention to Jesus and the law ("The Law of Moses"). Commenting on Matt 5:17, R. Fuller opts for the view favoring continuity ("The Decalogue in the New Testament," *Int* 43 [1989] 247). Otherwise, J. M. G. Barclay (*Obeying the Truth: A Study of Paul's Ethics in Galatians* [Edinburgh: T. & T. Clark, 1988] 234–35); and Douglas Moo ("Paul and the Law in the Last Ten Years," *SJT* 40 [1987] 287–307).

42. Especially since the work of E. P. Sanders there has been a fresh flurry of monographs and articles on the subject: E. P. Sanders, *Paul and Palestinian Judaism: A Comparison of Patterns of Religion* (London: SCM, 1977); idem, *Paul, the Law, and the Jewish People* (Philadelphia: Fortress, 1983); Heikki Räisänen, *Paul and the Law* (Tübingen: Mohr Siebeck, 1983); T. Gordon, *Paul's Understanding of the Law: A Tri-Polar Analysis* (Ph.D. diss., Union Theological Seminary in Virginia, 1984); Lloyd Gaston, *Paul and the Torah* (Vancouver: University of British Columbia Press, 1987); Stephen Westerholm, *Israel's Law and the Church's Faith* (Grand Rapids: Eerdmans, 1988); J. D. G. Dunn, *Romans* (2 vols.; WBC; Dallas: Word, 1988); and idem, *Jesus, Paul, and the Law* (Louisville: Westminster/John Knox, 1990). See the following works for helpful summaries: A. J. M. Wedderburn, "Paul and the Law," *SJT* 38 (1985) 613–25; John M. G. Barclay, "Paul and the Law: Observations on Some Recent Debates," *Themelios* 12 (1986) 5–15; Douglas Moo, "Paul and the Law in the Last Ten Years," *SJT* 40 (1987) 287–307; F. F. Bruce, "Paul and the Law in Recent Research," in *Law and Religion: Essays on the Place of the Law in Israel and Early Christianity* (ed. B. Lindars; Cambridge: James Clarke, 1988); Dunn, *Romans*, with extensive bibliography, lxiii–lxiv; and John Ziesler, *Paul's Letter to the Romans* (London: SCM, 1989).
Sanders showed that in modern biblical interpretation there was grave misunderstanding of the Judaism that Paul was attacking. Judaism was not preoccupied with a works righteousness, as often claimed. Judaism's self-understanding was of a salvation premised on God's grace, for through it the covenant relationship had come into being. Sanders maintained that this covenant was regulated by law, not in the sense that entry into covenant was by law, but that *staying in* called for law observance, a role for law he capsuled in the phrase "covenantal nomism" (*Paul and Palestinian Judaism*, 75). In my view, the law also has a wider function; law belongs to covenant, but law extends beyond covenant. With Sanders and the subsequent debate, interesting, even exciting proposals are emerging that to say the least are putting into question earlier, apparently too-facile answers.

overview article with the comment, "Scholarship on Paul and the law in the last ten years has witnessed a 'paradigm shift'."[43] As a result of this paradigm shift, better bridging between OT and NT on this issue is now possible. The angles of vision outlined by OT theologians can now be better correlated with what are the newer understandings in NT scholarship.

The fresh way forward in resolving the apparent contradictions about the law within Pauline literature has come with the adoption of a sociological approach. Drawing on anthropologists and sociologists such as Mary Douglas, attention has focused on the functions of law, two of which are summarized by the words "identity" and "boundary markers."[44] Laws that prescribe rituals, for example, give identity to a group. Prescriptions of this sort are also boundary markers. The ritual laws and their observance essentially draw sociological lines marking who belongs and who does not belong to the group. In much of Jewish history, overt practices, such as circumcision, dietary regulations, and Sabbath-keeping, as detailed in the law, gave to Jews their identity. These and other laws visibly distinguished Jews from Gentiles.[45] James Dunn argues that, when Paul spoke of the "works of the law," he had in mind the observances that were national identity and boundary markers. The phrase "works of the law" Dunn summarizes as belonging to "a complex set of ideas in which the social function of the law is prominent. The law serves both to identify Israel as the people of the covenant and to mark them off as distinct from the (other) nations."[46]

This view of "works of the law," given meaning sociologically rather than theologically, signals a need to rethink the agenda that Paul addressed in his letters. Commonly, working theologically and with the 16th-century Reformation questions in the forefront, we have understood Paul's words about the works of the law as answering the spiritually oriented question of how one is saved and how one finds acceptance with God. The platform for debate put the individual center stage. But the sociological approach sets the larger community center stage and means that Paul was attacking the exclusivism of

---

43. Moo, "Paul and the Law," 287.

44. These terms have been strategic in the discussion since the 1983 publication of James Dunn's article "The New Perspective on Paul," *BJRL* 65 (1983) 95–122. Dunn has developed his position in several articles, which are now collected in a single volume, *Jesus, Paul, and the Law*. In it, by means of "Additional Notes" appended to articles, Dunn answers his critics.

45. "These [circumcision, food laws, and sabbath] were not the only beliefs and practices which marked out Jews, but from the Maccabean period onward they gained increasing significance for their boundary-defining character, and were widely recognized . . . as particularly and distinctively characteristic of Jews" (Dunn, *Romans*, lxxi).

46. Idem, "Works of the Law and the Curse of the Law (Galatians 3:10–14)," *NTS* 31 (1985) 531 = *Jesus, Paul, and the Law*, 223.

people who tended to restrict God's favor to those whose mark of distinction was the law. In Dunn's interpretation, the nub of the issue in Paul is not merit-based righteousness; the nub is a closely cloaked national identity in which law and group identity are coterminous.[47]

Support for a sociologically oriented understanding of the "works of the law" can be drawn from Galatians. In the extant Pauline literature, the first use of "works of the law" is in Gal 2:16, which is in the context of a discussion of circumcision and dietary laws (Gal 2:1–14).[48] The contrast between works of the law and faith in Gal 3:10–14 has in view, as Dunn argues, not particular good works aiming at salvation, but an attitude whereby Israel is thought to be marked out by "law." "What he [Paul] is concerned to exclude is the *racial* not the *ritual* expression of faith; it is nationalism which he denies not *activism*."[49] Paul objects to a view in which there is no room for a covenant people bonded through faith quite independent of these outward law observances. That the Jewish exclusivism is the point at issue in Gal 3:10–14 is shown by the way in which the passage concludes—namely, with talk about the blessing of Abraham coming through Christ to the Gentiles (v. 14).[50] Paul's agenda is a missionary agenda.

This understanding of "works of the law," we can see, begins to ease the tensions that Bible readers have felt with Paul's assessment of the law, which is sometimes positive and sometimes negative.[51] Paul asserts the goodness of the law, for in it is the expression of God's will. Paul's interest is not to break from the law. Nor is it to fault the Jews for supposedly emphasizing the law as earning salvation. Nor is it to defend a distinction between ceremonial and ritual law. But Paul is critical of a use of the law that so emphasizes the identity and boundary-marking function that it erects a wall between the possessors of the law, the Jews, and all others and erects it so high that all others are

---

47. See Ziesler, "Moreover, when examined carefully, Paul's writings do not mount an attack on Law-obedience on the grounds that it leads to self-righteousness" (*Romans*, 43).

48. Dunn also notes how the language matrix for "works of the law," such as its parallel "of the flesh" (Rom 9:8, 11), comports with a sociological understanding ("Works of the Law," 30 = *Jesus, Paul, and the Law*, 222–23). Dunn argues that many of the crucial passages in Romans (e.g., 3:27–31; 7:14–25; 9:30–10:4) are more manageable given this sociological understanding (*Romans*, lxxii, and exegesis of relevant passages). The boasting of which Paul was critical is the boasting in national superiority, the Jew over the Gentile, not the boasting in merit-achieved righteousness. Paul is the great leveler between Jew and Gentile.

49. Idem, *Jesus, Paul, and the Law*, 198.

50. Idem, "Works of the Law."

51. Ibid., 531 = *Jesus, Paul, and the Law*, 223. Sanders (*Paul, the Law, and the Jewish People*, 13–14) and Räisänen (*Paul*, 94–96), though not in the same way, have overdrawn the tensions by describing them, as does Räisänen, as contradictions. See also Dunn, "Works of the Law," 523 = *Jesus, Paul, and the Law*, 215.

excluded. Paul's missionary efforts to bring Gentiles to faith were hindered by people who insisted that Gentiles must observe the election markers—circumcision and food laws. But in God's new people, identity markers are of a kind other than ethnic. Paul attacks the misuses of the law, in which its identity function has become central, determining, and all absorbing. Paul is not distancing himself from the law as such.

Paul's situation, one could add, was in some way parallel to Jeremiah's. Jeremiah, like Paul, took on a cherished theological dictum, one that was true but that had been perverted. Jeremiah's audiences had come to place trust in the temple (Jer 7:1–15). In an earlier day, under Isaiah, this move had not only been warranted but encouraged, given God's promises. The temple had functioned as a symbol of God's presence. By seizing on the explanation without paying attention to other realities, the generation of Jeremiah's day was being deceived. Jeremiah cried, "Do not be deceived, saying, 'The temple of the LORD, the temple of the LORD, the temple of the LORD'" (Jer 7:4). Similarly Paul warned, do not be deceived by anchoring your trust for salvation in your identity markers! At issue in Jeremiah's day, as also in Paul's time, was that the sound theology of a past generation had been perverted. That which was an aspect of Torah (namely, the marking of boundaries for a people) could not be defined as the essence of the Torah. Paul polemicized against the law because it separated Jew and Gentile. He was otherwise comfortable, it appears, in lauding the law. He could rail against law-keeping (Gal 3:10) and in the next breath (Gal 3:12) quote Lev 18:5 that "he who practices them shall live by them"—a statement comparable to Rom 2:13, that the one doing the law is justified.

Dunn's interpretation of "works of the law"—not as works of merit to achieve salvation but as deeds (circumcision, diet laws, and observances of festivals), which like badges keep Jews in and Gentiles out—has not gone unchallenged. Against Dunn's interpretation, H. Räisänen has urged that the continuity between Judaism and Paul has been overstressed, that Paul's attack is not really on an attitude toward law but on the law itself, and that the exegesis of Gal 2:16 is defective.[52] F. F. Bruce lodges a similar complaint about the exegesis.[53] Others, such as Peter Stuhlmacher and T. R. Schreiner, have noted that "works of the law" cannot be restricted to circumcision, food laws, and the Sabbath; and that the justification issue, rather than the nationality issue, is

---

52. Räisänen, *The Torah and Christ* (Helsinki: Finnish Exegetical Study, 1986) 168–84. The objections are summarized in Dunn, *Jesus, Paul, and the Law*, 207, followed by a reply.

53. Bruce, "Paul and the Law in Recent Research"; Dunn's summary and answer are found in his additional note, *Jesus, Paul, and the Law*, 212.

closer to the center of Paul's concern.[54] Even if these objections require further nuancing, the overall argument by Dunn, supported increasingly by others, carries considerable weight.[55] If the sociological argument can be sustained, an easy linkage with the OT can be forged, a consideration that could, in turn, make the position espoused by Dunn more creditable.

From the standpoint of the OT, we identified a color hue of law that was closely associated with covenant community and the identity of the people of God. Ronald Clements, basing his ideas on Deuteronomy, explained how law, inextricably bound with election and covenant, was constitutive for Israel. Israel's self-definition, as Paul Hanson underlined, incorporated an understanding of Torah. It is precisely this notion of Israel's self-definition that recent NT scholars have addressed. If the position sketched by Dunn and others holds, it would mean that a legitimate function of the law, that of giving identity, had in Paul's time become an obsession to the point that Gentiles were all but excluded from God's community, unless, of course, they took on the Jewish "badge." The grace of God had been restricted in nationalistic terms. There existed then a continuity of belief about the law from the OT into the age inaugurated by Christ, but it was a diseased continuity; a link yes, but one that needed to be sanitized. With the coming of Christ, the identity markers, or badges had changed; for the new people of God, the externals of circumcision or dietary laws were no longer of importance. In this respect one would need to speak of discontinuity between the OT and the NT.

Law: The Old Covenant Way to Eternal Life

The words of Jesus and Paul about law are not only positive in a general sort of way; Jesus explains, as Paul does also, that under the old covenant, embrace of law is life-engendering. Jesus and Paul reiterate, therefore, what was said of the law in the OT.

Jesus' explanation about the law and eternal life is given in response to the question by the rich ruler, "Good teacher, what must I do to inherit eternal

---

54. Summaries of correspondence and articles are given in Dunn, ibid., 212–13.

55. See A. Wedderburn, for example, who agrees that the antithesis of "works" and "faith" in some instances at least is in the context of the dispute over the admission of Gentiles into the church ("Paul and the Law," 618). John Barclay's conclusions from his study of Galatians are similar to Dunn's on the meaning of "works of the law" (J. M. G. Barclay, *Obeying the Truth: A Study of Paul's Ethics in Galatians* [Edinburgh: T. & T. Clark, 1988] 234–35). Barclay says, "In our analysis of the crisis in Galatia and Paul's response to it we have found no evidence to support the common theological interpretation of this letter, that Paul was fighting to maintain the principle of grace, received as a gift through faith, against the principle of merit, achieved through doing good works" (p. 235).

life?" (Mark 10:17–22 / Matt 19:16–22 / Luke 18:18–23). In reply Jesus points him to the commandments, specifically to a portion of the Decalogue.[56]

For our purposes, two observations are in order. The first pertains to the meaning of "eternal life." In Mark the teacher asks about "inheriting eternal life," a reference with an eschatological flavor. In Matthew, however, the language is of "having" or "getting" eternal life, hinting at that which is possessed in the here and now. An important key to living the good life here and now, both Hellenistic philosophy and Judaism would agree, would entail the observance of the second table of the Decalogue. But Jesus moves beyond the here and now by speaking about treasure in heaven, as in Mark, and thus highlights eschatology.[57] So, "eternal life" is defined partially as a life of virtue in the here and now, but more fully eschatologically, entailing treasure in heaven. I. Howard Marshall is correct to say that "life" is tantamount to salvation. "The thought is primarily of life with God after death."[58]

The second observation centers on the close linkage between eternal life and the Torah. To the ruler the answer is, "You know the commandments" (Mark 10:19). A similar incident with the lawyer prompts the response by Jesus, "What is written in the law (tō nomō)?" (Luke 10:26). The lawyer answers with citations from Deuteronomy and Leviticus. In both instances and without qualification, Jesus links the law with eternal life (Matt 19:17; Luke 10:26). Summarizing how the law and eternal life are connected, S. G. Wilson states: "For Luke the law can be adequately summarized in the two great commands and that obedience to them is sufficient qualification for entry into the kingdom."[59] Luke's Jesus corroborates what is the teaching of the old covenant, that to embrace the law fully is life-giving.

One is on similar turf if one moves into Pauline literature. Romans 9:30–10:4 is an example of an exposition that links law with faith and accords access to God via the law. Whatever Paul may say elsewhere of the law, here he clarifies under what circumstances the law leads to righteousness.

---

56. In a recent article, Reginald Fuller summarizes the results of Klaus Berger's tradition-critical work, whose conclusion is that the radical set of sayings, except for the quotation from the Decalogue, is authentic to Jesus. But Fuller points to evidence that supports the Decalogue reference as being authentic as well. Just as in the Sermon on the Mount where Jesus both quotes and then radicalizes the Decalogue, so also here he cites the Decalogue and radicalizes it ("The Decalogue in the New Testament," *Int* 43 [1989] 243–55, esp. p. 244.).

57. Ibid., 246.

58. I. Howard Marshall, *Commentary on Luke* (Grand Rapids: Eerdmans, 1972) 442.

59. S. G. Wilson correctly notes that some ambivalence emerges for the reader when in the story of the rich ruler the law is supplemented with the teaching about radical poverty, but this directive may be an explication of what it means to love the neighbor (*Luke and the Law* [Cambridge: Cambridge University Press, 1983] 15).

From this much-discussed passage, which has prompted doctoral theses and monographs, even on a single phrase, we draw the conclusion that acceptance with God is premised on faith in God through a faith-embrace of the law.[60] Without getting caught in the labyrinth of argument, we may view two propositions as sustaining the thesis. The first is that in this pericope the law, rather than being disparaged, is lauded. The second is that the contrast explicated is not on the works-faith axis but on a goals axis in which faith is common to both coordinates.

High praise for the law's role is attested in the expression 'law of righteousness' (*nomon dikaiosynēs*, Rom 9:31). The phrase *nomon dikaiosynēs* is a hapax legomenon in the NT. Often it is rendered as a law-kind of righteousness or as a righteousness established by law-keeping.[61] Quite a different interpretation is given by J. Toews and R. Badenas. Toews argues that the genitive *dikaiosynēs* must be a subjective genitive with the sense of a righteous law—that is, a law characterized as righteous. In the same context, the objective genitive is expressed differently: *tēn dikaiosynēn tēn ek tou nomon* 'the righteousness that arises out of law' (10:5). In a similar vein, Badenas sustains a high view of law. In several instances in which *nomos* is used in Rom 9–11, it is in construction with *dikaiosynē* and not in opposition to it. He notes that the background discussion of law in Rom 9–11, beginning with Rom 4, is always positive. He asserts, "The thrust of the passage then favors interpreting *nomon dikaiosynēs* as the Torah viewed from the perspective of the *dikaiosynē* it promises, aims at, or bears witness to" (see Rom 3:21).[62] So interpreted, Paul sees the law positively.

A further reason for regarding the law in a most favorable light is the statement "Christ is the end [*telos*] of the law so that there may be righteousness for everyone who believes" (Rom 10:4). This statement has been understood to mean that Christ has terminated the law; if so, the law appears in an unfavorable light. But quite the opposite is indeed the case. At issue is the term *telos*. Toews argues for a teleological rather than terminal meaning on four grounds: (1) Linguistically, in cognate literature, the teleological nuance is more basic than the terminal. (2) The context has goal-oriented language, for example,

---

60. See J. E. Toews, *The Law in Paul's Letter to the Romans: A Study of Romans 9:30–10:13* (Ph.D. diss., Northwestern University, 1977); and R. Badenas, *Christ, the End of the Law: Romans 10:4 in a Pauline Perspective* (JSNTSup 10; Sheffield: JSOT Press, 1985).

61. For a review of the traditional interpretation, see Toews, "Law in Romans," 117–24, and Badenas, *Christ*, 103 and the bibliography there. The RSV as well as the NRSV translate (erroneously, according to Badenas), "Israel who pursued the righteousness which is based on law did not succeed in fulfilling that law" (Rom 9:31).

62. Badenas, ibid., 104.

"pursue" (Rom 9:30, 31; see also 11:25–26). (3) The goal-oriented language characterizes the final part of the sentence, paraphrased as "Christ is the goal of righteousness unto everyone that believes." (4) Elsewhere in Romans, there is no hint that the law is invalidated.[63] Badenas concurs. Badenas allows, however, that *telos* is a dynamic polysemic word whose meaning is determined by context but "whose basic connotations are primarily directive, purposive, and completive and not temporal."[64] He concludes that the term *telos*, then, denotes purpose or fulfillment but never abrogation.[65] He offers a dynamic translation, "the law points to (or intends) Christ."[66] In this understanding, the law is definitely put in a favorable light.

The positive view of the law prepares one for the proposition that the faith-embrace of the law brings acceptance with God. This proposition becomes plausible when the contrasts in the passage are carefully noted.

First, the contrast in the passage is initially a contrast of goals (Rom 9:30–10:4). Paul asserts that the Gentiles obtained a righteousness that is by faith, but Israel, which pursued the law, did not attain the law because its pursuit was not characterized by faith (Rom 9:30–33). In the traditional interpretation, "the Gentiles obtained righteousness while the Jews did not because the former accepted the Messiah in faith in contrast to Jewish rejection of him."[67] Toews and Badenas, to cite two scholars, have offered a compelling reinterpretation.[68] The contrast that Paul draws is between Gentiles and Israel, but the distinction is not between a faith-kind of righteousness and a works-kind of righteousness. Rather, the distinction has to do with two goals: righteousness for the Gentiles; the law for Israel. The Gentiles strove after righteousness. The Jews were striving after the law, but inappropriately, in a manner we suggest, not unlike the Israelites in the wilderness for whom the brazen serpent, a gift for their healing, became an object of veneration. Israel's quest was indeed for the law, but they did not reach into the law's true meaning. The Jews' preoccupation was with law. The Gentiles reached for righteousness.

If there is a contrast in goals between Gentiles and Israel, there is in principle a common faith requirement for both. Paul underscores God's impartiality. The Gentiles were to respond in faith; so was Israel. What might seem to be a contrast is not a contrast, because, for both Gentiles and Israel, faith was the

---

63. Toews, "Law in Romans," 231–37.

64. Badenas, *Christ*, 79.

65. Ibid., 145–46. Moo ("Paul and the Law"), while recognizing the compelling nature of Badenas's arguments, tries to argue from this text (unconvincingly in my opinion) for discontinuity.

66. Badenas, *Christ*, 147.

67. Toews, "Law in Romans," 124.

68. Ibid., 125–204; Badenas, *Christ*, 101–51.

key component. The inference is clear: had Israelites pursued the law in a correct mode—namely, faith—they would have been the beneficiaries of God's saving activity. As it was, they seized on the law by "works." At issue is not the fulfillability of the law but the failure to embrace the law in a faith response to God's gift.[69] The problem then was not that Israel pursued the law; its problem was in the way it pursued it. Had Israel pursued the law in faith—embraced it as God's gift of grace—it would have been accepted by God.

A further support for the view that the law, when embraced by faith, results in God's saving activity comes from Lev 18:5, which Paul quotes in Rom 10:5: "Moses describes in this way the righteousness that is by the law: 'The man who does these things will live by them.'" One view is that with this OT quotation Paul inveighs against a works-kind of righteousness. Commentators arrive at this interpretation by importing some contrasts that Paul makes elsewhere between "works of the law" and "faith."[70] But this interpretation is flawed. Surely if the issue is righteousness by works of the law, as Lev 18:5 is purported to say, it is strange that Paul adduces this verse in support of the faith principle. Moreover, if Paul by means of Lev 18:5 were fingering works-righteousness, he would be setting the Deuteronomy quotation that immediately follows, "the word is near you" (i.e., the word of faith), against the Leviticus quotation as saying two opposite things. One, the Leviticus passage would stress doing; the other, the Deuteronomy passage, would stress believing. But it is not by contrast but by continuity that the two quotations are related, as the prepositions show.[71] The texts are complementary. "By putting these two references together Paul equated 'the righteousness taught by the law' with 'righteousness by faith' in a clearly new way, meaning thereby that doing the righteousness taught by the law is coming to Christ for salvation, and thus receiving life."[72] Or put another way, the embracing of the Torah by faith was to receive God's salvation. Law was a necessary vehicle, faith the sufficient condition for salvation. With the coming of Christ, this vehicle was superseded, of course, but as David's joy in salvation indicates, faith and law were not incompatible.

---

69. See Toews: "One's status before God is determined by one's stance to Torah as a statement of election, and not by performance of individual commandments" ("Some Theses toward a Theology of Law in the New Testament," in *The Bible and Law* [ed. Willard Swartley; Elkhart, IN: Institute of Mennonite Studies, 1982] 49).

70. See, for example, E. Käsemann, *Commentary on Romans* (Grand Rapids: Eerdmans, 1980).

71. Paul's use of *gar* to introduce the Leviticus quotation follows the statement that the law points to Christ. The subsequent preposition *de* in v. 5 is not disjunctive but conjunctive, which implies that vv. 6–8, the Deuteronomy quotation, is an elaboration of v. 5. That is, the Deuteronomy passage explains the Leviticus text.

72. Badenas, *Christ*, 125; for the sustained argument, see ibid., 118–25.

The view on Rom 9:30–10:4 that is adopted here is summarized by Toews: "Romans 9:30–10:13 read as a unit affirms . . . the law accepted in faith as a way to righteousness for the Jews, while at the same time declaring that Christ has fulfilled the law. It thus asserts two ways to righteousness, faith in God via the law and faith in God via Jesus Christ."[73] Paul's insistence on faith in Christ for salvation should not blind us to the earlier importance of law as Christ's counterpart with a similar, though time-bound, salvific function.

The principle that Paul enunciates, that salvation by faith in God is possible via the law, is of one piece with what the Jesus of the Synoptics told the rich ruler and the lawyer. Both in turn sustain the view elaborated in the OT. This view is that, when the law under the old covenant is embraced with a whole-hearted commitment to God, then righteousness and life are guaranteed. Clearly, with the coming of Christ a new reality obtains that far outstrips the law. Now the faith response, formerly to the law, is to Christ.

Conclusion:
Law in Biblical Theology—Continuity and Discontinuity

The positioning of law within biblical theology, as advocated here, takes greater account of the continuity between the OT and the NT than of the discontinuity that other law discussions have abetted.

The continuity for law is grounded in *Heilsgeschichte*, a notion premised on increments in God's revelation in history. To Abraham God appeared with a gift, the gift of a promise. Another disclosure came in the Exodus–Sinai event with God's gift of Torah. By it people may know the will of God. It was an advance over the gift of the promise in that it was more definitive and more elaborative, hence more of a disclosure of God. In the coming of Jesus, the incarnation, God gave the supreme gift. The person of Christ was more tangible than either promise or law. More than in promise and law, there was disclosed in Jesus Christ the will and purpose of God. So the increments in this holy history have their distinctive nodal points: the promise, the law, the Christ-

---

73. Toews, "Law in Romans," 106. Paul's statements elsewhere—e.g., Gal 2:21 and 3:21, which point at first sight to a different conclusion—must be understood in the sense that faith is the necessary and sufficient condition for salvation. The error that Paul speaks to is to make law both the necessary and sufficient condition for salvation. Once Christ has come, the function of law as critical for salvation ceases. Moreover, the term *law* is multivalent; its referent must be determined by the context. Some of Paul's supposed anti-law statements take on a different complexion once it is understood that "works of the law" are identity markers, as argued above. Much depends on how one sees the basic agenda in Romans and Galatians. We should follow scholars who see the agenda, not one-sidedly as soteriological, but primarily ecclesial. The agenda in both books is a Jew-Gentile agenda.

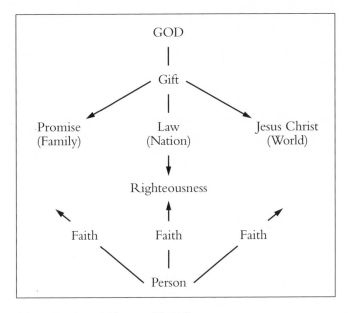

Fig. 1. Situating the law soteriologically.

event.[74] Each successive nodal point is within a larger sociological entity. The promise was given to a family; the Torah was given to an elect people (nation); the person of Christ is a gift to the world (see fig. 1).

Continuity in this holy history is not only in terms of God's gifts but also in terms of human appropriation. The gift of the promise was received in faith (Gen 15:6) and issued in righteousness. Similarly, the Torah, God's grace gift, when embraced by faith issued in righteousness (Rom 9:30–31). Clearly Jesus Christ, when received as God's gift through faith, brings righteousness (Gal 3:26; Rom 10:9–10). The principle of faith-response to God (namely, orienting oneself totally to God via his gift) remains unchanged. The faith-response is essentially an embrace of God; more specifically, it is an embrace of his gifts, be they promise, Torah, or Christ. To embrace the Torah is also to embrace the promise; to embrace Christ is to embrace the preceding gifts of promise and Torah. It is this recognition that gives to law an abiding ethical claim on the believer.

But to sketch the taxonomy in this fashion is also to recognize that with the coming of Jesus two functions of the law have been terminated. In the old

---

74. See Gal 3 for its broad contours of promise, law, and Christ.

covenant, the law made for national identity; it set out boundary markers. These boundary markers pertained to circumcision, dietary regulations, and festival regulations. No longer. Their function was temporary. In Christ, God's gift to the world, the boundaries between Jews and non-Jews are eliminated. Now the Holy Spirit is the boundary marker and the giver of identity (Rom 8:14–17). In the limited sense of law as a boundary marker, the law has been abrogated. In another sense also, discontinuity needs to be recognized. The embrace of law in the old covenant issued in God's acceptance—or eternal life, to use NT language. Law no longer functions this way, now that Christ has come. Christ has superseded the law.

A biblical theology of law is anchored in three theses: (1) Torah as good remains the expression of the will of God. (2) Torah was an identity marker for the OT people of God, and to the extent to which this became an obstacle the NT polemicized against it. (3) Torah, when embraced in faith, made for righteousness—the NT agrees—but is superseded now by Christ.

The view of law here elaborated means that, with respect to Paul's use of law, Heikki Räisänen's solution, that Paul is hopelessly contradictory, is unnecessary.[75] Nor is resolution to be found, as H. Huebner suggested, in positing a development of thought between Paul's writing of Galatians and his work on Romans.[76] Rather, Paul is fighting on two fronts: against the antinomians who hold that Christ's coming abrogates law and against supernationalists who maintain Jewish exclusivism on the basis of the law. Thus, Paul can be heard saying both "yes" to the law when its goodness is in question (even its earlier, life-bringing function) and "no" to the law at the points where it reinforces Jewish ethnic solidarity without making room, through Christ, for the Gentiles. Compared with the Gese-Stuhlmacher approach to traditions, the view here advocated sees less of a dichotomy between law and gospel. This exposition allows one to see more gospel in the law and more law in the gospel. The implications for Christian ethics that arise out of an endorsement of OT law are great but cannot be explicated here.[77]

We can summarize and restate our conclusions. In the OT, the law may be viewed from three perspectives: theologically, anthropologically, and so-

---

75. Räisänen, *Paul and the Law.* See now the articulate rebuttal of a major aspect of Räisänen's position by Jeffrey A. D. Weima, "The Function of the Law in Relation to Sin: An Evaluation of the View of H. Räisänen," *NovT* 32 (1990) 219–35.

76. H. Huebner, *Law in Paul's Thought* (Edinburgh: T. & T. Clark, 1984).

77. W. Kaiser's rehabilitation of the OT law for the Christian is to be heartily endorsed ("God's Promise Plan and His Gracious Law," *JETS* 33 [1990] 289–302). Among the helpful treatments are C. J. H. Wright, *Living as the People of God* (Leicester: Inter-Varsity, 1983) = *An Eye for an Eye* (Downers Grove, IL: InterVarsity, 1983); and Waldemar Janzen, *Old Testament Ethics: A Paradigmatic Approach* (Louisville: Westminster/John Knox, 1994).

teriologically. Theologically, the law is an expression of the will of God. The NT concurs. Anthropologically the law bonds a community. The NT partly demurs; it addresses an excessive preoccupation with the law in this respect and brings correctives. Soteriologically, the OT asserts the life-bringing function of the law. The NT concurs, emphasizing that this conclusion is warranted only when the law is embraced in faith and that the law is superseded by God's latest gift, Jesus, the Christ.[78]

---

78. Responses to this paper (though not always incorporated) are gratefully acknowledged from the following: Prof. Gerhard Hasel, Prof. John E. Toews, Prof. Howard Loewen, Mike Luper, Douglas Heidebrecht, Dean Williams, and students in the seminar "The Christian Use of the Old Testament."

God's Design and Postmodernism: Recent Approaches to Old Testament Theology

PAUL R. HOUSE

Associate Dean and Professor of Divinity
Beeson Divinity School, Samford University
Birmingham, Alabama

Prof. Elmer Martens's long and fruitful career has led him to accept many roles. He has served as teacher, leader, author, and mentor, to name a few. These are related ministries, to be sure, yet ministries that are rarely done well by a single individual. In all these roles he has proven to be a biblical theologian in the best sense of the term, for his ample understanding of the Bible's teachings has shaped his positive actions. For this and many other reasons, he is a person for whom his colleagues can give thanks to God—Father, Son, and Holy Spirit—with full hearts.

Perhaps Martens's most unique academic achievement is his 1981 volume on OT theology, *God's Design: A Focus on Old Testament Theology*.[1] After all, there were precious few OT theology volumes penned by evangelicals from 1962 to 1998.[2] Martens's early career unfolded in days when 20th-century North American–British-Australian evangelicalism was shaping its intellectual tradition. It is fair to conclude that NT scholars outpaced their OT colleagues in these years. Nonetheless, series such as the Tyndale Old Testament Commentary, the New International Commentary on the Old Testament, and the Bible Speaks Today allowed evangelical OT scholars to contribute excellent

---

1. Elmer A. Martens, *God's Design: A Focus on Old Testament Theology* (Grand Rapids: Baker, 1981). Subsequent editions appeared in 1994 and 1998. All citations will be from the 1st edition due to its historical significance and the fact that the 2nd and 3rd editions are not extensive revisions of the earlier work.

2. For a survey of the discipline and evangelicals' place in it, see R. C. Dentan, *Preface to Old Testament Theology* (rev. ed.; New York: Seabury, 1963); Gerhard F. Hasel, *Old Testament Theology: Basic Issues in the Current Debate* (4th ed.; Grand Rapids: Eerdmans, 1991); Ralph L. Smith, *Old Testament Theology: Its History, Method, and Message* (Nashville: Broadman and Holman, 1993) 21–71; and Paul R. House, *Old Testament Theology* (Downers Grove, IL: InterVarsity, 1998) 11–57. My own work was made much easier by these previous volumes.

analyses of individual books. Several fine monographs and introductions to
the OT also appeared. Yet only Walter C. Kaiser's *Toward an Old Testament
Theology*[3] and Martens's *God's Design* took on the task of offering whole-cloth
OT theologies during these years. Thus, Martens's volume has an important
place in the recent history of OT theology.

While several scholars were moving toward some version of canonical
analysis at this time,[4] in *God's Design*, Martens chose a key text (Exod 5:22–
6:8) from which he gleaned four significant themes that illustrate God's design
for Israel and the human race.[5] He charted these four themes, salvation, the
covenant community, knowledge of God, and abundant life in the land,
through the premonarchic, monarchic, and postmonarchic eras, thereby linking thematic and historical elements.[6] He concluded with observations on the
close relationship between the OT and the NT.[7] Thus, in this work Martens
reflects the type of thematic emphasis found in Walther Eichrodt's seminal
work and in the writers that followed his approach, as well as the ecclesio-
logical interests found in Gerhard von Rad's writings.[8]

Martens's analysis of God's design was unitary, theocentric, and humble. It
was unitary in that it tried to show the coherence of the nature and purposes
of God, to depict the thematic-historical wholeness of the OT, and to discuss
the relationship between the OT and the NT. It was theocentric in that
Martens asserted, "A theology of the Old Testament should lay bare, I believe,
the essence of the Old Testament message, a message that centers in Yahweh,
the God of Israel and the world."[9] He writes with great sensitivity about the
human need for deliverance, community, and joyful obedience, yet *Yahweh* is
the key figure in his volume. Indeed Martens claims that Yahweh meets the
needs of creation and that the four chosen themes illustrate how Yahweh does
so. Furthermore, the diversity of the purposes found in these themes indicates
that the unity of God's character allows for the completion of a diverse set of
goals. The book was primarily humble in nature because Martens understood

---

3. Walter C. Kaiser Jr., *Toward an Old Testament Theology* (Grand Rapids: Zondervan, 1978).

4. See, for example, James A. Sanders, *Torah and Canon* (Philadelphia: Fortress, 1972);
Ronald E. Clements, *Old Testament Theology: A Fresh Approach* (London: Marshall, Morgan, and
Scott, 1978); and Brevard S. Childs, *Introduction to the Old Testament as Scripture* (Philadelphia:
Fortress, 1979).

5. Martens, *God's Design*, 11–24.

6. Ibid., 39–248.

7. Ibid., 249–60.

8. Walther Eichrodt, *Theology of the Old Testament* (trans. D. A. Baker; 2 vols.; OTL; Philadelphia: Westminster, 1961–67); and Gerhard von Rad, *Old Testament Theology* (trans. D. M. G.
Stalker; 2 vols.; New York: Harper & Row, 1962–65).

9. Martens, *God's Design*, 3.

the enormity of the task at hand and did not count himself fully sufficient for the challenge that a project of this sort represents. Yet it was also humble because it was authority conscious. Martens placed his work under the authority of the God he described. He writes: "It is my conviction that, since the Old Testament is God's Word, a theology of the Old Testament should point beyond the description of the message to an indication of its importance for today's believer."[10] In other words, he placed himself under the authority of the text so that he might know and declare better the God whose words the text recounts.

Though I make no claims to have equaled Martens's facility in discussing OT theology, I have certainly "stood on his shoulders" when writing my own pieces on the subject. This essay is an attempt to do so once again. In the following pages I will discuss selected recent (1997–2006)[11] volumes on OT theology from the vantage point of one who, like Elmer Martens, strives to be committed to a unitary, theocentric, and authority-conscious reading of the OT. I will argue that such readings make the most sense of the literature and offer the most spiritual aid to our hurting world. Indeed, I believe that we have entered an era of scholarship that requires us to choose between two basic options or variations of these options. We must either learn to follow more thoroughly the biblical faith Martens calls "God's design" or attempt to redesign God according to postmodern conventions and follow the implications of that revision. In the spirit of honesty that includes as full a disclosure of personal belief as possible, I will begin with a summary of my own approach to OT theology, noting at times where my approach and Martens's method intersect.

A Proposed Methodology for Old Testament Theology

In my *Old Testament Theology*, I attempted three basic tasks.[12] First, I sought in the opening chapter and in an appendix to chart major methodological streams in OT theology before 1997 (11–53, 548–59). This survey was not exhaustive, for it focused primarily on projects devoted to treating the whole OT. Several monographs and seminal articles related to OT theology were mentioned, yet many other excellent materials were not included. One of the

---

10. Ibid., 4.

11. Due to time constraints, this survey was not able to include at least two important volumes published in 2006–7: Eugene H. Merrill, *Everlasting Dominion: A Theology of the Old Testament* (Nashville: Broadman and Holman, 2006); and Bruce Waltke, *An Old Testament Theology: A Canonical and Thematic Approach* (Grand Rapids: Zondervan, 2007).

12. All subsequent references in this section to page numbers in my *Old Testament Theology* will be noted in parentheses.

realities of doing scholarship today is choosing what to use among all the
quality works that exist or that one knows, all the while realizing that the
choices made will not lead to a perfect or totally comprehensive treatment.

Second, I offered a methodology for my own volume (53–57). This methodology includes ideas drawn from the history of the discipline and from the
contents of the OT. It affirms with Martens and others the need for *centering*
themes, though not for the need to argue for *one* central theme in the OT, as
did Eichrodt and others. It also affirms with the majority of writers of OT theology that centering themes ought to be grounded in history and in the contents of the OT, however difficult and imperfect the attempt to do so may be.

I chose the OT writers'[13] emphasis on Yahwistic monotheism as the
volume's centering theme, a choice made earlier by Westermann, Zimmerli,
and others.[14] It is important to assert that the OT writers' belief that there is
but one God is not a static, monotonous doctrine. Rather, the theme grows
and develops as the compassionate, covenantally faithful, just, stable, good, and
balanced nature of God emerges throughout the canon. It is also important to
note that arguing for monotheism's importance in the OT is not simply a
philosophical debate about definitions or a historical discussion about when
and how the Israelite writers came to believe in one God and to explicate the
implications of this belief. This theme gave the biblical writers a way of talking about and having a covenantal *relationship* with the one God. The same is
true today, for this theme has significance well beyond academic theology. For
example, it has ongoing importance for world evangelization, for it is now
impossible to assume monotheism when speaking with non-Christians in the
United States, much less in countries where polytheistic religions are historically prominent.

This methodology uses the threefold Hebrew canon as a structuring device,
a strategy that has been employed in the last thirty years by Clements, Childs,
Sailhamer, and others.[15] This is a viable option for working through the

---

13. I believe that the task of OT theology is to explicate what the canon's authors assert, not
to survey all that Israelites may have believed during the biblical era. In other words, I do not
equate OT theology and the history of Israel. For an excellent survey of the options available
for the study of the history of Israel and the ways that one might approach describing the many
religions in Israel during OT times, see Richard Hess, *Israelite Religions: An Archaeological and
Biblical Survey* (Grand Rapids: Baker, 2007) 11–80.

14. See Walther Zimmerli, *Old Testament Theology in Outline* (trans. Eliot Green; Atlanta:
John Knox, 1978); and Claus Westermann, *Elements of Old Testament Theology* (trans. Douglas
W. Stott; Atlanta: John Knox, 1982).

15. See Clements, *Old Testament Theology: A Fresh Approach*; Childs, *Introduction to the Old
Testament as Scripture* and *Old Testament Theology in Canonical Context* (Philadelphia: Fortress,
1986); and John H. Sailhamer, *Introduction to Old Testament Theology: A Canonical Approach*
(Grand Rapids: Eerdmans, 1995).

biblical material, though this is not the only useful option possible. As part of the canon, the OT is sacred Scripture. It is God's word written to and for his people.[16] The people receive the contents of the canon, but they do not create this word by their own impulse. They receive revelation that addresses the world in which they live.

This canonically oriented methodology seeks connections between biblical books and sections of the canon through quotations, allusions, and ongoing themes. Beginning at least as early as Deuteronomy, biblical writers refer to and build upon previous works. These verbal and thematic ties encourage OT theologians to read subsequent books in light of previous ones and to describe how ideas that span the whole of the canon develop. This type of intertextual study incorporates methods used by Childs, Seitz, Sailhamer, Harrison, Gese, and Fishbane.[17] It also utilizes formalistic literary methodology.[18]

When my *Old Testament Theology* was published, its methodology was intended as a precursor to later treatments of "Whole Bible" biblical theology. I view the OT as a discrete witness that leads to the next canonical step, which in my opinion is the NT. The Bible is one book, not two, so the OT and NT should be read in continuity. It is not necessary to read the OT as a separate witness, then to read the NT as a separate witness, and finally to compare the two. These convictions linked me in a subsequent project to other scholars, including Elmer Martens, who share similar commitments about the whole-ness of the Bible.[19]

Third, I applied the chosen methodology to each book and section of the OT (58–547). I desired to demonstrate the theological wholeness of each book and the way each individual book fits into the canon's portrayal of Yahweh,

---

16. Like Elmer Martens, I am a member of the Evangelical Theological Society, so each year both of us affirm our belief that the Bible is "inerrant in the original autographs."

17. See Childs, *Introduction to the Old Testament as Scripture* and *Old Testament Theology in Canonical Context*; Christopher R. Seitz, *Word without End: The Old Testament as Abiding Theological Witness* (Grand Rapids: Eerdmans, 1998); Sailhamer, *Introduction to Old Testament Theology: A Canonical Approach*; R. K. Harrison, *Introduction to the Old Testament: With a Comprehensive Review of Old Testament Studies and a Special Supplement on the Apocrypha* (Grand Rapids: Eerdmans, 1969); Hartmut Gese, *Zur biblischen Theologie* (2nd ed.; Tübingen: Mohr/Siebeck, 1983); and Michael A. Fishbane, *Biblical Interpretation in Ancient Israel* (Oxford: Clarendon, 1985).

18. See my *Unity of the Twelve* (JSOTSup 97; Sheffield: Sheffield Academic Press, 1990); Cleanth Brooks, *Community, Religion, and Literature: Essays by Cleanth Brooks* (Columbia: University of Missouri Press, 1995); and the works by John Goldingay and Stephen Dempster discussed below.

19. See Scott J. Hafemann and Paul R. House, eds., *Central Themes in Biblical Theology: Mapping Unity in Diversity* (Grand Rapids: Baker, 2007). Scott Hafemann, Elmer Martens, Roy Ciampa, Tom Schreiner, Frank Thielman, Stephen Dempster, and I contributed essays to this volume.

the only God. I hoped that this book-by-book format would aid preachers as well as students. Because of the emphasis on textual wholeness, I am aware that at times legitimate types of diversity were probably slighted. This was not my intention, because the variety of statements about Yahweh contributes to the OT's portrayal of God's oneness of character and action.

As was noted above, throughout *Old Testament Theology* I argued for the full authority of Scripture because I affirm the text's claims that they are the life-giving written words of God, the creator (see Deut 32:47; Isa 40–44; Ps 19:7–12; etc). Thus, like Martens I believe that OT theology must be descriptive: it should discuss and interpret the accounts given in Scripture. Yet I also believe that OT is normative because I embrace, albeit extremely imperfectly in my personal behavior, its claims to be the written word of the one God, the creator, the covenant maker, and the rightful, merciful judge of every person. In short, OT theology is unitary because it originates in the one unitary God[20] and because of its consistent literary contents. It is promissory in that it guides those who wish to serve God and because it anticipates future revelation.[21] In this way, it inspires people to serve Yahweh as a means of living in hope.

Since writing *Old Testament Theology*, I have explored briefly the Bible's overarching narrative.[22] I have noted that the Bible itself at several junctures presents a narrative that stretches from creation to new creation,[23] with stops along the way that include the exodus, the entering of Canaan, the rise of the Davidic monarchy, the fall of Israel, the Exile, the return from Exile, the coming of Jesus Christ, and the emergence and early work of the church. The coming new creation includes persons from the many nations of the world. This unified narrative includes a variety of threats and failures that make the plot quite diverse in presentation, yet the plot continues. Therefore, the plot is comic (positive) in the Aristotelian sense of the term.[24] For it to be so means that the positive result only comes after threats to its completion. Thus, this

---

20. On this point, consult Carl F. H. Henry, *God, Revelation and Authority, Volume Two: God Who Speaks and Shows, Fifteen Theses* (Wheaton, IL: Crossway, 1999) 69–76.

21. Scott Hafemann asserts that biblical theology revolves around our faith in present circumstances, which is grounded in our belief in God's provision in the past and his promises for the future. Thus, biblical theology consists of love, faith, and hope. See Hafemann, *The God of Promise and the Life of Faith: Understanding the Heart of the Bible* (Wheaton, IL: Crossway, 2001).

22. See my "Examining the Narratives of Old Testament Narrative: An Exploration in Biblical Theology," *WTJ* 67 (2005) 229–45.

23. This concept comes from William J. Dumbrell, *The Search for Order: Biblical Eschatology in Focus* (Grand Rapids: Baker, 1994) 9.

24. See my analysis of Aristotle's concept of the structure and development of comic plots as it relates to the Book of the Twelve in *The Unity of the Twelve*, 37–162. I believe that the prophetic literature's overall plot coincides with the plot found in OT narrative.

plot is a unity that includes much diverse content and that includes a positive result for all who trust Yahweh with their lives. It is also a cosmic comic plot that applies to everyone, which is an important trait to note in today's post-modern context.

The Search for a Moderate Postmodernism:
Walter Brueggemann

It is difficult to overstate Walter Brueggemann's prominence in American OT studies over the past three decades. He has authored and edited dozens of books, and his works are cited extensively in the discipline. Thus, the release of his 1997 *Theology of the Old Testament: Testimony, Dispute, and Advocacy* was a major publishing event.[25] Brueggemann's volume was not only the fruit of many years of study; it also marked the beginning of what is likely to be a long era of writers publishing what they consider to be postmodern OT theologies.

Brueggemann argues that scholarship cannot be anything other than a product of the predominant beliefs of its own times (xv, 1). Indeed, this fact is good, because it forces OT study to address the needs of its era. Given this conviction, Brueggemann argues that it is necessary for today's OT theologians to take a postmodern approach to the theological task. By *postmodern* he means primarily a method opposed to closure, certitude, and oppression and in favor of "processes, procedures, and interactionist potential" (xvi). Like reader-response critics and deconstruction advocates, he believes all interpretations involve advocacy, not just an individual author's perspective. All readings have agendas, whether their adherents know so or not (xvi). He claims recent literary approaches have determined that OT narratives may be read in many ways, and several of these ways can be legitimate (xv). These approaches not only reveal an unsettled epistemological situation but indeed indicate that "the unsettlement is a reflection of the nature of the Old Testament text itself and, speaking theologically, of the unsettled Character who stands at the center of the text" (xv).

Given these realities, Brueggemann concludes that one way to approach the text is to read it as a series of episodes that reveal both competing and complementary aims. God is a character in the story but no more and no less. The text creates God in this sense. The history of OT theological research reveals there are many ways to describe God's nature (61–80). Recent studies and 20th-century history indicate that reading the OT in a specifically Christian

---

25. Walter Brueggemann, *Old Testament Theology: Testimony, Dispute, Advocacy* (Minneapolis: Augsburg Fortress, 1997). All subsequent references to page numbers in Brueggemann in this section of the essay appear in parentheses.

way should be avoided, lest these interpretations be used against Jewish and other religious communities. Reading the OT as a final authority to be obeyed by all should also be avoided, lest interpretation be used to mistreat women, persons of color, or any other underrepresented group (81–114). To achieve these aims, it is best to set aside questions of historicity and ontology (118).

Brueggemann adopts a courtroom metaphor in which the various emphases in the text are read as voices offering testimony, dispute, and advocacy (xvi–xvii, 117–22). Taken together, these testimonies constitute Israel's confession of faith. Readers of these testimonies must determine which voice to heed in the sense that they must decide how the different voices apply to their own interpretive community. Presenting all the biblical witnesses is the fairest way for scholars to proceed, for no voice deserves priority over others. Anything less is interpretive coercion. Thus, the major rule that readers must observe is never to use their readings to harm others. Because of this concern, Brueggemann saves his most stringent criticism for scholars who offer what he considers methods that exclude others. For example, he cites Childs's approach to biblical theology as a singularly Christian discipline and calls it "massively reductionistic" (92).

Brueggemann follows his methodology carefully when examining the OT. He clearly and eloquently describes Israel's core testimony, which is that the Lord is sovereign and stable (122–313). Nonetheless, he concludes that there are other witnesses to be heard—witnesses that provide awkward and unsettling testimony (313). This countertestimony includes issues such as theodicy and perceived ambiguity in God's character (317–403). As one might expect, Brueggemann highlights the laments and the wisdom tradition in this section, though he also includes passages taken from the whole canon. He eventually discusses Israel's embodied testimony, which underscores the way Israel did and did not act as Yahweh's partner throughout their history (567–704). This section connects with Israel's core testimony in that God's goodness and Israel's flawed covenantal record are always part of the same story and the same discussion.

Brueggemann's final section is instructive for anyone wishing to chart the discipline's future (707–50). He addresses ongoing issues such as OT theology's relationship to historical criticism, the NT, the Jewish community, and ethics, particularly justice. The way forward, he believes, is to admit that pluralism is the wave of the future. Older views are being "disestablished." New ways of thinking are on the rise, and people who order their thinking toward Yahweh must find fresh ways of grasping reality. The important thing in the future will be to listen to all voices, always expectant that Israel's core testimony, Israel's countertestimony, and Israel's life before God will offer windows into ethical living today. At the same time, no one voice can have priority, lest certitude and its attendant abuse of others find their way back into interpretation.

As was noted above, Brueggemann's volume is the first major programmatic postmodern OT theology. As such it addresses unitary, theocentric, and authority-conscious theology. In some ways it does so positively, for it offers clear and artful descriptions of the wholeness of the character of Yahweh and the wholeness of the Bible. Indeed, Brueggemann considers these to be elements of Israel's "core testimony" (see above).

However, in the matter of authority Brueggemann implies that this core testimony must not be trusted completely because of what he considers competing, not just differing, voices in the OT. Despite multiple earlier scholars arguing the opposite, he thinks these differing voices destabilize the characterization of God and the text's claims to be from Yahweh for God's people on behalf of the creation. Brueggemann has determined that the differing voices do not need to be reconciled with the core testimony, which makes it impossible for these voices and the core testimony to be part of a multilayered plot and the resolution of the plot. In my opinion, he precludes the possibility of a complex comic plot too readily. He may do so because he believes that OT theology *must* reflect the current predominant intellectual scene, a scene that rebels against universally applicable narratives. He may think that changing others is not what the current climate requires—unless one sees the need to change "reductionistic" scholars' opinions (see above). It is more likely that he affirms the most generally accepted tenets of the current scene and believes that scholars who offer other solutions need to rethink their opinions.

Where does Brueggemann's approach to unitary, theocentric, and authority-conscious theology leave readers? I am concerned that it leaves them without a sure basis for reconciliation with God and neighbor, for dialogue alone cannot create and sustain the just world that Brueggemann so clearly and passionately advocates. His approach seems to claim that by voicing and attending to diverse views reconciliation can be achieved; and gratefully, when people do share their views, sometimes at least beginning points (presuppositions) or needs can be reconciled. Many of us wish this were always the case. However, reconciliation often occurs through acceptance of the authority of a person or persons who profess ideas that are "hard to take" because they do not currently satisfy our human longing to know, belong, and triumph. In short, sometimes reconciliation and/or justice come by an authority that orders it to happen.

Brueggemann's approach rightly treasures dialogue and testimony, which many prior works (including works by evangelicals such as Martens) value. However, to borrow his courtroom metaphor, it does not allow sufficient space for a very natural part of a courtroom scene to occur—the jury's verdict and the judge's sentence. And the Bible claims that the living God of the Bible is the judge who orders warring parties to accept reconciliation and community wholeness under the terms that God sets. Brueggemann's method leaves readers with no finally trustworthy witness, jurist, jury, or judge who can render an appropriate and clearly just decision. Though there is much injustice in human courts, even today, just witnesses, lawyers, juries, and judges exist.

By discounting fully trustworthy testimony and a fully trustworthy jury and judge, one may well postpone a verdict indefinitely. When one postpones a verdict indefinitely, one undercuts the community's ability to improve, heal, love, accept, and grow. Dialogue is an important part of any premodern, modern, or postmodern setting, but dialogue alone cannot bring reconciliation. Certitude is not the only devastating taskmaster; dialogue without decision can be devastating as well. One can trade the struggle to grasp the unity of Yahweh's character, the overall wholeness of the Bible, and an attitude of humility toward the text and receive talk alone, albeit thoughtful talk, as a result. One may trade trust in a completely trustworthy God for an exceedingly untrustworthy human race. If one precludes closure on vital issues indefinitely due to objections to older, oppressive, and perhaps failed interpretations, one may eventually find one's position in the service of dialogue just as inappropriately dogmatic and arrogant as earlier generations were in the service of closure.

Clearly, I do not think Brueggemann's approach gives full credit to the OT's own claims to unity, theocentric theology, and authority. It certainly does not provide a platform for overt evangelism. Of course, Brueggemann would probably use extreme caution in encouraging anyone to think that evangelism would be a good use of the OT in this era. Interestingly, Brueggemann troubles not only traditionalists such as me; his approach has already proven insufficiently revolutionary and dialogic for scholars who prefer certain types of reader-response and deconstructionist methods for reading the OT.[26] In the future, many interpreters will probably find Brueggemann too radical, others will find him too conservative, and still others will find him helpful in charting a course between traditional and newer approaches to the text. Regardless of his work's ongoing reception, however, I suspect that this skilled theologian's

---

26. For example, Carleen Mandolfo expresses great appreciation for Brueggemann, especially for his willingness to stress the OT's competing voices. Yet she concludes that in Brueggemann's work "one senses a real resistance to any kind of ultimate hermeneutical dialogism." She believes that his assertion of a positive core testimony that constitutes "a 'main theological claim' renders all calls to dialogic interpretation disingenuous" (*Daughter Zion Talks Back to the Prophets: A Dialogic Theology of the Book of Lamentations* [Atlanta: Society of Biblical Literature, 2007] 5 n. 10).

legacy will be in part his ability to make readers, even readers like me, think and act. In this particular way, he will thus have succeeded as a significant postmodern pioneer.

The Search for Contours of Old Testament Theology: Bernhard Anderson

Rather than use the postmodern methods that Brueggemann advocates, in his *Contours of Old Testament Theology*,[27] Bernhard Anderson attempts to incorporate more-traditional ways of examining OT theology into a current theological method beneficial to today's theological students, ministers, missionaries, and laypersons (vii). This volume appeared after Anderson had taught the OT for over four decades. Thus, like Brueggemann's *Theology of the Old Testament*, Anderson's work is that of a mature scholar.

Anderson defines the theologian's task as articulating and elaborating "the faith of the believing and worshiping community so that members of the community, or others interested, may understand who God is, God's relationship to the world and all that is in it, and the unfolding purpose of God from creation to consummation" (3). He desires to allow the OT to speak for itself in a way that will avoid overemphasizing discontinuity with the NT and avoid minimizing the distinctions between the testaments (9–13). Anderson considers Christology the main thematic link between the testaments and thinks that ideas such as holy war provide the greatest discontinuity (14). He hopes to avoid pitting the Jewish and Christian communities against one another without failing to deal with the vital doctrine of election (14–16).

Anderson understands that these aims hardly match some other current approaches. For example, he notes his agreements and disagreements with Brueggemann. On the one hand, he appreciates Brueggemann's creativity and concern that the entire OT testimony be heard (22–26). On the other hand, he questions Brueggemann's method for finding the core testimony, for he does not think that Brueggemann adequately explains why he chooses some texts for core testimony instead of others (26). He also believes that it is important *not* to bracket out historical concerns, that it is important to maintain OT theology as a Christian discipline, and that it is important to assert that the OT is revelation that comes from outside the community (26–27). He particularly maintains that revelation is not a matter of the community of faith

---

27. Bernhard W. Anderson, *Contours of Old Testament Theology* (Minneapolis: Augsburg Fortress, 1999). All subsequent references to page numbers in Anderson in this section of the essay appear in parentheses.

deciding that the Bible is revelation. Rather, God's revelation transcends the community and calls the community to the Lord (27).

Anderson observes that his volume must deal with basic issues to be effective. He notes four methodological requirements for a sound OT theology: finding a valid starting place, ascertaining the text's fundamental witness, demonstrating the text's unity and diversity, and showing the continuity and discontinuity between the testaments (39).

With regard to the first point, he begins with the Torah's assertion that Yahweh is the holy one of Israel, because the Torah is Israel's fundamental Scripture and because this theme appears in the Prophets and Writings (39–40). From this core affirmation, Anderson then traces other assertions about Yahweh, including his names, character, and depiction in the Scriptures (40–73). He duly notes the various aspects of Yahweh's nature (mercy, wrath, etc.) and concludes that God's holiness means that "there is no antithesis between divine wrath and divine mercy" (62). In a manner reminiscent of G. Ernest Wright, to whose memory the volume is dedicated, he thinks Yahweh's great acts in history identify him as quite different from the other gods described in ancient texts (63–73).

For the second and third primary tasks, he outlines three great covenants, great historical figures associated with them, and great prophets who profess these covenants' principles. Thus, he connects Abraham and Sarah to the priestly elements of the Abrahamic Covenant and emphasizes Ezekiel's expounding of priestly theology. He links Moses, Aaron, and Miriam to the Deuteronomistic Covenant and details Hosea's and Jeremiah's teaching of that covenant's principles. Finally, he ties David to the Psalms and Chronicles and discusses Isaiah's commitment to Davidic and Zion theology. Through this strategy, he manages to cover major segments of the Law, Prophets, and Writings (34, 81–249). Anderson believes that the Babylonian Exile led to a crisis of faith that gave rise to canonical Wisdom Literature. Thus, he asserts that the nation's love for Torah led to wisdom writings and new prophetic voices such as exilic Isaiah (253–301). Eventually the people's frustration with their political and spiritual situation resulted in the emergence of apocalyptic, a literary tradition that looked for a cosmic solution to the woes that the exiles faced (302–24).

This leads us to his fourth methodological concern, and Anderson argues that apocalyptic literature is an excellent bridge between the testaments. Apocalyptic literature's emphasizing of cosmic divine victory, resurrection, and the coming Son of Man (see Dan 7:13–14) all provide links to the NT (325–36). It thus leads to reflection on Jesus, who is prophet, priest, and king—the one who thereby links the testaments (337–44).

Anderson's volume is a vital contribution to unitary, theocentric, and authority-conscious OT theology. His ability to reveal thematic, historical, canonical, and messianic continuity in the text demonstrates the vibrancy of traditional approaches. His linking of text, covenant, and prophet is a unique way of discussing OT unity. At the same time, stressing different emphases allows him to avoid an improper overstating of this unity. Diversity does exist. Nonetheless, he correctly concludes that diversity of presentation does not exclude underlying connections. The nature of God, his relationship with Israel and the nations, and his promises for the future take many forms in the OT. To view these as competing voices, however, does not do justice to their common aims—what Brueggemann calls Israel's "core testimony" and what Elmer Martens calls "God's design." Despite my disagreements on matters such as his dating of many parts of the OT and the implications of his historical conclusions for the authority of the Bible that he clearly values, I believe that he indeed demonstrates that there are specific enduring contours in OT theology.

The Search for Pluralistic Old Testament Theologies: Erhard Gerstenberger

Like Brueggemann and Anderson, Erhard Gerstenberger is an established OT scholar. He has written major commentaries on Leviticus, Psalms, and Lamentations. Thus, he has done the sort of wide-ranging work on the OT that often serves as excellent preparation for writing OT theology. These prior contributions, supplemented by lecturing outside his native Germany, have led him to contend for a pluralistic approach to the discipline. The English title of his OT theology volume, *Theologies in the Old Testament*,[28] announces his convictions, as does the subtitle of the German edition, *Pluralität und Synkretismus alttestamentlichen Gottesglaubens*. As his volume unfolds, it becomes clear that he advocates a broader brand of postmodernism than Brueggemann.

Gerstenberger desires to write a theology that contributes to an "ecumenical quest for a responsible theology," and by "ecumenical" he means religion that incorporates different cultures and different religions. His main goal is to "help us find authentic answers of faith in a torn-apart and confused world" (ix–x). Thus, he wants to reach out to Christians and non-Christians alike. To do so, he begins with the bold declaration, "The Old Testament, a collection of many testimonies of faith from around a thousand years of the history of ancient Israel, has no unitary theology, nor can it" (1). He adds that any "unity

---

28. Erhard S. Gerstenberger, *Theologies in the Old Testament* (trans. John Bowden; Minneapolis: Fortress, 2002). All subsequent references to page numbers in Gerstenberger in this section of the essay appear in parentheses.

of belief in God . . . does not lie in the texts themselves, even in the collected writings or the canon, but solely in our perspective" (1). These ancient testimonies are fragmentary, heavily edited, and syncretistic. Gerstenberger considers these conclusions "an extraordinary stroke of good fortune," for this knowledge frees readers to dialogue with other world religions without the burden of certitude and the need to find permanent, binding statements (1–2). It calls Christians to "refrain from claiming to be sole representatives and acknowledge that other traditions, interpretations and theological formulations have equal rights" (3). Gerstenberger's commitment to a community-oriented, dialogic, reader-response approach to the text could hardly be stated more plainly.

Gerstenberger's method includes three basic points. First, he asserts that he does not begin with the revealed word of God, because it is impossible to know that this is what the OT is. Second, he begins instead from the social conditions in ancient Israel, which he reconstructs from the Bible and the principles of selected current sociological theories. He believes that the main sources for Israel's theologies were the family, village, tribal alliance, kingdom, and postexilic community (19–24). He treats these groups in the OT as competing parties that wrote or influenced the writing of the text. Third, he claims that "the different interests of the individual social groupings, often existing side by side, produced group-specific theologies which also existed side by side" (24). He defines these theologies largely by the way he believes they used their depiction of God to protect their group. His analysis of the theologies in the OT (25–272) then uses these groups as reference points.

Gerstenberger's final two chapters summarize what these assertions mean for contemporary readers. In "Polytheism, Syncretism, and the One God," he concludes that the OT is syncretistic in that no matter how much the canon may speak of the one God its texts are actually written to maintain the existence of a community, not to declare the nature of God (274). Further, failure to recognize this point can lead to one group using "the truth" to oppress another, as was the case in Nazi Germany (274–75). Given the Bible's and our commitment to self and community preservation, we "are and remain born polytheists, regardless of how much lip-service we pay to the one God" (275). He thinks that wars based on what people claimed to believe about God are proof of this polytheism. He also considers the monotheistic claims of postexilic Israel dangerous in that they were used to oppress those in Israelite society who disagreed. From seeds such as this, religious intolerance is born, and to this day intolerance "has unleashed orgies of persecution and extermination from the side of the dominant majority and state religions, time and again, and with explicit reference to the religious sources of antiquity" (280–81).

In his final chapter ("Effects and Controversies"), Gerstenberger suggests ways that this theology can affect the world today. Stated briefly, he hopes that this theology can sustain the many social groups in the world. He hopes that clans, families, tribes, and nations can coexist without intolerance and oppression. He notes that there are many definitions of God today and believes that Christians should create a "God for all" (305). Christians must stress human equality, engage helpfully with other faiths, work for the good of all human beings, and hope in the future improvement of human life (306). There is no question that Gerstenberger wishes to foster peace, tolerance, and kindness among differing theological groups. There is also no question that he believes that specific theological beliefs that are held to be revealed by God lessen the potential for these positive changes to emerge.

Because the earlier parts of this essay make plain many of my disagreements with Gerstenberger's approach to unitary, theocentric, and authority-conscious theology, I will not raise these concerns in detail at this point. But I will note three issues related to the potential of Gerstenberger's program to meet his own objectives. First, Gerstenberger's volume, like Brueggemann's, reveals and criticizes the way professing Christians have abused others. God's name has been used to mistreat other people. Wars having nothing to do with true and accurate biblical theology have been fought based on theological claims. Theology has indeed been used both to suppress and to create opposition to established governments. Thus, we can agree that God's name has thereby been taken in vain. Perhaps no one would agree with these conclusions more than Elmer Martens, whose pacifist convictions embody his opposition to these sorts of misuses of theology.

Second, in my opinion the type of postmodern approach that Gerstenberger advocates cannot produce the peace and harmony that he desires. Gerstenberger mentions Nazi Germany and its atrocities. I have merely read about and reflected on these events rather than experiencing their unfolding and their immediate aftermath. Nevertheless, I believe these terrible events, or at least the participation of Christians in them, might have been minimized or might never have occurred if interpretations of the Scriptures such as Schlatter's, Barth's, Niemoller's, and Bonhoeffer's had been heeded. Their views were more in keeping with the structure and genre of the Bible and with its presentation of the character of God than "Nazified" readings. They were truer to the text. These theologians did not just represent competing community voices. Their voice was in concert with the Bible, and they rightly asked the people of their day to decide between the power of light and the power of darkness. Without decisions of this sort, there can be no peace and wholeness in times of severe trial.

Third, Gerstenberger's call for pluralistic OT theologies is in effect a call to
syncretistic religion that if heeded will greatly curtail or even eliminate biblical
faith. The definition of "God" that his method allows (and may indeed call
for) is not the definition given by the mainstream of history's interpreters of
the Bible. It is not the definition offered in the great creeds of church history
or in the historical Christian spiritual disciplines. It is not a definition of the
God of neo-orthodoxy or evangelicalism—or indeed of confessing Christianity in general. Of course, Gerstenberger may believe that this is precisely
the point he wishes to make. It may be that this type of re-formed religion is
what he thinks is needed. If so, we must question whether a new religion
would produce less oppression, even if we accepted the premise that a belief in
the value and effectiveness of human dialogue and decision-making serves the
true needs of humanity better than a belief in divine revelation and its attendant ethics of love.

Contending for the Old Testament's Theological Narrative: Stephen Dempster and John Goldingay

Volumes published in 2003 by Stephen Dempster and John Goldingay
sought to chart the OT's unitary theological narrative and anchor that narrative in the OT's unitary presentation of God and his authority. Both used
formalistic literary methods, and both highlighted legitimate diversity within
the unity they described. Both wrote from a broadly evangelical framework,
and both presented a clear alternative to the postmodern approaches offered
by Brueggemann and Gerstenberger. Their emphasis on the OT's overarching
narrative also separated them a bit from Anderson's thematic approach, though
their work is compatible with his. Both writers contended for unitary reading,
took a theocentric approach to their task, and asserted the OT's authority,
though they took differing paths on the latter issue.

Stephen Dempster's *Dominion and Dynasty: A Theology of the Hebrew Bible*
is the fruit of many years of teaching and writing about biblical theology.[29]
Like Elmer Martens's *God's Design*, Dempster's work is compact. In his introductory chapter, Dempster freely acknowledges that the OT contains diverse
material and will thus be viewed differently by different scholars (15–16).
Nonetheless, he denies that unity means "sameness" or that diversity means

---

29. Stephen G. Dempster, *Dominion and Dynasty: A Biblical Theology of the Hebrew Bible*
(NSBT 15; Downers Grove, IL: InterVarsity, 2003). All subsequent references to page numbers
in Dempster in this section of the essay appear in parentheses.

"competing ideas" (16–24). Rather, he believes that by adapting formalistic literary methods he will be able to describe the OT's structural, generic, and theological-conceptual unity (24–51).

With this methodology in place, Dempster then uses the threefold order of the Hebrew Bible that appears in the Talmud to structure his discussion (33–35). He claims that the Law (Genesis–Deuteronomy) and Former Prophets (Joshua–Kings) announce "Dominion Lost: The Rise and Fall of Israel" (55–156). The Latter Prophets (Jeremiah–Book of the Twelve) and first portion of the Writings (Ruth–Lamentations) describe "Retrospect and Prospect: A Stump and a Shoot" (159–210), while Daniel–Chronicles, also part of the Writings, discuss "Dominion Regained: The Fall and Rise of Israel" (213–34). He thereby treats Genesis–Kings as the story of Israel's rise, possession of the land, and loss of the land. He treats the prophetic and poetic materials as commentary on those events. Finally, he treats Daniel–Chronicles as the description of Israel's return to its land. Throughout his analysis, Dempster focuses on the text's historical setting, not just its overarching literary context. He clearly believes that history must inform an accurate and compelling literary theory of the OT.

Dempster's work has several strengths. First, it helps readers grasp the wholeness of the OT without losing a sense of the multifaceted nature of its plot. For Dempster, "unity" and "diversity" are not competing claims. This viewpoint coincides with the views of the majority of practitioners of ancient and recent literary criticism. Second, the book's compactness makes it an effective tool for students who have not grown up with knowledge of the Bible's basic contents or studied its contents previously in an academic setting. Readers can use this volume to gain a sense of the entirety of the OT's theological witness before endeavoring to make decisions about its specific theological details. Third, this volume links literary and historical data effectively. Dempster rightly understands that the OT's literary nature is in many ways inextricable from its historical reflections. Fourth, Dempster discusses the need for readers to obey the God described in the OT for the OT to be an effective tool for societal renewal. His emphasis on an appropriate sense of and response to authority is, like his emphasis on the wholeness of God's character and the unity of the OT's plot, stated gently but persistently. He guides; he does not berate. In these ways, his writing and Elmer Martens's are very much alike.

In my opinion, Dempster's work could be improved by the inclusion of more-specific thematic elaboration. There are thematic elements in the book to be sure, yet the broader implications of the parts could be made plainer. Perhaps these matters will be taken up in a subsequent work. His recent work on the "servant of Yahweh" in biblical theology is the sort of quality, whole-cloth analysis of which he is capable.[30] His contribution to unitary, theocentric, and authority-conscious OT theology will no doubt grow over the next few years.

John Goldingay has had a long and productive scholarly career, having written significant commentaries and hermeneutical volumes on the OT. His *Old Testament Theology, Volume One: Israel's Gospel* is the first installment of a three-volume project.[31] This first volume surveys the OT's narrative books, which Goldingay believes reveal God's acts on Israel's behalf that constitute the nation's gospel. The second volume, which appeared in 2006 (see below), discusses "Israel's Faith," which in this case means Yahweh and his relationship with Israel, creation, and the nations of the earth. This volume features the Pentateuch and prophetic literature to a much greater extent than the previous one. The projected third volume is slated to analyze Israel's ethics and to use more of the OT's wisdom and worship-oriented materials. When finished, Goldingay's project will be one of the most comprehensive in the history of the discipline. If completed as planned, it will also be very much in keeping with Elmer Martens's concerns. After all, the first volume focuses on unitary theology, the second volume emphasizes theocentric theology, and the third volume intends to stress authority-conscious living in God's world.

As for his methodology, in the 2003 volume Goldingay writes that the task of OT theology is to begin with the contents of the OT (16) and work toward being able "to see what greater whole can encompass the diversity within the Old Testament" (17). Though this task is critical and analytical, it is not just that. Rather, it is a reflective exercise that he believes "has a capacity to speak with illumination and power to the lives of communities and individuals" (18). As part of his reflective work, Goldingay desires to "formulate a statement that is theological in the sense that it expresses what we can believe and live by and not merely one that restates what some dead Israelites believed" (18).

To support this reflective work, he identifies "with those Christians who affirm the entire trustworthiness and authority of Scripture" without expecting others to take his comments at face value without sufficient evidence (19). He also wishes to criticize the actual practice of Christians who do not agree that Scripture is authoritative and trustworthy, because he does not believe that they have come to grips with the unity of the Bible, the thematic elements the OT reveals as part of the biblical story, or the OT's realistic descriptions of

---

30. See Stephen Dempster, "The Servant of the Lord," in *Central Themes in Biblical Theology: Mapping Unity in Diversity* (ed. Scott J. Hafemann and Paul R. House; Grand Rapids: Baker, 2007) 128–78.

31. John Goldingay, *Old Testament Theology, Volume One: Israel's Gospel* (Downers Grove, IL: InterVarsity, 2003). All subsequent references to page numbers in Goldingay in this section of the essay appear in parentheses.

life in God's world (20–23). Goldingay believes that the OT and the NT tell a unified story of God's gospel that includes the definitive work of God in Jesus Christ and that an "under reading" of the OT minimizes the full force of the gospel. Thus, he concludes, "The Old Testament is not basically hard or demanding news to swallow, but good news that has not been heard" (23). It is with these principles in mind that Goldingay argues that the OT and the NT are authoritative interpretations of one another (25) and that early Christians considered "Jesus' story as 'gospel'" because they "were thinking of his story in terms that had already applied to Israel's story" (28).

He believes that to attempt the theological task he envisions in a postmodern context, it is important to begin with the OT's grand narrative, which he believes has the added benefit of forcing him to work with the whole canon, not just with themes (18). He thinks that as one examines Genesis–Kings one discovers that these books depict the good news that God loves Israel and the whole of creation and works for their redemption (29–33). Examining this narrative leads readers to scrutinize the character of God and of Israel, for these are the narrative's primary characters (29–33). Furthermore, this exercise underscores how narrative texts often force readers to think for themselves about their meaning (38–39).

Though Goldingay clearly respects Brueggemann and other self-professed postmodern scholars, he does not accept their approach. Goldingay appreciates postmodernism's emphasis on narrative and on the fact that interpreters operate from presuppositions and from within social settings (41). He finds it important to state one's foundational principles and commitments. But he disagrees with Brueggemann's assertion that biblical interpretation is inevitably a deconstructive task (22). Rather, he claims, it is a reconstructive endeavor, for "The Old Testament tells us who God is and who we are through the ongoing story of God's relationship with Israel" (30).

Interestingly, as was noted above, he claims that many conservative Christians take what amounts to a deconstructive postmodern approach to the OT, for they cut off the OT from the NT (22, 40–41). The better way, he argues, is to read the Bible forward. That is, one should read the OT as the first portion of revelation, rather than reading the text backwards, as I sense that some "Old-Testament-in-the-New" advocates do. The OT is an incomplete story without the NT, but the NT is likewise an incomplete story without the OT. Therefore, readers should follow the OT's agenda, not impose an agenda of their own on the text (25–41).

I find it impossible to describe the contents of this lengthy volume in detail in this essay. Nonetheless, it is important to note that while discussing the OT's narrative Goldingay focuses on certain subjects, all of which treat God as the main character in an unfolding depiction of God's work in the world through Israel for the benefit of the nations. He addresses the OT's assertion that God's redemptive work began with creation, began again after humanity's sin, promised Israel's ancestors blessing and relationship, delivered Israel at the time of the exodus, sealed Israel as his people at Sinai, gave Israel land, accommodated Israel's frailties from the conquest of Canaan to the time of David, wrestled with Israel due to their covenant-breaking ways from Solomon's era to the Exile, preserved Israel during the Exile, and sent Jesus to herald God's reign (42–858). It is hard for any interpreter to choose which themes to stress when emphasizing the OT's unified message; Goldingay chooses well. He also does a solid job of detailing the implications of the themes as they appear in the text. Like Dempster, he offers readers an excellent view of the wholeness of the OT's contents.

In the second volume,[32] Goldingay first reflects on how the previous one has been received and states his method for the new book. He notes that his approach in the first volume led one Jewish reviewer to conclude that he was too Christian in his approach and one Christian reviewer to decide that he was not Christian enough (13–14)! He responds, "I believe the two Testaments are fundamentally at one in their understanding of God and humanity and the relationship between them. The New Testament confirms the perspectives of the First Testament and shows how God brought to its climax the purpose that God had been pursuing with Israel" (14). Reviewers can certainly dispute how well Goldingay fulfilled his goals, and the conviction that he did so poorly may contribute to the critiques he mentions. But other issues are likely in play as well. Christians who wish to divide the testaments more radically than Goldingay does will perhaps find him not Christian enough. Interpreters who do not find the fulfillment of Israel's story in Jesus and/or who believe that OT theology should contribute to societal well-being through consensus with other religions may well find his first volume too Christian. By sticking to a unitary reading and to an authority-conscious posture, he does not please everyone, no matter how irenic his tone may be. However, I believe he is faithful to the narrative he discusses by doing so.

Goldingay proceeds to explain how he will describe, "not what Israelites actually believed, but what the First Testament suggests they should have believed" (16) about God. In this volume, he strives to focus on who God is, whereas in the first volume he emphasizes what God has done (16). He rec-

---

32. John Goldingay, *Old Testament Theology, Volume Two: Israel's Faith* (Downers Grove, IL: InterVarsity, 2006). All subsequent references to page numbers in Goldingay vol. 2 in this section of the essay appear in parentheses.

ognizes that the current postmodern context forces scholars to recognize that all theological reflection is "partial and fragmentary" yet disagrees with Brueggemann's belief that the implication of this partial knowledge is that it is impossible to articulate a coherent unified faith in the OT (17). As in the first volume, he affirms that Jesus is God's supreme revelation while at the same time denying that Jesus came to bring a completely new message (18–19). Rather, Jesus came to provide a visible embodiment of God's message, "a huge distinction indeed" (19), which forced humanity to deal with "God's rule in the world" (19). He concludes his introductory remarks with the thought-provoking suggestion that the closeness of content in the OT and the NT makes it possible to treat them separately without losing too much of the whole biblical message (20). He then proceeds to analyze God, Israel, Israel's nightmare (exile), vision (renewal), humanity, the world, and the nations in the rest of the book (21–833).

The length of Goldingay's work makes it impossible for me to describe the contents of this volume in detail. It is important, however, in light of this essay's interest in theocentric theology, to mention his chapter on God (21–172). After a perceptive and text-saturated discussion of God's goodness, love, and wisdom, he stresses God's hostility to sin and wickedness. With these issues in mind, he draws on Lam 3:21–33 to observe that Yahweh never judges "from his heart" (165–66). God's heart and his actions thereby seem to be asymmetrical from a human standpoint, so the postmodernist's concern that the OT does not offer a unified portrayal of God becomes more understandable (166–68). Goldingay addresses this concern by using a parental metaphor. Like children, who do not understand their parents or themselves fully, we may not understand God or ourselves when we experience God's asymmetry (168–70). God's agenda is a broad one, and it includes inexplicable blessing and unexplained woe (170). Maturity becomes necessary, as does faith (170). Protest is part of the OT's witness to God, and it is an allowable part of maturing faith today (170).

Goldingay certainly contends for unitary, theocentric, and authority-conscious OT theology. Indeed, in his conclusion to the volume he writes, "What emerges is an account of a God who is transcendent but involved, sovereign but flexible, faithful but tough" (834). This God chooses a people to bless all nations; this God judges his people so that renewal may occur; this God expects his word to shape one's personal, familial, and societal behavior (834). Thus, this God's acts and teachings provide a coherent narrative that shapes all of human life. And this God's acts include revealing the uniqueness of Jesus. Obviously, I do not agree with Goldingay at every point. For example, I do not share some of his historical conclusions, and I believe that some of these conclusions undermine his analysis. I am also more inclined to have the Hebrew canon shape theological reflection than he is and less reticent about equating the Bible with God's word. Nonetheless, these differences do not lessen my gratitude for his careful, in-depth analysis. They do not lessen my sense that he gives me and other writers a model for comprehension of and commitment to perceptive analysis well worth emulating. He provides a sensitive, strong, and viable alternative to theologies committed to biblical diversity without unity.

Both Dempster and Goldingay offer budding and veteran OT theologians a text-based methodological option. Quite significantly, they also offer a narrative to a narrative-less society. The fact that they do so while maintaining a charitable and helpful spirit indicates that authority-conscious works are not of necessity coercive and domineering. In this way, they share the irenic spirit that Elmer Martens displays. They recognize the importance of historical matters such as the author, setting, and audience. They are not oblivious to the way readers approach the text in today's world. But their main focus is on the OT text. They highlight the way the text unfolds and how its grand narrative depicts God and his deeds in the history of Israel. In other words, they have produced works that integrate history, literature, and theology in a way that may inspire future works based on their own.

Contending for Canon and Theology: Rolf Rendtorff

I conclude this survey of recent treatments of OT theology with Rolf Rendtorff's *Canonical Hebrew Bible: A Theology of the Old Testament*, which appeared in German in 2001 and in English in 2005.[33] Rendtorff did not write this volume for technical scholars, though its length (over 800 pages) and methodological comments toward the end of the book may make it a bit forbidding to nonspecialists. Like Brueggemann, Gerstenberger, Anderson, and Goldingay, Rendtorff has enjoyed a long and productive scholarly life. He has contributed an impressive body of work to OT studies. While he has many sympathies with the former two authors, his method and its application have much more in common with the latter two writers. His aim is to demonstrate the diversity of the threefold canon while demonstrating how theological reflection leads to several unifying principles in the OT. Thus, he contends for the importance of canon and of thematic theology.

---

33. Rolf Rendtorff, *The Canonical Hebrew Bible: A Theology of the Old Testament* (trans. David Orton; Tools for Biblical Study 7; Leiden: Deo, 2005). All subsequent references to page numbers in Rendtorff in this section of the essay appear in parentheses.

Rendtorff operates from several specific methodological concerns. First, he is determined to explicate the contents of the Hebrew canon. He recognizes the value of historical-critical exegesis, yet he does not consider historical reconstruction of sources and/or redactional processes the primary goal of theological analysis. Diachronic details of this sort "are considered in relation to the contribution they may make to the understanding of the texts in their present, final, form" (1–2). After all, it is the canon of the OT that has served as a basis for Judaism and Christianity (2).

Second, Rendtorff chooses the Hebrew order of the canon, though he recognizes that there are other prominent orderings in the history of Judaism and Christianity. He believes this order not only has historical and biblical backing, it also emphasizes the primacy of the *Torah* in the canon. Indeed, he writes, "One can even say that most of the books of the canon of the Hebrew Bible could not be fully understood without knowledge of the Pentateuch to which they frequently directly or indirectly refer" (6).

Third, Rendtorff believes that the threefold Hebrew canon provides "three ways of speaking of and with God" (4). The various genres, historical settings, and literary contexts give readers a diversity of material about God. This material includes God's revelation to human beings and divulges a number of attempts that humans have made to walk faithfully with God (7–8).

Fourth, Rendtorff believes that despite the diversity of perspective in the canon its parts "stand in a constant mutual relationship," as is reflected by the fact that several key themes "appear in some way in several or all parts of the canon" (8). Therefore, the canon provides unity and diversity, not just one or the other trait. He writes, "Thus the variety of voices within the Hebrew Bible gains its quite specific structure through the arrangement of the canon" (8). All the OT's voices should be heard, but they should not be heard without reference to their coherence (413–14).

With his methodology in place, Rendtorff proceeds to describe the contents of the canon in order (9–413). At several points, he brings together common ideas and themes found in several passages. This descriptive portion of the book is accessible to any reader interested in studying the rich texture of the OT canon. He then discusses primary themes that crisscross the canon, such as creation, covenant and election, Israel's fathers, the promised and entrusted land, the first and second exodus, the Torah as the center of Israelite life, the cult as life before God, the Mosaic Covenant, the Davidic Covenant, the role of Zion, and so forth (415–715). He concludes the volume with methodological considerations for future analysis of OT theology and biblical theology, both of which he conceives of in holistic terms (717–56). One of the strengths of this analysis is Rendtorff's dealing with issues related to Jewish and Christian interaction (740–56), a subject that has been a special concern for him throughout his academic career.

Rendtorff's is a hopeful volume that places great emphasis on and significant trust in the power of the text to shape healthy postmodern life. He seems to believe that the text has not been followed; and this is the case even though the text does not present too many conflicting voices to provide solutions to contemporary issues. In this way his unitary, theocentric, and thematic approach coincides with the approaches of Martens, Anderson, Dempster, and Goldingay. He does not discuss OT authority as overtly as they do, yet his determined focus on the text leads toward the inevitability of some form of strong biblical authority. At the same time, his interest in Jewish-Christian dialogue and in the diversity of the canon's contents shields him somewhat from charges of certitude and oppression. This approach can thus promote dialogue without counting on dialogue alone to solve human problems.

Old Testament Theology in the Future

Caution and humility ought to characterize any predictions concerning or statement of hope for OT theology. I do not claim to be omniscient, and I recognize that my hopes may be mere selfish reflections. Even a scholar seeking to be humble must take a stand, however, so I will attempt several assessments, concerns, and hopes.

My assessments and predictions will probably not surprise the reader by now. I am grateful for many of the insights that Brueggemann, Gerstenberger, and other postmodern scholars have brought to the discipline. They expose interpreters who act as if they have no presuppositions, act as if they are truly disinterested, and act as if they are totally objective. They express the fears, hurts, and dangers that exist in today's world. They detail ways that interpreters have used the Bible for their own ends. They interpret the Bible's "core testimony" effectively. They keep OT theologians honest, and this is no small feat.

On the other hand, they probably overstate the inevitable triumph of postmodernism in intellectual life. It is not true that reader response and deconstruction have swept the hermeneutical field. Thus, I wonder if accepting the current context as they describe it is the best way to address the very real concerns they raise. I am afraid their approach has the potential to encourage readers to reject the authority that the OT claims for itself—a comment with which they might agree. But a text that has only the authority to call into account people who already accept the text as authoritative does not have the power to call other communities into account, and Brueggemann and Gerstenberger rightly desire to call truly abusive interpreters into account. Reader-response and deconstruction approaches leave readers with pieces of theology, just as they leave readers with pieces of texts. Thus, they can add to the fragmentation of life. Putting the pieces together is part of the teaching and healing process. Replacing interpretation-leading-to-authority with dialogue may prolong the need to make a decision that is valid for all, and it may temporarily lessen the anger between communities, but dialogue alone will not remove the need for the decisions.

Postmodern readings, both moderate and radical, will continue to appear and to have appeal. Radical readings of God's character and of biblical writers are in vogue in many American graduate schools. Therefore, scholars committed to unitary, theocentric, and authority-conscious theology will continue to contribute to the field. In the future, as in the past, the issue will not simply be whether one wants *to be* a scholar or not. It will be a matter of choosing *what sort* of scholar one wants to be.

I believe that Anderson, Dempster, Goldingay, and Rendtorff provide more-productive examples of helpful OT theology. We do live in a fragmented world that pits one group against another. Thus, what is needed is a theology that underscores the unity of the human race that comes through serving the one living God of the Bible. What is needed is a theology that calls all nations to a love for one another that is based on love for God the Father, Son, and Holy Spirit. What is needed is a theology that speaks against competing interests that fragment cultures and the world community. At the same time, theology that participates with complementary traditions rather than theology that seeks to become prominent by proving all others inadequate is needed.

For this theology to emerge, scholars must begin with an authoritative text based on the character of a good God. This authoritative text requires its adherents to love and embrace others, yet it also speaks of judgment for people who reject its message. Since this authoritative text commands love for neighbors, this text requires its adherents not to hate those who disagree with them. It is important to claim that theologians who use the text to abuse others disobey the text. Once again, as Elmer Martens's pacifist convictions and his writings about God's people in God's world remind me, the better option is to suffer loss of life in the pursuit of sharing biblically defined love.

Taken together, the methods of Anderson, Dempster, Goldingay, and Rendtorff allow readers an excellent framework for OT theology. Their methodologies stress that interpreters should ask *how* they should seek to uncover the OT's unity, not *whether* they should seek to do so. Dempster's approach to narrative allows one to examine the unity of the OT even as one determines how tension, irony, and new settings help produce that unity. The same is true of Goldingay's approach. Anderson's linking of theme, prophet, and blocks of text provides a way for interpreters to analyze the OT's interlocking ideas and characters. Goldingay's expansive treatment of the text gives readers ample opportunity to reflect on the way individual texts relate to the whole canon's broader themes. Rendtorff's approach does the same. In short, I agree in principle with the desire to use the shape of the Hebrew canon as a structuring device, to use literary methods as a conceptual device, and to use OT themes as examples of authoritative divine utterances. These experts' efforts at linking the OT and the NT will bear fruit as they continue their work and as other writers respond to their ideas.

I sincerely hope that future OT theology books built on these scholars' works and other similar works continue to appear. In fact, I believe that this will be the case. Whole-cloth treatments of the text continue to appear. *Whole Bible Theology* is being emphasized in many parts of the world. This ongoing movement will need to be courageous, for it will be opposed in many influential places. However, its adherents can be confident that there are philosophers, theologians, and biblical scholars who support unitary readings. It can also be confident that a hurting world can best be saved from sin and sorrow and division through belief in the Bible's presentation of a stable God whose word is trustworthy and whose word calls all the nations of the world to be one believing community encompassing the globe, not competing communities. In other words, the theological legacies of Elmer Martens and of scholars who hold his general viewpoint should have a significant place in future OT theology that seeks to heal, not harm, readers and their world.

Educating to Become Wise:
Intercultural Theological Education

Professor of Practical Theology
Facultad de Teología de la Universidad Evangélica del Paraguay
Asunción, Paraguay

Education in general and theological education in particular has entered an era in which cultures impinge on one another in the global village.[1] One of the consequences of this reality is that classrooms tend to be multicultural, bringing with them new challenges. The growing diversity means that curricula need to be internationalized, and the social requirements of "political correctness" need to be addressed. Some see these accommodations as an "additional burden."[2] Others fear that "academic excellence" may suffer as educational quality is lowered in order to attract the added sources of income

---

Author's note: As a student of Elmer Martens at MB Biblical Seminary (1982–86), I was touched by his interest in international students and his faithful witness to Christ. Later, during my doctoral studies in the United States (1999–2003), he also stayed in contact with me and encouraged me in various ways. In a recent e-mail (December 2007), he mentioned that he and Phyllis had gone to a Christmas musical; and at the end, he wrote: "We had with us our African-American neighbors." Indeed, Elmer and Phyllis have a special love for people of different cultural backgrounds. Besides serving for many years on the international board of mission of the MB Missions/Services International, he continues to teach in various parts of the world. In 1998, he was commissioned to facilitate MB international teacher exchanges. In this capacity, he started the *International Teacher Exchange Newsletter*, which continues to link educators to teaching opportunities globally. In light of the above, it is a privilege for me to reflect on educational issues in intercultural theological education and to dedicate this essay to Elmer.

1. In 2006–7, 28.7% of all students enrolled in the member schools of the Association of Theological Schools (ATS) in North America identified their ethnic background as Asian, Black, Hispanic, or Native American, including people admitted on student visas. The percentage could even be higher, because 11.8% did not report their race or ethnic background. See *www.ats.edu* for updated figures.

2. Jui-shan Chang, "A Transcultural Wisdom Bank in the Classroom: Making Cultural Diversity a Key Resource in Teaching and Learning," *Journal of Studies in International Education* 10 (2006) 369.

that international students bring to Western countries.[3] And people who do welcome the multicultural flavor within education lament the tokenism that is sometimes evident when different viewpoints are sought "solely because they are different or exotic" but are "not taken as serious . . . dialogue," because "the conflicts produced by real diversity are often avoided through the elevation of relativism."[4]

Furthermore, higher education is increasingly confronted with the limits of scientific knowledge based on the Cartesian supremacy of reason.[5] Voices—such as Eliot's—cry out:

> Where is the life we have lost in living?
> Where is the wisdom we have lost in knowledge?
> Where is the knowledge we have lost in information?
> The cycles of Heaven in twenty centuries
> Bring us farther from God and nearer to the Dust.[6]

Maxwell even goes so far as to affirm that "*the* crisis of our times, in short—the crisis behind all the others—is the crisis of science without wisdom."[7] Voices within theological education make similar claims. For instance, Treier regrets the historical development of theological education as follows: "once theology was sapiential, then strove to be scientific."[8] For Treier, theology must recover its sapiential character—as an enterprise for the whole people of faith with a more global Christian construal. Similarly, Cannell—after assessing major problems in theological education—emphatically points out that "the

---

3. In Australia, education was the second largest export industry within the services sector for 2005. By 2025, it is expected that international students (mostly coming from Asia) will inject $38 billion into the Australian economy (W. Martin Davis, "Cognitive Contours: Recent Work on Cross-Cultural Psychology and Its Relevance for Education," *Studies in Philosophy and Education* 26 [2007] 18).

4. Theodore Hiebert et al., "The Tower of Babel and Cultural Diversity: A Case Study on Engaging Diversity in the Classroom," in *Shaping Beloved Community: Multicultural Theological Education* (ed. David V. Esterline and Ogbu U. Kalu; Louisville: Westminster/John Knox, 2006) 138.

5. Miriam K. Martin and Ramón Martínez de Pisón, "From Knowledge to Wisdom: A New Challenge to the Educational Milieu with Implications for Religious Education," *Religious Education* 100 (2005) 157–73.

6. T. S. Eliot; quotation from the choruses of *The Rock.* Quoted in Patrick Slattery, *Curriculum Development in the Postmodern Era* (New York: Garland, 1995) 76.

7. Nicholas Maxwell, "A Revolution for Science and the Humanities: From Knowledge to Wisdom," *Dialogue and Universalism* 15 (2005) 32.

8. Daniel J. Treier, *Virtue and the Voice of God: Toward Theology as Wisdom* (Grand Rapids: Eerdmans, 2006) 27–28.

real challenge is to enable *holistic learning toward informed wisdom*"[9] and to do so in dialogue with non-Western communities.[10]

The call to recover wisdom and to take seriously diverse cultural backgrounds in theological education so that wisdom becomes intercultural—and not just loosely multicultural—gains even more *pathos* in light of Ben Ollenburger's suggested interpretation of Gen 11:1–9 in this festschrift. He suggests that God's final act of creation with primeval history was to make distinct the language and place of people. In fact, it was an act done in "defense of creation and peace."[11] And it is here that I want to weave in the call for education to be about becoming wise, because to be wise has to do with discerning the divine creation order and all that is necessary for wholeness, peace, and life. This also is the aim of theological education. We begin by looking at one of the cultural differences that plays a large role in educational settings: namely, reasoning.

Sociocultural Variations in Reasoning: Analytic and Holistic Cognition

Richard Nisbett and his colleagues[12] have indicated that for too many years psychologists have wrongly assumed that cognitive processes are the same across cultures. Through empirical research among college students,[13] they found that European-Americans (Westerners) and East Asians (Easterners) have a tendency to focus on different things in the environment and to use different patterns of

---

9. Linda Cannell, *Theological Education Matters: Leadership Education for the Church* (eBook ed.; Newburgh, IN: CanDoSpirit, 2006) 106.

10. Hence, the title of her last chapter is: "Toward an International 21st Century Theological Education" (Cannell, ibid.).

11. Ben C. Ollenburger, "Creation and Peace: Creator and Creature in Genesis 1–11," in this volume, p. 157.

12. Richard E. Nisbett et al., "Culture and Systems of Thought: Holistic versus Analytic Cognition," *Psychological Review* 108 (2001) 291–310; and Richard E. Nisbett, *The Geography of Thought: How Asians and Westerners Think Differently . . . and Why* (New York: Free Press, 2003).

13. They chose college students as their population, reasoning that they "would be expected to be more similar to one another than to more representative members of their parent populations" (Nisbett et al., "Culture and Systems," 305), because "higher education around the globe is likely to expose students to a similar set of experiences, values, and knowledge" (Ara Norenzayan, Incheol Choi, and Richard E. Nisbett, "Eastern and Western Perceptions of Causality for Social Behavior: Lay Theories about Personalities and Situations," in *Cultural Divides: Understanding and Overcoming Group Conflict* [ed. Deborah A. Prentice and Dale T. Miller; New York: Russell Sage, 1999] 259).

inductive and deductive reasoning to process what they see.[14] They named these systems of thought Analytic and Holistic Cognition. Furthermore, they suggested that social organizations along with their practices—such as those that reflect individualistic and collectivistic orientations—support cognitive content and processes in ways that can sustain sociocognitive homeostatic systems for millennia. Analytic reasoning can be traced back to influence of the ancient Greeks, who developed a sense of personal agency and a tradition of debate that was oriented toward control. Holistic reasoning can be traced back to the influence of the ancient Chinese, who developed a sense of group agency and discouraged confrontation and debate—all of which was oriented toward harmony. Their research produced results in the following five areas.

Attention and Control (Inductive Reasoning)

Reasoning processes start with attention to the surrounding setting. Attending to one's environment is necessarily selective, because it is impossible to attend to everything all the time. However, that to which one pays attention is influenced by naïve metaphysics and sociocultural organization. Table 1 summarizes the findings.[15]

Table 1. Metaphysics, Attention, and Control

Analytic System of Thought	Holistic System of Thought
1. Life is consistent; *A* must be *A*, regardless of the context.	1. Life is changing; to be is not to be, and not to be is to be.
2. Models of the world are simple and specific.	2. Models of the world are complex, interactional, and immune to contradiction.
3. Attention is given more to the salient target object.	3. Attention is given more to the field.
4. See the parts. Isolate and analyze an object, while ignoring the field in which it is embedded.	4. See the whole. Detect covariation (perception of relationships within the field).

---

14. I should clarify at the outset that analytical reasoning is not limited to Western populations, and holistic reasoning is not limited to East Asian populations.

15. Li-Jun Ji, Kaiping Peng, and Richard E. Nisbett, "Culture, Control, and Perception of Relationships in the Environment," *Journal of Personality and Social Psychology* 78 (2000) 943–55; Takahiko Masuda and Richard E. Nisbett, "Attending Holistically versus Analytically: Comparing the Context Sensitivity of Japanese and Americans," *Journal of Personality and Social Psychology* 81 (2001) 922–34.

Table 5. Dialectics versus Law of Noncontradiction

Analytic System of Thought Folk Western Logic (based on Aristotelian logic)	*Holistic System of Thought* Folk Chinese Logic (based on Chinese dialecticism)
1. The law of identity: a thing is identical to itself.	1. The principle of change: reality is a process that is not static but is dynamic and changeable. A thing need not be identical to itself at all because of the fluid nature of reality.
2. The law of noncontradiction: no statement can be both true and false.	2. The principle of contradiction: because change is constant, contradiction is constant. Thus, old and new, good and bad exist in the same object or event, and indeed they depend on one another for their existence.
3. The law of the excluded middle: any statement is either true or false.	3. The principle of relationship or holism: because of constant change and contradiction, nothing either in human life or in nature is isolated and independent, but instead, everything is related. Attempting to isolate elements of some larger whole can only be misleading.
4. When presented with a situation of interpersonal conflict, there is a tendency to be uncompromising and to favor one or the other side within a conflict situation.	4. When presented with a situation of interpersonal conflict, there is a tendency to be compromising and to seek the "middle way."

The logical ways of dealing with contradiction may be optimal for scientific exploration and the search for facts because of their aggressive, linear, and argumentative style. On the other hand, dialectical reasoning may be preferable for negotiating intelligently in complex social interactions. Therefore, ideal thought tendencies might be a combination of both—the synthesis, in effect, of Eastern and Western ways of thinking.[21]

They seem to be on track, because an analysis of the Noble Prize winners for medicine between 1978 and 2007 (30 years) yields the following results: in all but 3 years (i.e., 27 years), it was awarded to people from the U.S.A. and/or Europe; one year the prize went to Argentina and the U.K. (1984), one year

---

21. Peng and Nisbett, "Culture, Dialectics," 751.

to Japan (1987, although the person was working in the U.S.A.), and one year to Australia (2005).[22] However, during this same 30-year period, the Noble Peace Prize was awarded 21 times to individuals from non-Western countries; 6 times organizations were awarded the prize, and only 3 times was it awarded to individuals from Western countries: Northern Ireland (1998) and U.S.A. (2002, 2007).[23]

Peng and Ames remind their readers that even Immanuel Kant "maintained that logical reasoning is very effective within the confines of science, but 'all the worse for the beyond.'"[24] Hence, we would do well not to exclude holistic ways of reasoning from theological education.[25] In fact, Vanhoozer suggests that, to provide a "richer appreciation of the historical meaning of the text,"[26] it is necessary for different cultures to come together to interpret the Bible.

Coming together is possible because, besides having a common Christian world view in theological education, analytic and holistic systems of reasoning have not only differences (diachronic elements) but also commonalities or structural similarities (synchronic elements): namely, wisdom and dialectics. When Nisbett and his colleagues present their findings about culture, dialectics, and reasoning, they acknowledge that the principles that underlie dialecticism (which are part of holistic cognition) are not foreign to Western epistemology. They admit that:

> Western developmental psychologists . . . have argued that such "post-formal" principles are learned in late adolescence and early adulthood to one degree or another by Westerners and that "wisdom" consists in part of being able to supplement the use of formal operations with a more holistic, dialectical approach to problems.[27]

---

22. See http://nobelprize.org/nobel_prizes/medicine/laureates (accessed on December 27, 2007).

23. See http://almaz.com/nobel/peace/peace.html (accessed on December 27, 2007).

24. Immanuel Kant, *Critique of Pure Reason* (trans. N. Kamp Smith; New York: St. Martin's, 1965). Quoted by K. Peng and D. Ames, "Dialectical Thinking, Psychology Of," *International Encyclopedia of the Social and Behavioral Sciences* (ed. Neil J. Smelser and Paul B. Baltes; New York: Elsevier, 2001) 3634.

25. For more details, see my "Many Counselors Bring Success: Making Room for Holistic and Analytic Reasoning," *Direction* 33 (2004) 70–84; idem, "Recovering the Wisdom Tradition for Intercultural Theological Education," *Journal of European Baptist Studies* 5/3 (2005) 5–23; and idem, "'Now I Know in Part': Holistic and Analytic Reasoning and Their Contribution to Fuller Knowing in Theological Education," *Evangelical Review of Theology* 29/3 (2005) 251–69.

26. Kevin J. Vanhoozer, "The Voice and the Actor: A Dramatic Proposal about the Ministry and Minstrelsy of Theology," in *Evangelical Futures: A Conversation on Theological Method* (ed. John G. Stackhouse Jr.; Grand Rapids: Baker, 2000) 81–82.

27. Nisbett et al., "Cultures and Systems," 301.

Because of this commonality, Westerners and Easterners can aim for complementarity and move beyond multicultural to intercultural education and relationships—that is, if we are willing to accept a critical-realist epistemology with its emphasis on rationality as "a many-splendored thing."[28] According to this epistemology, rationality is not reduced to computer-like calculations but is seen *as a form of wisdom*, which carefully weighs many different variables, makes informed judgments, and allows for mystery, as it recognizes that reality also has dimensions that cannot be directly perceived and conceived by science.[29] Hence, we now turn our focus to wisdom. We do so by looking at wisdom competencies within psychology and the Bible that have a bearing on the subject of this study.

Wisdom Competencies in Psychology

Wisdom literature can be found in most ancient civilizations. According to Elwell, it "is the most international and cosmopolitan in both form and content."[30] It has been the focus of attention of sages, philosophers, and theologians alike. However, during "the Enlightenment and the process of secularization, wisdom lost its salience as one of the fundamental categories guiding human thought and conduct."[31] The situation is changing. Since the 1980s, wisdom has received new attention in psychology and theology.[32]

Although researched by many, wisdom is most prominently defined based on the operationalization and measurement developed by Paul Baltes, along with his colleagues at the Max Planck Institute (MPI) in Berlin.[33] Their definition of wisdom has been analyzed by Monika Ardelt. She claims that, when measuring wisdom, "the Berlin group does not conceptualize wisdom as a personality characteristic or a combination of personality qualities but as an expert knowledge system which belongs to the cognitive pragmatics of the mind."[34]

---

28. Paul G. Hiebert, *Missiological Implications of Epistemological Shifts: Affirming Truth in a Modern/Postmodern World* (Harrisburg, PA: Trinity Press International, 1999) 87.

29. Ibid., 91–94.

30. W. A. Elwell, "Wisdom, Wisdom Literature," *Baker Encyclopedia of the Bible* (4 vols.; ed. Walter A. Elwell; Grand Rapids: Baker, 1988) 2.2151.

31. Ibid., 2.1144.

32. Ibid., 2.1144; Monika Ardelt, "Wisdom as Expert Knowledge System: A Critical Review of a Contemporary Operationalization of an Ancient Concept," *Human Development* 47/1 (2004) 257.

33. P. B. Baltes and U. M. Staudinger, "Wisdom: A Metaheuristic (Pragmatic) to Orchestrate Mind and Virtue toward Excellence," *American Psychologist* 55 (2000) 122–36.

34. Ardelt, "Wisdom," 259. She does acknowledge, however, that in their theoretical writings about wisdom they also tend to include emotions, motivations, and virtues as aspects of

Findings by the Max Planck Institute

Baltes and his colleagues ask respondents to find solutions to problem situations and then measure their answers by 5 criteria: (1) rich factual knowledge (e.g., coordination of the well-being of oneself and that of others), (2) rich procedural knowledge (e.g., how to deal with the meaning and conduct of life), (3) life-span contextualism (education, family), (4) relativism of values and life priorities (e.g., tolerance for value differences), and (5) recognition and management of uncertainties of life. The answers are measured on a 7–point scale.[35] This way of measuring wisdom suggests that wisdom is linked to expert knowledge.

The Berlin group found that wisdom-related performance was influenced by 5 factors: (1) intelligence (e.g., fluid intelligence), (2) personality-intelligence interface (e.g., creativity, cognitive style), (3) personality traits (openness to experience, psychological-mindedness), (4) life experience (general and professional), and (5) age (adulthood).[36] They also found that respondents who discussed dilemmas with trusted friends and co-workers showed a better performance than individuals who think alone, suggesting that "wisdom is a social and collective phenomenon."[37]

Findings by Monika Ardelt

Ardelt draws on theories from Eastern wisdom traditions as well as other theories—and this is important for us, because we are testing wisdom as the common ground between Western and Eastern reasoning variations.[38] Research conducted with Western (Americans and Australians) and Eastern (Indian and Japanese) samples suggested that the former focus more on knowledge and analytical ability, but the latter tend to emphasize the need to balance cognitive, reflective, and affective aspects of wisdom.[39] Hence, Ardelt proposes a three-dimensional wisdom scale that measures cognitive, reflective,

---

wisdom. The reason that we will concentrate on the findings of MPI and Ardelt is that, to my knowledge, their research is rooted in the work of the most-quoted studies of previous researchers. In fact, Sternberg suggests that, "for a number of years, Paul Baltes and his colleagues have been the world leaders in the study of wisdom. . . . Ardelt is a young scholar who is challenging the benevolent monopoly of the Baltes group" (Robert J. Sternberg, "Words to the Wise about Wisdom? A Commentary on Ardelt's Critique of Baltes," *Human Development* 47/5 [2004] 286).

35. Baltes and Staudinger, "Wisdom."

36. Ibid.

37. Monisha Pasupathi and Paul B. Baltes, "Wisdom," *Encyclopedia of Psychology* (8 vols.; ed. Alan E. Kazdin; Oxford: Oxford University Press, 2000) 8.2151.

38. Monika Ardelt, "Development and Empirical Assessment of a Three-Dimensional Wisdom Scale," *Research on Aging* 25 (2003) 275–324; idem, "Wisdom."

39. M. Takahashi and P. Bordia, "The Concept of Wisdom: A Cross-Cultural Comparison," *International Journal of Psychology* 35 (2000) 1–9.

Table 6. Definition and Operationalization of Wisdom as a Three-Dimensional Personality Characteristic

Dimension	Definition	Operationalization
Cognitive	An understanding of life and a desire to know the truth: to comprehend the significance and deeper meaning of phenomena and events, particularly with regard to intrapersonal and interpersonal matters. Includes knowledge and acceptance of the positive and negative aspects of human nature, of the inherent limits of knowledge, and of life's unpredictability and uncertainty.	Items or ratings should assess: • the ability and willingness to understand a situation or phenomenon thoroughly; • knowledge of the positive and negative aspects of human nature; • acknowledgement of ambiguity and uncertainty in life; • the ability to make important decisions, despite life's unpredictability and uncertainty.
Reflective	A perception of phenomena and events from multiple perspectives. Requires self-examination, self-awareness, and self-insight.	Items or ratings should assess: • the ability and willingness to look at phenomena and events from different perspectives; • the absence of subjectivity and projections (i.e., the tendency to blame other people or circumstances for one's own situation or feelings).
Affective	Sympathetic and compassionate	Items or ratings should assess: • the presence of positive emotions and behavior toward others; • the absence of indifferent or negative emotions and behavior toward others.

and affective dimensions of "the ideal type of a *wise person* rather than the ideal type of *wisdom related knowledge*."[40] She summarizes these dimensions as shown in table 6.[41] Ardelt found that the measurement of characteristics such as in table 6 could serve as effective indicators of wisdom; people who scored high on one of the dimensions also scored high on the other two. In fact, she

---

40. Monika Ardelt, "Where Can Wisdom Be Found? A Reply to the Commentaries by Baltes and Kunzmann, Sternberg, and Achenbaum," *Human Development* 47 (2004) 306.

41. Idem, "Wisdom," 275.

proposes, "they appear to be *sufficient* for wisdom to emerge"[42] as well as *necessary* for the acquisition of wisdom, because:

> Cognition alone might make a good scientist or businessperson but it is not
> a guarantee for wisdom. Individuals who combine cognition and reflection,
> especially self-reflection, might overcome their subjectivity and projections
> to a certain degree, but if their ultimate goal is more power, wealth, fame,
> etc. rather than the quest for truth, their self-centeredness will ultimately
> increase rather than decline . . . [and prevent] them from developing sym-
> pathy and compassion for others and the pursuit of a common good. . . .
> Finally, individuals who [are reflective and affective] might still be unable
> to acquire wisdom if their primary interest is not the pursuit of truth. An
> example might be members of various religious sects [since in] those circles,
> objectivity and rational analysis are often viewed as enemies of self-discovery
> and love.[43]

She continues to emphasize that, while cognitive competencies are important,
wisdom-related knowledge needs to be *realized* by the individual. Moreover,
responding to a reply of Achenbaum,[44] Ardelt predicts that wisdom as a personality quality (affective dimension) is positively related to forgiveness.

Preliminary Conclusions

When analyzing the above findings, I suggest that wisdom competencies
integrate aspects of both cultural variations of reasoning and avoid their ex-
tremes: the linear-control orientation within analytic reasoning and the relativism of harmony orientation within holistic reasoning. Furthermore,
these character traits probably are best pursued in intercultural communities
of wisdom, because here, individuals can correct each other better. And last,
wisdom competencies are not so much about wise *expert knowledge* as they are
about wise *people* who live in ways that foster life and peace.

Wisdom Competencies in the Bible

Biblical wisdom has common features with wisdom in other ancient Near
Eastern cultures, but as we will see it is also distinct from these and from
wisdom in psychology. While distinct, it is nevertheless ecumenical, in that:

> It is the antithesis of polarization, for it assumes that both parties have some-
> thing to learn from each other, that both come prepared not to change the

---

42. Ibid., 280.
43. Ibid., 279.
44. W. Andrew Achenbaum, "Wisdom's Vision of Relations," *Human Development* 47 (2004)
300–303.

other, but to be changed, to be open, to receive new perspectives and new insight. . . . It is dialogue, not as a technique but as a way of life.[45]

Much could be written about biblical wisdom and wise living. However, we will limit ourselves to giving a summary of core competencies that need to be pursued in intercultural theological education.

In the OT, wise people respond to divine communication. This affects the character of the community in such a way that there is harmony among them as they seek to live according to the cosmic order of God's creation with "whole holiness" or "holy wholeness."[46] Similarly, when analyzing wisdom in the NT, James concludes that a wise person has a character that is peace-loving, gentle, impartial, willing to yield, and ultimately engenders "a community of peace and righteousness whose arms can stretch wide enough to welcome the Kingdom of Peace."[47]

To live in this way is closely related to *phronēsis*. Hence, a wise person is someone who has "the ability (which includes knowing but is not limited to knowing) to say or do the right thing in a specific situation."[48] In other words, wise people are able to make good judgments, and judgments "are neither expressions of private feelings nor are they universal statements of theoretical truths. . . . Right theological judgment is the product of human cognitive action that has been nurtured by divine canonical action concerning right covenantal relations."[49] In Schipani's words, they have a spiritual and moral intelligence.[50]

It may be said that wise people have a 'skill or craft which secures success' (*technē*) or the instrumental virtue of 'prudence' (*phronēsis*) that enables them

---

45. Walter Brueggemann, "Scripture and an Ecumenical Life-Style: A Study in Wisdom Theology," *Int* 24 (1970) 4–5.

46. Daniel J. Treier, "Wisdom," *Dictionary for Theological Interpretation of the Bible* (ed. Kevin Vanhoozer; Grand Rapids: Baker Academic, 2005) 845; William P. Brown, *Character in Crisis: A Fresh Approach to the Wisdom Literature of the Old Testament* (Grand Rapids: Eerdmans, 1996) 158; C. Richard Wells, "Hebrew Wisdom as a Quest for Wholeness and Holiness," *Journal of Psychology and Christianity* 15 (1996) 59; and H. N. Malony, *Wholeness and Holiness: Readings in the Psychology/Theology of Mental Health* (Grand Rapids: Baker, 1983). Hence, Brueggemann suggests that wisdom education is "nurture in perspective." This includes: recognizing that life is coherently interrelated, acknowledging the transcendent mystery within the interconnectedness of life, knowing and practicing a critical unmasking of that which is held to be known and to lead to trustful submission and yielding to God (Walter Brueggemann, "Passion and Perspective: Two Dimensions of Education in the Bible," *ThTo* 42 [1985] 172–80).

47. Brown, *Character*, 164.

48. Vanhoozer, "The Voice," 81–82.

49. Ibid., 83, 85.

50. Daniel S. Schipani, "Sabiduría a la luz de Dios: La inteligencia moral y espiritual como contenido esencial de la educación," *Kariós* 38 (Enero–Junio 2006) 99–105.

to make right judgments as it regulates other virtues, criteria, and skills. However, ultimately, wise people order their lives in light of the fear of the Lord.
In the NT, to be wise requires both listening/knowing *and* obeying/doing
(Matt 7:24–27; Jas 1:22–25). Wisdom has its embodiment in Jesus Christ.
Hence, it is cruciform, forgiving, nurtured by humility, has charity as its Christian *telos*, and oscillates between *sophia* 'vision, as in bringing understanding of
the case and the rule' and *phronēsis* 'discernment, virtue'.[51]

Wisdom competencies according to psychology and the Bible have factors
in common, both stressing especially the need to bring cognitive, reflective,
and affective dimensions together into action. However, there are differences.
According to the Bible: (1) wise people interpret experience *theologically*;
(2) they "fear the Lord" and live with "whole holiness" or "holy wholeness"
within the framework of Israel's covenantal life; and (3) ultimately, they follow
Jesus Christ, who is wisdom's cruciform embodiment.[52]

Educational Implications

If we want education to be about becoming wise, educational facilitators
first need to become wise themselves, because only the wise can lead others
to wisdom. However, it is not a matter of first "becoming" wise, as though
wisdom were an acquisition that, once owned, is owned forever. Rather it is
a process; it is "what one *does* moment by moment . . . [because it] is a bit of
a 'use it or lose it' category."[53] There is no clearer example of this reality than
Solomon, who began as a person who "was wiser than any other man" (1 Kgs
4:31).[54] However, toward the end of his life, people could only refer to the
wisdom he *had* displayed, which was "written in the Book of the Annals of
Solomon" (1 Kgs 11:41). Solomon died a fool, because "his heart was not fully
devoted to the Lord his God . . . [and] turned away from the Lord" (1 Kgs
11:4, 9). The wise according to the Bible cannot *be* or *become detached* in this
way from the "fear of the Lord" (Prov 1:6) or from "Christ crucified . . . the
wisdom of God" (1 Cor 1:23–24).

In order for education to be about becoming wise, we must begin by asking ourselves: Am I a wise person? Do I *desire* to become wise? Do I *thirst* for
wise living as the deer pants for streams of water? Am I *willing* to pay the price?
And not last, we must ask the question that sums up everything else: Do I *value*

---

51. Treier, "Wisdom," 845; Treier, *Virtue*, 31–66.

52. Wells, "Hebrew"; Daniel S. Schipani, *The Way of Wisdom in Pastoral Counseling* (Elkhart,
IN: Institute of Mennonite Studies, 2003) 40–41; and Treier, "Wisdom," 845.

53. Adam Blatner, "Perspectives on Wisdom-ing," *ReVision* 28 (2005) 29.

54. Unless otherwise noted, all Bible quotations are from the New International Version.

wisdom?[55] Education that aims at becoming wise is not as much a matter of allowing students to encounter something as to encounter someone.[56] Having asked ourselves these questions, we may consider other implications, especially in the areas of goal-setting and assessment, because the way that we set goals and assess the educational process is fundamental to the promotion of education focused on becoming wise.

Goal-Setting and Becoming Wise

Schipani suggests that educating to become wise may be linked to using new categories for goal-setting: namely, seeing/knowing, valuing/being, and doing/living. These may be expressed in fresh ways by linking them to a three-fold pattern of the human spirit based on the triune God: to have *the vision* of the living God (i.e., increasingly to see reality with the eyes of God), *the virtue* of Christ (i.e., becoming conformed to the heart of Christ), and *the vocation* of the Spirit (i.e., increasingly to participate in the life of the Spirit in the world).[57] By suggesting this route, Schipani tries to go beyond mere human science in formulating objectives and to promote what Cannell calls one of the major challenges for contemporary theological education: "the desire to hold together reason and piety, academy and church, virtue and service."[58]

What would happen if we always asked: What/whom do I/we need to see as God sees it/her/him? What virtue of Christ do I/we need to incarnate? What vocation of the Spirit do I/we need to practice? What if we continuously asked these questions on a personal, class/course, institutional, and societal level? Moreover, what would happen if these or other questions were asked in small groups comprising people who have different ways of reasoning from ours?[59]

There are also other options. Wiggins and McTighe, for instance, propose that a teaching/learning process is not obligated to begin with objectives or

---

55. Maxwell would phrase it: Do I *realize* what is of value? This is "to be interpreted to mean both 'to become aware of what is of value' and 'to make real and actual what is of value potentially'" (Maxwell, "A Revolution," 49).

56. Thomas reminds us that in Proverbs wisdom is a woman (8:22–31) and is asked to be loved as a sister (7:4); and in John the *Logos* is incarnated by Jesus (Jesse J. Thomas, "Wisdom Literature and Higher Education," *Journal of Interdisciplinary Studies* 14 [2002] 128–31).

57. Daniel S. Schipani, "The Purpose of Ministry: Human Emergence in the Light of Jesus Christ" (paper presented to the faculty of Associated Mennonite Biblical Seminary; Elkhart, IN, 1995) 8–23; idem, "La juventud y su contexto," in *Comunicación con la juventud: Diseño para una nueva pastoral* (ed. Daniel S. Schipani et al.; San Juan, Seminario Evangélico de Puerto Rico, 1994) 35–38; and idem, *The Way*, 54.

58. Cannell, *Theological Education*, 98.

59. For concrete examples of intercultural communities of learning of this sort, see Chang, "A Transcultural"; and Hiebert et al., "The Tower."

outcomes. They suggest that the focal point is discerning what information has priority and can be classified as "enduring understanding." Once this has been determined, some key questions are formulated that serve as doors to rooms of inquiry. This conception of the teaching/learning process only provides an overall direction, allowing students to explore the field around this direction in many ways by using a variety of sorts of reasoning.[60] Hence, Duckworth suggests that teaching

> must seek out, acknowledge, and take advantage of all the pathways that people might take to their understanding. We cannot plan for "the logical sequence" through a set of ideas, especially if we want schools to make sense for students whose backgrounds differ from our own. We must find ways to structure subject matter so as to enable learners to get at their thoughts about it. Then we must take those thoughts seriously, and set about helping students to pursue them in greater breadth and depth.[61]

Thus, Maxwell would probably argue that, if we want to move toward becoming wise, we need to nourish students' "holy curiosity," because passion, emotion, and desire cannot be fragmented from wisdom-inquiry unless we want "to reduce education to a kind of intellectual indoctrination."[62] Furthermore, when articulating *problems of living* in ways that are more fundamental than *problems of knowledge*, we need to promote empathic understanding of people "by putting ourselves imaginatively into their shoes, and experiencing, in imagination, what they feel, think, desire, fear, plan, see, love, and hate."[63] These (among other proposals that he gives) could help us move from what he calls mere "knowledge-inquiry" to "wisdom-inquiry." And I must add that the context for inquiry of this sort is obedient and worshipful reverence in the presence of God, from whom all wisdom proceeds, and who searches the heart! This takes us to the last point.

Assessment and Becoming Wise

Assessment requires a special degree of wisdom from educators. It is relatively easy to "measure" assignments that reflect analytic reasoning, especially if they correspond to linear, algorithmic, and formal ways of organizing and presenting information and if they fit very specific, measurable criteria. Under these circumstances, assessment is a matter of checking the presence or absence

---

60. Grant Wiggins and Jay McTighe, *Understanding by Design* (Alexandria, VA: Association for Supervision and Curriculum Development, 1998).

61. Eleanor Duckworth, *"The Having of Wonderful Ideas" and Other Essays on Teaching and Learning* (New York: Teachers College, 1996) xii.

62. Maxwell, "A Revolution," 52.

63. Ibid., 53.

of requested criteria, of doing so in a "fair" manner (usually defined as being egalitarian), and of assigning a "final" grade. However, this type of assessment raises many questions for theological education that attempts to be wise and intercultural. What would it look like for wisdom to inform assessment? What does it mean to be "fair" when assessing? In what ways can assessment be wise and "fair"? Who sets the criteria? And perhaps an even more important question: What is the purpose of assessment after all?

Cannell, referring to Harris who is a noted specialist in educational assessment, reminds us "that grades don't correlate with much of anything except other grades."[64] She recognizes that looking for alternative forms is difficult, but it is possible if "teams of faculty, educational specialists, congregational leaders, and students . . . study current practices, examine options, and propose alternatives."[65]

One alternative worth exploring is portfolio assessment. It may include teacher observations, collections of student work, self-evaluations, peer-evaluations, questionnaires, dialogue with the professor, and other items.[66] It does not exclude the establishment of criteria, but it allows for a more holistic evaluation.[67] Ott suggests that assessment is most effective when accompanied by mentoring.[68]

Conclusion

Is excellence possible in intercultural theological education? Hiebert and his students in the course "Babel and Diversity" responded this way: "diversity actually raised the bar of excellence for academic study and discourse."[69] Does cultural diversity contribute to becoming wise? Their answer was as follows:

> It was important for members of our class to discover that true learning is not about competing for a grade or buying into a dominant understanding of an issue. More importantly for McCormick and the process of theological education, on the other hand, is the broader experience of the relationship between diversity and standards that the participants of our class will take away to their future communities of faith and work. The real knowledge we gained was that valuing diversity does not consist of an "anything goes" attitude; it consists, rather, of a real willingness to engage in a respectful

---

64. Cannell, *Theological Education*, 299.
65. Ibid., 300.
66. Emily Grady, *The Portfolio Approach to Assessment* (Bloomington, IN: Phi Delta Kappa Educational Foundation Report, 1992).
67. Seung-Yoeun Yoo, "Using Portfolios to Reflect on Practice," *Korea* 58/8 (2001) 78–81.
68. Bernhard Ott, *Handbuch Theologische Ausbildung* (Wuppertal: Brockhaus, 2007) 313–19.
69. Hiebert et al., "The Tower,"128.

process of mutual transformation that can happen only with those who are from worlds entirely not our own.[70]

If we want to aim toward becoming wise in intercultural theological education, for one thing we must invest more time and energy. Therefore, the question needs to be asked again: Do we place enough *value* on becoming wise to be willing to pay the price? Sternberg answers that this is not an option but a necessity! "[I]n a world torn with strife and warfare . . . wisdom may be the only hope out of the bloodshed."[71] Of course, it is easier to stay where we are and continue building the "tower" in a vertical but not cruciform shape. However, will God allow us to do so? Or will God intervene in theological education as he did on the plains of Shinar (Gen 11:1–9), for the purpose of promoting order (peace) and for the sake of creation? Whatever God decides to do now, one thing about the future is clear: those who worship before the Throne will come "from every tribe and language and people and nation." In a loud voice, they will sing together: "Worthy is the Lamb, who was slain, to receive power and wealth and wisdom and strength and honor and glory and praise!"[72] Thus, educating to become wise has everything to do with the *slain* Lamb!

---

70. Ibid., 140.
71. Sternberg, "Words," 286.
72. Revelation 5:9, 12.

To Know or Not to Know:
Hosea's Use of ydᶜ/dᶜt

M. DOUGLAS CAREW

Vice Chancellor
Nairobi Evangelical Graduate School of Theology
Nairobi, Kenya

Finding a precise definition for *yādaᶜ/daᶜat* 'knowledge/know' in Hosea has been problematic, despite wide acknowledgment of the importance of the term for Hosea's discourse and the almost exclusive Hosean use of the phrases "know Yahweh" and "the knowledge of God."[1] This problem of determining the sense of the lexeme is the primary concern of this essay. I argue that the semantic domains in which the lexeme is employed range from the experiential to the moral-ethical to the cognitive. The phrases "know the LORD" and "knowledge of God" are related in meaning but carry distinct senses. Consequently, Hosea's use of *yādaᶜ/daᶜat* is consistent but not uniform.

With its origins in the exchange between Baumann and Wolff, the debate on this issue has centered on the meaning of the phrases *yādaᶜ ʾet-YHWH* 'know Yahweh' and *daᶜat ʾĕlōhîm* 'knowledge of God'.[2] Wolff succinctly articulates

---

Author's note: Prof. Elmer Martens had a formative influence in my theological education. It is a pleasure and privilege to contribute this essay in honor of not only a teacher *par excellence* but also a scholar, mentor, friend, and faithful follower of the Lord Jesus Christ.

In this essay, chapter and verse numbers follow the versification of the Hebrew Bible.

1. The lexeme occurs a total of 20 times in the 14 chapters of the book and is one of the most frequently used terms, second only to the lexeme *šûb*, which appears 22 times. It appears in Qal 15 times: in 2:10, 22, 5:3, 4, 6:3 (twice), 7:9 (twice), 8:2, 4, 9:7 (a contested reading), 11:3, 13:4, 5, and 14:10. Hiphil is used in 5:9. The nominative *daᶜat* is found in 4:2, 6 (twice), and 6:6. *Wĕyādaᶜat ʾet-YHWH* is used in 2:22 and *wĕnēdᶜâ nirdĕpâ lādaᶜat ʾet-YHWH* in 6:3. The negative form *wĕʾet-YHWH lōʾ yādāᶜû* is found in 5:4. *Daᶜat ʾĕlōhîm* appears in 4:1 and 6:6, with the absolute form *haddaᶜat* occurring in 4:6 (twice).

2. Eberhard Baumann, "*Yādaᶜ* und seine Derivate," *ZAW* 28 (1908) 22–41, 110–43; idem, "'Wissen um Gott' bei Hosea als Urform der Theologie?" *EvT* 15 (1955) 416–25; Hans Walter Wolff, "'Wissen um Gott' bei Hosea als Urform von Theologie," *EvT* 12 (1953) 533–54; idem, "Erkenntniss Gottes im Alten Testament," *EvT* 15 (1955) 426–31; and idem, *Hosea* (trans. Gary Stansell; Hermeneia; Philadelphia: Fortress, 1974).

the core problem in the discussion when he asks whether the term *da'at 'ĕlōhîm* should be understood objectively or subjectively.[3] Three positions have been taken.

(1) *Yāda' as subjective.* Against the background of Hosea's marriage, Baumann argues that *yāda'* in Hosea underscores a personal relationship with Yahweh and emphatically rejects the notion that knowledge of God in 4:1 is an intellectual activity.[4] He takes 'knowledge of God' as indicating "communion with God in the living sense of the words" and proffers this conclusion:

> We can now summarize the results: In Hosea, the expression *'ĕlōhîm*, more precisely *da'at 'ĕlōhîm*, indicates not (intellectual) knowledge of God (*die Gotteserkenntnis*), but connection with God, communication with God, and with the exception of 2:22 generally turns out to be subjective as respect, love, and trust displayed toward God.[5]

A similar position is adopted by J. Hänel ("concern for God and his will"), Robinson ("personal sense of communion relationship"), Weiser ("practical communal life with God"), and Martin Buber, who suggests "intimate contact of both partners."[6] More recently, Nicholson has taken *yāda'* in the sense "know someone for one's own, choose and make someone one's own."[7]

(2) *Yāda' as objective.* The objective view is advocated by Wolff, followed by Holt.[8] Both in his seminal article and in his commentary, Wolff argues that

---

3. Wolff, "Wissen um Gott," 533–54. Five principal points attend the discussion: (1) the nature of *yāda'/da'at*—the question whether the term is objective or subjective; (2) the question whether "knowledge of God" is different in meaning from "knowledge of Yahweh"; (3) the issue of the content of "knowledge of God"; (4) the question of the proper context for understanding the lexeme. Does Hosea's use of *yāda'/da'at* fit best in a marriage, priestly, prophetic, or ANE treaty context? (5) the matter of the pattern of Hosea's usage. Is the sense of the lexeme in all of its occurrences the same or not? Space limitations allow for discussion of only the first point.

4. Baumann, "*Yāda'* und seine Derivate," 22–41, 110–43.

5. Ibid., 124.

6. Cited in Wolff, "Wissen um Gott," 536; J. Hänel, "Das Erkennen Gottes bei den Schriftpropheten," in *Die Ebed Jahwe-Lieder in Jesaja 40ff.* (BWANT 4; Leipzig: Hinrichs, 1913) 224; T. H. Robinson, *Die zwölf kleinen Propheten* (HAT 14; Tübingen: Mohr, 1938) 19, 27; A. Weiser, *Das Buch der zwölf kleinen Propheten* (ATD 24; Göttingen: Vandenhoeck & Ruprecht, 1949) 29, 45; and M. Buber, *Der Glaube der Propheten* (Zurich: Manesse, 1950) 165.

7. Ernest W. Nicholson, *God and His People: Covenant and Theology in the Old Testament* (Oxford: Clarendon, 1986) 78–80. Other recent scholars who hold a similar view include: Thomas McComiskey, "Hosea," in *The Minor Prophets* (ed. Thomas McComiskey; Grand Rapids: Baker, 1992) 44–45; Francis I. Andersen and David Noel Freedman, *Hosea* (AB 24; Garden City, NY: Doubleday, 1980) 283–84; and A. A. Macintosh, *Hosea* (ICC; Edinburgh: T. & T. Clark, 1997) 83–85.

8. Else Kragelund Holt, *Prophesying the Past: The Use of Israel's History in the Book of Hosea* (JSOTSup 194; Sheffield: Sheffield Academic Press, 1995) 53; and E. K. Holt, "*d't, 'lhym* und *ḥsd* im Buche Hosea," *SJOT* 1 (1987) 87–103.

by *daᶜat ʾĕlōhîm* Hosea means knowledge of Yahweh's divine activity and "the intimate knowledge of the revealed law of God."[9] He points out that *daᶜat* is identical with *tôrâ* in 4:6, while in 13:4 the covenant law of ancient Israel is the main component of Israel's knowledge. In 2:10, the indication is that Yahweh's divine activity, "the knowledge of God's saving works handed down to Israel," is the object of the knowledge that Israel lacks.[10] He concludes that the content of *daᶜat ʾĕlōhîm* is both divine action reflected in the covenantal traditions and the revealed divine law.[11] In supporting Wolff's position, Else Kragelund Holt argues that Yahweh's dealings with Israel in history, now embodied in Israel's historical traditions, are the content of *daᶜat ʾĕlōhîm*.[12]

(3) *Yādaᶜ as both subjective and objective.* Eichrodt, while lending some support to Wolff's insistence on the cognitive character of Hosea's *yādaᶜ*, identifies a serious weakness in this position: namely, an insufficient appreciation of the dynamics between this sort of knowledge and God as its object.[13] For Eichrodt, the knowledge of God is not simply theoretical knowledge concerning the nature and will of God. Rather, it is "the practical application of a relationship of love and trust, as this is seen at its loveliest in the association of a true wife and her husband."[14] In addition, he sees it as "the experience and recognition of God's succoring acts, which ought to lead to obedience and trust, and as such bears a strongly noetic character."[15] Thus, in Eichrodt's opinion, Hosea's use of *yādaᶜ* combines both the objective and subjective dimensions. Similarly,

---

9. Wolff, "*Wissen um Gott*," especially pp. 543–49, where he argues for *tôrâ* as the specific content of knowledge of God. See also Wolff, *Hosea*, 67. Herbert B. Huffmon assumes Wolff's view but adds that the proper context for understanding the usage is that of the ANE treaties (Huffmon, "The Treaty Background of Hebrew 'YADA'," *BASOR* 181 [1966] 31–37). See also Herbert B. Huffmon and Simon B. Parker, "A Further Note on the Treaty Background of Hebrew 'YADA'," *BASOR* 184 (1966) 36–38.

10. Wolff, "Wissen um Gott," 545–46; and idem, *Hosea*, 37.

11. To this end, Wolff states: "The divine law is surrounded and carried by the divine activity that can be described in sum as the conclusion of the covenant. Hosea . . . understands this gift of Yahweh, early in time, as the actual summary of that *daᶜat ʾĕlōhîm*, which he misses among the priests and people" ("Wissen um Gott," 546).

12. Holt, *Prophesying the Past*, 140–41. Unlike Wolff, Holt does not see *tôrâ* as part of the content of "knowledge of God."

13. Walther Eichrodt says of Wolff: "Nevertheless his own interpretation of the knowledge of God as coming down to the priest via the cult tradition, and being passed on by him to the people, fails to do justice to the deep interior dynamic which links this knowing to its object, and because of which it attains its full content only when it is knowledge which has become concrete in action" (*Theology of the Old Testament* [trans. J. A. Baker; OTL; 2 vols.; London: SCM / Philadelphia: Westminster, 1961–67] 2.292 n. 1).

14. Eichrodt, *Theology*, 2.291.

15. Ibid., 2.292.

Craghan sees Wolff's insistence on the priority of the cognitive as being detrimental to the "subjective and volitional dimensions of the term."[16]

The Meaning of yāda‛/da‛at

The discussion that follows examines the use of *yāda‛/da‛at* within the discourse framework of chaps. 2, 4, and 6, in particular. Though these chapters do not exhaust the use of *yāda‛/da‛at* in Hosea, the occurrences in them are important for understanding the use of the lexeme in the entire book. In addition to these chapters' being pivotal in the discourse structure of the book, the key senses of the lexeme, including all the senses that are in dispute, occur in them. Chapters 4 and 6 are of signal importance in determining the sense of *yāda‛/da‛at* in particular.

The Meaning of yāda‛ in Hosea 2:10

In its occurrence in 2:10, *wĕhî' lō' yād‛â*, the lexeme appears in collocation with *kî 'ānōkî nātattî*. The syntagmatic relations among the elements of these clauses are important. First, the marked subject *hî'* is also the subject of the verb *'āmrâ* in vv. 7b and 9b. In addition, *'āmrâ* is used in the cognitive sense and could be an overlapping synonym with *yād‛â*.[17] This possibility is increased when the collocation with *nātan* is considered. In all three of its occurrences, vv. 7b, 10, and 14b, this lexeme is collocated with the good gifts. In two of these cases, vv. 7b and 14b, it is in syntagmatic relations with both *'āmrâ* and *mĕ'ahăbāy* 'my lovers', thus indicating that Gomer perceives her lovers to be the providers of her gifts. The emphatic personal pronoun *'ānōkî* is the subject of *nātan* in v. 10 and stands in contrast to "her lovers." The meaning suggested by these collocations is that the perception of "her lovers" as providers of her gifts stands in contrast to her failure to perceive Yahweh as the true provider. If this holds, then *yāda‛* in this context primarily carries the sense 'to acknowledge, understand, perceive'.[18] Along with the cognitive nature of the usage,

---

16. John F. Craghan, "An Interpretation of Hosea," *BTB* 5 (1975) 205. For Craghan, the parallelism and association of both *ḥesed* and *'ĕmet* with *da‛at 'ĕlōhîm* in 4:1 and 6:6 indicates that the primary domain is moral ("The Book of Hosea: A Survey of recent Literature on the First of the Minor Prophets," *BTB* 1 [1971] 81–100, 145–70).

17. Three types of synonymous relations are distinguished by Silva: overlapping, contiguous, and inclusive (Moisés Silva, *Biblical Words and Their Meaning: An Introduction to Lexical Semantics* [Grand Rapids: Zondervan, 1983] 119).

18. The same position is adopted by Davies, who holds that the lexeme signifies "an appropriate response to what is perceived as well as the perception itself" (G. I. Davies, *Hosea* [NCB; Grand Rapids: Eerdmans, 1992] 74). Others in favor of this view are James Luther Mays, *Hosea* (London: SCM, 1966 / Philadelphia: Westminster, 1969) 40; Macintosh, *Hosea*, 54–56; and Andersen and Freedman, *Hosea*, 242.

I suggest that the content of this cognitive activity is the misperception of the source of blessings, rather than the blessings themselves.[19]

The Meaning of yāda⁽ *in Hosea 2:22*

In Hos 2:22, the lexeme appears in the climactic utterance *wĕyādaʿat ʾet-YHWH* 'and you shall know the LORD'. The sphere of activity in vv. 21–22 is personal relationship. Righteousness and justice, kindness, compassion, and faithfulness are to characterize the new relationship between Yahweh and Israel.[20] All of these are relational, moral, and ethical qualities. As the culmination of the betrothal act, a personal subjective relationship, the likelihood is that "You shall know the LORD" speaks of a similarly subjective relationship.

Consideration of the relationship between *yāda⁽* in this verse and *šākaḥ* 'forget' in 2:15 confirms this view. Wolff contends not only that *šākaḥ* is the opposite of *yāda⁽* in Hosea but that to forget Yahweh is to forget both the *tôrâ* and the gifts provided by Yahweh.[21] He arrives at this conclusion by linking 2:15 with 2:10, 4:6, 8:14, and 13:4–6. Observing that the meaning is the plain and usual sense of a mental activity in all of the occurrences of *šākaḥ* outside chap. 2, he concludes that *šākaḥ* in 2:15 is also an intellectual and theoretical activity and is the opposite of *yāda⁽* in 2:10.[22]

It is possible, however, to understand the relationship between 2:10 and 2:15 differently. First, the linkage is between the ideas expressed in the verses, not simply the two words. Verse 15 complements and advances the point made in v. 10. Not only has Israel failed to acknowledge the true source of her gifts, 2:10, she has forsaken (*šākaḥ*) the provider himself for other gods, 2:15. Second, *šākaḥ* is used in synonymous parallelism with *wattēlek ʾaḥărê mĕʾahăbeyhā* 'and she went after her lovers'. Schottroff notes that *šākaḥ* is often used with respect to turning to and worshiping other gods.[23] In Deut 8:19, for example, the two

---

19. Contra Wolff, who takes the content of this knowledge as the "historical works and gifts of Yahweh" (*Hosea*, 36–37).

20. My reading assumes a *beth essentiae* rather than a *beth pretii*. Ortlund notes that Rashi's comment, "with which you will conduct yourselves," puts the emphasis on Israel's horizontal relations (Raymond C. Ortlund Jr., *Whoredom: God's Unfaithful Wife in Biblical Theology* [New Studies in Biblical Theology; Grand Rapids: Eerdmans, 1996] 71 n. 74). He rightly questions whether Rashi captures the primary thrust of the verse. Rashi's observation is certainly more suited to 4:1, which is perhaps anticipated here. Ortlund's preference for Calvin's emphasis on God as the subject of betrothal, however, is also subject to query. If the prepositional phrases qualify the entire clause, "I will betroth you to me forever," as he maintains, then it may be more satisfactory to identify the emphasis as falling on the exchange process rather than the subject of the clause. So, whereas it is true that Yahweh is the "ultimate explanation" for the change, the emphasis here is on the quality of the new relationship.

21. Wolff, *Hosea*, 40.

22. Idem, *"Wissen um Gott,"* 536.

23. W. Schottroff, *"šākaḥ,"* TLOT 3.1322–26.

verbs are used together in this sense with respect to turning away from Yahweh to other gods, which is clearly a relational and subjective use. Third, *šākaḥ* in v. 15 is the opposite not of *yādaʿ* in 2:10 but of *yādaʿ* in 2:22.[24] Hosea 2:22 reverses 2:15, so where in 2:15 Israel's turning away from Yahweh breaks the relationship, in 2:22 Yahweh's turning to Israel restores the relationship. Thus both *šākaḥ* and *yādaʿ* are subjective, relational terms as used in these verses.[25]

Within this subjective and relational sphere, the specific sense of *wĕyādaʿat ʾet-Yhwh* 'you shall know the LORD' in 2:22 is 'you will be devoted/committed to the Lord'. This climactic utterance sharply contrasts with the basic charge of harlotry that pervades the discourse. At the heart of the imagery of harlotry is the reality of Israel's unfaithfulness to her covenant relationship with Yahweh. It is this unpleasant reality that Yahweh, of his own free will, turns around in vv. 15–25. To play the harlot, therefore, must be understood as the direct opposite of knowing Yahweh. Israel's failure to perceive that the two are mutually exclusive is a fundamental mistake.

The Meaning of *daʿat* in Hosea 4:1 and 4:6

The occurrences of *daʿat* in 4:1 and 4:6 are crucial to the debate on Hosea's use of the term. The proposed senses in these occurrences include "knowledge of covenant obligation" (Huffmon), "presence or epiphany of Yahweh"

---

24. I do not dispute that *yādaʿ* and *šākaḥ* are antonyms in some of the other texts that Wolff cites. My contention is that the antonymy relationship does not hold in this specific case, given my judgment of the objective and cognitive nature of *yādaʿ* in 2:10 and the subjective, relational nature of *šākaḥ* (a metaphorical usage) in 2:15.

25. Commenting on Hosea's perspective on Israel's guilt, Wolff poignantly states: "Guilt is for him above all the destruction of personal harmony of Israel with its God, who has turned to Israel in its history in personal love, as is most clearly seen in the great Yahweh similes of the loving husband (2:2–20), the father (11:1ff.), and the healing physician (14:4; 7:1; cf. 5:13; 6:1; 11:3)" (Wolff, "Guilt and Salvation: A Study of the Prophecy of Hosea," *Int* 15 [1961] 274–85; quotation from p. 281). In view of this, it is interesting that Wolff adopts the objective, cognitive sense for *yādaʿ* in 2:22, claiming: "2:22 is final confirmation that the object of *daʿat ʾĕlōhîm* in Hosea are those events and conditions which had established the Yahwhistic covenant of the Israelite tribes in the early period between Egypt and the conquest of the land. We should therefore take leave of every psychological interpretation of the idea that suggests 'devotion of the heart', 'intimate intercourse with God', 'intimate contact', and such" ("Wissen um Gott," 549). This conclusion is predicated on two points. First, Wolff assumes that the use of *yādaʿ* in chap. 2 should be understood in terms of the "common Hoseanic" cognitive usage in chaps. 4–11 ("Wissen um Gott," 437–39; idem, *Hosea*, 53). Second, he opts for a *beth* of price (*pretii*) in vv. 21–22 and understands the five associated nouns as the objects of *yādaʿ*. These objects, which are linked with Yahweh's divine activity and law, are presented to Israel as Yahweh's bridal price. It may be noted that even with a *beth pretii* other understandings are possible. Macintosh, for example, prefers a *beth pretii* but holds that these gifts that Yahweh offers "indicate the quality of the marriage" (*Hosea*, 83–84).

(Crotty), "knowledge of his teachings as the source of a harmonious community life" (Wolff), and "knowledge of God's will revealed in the law" (Sakenfeld).[26]

Daʿat ʾĕlōhîm appears in 4:1.[27] In 4:6, the noun appears twice with the definite article and without the genitive *ʾĕlōhîm*. Many commentators agree that the two forms are the same term.[28] Consequently, the knowledge that is rejected in 4:6 is the knowledge of God predicated as being absent in 4:1.

The construct relation in *daʿat ʾĕlōhîm* may be understood as subjective genitive, which describes the knowledge that God gives.[29] This construal of the construct relation approximates to Wolff's suggestion that *daʿat ʾĕlōhîm* be understood as the knowledge of the revealed will of God.[30] There is more to the term than this, however. In v. 1, the term appears in collocation with the covenant virtues of *ʾĕmet* 'truth' and *ḥesed* 'goodness' and appears in a climactic position. In addition, the triad of covenant virtues contrasts with the five vices in v. 2. These observations have a twofold significance. First, they suggest that, along with the other virtues and vices, *daʿat ʾĕlōhîm* is to be understood in a moral-ethical sense, as McKenzie advocates.[31] Second, they point to an understanding of *daʿat ʾĕlōhîm* as a quality that can be put into practice. Thus, along with "truth" and "goodness," Israel has failed to practice *daʿat ʾĕlōhîm*. Instead, the practice of robbery, murder, and so on is rampant. Thus, *daʿat ʾĕlōhîm* is not only knowledge that God has revealed; it is also moral and ethical conduct.[32]

---

26. Huffmon, "The Treaty Background of Hebrew 'YADA'," 36–37; R. Crotty, "Hosea and the Knowledge of God," *ABR* 19 (1971) 1–16; and Wolff, *Hosea*, 67, 79. Wolff maintains a single meaning for *daʿat ʾĕlōhîm*, namely, "knowledge of God's revealed will," but with two senses: (1) the divine law, which is ethical in nature, and (2) the historical covenant traditions; Katharine Doob Sakenfeld, *The Meaning of Ḥesed in the Hebrew Bible: A New Inquiry* (HSM 17; Missoula, MT: Scholars Press, 1978); and idem, *Faithfulness in Action: Loyalty in Biblical Perspective* (OBT; ed. Walter Brueggemann and John R. Donahue; Philadelphia: Fortress, 1985) 108. James Ward, like Sakenfeld, admits different senses for Hosea's use of the lexeme; a subjective, relational sense and an objective, cognitive sense (Ward, *Hosea: A Theological Commentary* [New York: Harper & Row, 1966] 82–90).

27. Hosea 6:6 is the only other place in Hosea where it occurs.

28. Those who take this view include, among others, Wolff, *Hosea*, 79; Macintosh, *Hosea*, 139; McComiskey, "Hosea," 56; and Mays, *Hosea*, 63, 69. I do not find any significant reason to dispute this position.

29. See J. C. L. Gibson, *Introductory Hebrew Grammar-Syntax* (Edinburgh: T. & T. Clark, 1994) §32; and Bruce K. Waltke and Michael P. O'Connor, *Introduction to Biblical Hebrew Syntax* (Winona Lake, IN: Eisenbrauns, 1990) 143. A less likely option, in my view, is to assume an objective genitive.

30. Wolff, *Hosea*, 79.

31. J. L. McKenzie, "Knowledge of God in Hosea," *JBL* 74 (1955) 22–27, 26–27.

32. The notion of practice is amplified by the use of the five infinitive absolutes in v. 2.

A related issue that demands consideration is the relationship between *hadda'at* and *tôrat 'ĕlōheykā* 'the law of your God'. That *hadda'at* is a specific rather than a nebulous entity is confirmed by its parallelism with *tôrat 'ĕlōheykā*. This parallelism in itself cannot be the final arbiter of the content, because a number of scholars note the parallelism but proffer different understandings of "Torah."[33] Two relationships best indicate the content of Torah in this discourse. The first is the cataphoric relationship between the lack of *tôrat 'ĕlōheykā* and the list of vices in 4:2. The practice of these vices amounts to a rejection of Yahweh's *tôrâ*. Furthermore, the vices are basically illustrations of what the Sinai law opposes.[34]

The second relationship is the link between *da'at*, *tôrâ*, and *bĕrît*. In 4:6, the link is between *da'at* and *tôrâ*; 6:6 and 6:7 link *da'at* and *bĕrît*. In 8:1, the link is between *tôrâ* and *bĕrît*. As Nicholson argues, there is good reason to assume that the breach of *bĕrît* in 6:7 is a breach of Yahweh's Torah.[35] In all three verses, the links outlined appear in a context of moral and ethical virtues and/or vices. Furthermore, each linked pair is closely associated with Yahweh. What these considerations suggest is that the Torah in each of these occurrences is Yahweh's Torah, as distinct from the Priestly Torah.[36] Second, they suggest that Torah must be understood as the ethical and moral component of Yahweh's teaching. Thus, the most appropriate contextual meaning of *tôrâ* is the revealed moral and ethical teachings of Yahweh, the concrete moral-ethical framework that guides appropriate conduct. *Da'at 'ĕlōhîm*, then, could be considered moral and ethical conduct in accordance with the teachings of Yahweh's Torah.

In addition, the discourse connection between 4:1 and 2:22 is important for a final determination of the meaning of *da'at 'ĕlōhîm*. McKenzie maintains that *wĕyāda'at 'et-Yhwh* and *da'at 'ĕlōhîm* are different in meaning.[37] Other scholars find this distinction wanting and maintain that the two expressions are

---

33. Linking it to the Priestly Torah, McKenzie understands the content of Torah to be moral and ethical in nature ("Knowledge of God," 24–26). Wolff, for his part, understands the content of Torah to be the "instruction of your God" or the divine law (*Hosea*, 79). On the basis of the parallelism between both terms in 8:3, Crotty proposes "the saving experience of knowing" ("Hosea and the Knowledge of God," 14–15).

34. So Walter Brueggemann, "*Tradition for Crisis: A Study in Hosea* (Richmond, VA: John Knox, 1968) 37–43; Wolff, *Hosea*, 67–68; Andersen and Freedman, *Hosea*, 336–37; D. K. Stuart, *Hosea–Jonah* (WBC 31; Waco, TX: Word, 1987) 75–76; McComiskey, "Hosea," 56; and Macintosh, *Hosea*, 130–31; and contra Holt, *Prophesying the Past*, 53.

35. Nicholson, *God and His People*, 183–88.

36. For a distinction between Yahweh's Torah and the Priestly Torah, see G. Liedke and C. Petersen, "*tôrâ*," *TLOT* 3.1418–20.

37. McKenzie, "Knowledge of God in Hosea," 22–24. Andersen and Freedman agree: *Hosea*, 336. The distinction goes back to Wellhausen.

identical in meaning.[38] I have advocated above that *daᶜat ʾĕlōhîm* in 4:1 and 4:6 be understood in the sense "conduct that is appropriate to devotion/commitment to God." Before that, I advocated understanding *wĕyādaᶜat ʾet-Yhwh* 'you shall know the Lord' as "devoted/committed to the Lord." In 4:1 and 4:6, the nominal usage carries the sense of conduct that flows out of this commitment. Thus, the difference in Hosea's usage can be explained as a nuance somewhere between the verbal and the nominal uses. In view of this, I have reached the conclusion that the two phrases are different terms in the same semantic domain.

To summarize, *daᶜat ʾĕlōhîm* in 4:1 and 4:6 is to be understood as conduct that issues out of and is appropriate to covenantal devotion to the Lord and rooted in Yahweh's divine teachings. It implies action: that is, the practice of moral qualities that reflect commitment to the will, person, and nature of Yahweh. In other words, it designates conduct reflecting faithful commitment to Yahweh.[39] This conduct requires knowledge of God's law (which has in the context been rejected and spurned) and issues from knowing God. So, because the people of Israel do not "know God" (lack an intimate relationship with God, à la 2:22), they do not conduct themselves in a manner that conforms to the ethical and moral requirements of God.

The Meaning of yādaᶜ/daᶜat *in Hosea 6:3*

Hosea 6:1–6 brings together the verbal and nominal uses of the lexeme for the first and only time in the book. *Yādaᶜ* is used two times in 6:3, once in the cohortative and once in the infinitive form. The object of both verbal forms is *ʾet-Yhwh* 'the Lord'. Thus, the usage recalls *wĕyādaᶜat ʾet-Yhwh* in 2:22. I have argued above that in 2:22 the term is relational and subjective, carrying the sense 'be devoted/committed to the Lord'. The same sense should be understood in this usage.[40]

The associated lexical field confirms that this proposed sense is accurate. The *šûb* 'return' motif contributes significantly to the relational sense and context.[41] The purpose of the summons to "return" in vv. 1–3 is that Israel will be devoted to the Lord. Significantly, in Hos 5:4, where *šûb* is used

---

38. Ward (*Hosea*, 85 n. 3); Wolff (*Hosea*, 67; idem, "Wissen um Gott," 537), and Macintosh (*Hosea*, 128) are among recent scholars who hold this view.

39. See also Ward, *Hosea*, 85; Willem A. VanGemeren, *Interpreting the Prophetic Word* (Grand Rapids: Zondervan, 1990) 111; Stuart, *Hosea–Jonah*, 78. BDB suggests that *daᶜat* could refer to skill and obedience (395b).

40. It is "single-minded loyalty" to Yahweh and to his "ethical nature" (Macintosh, *Hosea*, 226).

41. For Hosea's use of the lexeme in a covenantal context, see William L. Holladay, *The Root ŠÛB in the Old Testament* (Leiden: Brill, 1958) 120–26.

along with "know the LORD" and "spirit of harlotry," the claim is that Israel does not "know the LORD" because she is enticed by a spirit of harlotry. "Know the LORD" is used in contrast to a "spirit of harlotry" to make the point that the "spirit of harlotry," Israel's guiding principle, leads to evil deeds, which in turn leave her without the capacity to return to Yahweh. To return to Yahweh as summoned in 6:1, therefore, is to turn away from apostasy and unfaithfulness and be devoted and faithful to Yahweh. Thus, the use of the lexeme *šûb* in both 5:4, and 6:1 clearly reflects its frequent theological use in the OT, depicting a relationship between Yahweh and Israel.[42]

The Meaning of da‛at ’ĕlōhîm *in Hosea 6:6*

Apart from this text, the only other places where Hosea uses *da‛at ’ĕlōhîm* are 4:2 and 4:6.[43] This limited use of the term readily suggests that the same sense obtains in each usage.[44] In considering 4:2 and 4:6, I advocated the sense "conduct that is appropriate to covenantal devotion to the Lord." My analysis of 6:1–10 suggests that the same sense holds in v. 6.

The logical-semantic or consecution relations in 6:1–10 structure the discourse as a two-act interactive drama between Israel and Yahweh. In act one, vv. 1–3, Israel expresses the resolve to return to and "know the LORD." This theme of "know the LORD" links acts one and two. In act two, vv. 4–10, Yahweh responds to Israel's resolve with four propositions. The first proposition declares Yahweh's assessment of Israel; Israel is fickle in her resolve to return to Yahweh and know him, vv. 4–5. Proposition two is that offering cultic ritual sacrifices does not mean "knowing Yahweh," v. 6. The point is made by setting *ḥesed* and *da‛at ’ĕlōhîm* in contrast to cultic sacrifices. The next proposition defines what "knowing Yahweh" is, as distinct from "knowledge of God."[45] To this end, proposition three states that "knowing Yahweh" entails practice of *da‛at ’ĕlōhîm* and *ḥesed* (v. 6).

---

42. J. A. Thompson and Elmer Martens, "*šûb*," *NIDOTTE* 4.55–59. Crotty's "presence" motif augments the point that "to know Yahweh" goes beyond the cognitive dimension into the relational—the spiritual/religious, even cultic relationship between Israel and Yahweh. Crotty is wrong, however, to conclude that "knowledge of God" means Yahweh's presence ("Hosea and the Knowledge of God," 1–16). In the dynamic of "knowing Yahweh," Yahweh's presence in cultic worship is an act of grace that facilitates devotion and faithfulness to Yahweh but does not in itself constitute "knowledge of God."

43. The absolute form *hadda‛at* used in 4:6 is parallel to *da‛at ’ĕlōhîm* in 4:2, so the former is considered a legitimate listing of the full phrase.

44. Indeed, virtually every commentator has understood the same sense in all of these occurrences. Nevertheless, the following analysis does not take this consensus for granted.

45. These two propositions are essentially complementary, presenting first the negative then the positive definition.

Proposition four describes the content of *da⁽at ʾĕlōhîm* and *ḥesed* as observance of covenant and its ethical virtues, vv. 7–10. This is done by means of
the rhetoric of reversal and negation. Yahweh's desire for these ethical virtues
is set against Israel's breach of covenant and ethical vices in vv. 7–10. The juxtaposition serves to define the content of knowledge of God by detailing the
practices that mark its absence, à la 4:2. In other words, the covenant breach
and ethical vices are the antithesis of "knowing Yahweh." By way of reversal,
therefore, covenant observance and the practice of ethical virtues constitute
da⁽at ʾĕlōhîm and *ḥesed*. In 8:1, covenant is linked with Torah. For this reason,
it is fair to say that Hosea views the vices detailed in vv. 8–10 as breaches of
Torah. This ethical context shows similarity to the context in 4:2.

To summarize, "know Yahweh" (6:3) and "knowledge of God" (6:6) are
used in the same senses as in their previous occurrences in 2:22, 4:1, and 4:6,
respectively. To "know Yahweh" means to be devoted to the LORD, and
"knowledge of God" speaks of conduct that is in keeping with commitment
to the LORD and the Torah. The two terms are linked with *ḥesed*. Within this
linkage, both "goodness" and "knowledge of God" are appropriate responses
to the LORD from those who "know Yahweh." Thus, the personal relationship
between Yahweh and Israel demands not impersonal manipulatory rituals but
the personal, socioethical commitments embodied in "goodness" and "knowledge of God."[46]

Conclusion

In addition to the passages considered above, *yāda⁽/da⁽at* appear in 5:3, 4, 9,
7:9, 8:2, 4, 9:7, 11:3, 13:3, and 14:10. The proposed sense in these appearances is included in the summary below without the supporting justification.[47]
The senses of *yāda⁽/da⁽at* that arise out of the study can now be set out as
follows:

Cognitive (Objective)

1. *yāda⁽* 'to acknowledge'. This sense is employed in 2:10, 7:9 (×2), 8:4, 11:3
2. *yāda⁽* 'to be aware' (5:3)
3. *yāda⁽* 'to perceive, understand'. It is used in this sense in 9:7 and 14:10
4. *yāda⁽* 'to experience/know by experience' (13:4)

---

46. The point is elegantly made by Plank in terms of Martin Buber's "I-it" and "I-Thou"
descriptions (Karl A. Plank, "The Scarred Countenance: Inconstancy in the Book of Hosea,"
Judaism 32 [1983] 343–54, 352–53).

47. The argumentation is left out primarily because of space limitations. With the exception
of Hos 9:7, with its attendant textual difficulties, these occurrences do not pose any significant
interpretive challenges.

Relational (Subjective)

1. Experiential: *yāda*ʿ 'be devoted/committed'. The verbal form is used this way in 2:22, 5:4, 6:3 (×2), 8:2, and 13:5
2. Volitional: *daʿat ʾĕlōhîm* 'conduct appropriate to commitment to Yahweh'. The nominal collocation carries this sense in 4:1, 4:6, and 6:6

The analysis shows that in 11 out of the 16 uses of *yāda*ʿ, the senses are cognitive in nature. Four distinct senses are used: perceive, acknowledge, be aware, and experience. A total of 9 cases of relational usage are observed. All 4 of the uses of *daʿat* fall in this category, as do all the uses of "know Yahweh." Thus, the subjective relational usage is almost exclusive to the phrases *yāda*ʿ *ʾet-YHWH* and *daʿat ʾĕlōhîm*. In only 2 other cases, 8:2 and 13:5, is the subjective usage of *yāda*ʿ observed. In both of these cases, the relational domain is also prominent. Two clear senses obtain in this category of relational usage: namely,, commitment and conduct worthy of the commitment.

It is significant that the lexeme is almost exclusively used in a religious rather than secular sense.[48] Israel is the knowing subject in 12 out of the 16 cases where the verb is used.[49] In the other 4 verbal uses, Yahweh is the knowing subject.[50] The reverse is true in terms of the object of knowing. Yahweh is the object of knowing in 13 instances, while there are only 2 clear cases in which Israel is the object.[51] In one case (14:9), neither Yahweh nor Israel is the object of knowing, the object being the prophetic proclamation.

The evidence garnered indicates that the use of *yāda*ʿ/*daʿat* in Hosea is consistent but not uniform. The verbal collocation "know the LORD" and the nominal collocation "knowledge of God" are related in meaning but carry distinct senses. The former is best understood within the sphere of the exclusive covenant relationship between Yahweh and Israel. It defines the essence of a relationship with God, "a personal relationship growing out of a living encounter with God."[52]

To know Yahweh is in fact a three-strand cord. The cognitive is woven together with the experiential and the moral-ethical/volitional strands. All

---

48. The one use that comes closest to a secular usage is 7:9. This religious realm of use is the one uniform element in Hosea's use of the lexeme.

49. Hosea 2:10, 22; 5:4; 6:3 (twice); 7:9 (twice); 8:2; 9:7; 11:3; 13:4; and 14:10.

50. Hosea 5:3, 9; 8:4; and 13:5.

51. Israel is clearly the object in 7:9 and 9:7.

52. Botterweck, "*yāda*ʿ," *TDOT* 5.448–81. Eichrodt similarly understands "true 'knowledge of God'" as "a relationship to God which will develop in obedience, faithfulness, and returned love and thus put an immediate spiritual correlation in the place of material accomplishments" (Eichrodt, "'The Holy One in Your Midst': The Theology of Hosea," *Int* 15 [1961] 259–73, especially p. 270).

three strands are found in Hosea's understanding and treatment of the nominal collocation *da⁽at ʾĕlōhîm* 'knowledge of God'. For this collocation, I have advocated the sense "conduct that is in accordance with a relationship to Yahweh and guided by the Torah." The link with Torah provides the moral-ethical and cognitive connections. Hosea speaks not only of Yahweh's Torah but specifically of the moral and ethical teachings of Yahweh's Torah. In this respect, Mckenzie is right to conclude that "knowledge of God" is moral integrity.[53] Knowledge of Torah, therefore, was essential to "knowledge of God" but did not constitute "knowledge of God."

Hosea's use of knowledge of God/Yahweh becomes a metaphor for Yahweh's possession of and relationship with Israel. For Hosea, the relationship is to be characterized by exclusive allegiance to Yahweh, faithfulness in worship, and moral integrity in social conduct and relationships. In calling Israel to know Yahweh, Hosea calls Israel to return to her relationship with Yahweh, a unique and exclusive relationship founded on covenant and election.

---

53. McKenzie, "Knowledge of God in Hosea," 27.

The Problem of Preaching the Old Testament

FRANKLYN L. JOST

Academic Dean and Associate Professor of Old Testament
Mennonite Brethren Biblical Seminary
Fresno, California

Preaching the OT presents a problem to Christians. The problem is interpretation. It is a canonical question: what is the relationship of the OT to the NT? We confess that the OT is part of the inspired, Christian scriptural canon. The Hebrew Bible is the written Word of God and reveals God to us. We also confess that the OT is preparatory, bearing witness to Messiah Jesus, who brings continuity and clarity to the two testaments.

How do Christians describe the relationship between the OT and the NT? Luther suggested a contrast between law and grace. Caricatured, Luther becomes the authoritative excuse to read the OT primarily as law, which defines the human problem with sin; here the NT is read as a witness to God's grace in Jesus Christ. Calvin spoke of old and new covenants, suggesting the possibility of an interpretive approach labeled supersessionism; here the NT is read as superceding the OT. Anabaptists are particularly susceptible to the latter. Jesus is the starting point for interpretation; Jesus is the hermeneutical key, making the NT primary. In this reading, the OT is *old*—old news and worn out.

How does one use the Hebrew Bible to preach? Prof. Elmer Martens gave direction to a generation of OT preachers. Years ago he pointed students to a helpful book by Donald Gowan, *Reclaiming the Old Testament for the Christian Pulpit*.[1] Gowan encourages the preacher to match the message and the sermonic approach to the text's genre. Martens also encouraged students to give attention to Elizabeth Achtemeier's counsel that the preacher should always pair a NT text with the preached text of the OT.[2] This seemed an improvement to my undeveloped, largely undirected homiletic approach. The

1. Donald E. Gowan, *Reclaiming the Old Testament for the Christian Pulpit* (Atlanta: John Knox, 1980).

2. Elizabeth Achtemeier, *Preaching from the Old Testament* (Louisville: Westminster/John Knox, 1989) 56–58.

NT would give direction, serving to protect against legalistic or overly earthy or earthly messages.

Later graduate school training pointed out the weakness of Achtemeier's dictum. By insisting on a NT text to tutor or supervise the message, we were undercutting OT authority. The OT, if it is God's Word, does not need NT scaffolding for support. In fact, many scholars avoid the term "Old Testament," because it can be heard as pejorative, and instead they prefer the term "Hebrew Bible."

When I visited India, I was intrigued by the system of chapel preaching at MB Centenary Bible College under the tutelage of Principal V. K. Rufus. The sermon was followed by an open session of critique. I soon learned that it was woe to the preacher who preached an OT text that did not lead to Jesus. I discovered that the insistence was born of an apologetic demand. The Indian church had been influenced by liberal interpretation in the national Christian seminary system. People had been taught that the OT was the Jewish holy book that was the precursor to the Christian Scriptures in a way that corresponded to the Indian holy book of the Vedas, Upanishads, and Bhagwad Gita. Although Mennonite interpreters did not completely buy the argument that the OT was on a par with Hindu literature, they did accept the need to play the Jesus trump card in every sermon. But does not the OT enjoy a privileged position in the Christian Bible? The OT is not simply preparation for the true divine Word. If we are listening for God's voice, is not the authority of the Father of Jesus who speaks in the Hebrew Bible as great as that of God's Son who speaks in the NT?

In this essay, my aim is to encourage OT preaching by claiming its place as a full partner with the NT. My proposal aims to develop what Paul House describes as "Whole Bible Theology" (the Bible is considered one book with the two testaments read in continuity).[3] I propose to begin reading in a manner that may initially seem counterintuitive—by reading first the NT text of Matt 19 rather than reading an OT text. Through this "Whole Bible theological reading," I hope to show that the OT is more than important background for the NT. Rather, OT theological voices continue in conversation with one another into the NT (and beyond!).

Before proceeding to the text, let us review some of the perspectives that inform this reading. Walter Brueggemann's *Theology of the Old Testament* makes the case for testimony and countertestimony within the text.[4] The OT is a

---

3. Paul House, "God's Design and Postmodernism: Recent Approaches to Old Testament Theology," in this volume, pp. 29–54.

4. Walter Brueggemann, *Theology of the Old Testament: Testimony, Dispute, Advocacy* (Minneapolis: Fortress, 1997).

dialogue—perhaps a chorus of voices. Brueggemann claims that his is a "non-foundational" reading, one that refuses to be predetermined by Enlightenment categories such as historicity, historical criticism, and Christian doctrine. He argues for an alternative reading that opposes the ideological assumptions that privilege the reading of the powerful. According to Brueggemann, nonfoundationalism is not an attempt to imagine a world without God but rather "an attempt to give voice to a deep alternative that is given in the text and that is not particularly respectful of our preferred inclinations and modes of reasoning."[5] Brueggemann suggests the metaphor of *guerilla theater* (suggesting, revealing, and yet concealing surprises) to describe his approach.[6]

From Brueggemann, we gain the perspective that recognizes currents and crosscurrents. Not everyone perceives God's reign in the same way. More than one voice is allowed to speak.

An example of this is 1 Sam 8–12, which seems to preserve both pro-monarchic and antimonarchic voices. Brevard Childs, who counters Brueggemann's testimonial reading with the "canonical" approach, reads 1 Sam 8–12 in a way that smooths the final edition. Childs resolves the tension within the text by identifying editorial shaping that privileges the antimonarchical voice, yielding "a literary and theological solution."[7] Brueggemann, on the other hand, recognizes an ongoing "sharp interpretive dispute" in the text.[8] The problem is not "solved" but highlighted.

The second perspective is that of N. T. Wright. Wright argues that the mission of Jesus is to embody and to call into being a new people, a restored Israel, a returned-from-exile people of God.[9] To understand Jesus' mission, one must grasp God's purposes for the OT people of God. Borrowing from Wright, Walsh and Keesmaat argue that the canonical story is a unified drama in six acts. Act one is creation followed by human rebellion. Act two has God calling out a people and giving them a covenant and a land with a mission to be a blessing to all nations. Act three describes the exilic loss of land as judgment of Israel's failure to fulfill its divinely appointed mission. Act four shows how the Messiah Jesus reverses Israel's exile, fulfills Israel's mission, and conquers the enemy power that had enslaved all of humanity. The Messiah acts to

---

5. Idem, *Ichabod toward Home: The Journey of God's Glory* (Grand Rapids: Eerdmans, 2002) 88–89.

6. Ibid., 110.

7. Brevard S. Childs, *Introduction to the Old Testament as Scripture* (Philadelphia: Fortress, 1979) 277–78.

8. Brueggemann, *Theology*, 602.

9. N. T. Wright, *The Challenge of Jesus: Rediscovering Who Jesus Was and Is* (Downers Grove, IL: InterVarsity, 1999) 41.

accept the world's violence, dies, and rises from the dead. We presently participate in the drama in act five, which began with the biblical book of the Acts of the Apostles and continues into the present church age. Act six, the consummation, is still to come.[10] In each of these six acts, God's purpose remains to create a covenant people.

The six-act-drama perspective shows that the OT is important not simply because it provides historical context for the NT story. The OT is part of the story. It *is* the story. From the OT, we learn about God's creation objectives, God's redemptive purposes, and God's judgments of human failure to fulfill these purposes. Neither law versus grace nor old versus new covenant is sufficient to understand the story. Wright's drama metaphor encourages reading with deliberate *intertextuality*. Because the drama is unfolding, the interpretation of an OT text may be informed by events that occur in another act of the drama. This may in fact pair an OT text with a text from the NT—or it may pair OT texts.

A third perspective informs this "Whole Bible" reading. Elmer Martens's reading of God's purpose in Exod 5:22–6:8 enriches the perspectives of Brueggemann and Wright.[11] What is God about in the six acts of the biblical drama? How do we gain footing in this kind of nonfoundational reading? What alerts us to the voice of the oppressed? Martens's observation of the fourfold design of God in deliverance, covenant community, knowledge of God, and abundant life in the land offers a grid that gives direction to Brueggemann's iconoclastic, deconstructionist perspective. It clarifies the purpose of Wright's drama in six acts.

A "Whole Bible" Reading of Matthew 19

Having set out these parameters for reading, I now want to pursue a "Whole Bible" reading of Matt 19. At first it may seem counterintuitive to claim a NT text for this reading. Matthew 19 is chosen for three reasons. First, Matthew is a NT text used by Martens in *God's Design* to test the fourfold design in the NT.[12] Second, Matthew not only uses the OT extensively to write to an apparently Jewish audience, but he also includes in the Sermon on the Mount Jesus' teaching on the greater righteousness that fulfills the law and the prophets—Jesus' Bible! Third, Matt 19 is chosen because in it we find Jesus

---

10. Brian J. Walsh and Sylvia C. Keesmaat, *Colossians Remixed: Subverting the Empire* (Downers Grove, IL: InterVarsity, 2004) 133.

11. Elmer A. Martens, *God's Design: A Focus on Old Testament Theology* (3rd ed.; N. Richland Hills, TX: Bibal, 1998).

12. Ibid., 341–46.

himself twice reading OT texts—citations from the creation story (Gen 1:27 and 2:24 with an allusion to Deut 24) and a citation of the second tablet of the Ten Words from the law (Exod 20 and Deut 5). Can the reading that Jesus gives these texts help us evaluate the primitive, OT hermeneutic outlined above in this essay?

Matthew 19 contains three narratives, a controversy story regarding divorce (19:1–12), a pronouncement story (19:13–15), and a call story (19:16–30).[13] The chapter opens with the typical Matthean concluding formula for Jesus' authoritative sermons, a geographical marker emphasizing Jesus' movement to Judea, and a report of crowds who witness Jesus' healing ministry.

Reading Matthew 19:1–12

Matthew portrays the relationship of the Pharisees with Jesus as a continuation of the testimony/countertestimony of the Hebrew Bible. Jesus, with authority, claims to adjudicate among the possible readings. The Pharisees' question assumes that Jesus will become embroiled in the continuing rabbinic argument between the conservative Shammaites and the more liberal Hillelites regarding proper grounds for divorce.[14] Jesus refuses to take the Pharisees' bait, avoids the contemporary controversy, and focuses on the question he considers more central by asking them about the twin references to the creation stories. To read Jesus' answer is to read the Hebrew Bible. Or, again, to read Jesus' answer requires that we grasp the argument of the Hebrew Bible. To read Jesus is to do a "Whole Bible" reading.

In Matthew's account, Jesus begins with the text that sets the paradigm. Creation theology is the larger rubric within which Jesus addresses this ethical issue. By quoting the creation story, Jesus is claiming that the solution to this ethical dilemma comes from God's purpose for all humanity. The first act (creation) of the six-act drama gives essential guidance to Jesus (who acts as a character in act four, according to the schema outlined above).

Jesus quotes first the final phrase of Gen 1:27. While the emphasis on "male and female" fits the divorce controversy, we do well to understand the allusion in its biblical context. Genesis 1:27 states that "God created human beings in his own image." What do we need to know about Gen 1 to read Jesus?

J. Richard Middleton posits that Gen 1:27 is the rhetorical climax of the creation story. Middleton argues that Barth's focus on "male and female" has value for insight into human relationships but disagrees with Barth's conclusion that the phrase explains that the fundamentally relational, interpersonal,

---

13. Lamar Williamson Jr., *Mark* (Interpretation; Atlanta: John Knox, 1983) 178, 183.
14. M. Eugene Boring, "The Gospel of Matthew," *NIB* 8.385.

intercommunal character of humanity is the essence of being created in God's image.[15] Rather, according to Middleton, the reference in Gen 1 to being created in God's image is best understood by reading it in context with the succeeding verse, with its mandate to "rule" and "subdue" the earth.[16] Middleton concludes that the concept of human beings created in God's image must be connected to the divine ruler metaphor. The notion of likeness to God as ruler is both "representational" (an analogy between God and humans) and "representative" (a task delegated to humanity by God).[17] Humans created in God's image are rulers together of God's creation.

Middleton's conclusion that being created in God's image has to do with the human function of ruling creation leads to several implications. First, humans as rulers are also creators, following the model of God's creativity.[18] Second, the image of God includes a priestly dimension in God's cosmic sanctuary as they mediate blessing to creation.[19] Third, the biblical language of ruling creation in God's image is essentially democratic (anti-imperial) and extends this royal priesthood to all humanity through their first parents.[20] Fourth, "Genesis 1 constitutes a normative framework by which we may judge all the violence that pervades the rest of the Bible." It "provides a framework for judging human violence" as a "contradiction to the disclosure of God's power in Genesis 1."[21]

Though Jesus does not comment further on the quotation from Gen 1, the implications for marriage are striking. Humans are created for a purpose, a divinely imagined role that implicates them as servants to others. Their task of ruling and subduing the earth, of tilling and keeping the soil moves them beyond the selfish confines of self-pleasure within marriage. Following the model of God's creativity invites humans to develop creatively within their marriage relationship as well as serve others. As mediators of blessing, husband and wife together lead within the home and within the faith community to extend God's blessing to others. Not only Gen 1 emphasizes that humans male and female are created in God's image—thus implying egalitarian status—but the Babylonian *Enuma Elish* account also prefers egalitarian power structures over imperial. The implications for marriage are egalitarian. If Gen 1 judges

---

15. J. Richard Middleton, *The Liberating Image: The Imago Dei in Genesis 1* (Grand Rapids: Brazos, 2005) 49.

16. Ibid., 50.

17. Ibid., 88.

18. Ibid., 89.

19. Ibid., 89.

20. Ibid., 231.

21. Ibid., 269.

violence, Jesus' citation of Gen 1 reinforces a stance against domestic violence—a common complaint in divorce proceedings.

Jesus also quotes Gen 2:24, this verse in its entirety. Following the principle used above, we can posit that Jesus in quoting a single verse is alluding to the larger context. Without an exhaustive study of the second creation account, one can again identify elements of the story that inform Jesus' comments in the divorce controversy.

As noted above, Gen 2 reinforces the notion that human beings have responsibility for the well-being of the environment. If Gen 1 emphasizes the royal nature of the human created in the image of God, Gen 2 gives the 'human' (*'ādām*) responsibility to till and keep (guard or protect) the 'soil' (*'ădāmâ*, 2:15).[22] Work and service are part of the good created order, not a result of human transgression.[23]

Genesis 2 recognizes that it is not good that the man is alone—in contrast to all the good that God saw in Gen 1. A companion for relationship is needed. The woman is called a "helper" who is a "partner." Because the term 'helper' (*'ēzer*) is used for God (Ps 121:1–2), the word does not imply lower status for the woman, nor does it collapse the role of helping into merely procreation.[24] The process of creating the woman also implies egalitarian complementarity. God designs and "builds" the woman to complete the creation design.

Verse 23 records the man's first words about the woman. Everything the man has to say about creation concerns his helper: She is "bone of my bones and flesh of my flesh," he says. Hamilton suggests that, while flesh is often a symbol for weakness and frailty, bones may be a symbol of an individual's strength.[25]

Alternatively, "flesh and bone" may express relationship.[26] Brueggemann has argued that the term is actually a covenant formula. It speaks of reciprocal loyalty.[27] When representatives of the Northern tribes approach David, they say, "We are your bone and flesh" (2 Sam 5:1). This is a pledge of loyalty. In Gen 2:23 Adam is pledging covenantal commitment to the woman. Hamilton again suggests that this corresponds to the modern wedding commitment to

---

22. Theodore Hiebert, "Creation, the Fall, and Humanity's Role in the Ecosystem," in *Creation and the Environment: An Anabaptist Perspective on a Sustainable World* (ed. Calvin Redekop; Baltimore: Johns Hopkins University Press, 2000) 115–17.

23. Victor P. Hamilton, *The Book of Genesis Chapters 1–17* (NICOT; Grand Rapids: Eerdmans, 1990) 171.

24. Terence E. Fretheim, "Genesis," *NIB* 1.352.

25. Hamilton, *Genesis*, 179.

26. Ibid., 179.

27. As cited by Hamilton in ibid.

be true "in weakness and in health." Strength and weakness are not attributed to male or female alone.[28]

Verses 24–25 emphasize the closeness of the male-female bond. The text does not mention procreation but focuses on the closeness and intimacy of the man-woman relationship. Although the text envisions the future day in which children will leave parents, the emphasis here is on the marriage bond, not family life.[29]

The "leave" and "cling" language challenges interpreters. Why is the man the one who is said to leave? Does the text envision a matrilineal society? Because it was more common in Hebrew society for the woman to leave her parental home, perhaps the term alludes to emotional detachment or to forming a new identity.[30]

Hamilton emphasizes the significance of the covenant relationship. Israel is said to "leave" its covenant relationship with Yahweh (Jer 1:16; 2:13, 17), but the verb "cling" designates maintenance of the covenant relationship (Deut 4:4; Ruth 1:14). To leave father and mother and to cling to one's wife is to end one loyalty and to enter into another.[31]

In Matt 19:6, Jesus concludes his opening statement by interpreting and applying the creation accounts to his contemporary context. In the tradition of the Hebrew Bible, Jesus gives testimony to God's purpose. God's purpose involves covenant community. Jesus embodies and models faithfulness. Jesus uses the image he finds in the OT creation story to reinforce the covenant loyalty inherent in community relationships. For Jesus, as Paul makes explicit in Eph 5:25–32, the marriage relationship of husband to wife is to be a model for community relationships.

The Pharisees, as good OT scholars, raise the countertestimony. Conceding for the moment, perhaps, the creation narrative's ethic of lasting covenant bonds, they raise the question of the Mosaic command to issue divorce papers when husbands leave wives. Surely Jesus recognizes that the ideals of Gen 1–2 must face the reality of Deut 24:1–4! Legal rulings about conditions for divorce restrict the flippant and cavalier breaking of legal bonds, but they also concede the reality that marriage covenants will break down. The Pharisees challenge Jesus' creation ideals with traditional OT countertestimony.

Jesus' reply adjudicates between competing OT traditions. Jesus uses creation theology to trump Mosaic legal tradition. Both ancient traditions revolve around covenant. In his first statement of rejoinder to the pharisaic

---

28. Ibid., 180.
29. Fretheim, "Genesis," 1.354.
30. Hamilton, *Genesis*, 180; Fretheim, "Genesis," 1.354.
31. Hamilton, *Genesis*, 181.

objection, Jesus reads creation theology as more authoritative than Sinai theology on the basis of priority. Creation theology reveals the purpose of God for relationship within covenant.

Jesus' second statement to the pharisaic objection changes the focus from creation theology to Sinaitic covenant theology. Jesus teaches that divorce and remarriage constitutes a breach of the Ten Words regarding adultery. Ultimately, according to Jesus, identification of conflict between creation theology and Sinaitic covenant theology is a misreading of the traditions. Jesus' teaching in Matt 19 is fully consistent with his third antithesis in the Sermon on the Mount (Matt 5:31–32). Jesus engages the OT testimony, he reinterprets it, and he seeks to establish a consistent application that depends on what he considers primary and authoritative.

The controversy pericope concludes with Jesus' answer to a private question from his disciples. Without trying to interpret what Jesus' message about becoming eunuchs for the kingdom might involve, we do get a sense that Jesus recognizes the pluralistic context in which he speaks. He opens his statement with the phrase, "Not everyone can accept this teaching." He concludes with the sentence, "Let anyone accept this who can." Perhaps the reply to the disciples involves only their recommendation that it is best not to marry. Nonetheless, Jesus appears to be recognizing that a diverse community will not respond uniformly.

The divorce controversy illustrates Jesus' use of the OT tradition. Jesus uses creation theology to establish the governing paradigm. His citations have been read in this essay as a witness in favor of egalitarian marriage relations and the primacy of covenant faithfulness. Jesus recognizes that there is testimony and countertestimony within the tradition. He makes an authoritative claim in favor of his interpretation.

Reading Matthew 19:16–30

Postponing for the moment attention to the brief pronouncement story, we next consider the third pericope in Matt 19. It is the call story of the young man with many possessions, a text containing extensive citations from the Hebrew Bible. This scandalous text presents plenty of problems for preaching to middle-class congregations in North America, setting aside for the moment the problem of the OT in preaching. Most northern/Western readers are uncomfortable with Jesus' declaration that it is difficult for a rich person to enter the kingdom. Perhaps our audience (and this may include the preacher) is more attuned to the grieving response of the young man than to the hopeful word of Jesus that God makes all things possible.

The young interlocutor approaches Jesus with the question about a good deed that he must do to have eternal life. Jesus' reply does not condemn the man for works righteousness. He does allude to the monotheistic confession of Deut 6:4 that Yahweh alone is God. Then Jesus makes the bold declaration that the way to life is through obedience to the Torah. This answer of Jesus need not surprise the reader. It reinforces the notion of "Whole Bible" theology, that the OT expresses God's gracious gift of life. Jesus' answer is consistent with his six antitheses in Matt 5:17–48. Jesus is here to fulfill the OT. Jesus' fulfillment includes an authoritative interpretation of the Torah, a testimony that stakes a claim for truth within the diverse voices of OT testimony and countertestimony. Yet Jesus offers a humble, nonfoundational answer, recognizing that God alone is a good authority. Jesus tells his questioner that the commandments are the way to life.

When the young man presses him to be more specific, Jesus quotes the second tablet of the Ten Words, the heart of the Torah. Curiously, Jesus does not cite the first four Words, all of which address human worship of God. Jesus moves the order of the commandment regarding honoring parents from first to last in his list. Jesus replaces the Word(s) prohibiting coveting with a single command to love neighbor (Lev 19:18). In Matt 22:34–40, when asked to summarize the Law, Jesus quotes the OT commandments calling for love of God and neighbor, again summarizing the second tablet of the Ten Words with the command to love neighbor. Jesus teaches that keeping the Torah is the way to life.

While commentators might speculate on the rhetorical effect of placing the command to honor parents in the penultimate position and replacing the command prohibiting coveting with the one that commands love for neighbor, interpretation of the ensuing conversation does not seem to depend on this sort of analysis. When the young man insists on more specificity, Jesus issues the call to follow him as a disciple. Preparation for discipleship requires the rich young man to practice OT Jubilee principles.

Jesus prefaces his Jubilee call with the conditional phrase, "If you wish to be perfect." The adjective 'perfect' (*teleios*) is used elsewhere in Matthew only in 5:48, where Jesus calls his followers to be perfect, because the Father is perfect. This construction parallels the construction of Lev 19:2: "You shall be holy, for I the Lord your God am holy." The Jubilee legislation follows in Lev 25. The Jubilee year is holy (Lev 25:12).

The Jubilee legislation is the great social and economic leveler, a program for social justice. The Deuteronomistic parallel to Jubilee is the sabbatical year. Here again the emphasis is on justice and generosity within the community. Deuteronomy calls for remission of debts, release of slaves, and soft-hearted, open-handed, liberal, and ungrudging giving to the needy neighbor (Deut 15:1–17). Such generosity, Moses claims, will lead not to hardship but to God's blessing in all that the faithful do.

Psalm 72 reinforces the link between justice and generosity to the poor. The righteous king "delivers the needy," "has pity on the weak," and "saves the lives of the needy" (72:12–13). He enjoys long life (72:15)! Linking righteousness to care for the poor demands notice, given Jesus' frequent use of the term in Matthew's Gospel (5:6, 10, 20; 6:33).

The prophets reinforce the call to distributive justice that favors the poor. Isaiah calls for Israel to "learn to do good; seek justice, rescue the oppressed, defend the orphan, plead for the widow" (1:17). Amos speaks woe to hearers who live a luxurious lifestyle (6:4–8). Jeremiah speaks woe to people who build luxury homes by unrighteousness and commends the king who does justice and righteousness and judges the cause of the poor and needy. He declares that this is what it means to know Yahweh (22:13–16).

Preachers often feel compelled to relativize or mitigate the effect of Jesus' words to the rich young man. These words are spoken to a single individual with a particular need, we say. They are unreasonable, we argue. How would we live if everyone sold everything? Preachers and other readers seek to avoid Jesus' word as a word to us today.

A "Whole Bible" reading of the words of Jesus reinforces their contemporary relevance. Jesus confirms the testimony of Moses, interpreting the Ten Words as leading to Jubilee practices. Jesus inaugurates the kingdom of heaven with royal justice described in Psalms and Jeremiah. Jesus speaks in a manner consonant with the OT prophets. Jesus' words cannot be relegated to the sidelines as a specific message to an isolated individual.

Jesus' response to Peter closes the OT link and reinforces the notion that Jesus is deliberate in his OT contextualizing. Eternal life in the kingdom will involve just rule. Because of their own faithful following after having experienced the Jubilee freedom of God's grace, the disciples will judge all Israel. Matthew 19 concludes with an eschatological reference to Israel.

Reading Matthew 19:13–15

The brief pronouncement story does not have an obvious link with the Hebrew Bible. Unlike the other two pericopes in Matt 19, in Matt 19:13–15 Jesus does not quote an OT text. Further, one wonders why Matthew places this pericope where he does unless one attributes its placement to Matthew's slavishly following the lead of his Markan source (which pushes the question of placement back one generation to Mark's Gospel).

In the reading that follows, I will, by necessity, take a different direction from my reading of the other two pericopes, which investigate OT quotations and allusions. While one might profitably read Matt 19:13–15 in light of other OT texts that deal with parents and children (e.g., Ishmael and Hagar, the Hebrew midwives, Jacob's blessing of Joseph's children), the analysis that follows reads this text in parallel with Samuel.

Barbara Green, interpreting 1 Samuel with a reading guided by the Russian literary critic Mikhail Bakhtin, suggests that the genre of the story of Saul is best identified as a riddle.[32] It is a riddle that attends to the *sons* in the book of 1 Samuel, particularly the riddle located in the wordplay that gives Samuel and Saul their names. 1 Samuel 1:20 reports that Hannah gave her son the name Samuel (the name itself sounds like "heard of God") because, she said, I have *asked* (this verb sounds like "Saul") him of Yahweh. Green suggests that the riddle reminds the reader of both the hope and the eventual disappointment that is experienced by the reader with the sons of Eli, Samuel, Saul, and David. It also raises questions, in Green's analysis, of the role and appraisal of kings in Israel and Judah.

Pursuing Green's analysis at length would take us too far from our focus. However, Green's theological conclusion regarding both Hannah and the king-Israel nexus is worth considering for our reading of Matt 19:13–15. She asks why Hannah weeps in 1 Sam 1:3–18. Green considers the apparent remedy of offspring when Hannah bears a child as a way of "faking out" the reader. After all, Hannah immediately gives the child back to Yahweh. Green claims to detect what both Elkanah and Eli are too blind to see. Eli mistakes Hannah's tears for drunkenness, a disorder that more nearly describes the sons of Eli than Hannah. Elkanah tries to solve the problem with additional sacrificial portions. Green concludes that what Hannah is truly seeking in her prayer before Yahweh is a relationship. Reading the riddle of the life of Saul, Green concludes that "the vitality of the relationship between God and humans is more central" than other issues or questions interpreters have brought to the text. "The son is a way of Hannah's asking God for what she lacks."[33] The basic relationship of God and Israel should be the point of kingship as well (1 Sam 12:14–15, 24).

Just as I have raised a question about the place of Matt 19:13–15 in its context, so scholars have been skeptical of the place of the poem of Hannah (1 Sam 2:1–10) within the original Samuel narrative. Scholars have also re-

---

32. Barbara Green, *King Saul's Asking* (Interfaces; Collegeville, MN: Liturgical Press, 2003) xvi.
33. Ibid., 16.

garded 2 Sam 21–24 as a later addition, an epilogue that interrupts the narrative. Robert Polzin, acknowledging his debt to Mikhail Bakhtin, claims that a "literary study" of Samuel locates the Samuel story within the context of kingship criticism. Polzin appreciates the care with which the Song of Hannah is "inserted" into the prose narrative. Following Bakhtin, Polzin detects a "polyphonic composition" in the Song of Hannah; it is a "chorus" of voices including the rejoicing mother, Hannah; the exultant king; and the Deuteronomist, the "author" of the current text.[34]

The voice of Hannah appears at the most superficial level, a once-barren woman exultant in the birth of her child. Like the parents who bring their children to Jesus, Hannah rejoices in the life of her son.

Polzin notes, at a deeper level, that the language of 1 Sam 2 is strikingly monarchic and develops parallels between Hannah's Song and the royal psalm found in 2 Sam 22 (part of the so-called epilogue). Both praise the victory of kingship in Israel.[35] Polzin notes other connections between the royal voice of 1 Sam 2 and the rest of the book of Samuel. For example, Hannah sings, "Do not multiply your words, 'Tall! Tall!'" (Polzin's translation of 2:3). We are reminded of Saul's stature (and Goliath's) and of Yahweh's warning to Samuel not to give attention to appearance when he seeks to anoint one of Jesse's sons. Eli has already made a mistake about appearances when he accused Hannah of drunkenness. Thus, the exaltation of the lowly and the debasement of the mighty can be traced throughout Samuel (and Kings).[36]

Polzin, on a still deeper level of reading, perceives a more melancholy voice in the song. This is the voice of the Deuteronomist, who anticipates the failure of the monarchy and the eventual exile. Jehoiachin in exile is alternately hungry and well fed at the king's table. The people who remain in Jerusalem are the poor, the barren in Israel.[37]

Reading the book of Samuel in conversation with Matt 19:13–15 is the aim of this "Whole Bible" analysis. Note that the reading of Samuel with Matt 19:13–15 succeeds on two levels. First, it provides depth of insight to the pronouncement story. Second, it connects Matt 19:13–15 with the pericopes that precede and follow it.

A brief summary aims to integrate these fresh insights. First, the aim of Hannah's prayer is consistent with the aim of Jesus' blessing of the children—what is needed is a renewal of the relationship that Israel has with its God.

---

34. Robert Polzin, *Samuel and the Deuteronomist: A Literary Study of the Deuteronomic History, Part Two: 1 Samuel* (San Francisco: Harper & Row, 1989) 30.

35. Ibid., 33.

36. Ibid., 32–35.

37. Ibid., 36–39.

Further, in both the divorce controversy and the call story, we see that covenant relationships within Israel are primary. Self-giving compassion and loyalty
to the "other" are expressions of right relations with God. Second, the sons
of this world may disappoint (hard-hearted divorcing men and grieving rich
young men), but Jesus gives hope by blessing a new generation of children.
Third, Jesus continues God's policy of reversals, of raising the humble and
sending the proud and the rich away empty. Fourth, Jesus comes to embody
and call out a new Israel that reverses exile. The final reversal does not end in
Babylon but in Jerusalem with a new kingdom. In this new kingdom, covenant
relationships are honored, children are blessed and exalted, and thrones are
given to those who have left all to follow Jesus.

Conclusion

The purpose of this essay has been to assist the preacher (teacher) who has
struggled with preaching (teaching) the OT as authoritative. By interpreting
one NT chapter in light of the OT, I have attempted to demonstrate one way
to read the testaments in continuity. The task of using this reading to craft
sermons is the challenge that awaits preachers. Additional guidance in this task
remains a future project.

Brueggemann's approach to nonfoundational assumptions has guided our
reading of Jesus' appropriation of the OT tradition. Jesus taught in a pluralistic
context, well aware that his was not the only reading of the tradition. He spoke
with authority but explicitly gave freedom of response to his audience. He also
made claims regarding the testimony of Israel with particular attention to justice
for discarded wives, unappreciated children, and disenfranchised poor persons.

Wright's insight regarding the six acts of the story, with Jesus seeing himself
as the embodiment of and caller to a newly reconstituted Israel also shaped this
reading. Jesus is calling a new community that lives in covenant loyalty. This
new people develops within the story begun in the earlier acts of creation and
the formation of Israel's covenant community. The story anticipates a sixth act
in which an eschatological community rules with justice in the reign of God.

Martens's attention to God's purpose has informed our reading throughout.
Martens's contribution to our understanding of God's fourfold design punc-
tuates this essay. We see God's act of *deliverance* in the concern for justice for
divorced wives and blessing for disregarded children. The justice theme is
more dominant in the story of the rich young man, who is called to act with
Jubilee care for the poor. We see God's concern for *covenant community* in the
primary theme of relationship. Just as Hannah prayed for a son when she
yearned for relationship, so Matt 19 emphasizes that community relations ex-

press right relations of the community with God. Divorce is forbidden because it breaks covenant. Children are blessed in order to facilitate relationships with God. The rich young man is called to be loyal to covenant commitments by selling his excess to provide for the needy in the community. We see how God's concern that the *knowledge of God* be growing relationally overlaps with the preceding pillar of the fourfold design. Suffice it to say that Jesus emphasizes that knowledge of the one who is good (holy) leads to life. We see God's concern for *land* in the Jubilee expressions of the final pericope. The young man seeks life eternal—the abundance of life in the land. Jesus offers a kingdom—a kingdom that anticipates the renewal of all things.

On Truth-Telling and Biblical Theology

ROLF P. KNIERIM

Professor of Old Testament, Emeritus
Claremont School of Theology and Claremont Graduate University
Claremont, California

The Bible presents legal cases of all sorts but as a whole presents no systematized theology of any sort regarding truth-telling.[1] Although everywhere it speaks about, refers to, and implies truth, nowhere does either of the two Bibles, Jewish or Christian, declare itself on the subject of truth in one treatise that systematizes all the perspectives.

To develop a biblical approach to truth, the biblical materials must be systematized by their interpreters, by us, readers of the Bible from generation to generation. This is what has always been done in one way or another, because the biblical writers themselves have not done it for us.[2]

Author's note: I am happy to respond to the invitation to contribute an essay to a festschrift in honor of Prof. Elmer Martens, with whom I have been connected through some four decades, beginning at Claremont Graduate University and followed by many years of mutual attention to our vocational and professional careers. This essay comes to Prof. Martens with my recognition of his service to Christian faith and life as well as to his work in biblical theology and with my best wishes for him and his wife.

1. On March 10–15, 2002, the Claremont School of Theology conducted a five-day conference on *Truth: Interdisciplinary Dialogues in a Pluralistic Age*. At the conference, an international range of scholars from the major fields of theology and philosophy of religion were assembled. One of the main lectures was given by Marjorie Hewitt Suchocki on the topic *To Tell the Truth*. Her paper was later published under the title, "To Tell the Truth," in *Truth: Interdisciplinary Dialogs in a Pluralist Age* (ed. Christine Helmer, Kristin De Troyer, and Katie Goetz; Studies in Philosophical Theology 22; Leuven: Peeters, 2003) 217–31. I gave a formal response to her original paper at the conference, and this essay is the essential part of my response to her published paper.

2. It needs to be said that using unitary terms such as "the Bible" or "biblical study" without explicit reference to different Bibles is indefensible, for basically two reasons. First, the Jewish people have their own threefold TaNaK, consisting of Torah (Instruction, Law), Nebiim (Prophets), and Ketubim (Writings). The TaNaK is their Bible, their only one, and only their Bible. They have no Testament at all like the Christians, neither an Old nor a First nor a Former one, let alone a New Testament. Their Bible is best described as the Bible of the Jewish people. It will henceforth be called TaNaK in this essay. By contrast, the Bible of the Jewish people is

In this essay I want to discuss a few perspectives, predominantly from the TaNaK, that appear to relate to the topic of telling the truth. That truth statements can be made on the level of verifiable facts has been a tenet throughout the ages, and the TaNaK also provides uncounted examples of this sort. These statements are held true because they are first of all confirmed/confirmable as correct. In the Bible, statements of this sort rest on the "simple," common-sense assumption that a told fact "is there," whether or not I know, see, or like it.

The people who make these statements—as individuals or as a group—speak about facts of the world, about the sun, moon, and stars, about the earth, plants, animals, mountains, valleys, and about humans and what they think, say, and do. Their statements are true because they were and are verifiable, not because the statements were or are made. The relation of these statements to the factuality of things is fundamental at the outset because it shows that they, like we, are bound by factuality and cannot escape it. Factuality binds our language and our rhetoric to the reality that is external to it.

One particular aspect of truth has to do with the materiality of facts. By and large, the thousands of biblical references to material realities have played little if any role in biblical theologies or in discussions about truth in the Bible. Books that record the *materialia* mentioned in the Bible have not typically been granted theological significance. How can one speak about creation without the *realia* of the world?

A consciousness of the materiality of facts, however, is found in the evidence for the scientific affairs of that time in the TaNaK and the relevance of this evidence for the understanding of reality as the relationship between God and world, and for telling truth. By contrast, very little of this sort of evidence is found in the NT. Any discussion of science in the time of the TaNaK is

---

the first of the two Testaments of the Christian Bible. Truth demands that the integrity of the one Bible of the Jewish people be recognized just as much as the integrity of the one Bible of the Christians in its two Testaments.

Second, the perspectives of Christians in the NT are fundamentally different from those in the Bible of the Jewish people. The NT's world view is not the one of the TaNaK, and the Jewish world view is not Christian. The separation of the two world views outweighs everything that both traditions may be or have been said to have in common. This claim applies especially to the area of the so-called traditiohistorical study, in which many threads of tradition from the TaNaK via "intertestamental" evidence to the NT have been studied. These threads show that certain notions or motives are united by being linked in ongoing processes, but this uniting as linkage demonstrates as yet nothing about whether their conceptual identity has remained the same throughout, even as it may have experienced modification while remaining the same, or—a decisive issue widely missed in exegetical studies—whether one conceptual identity has at some point been replaced by a new one, which is basically the case in the difference between the world views of the TaNaK and the NT.

almost completely neglected in our biblical theologies, a serious deficiency in their design. It is as though, then and today, God, as long as God is considered a decisive criterion for truth-telling, had nothing to do with science. I am speaking of scientific systems in the literature of the TaNaK.

Thus, according to criteria such as rationality in argumentation, consistency between thought and language, verifiability by external factors, predictability of recurring conditions, implementability of theory in practice, or confirmation of theory or proof of its failure by undeniable facts—according to these criteria, many texts of the TaNaK not only refer to innumerable materials in stating one fact after another; they also rest on, reflect, and directly presuppose the science of collecting and ordering all sorts of materials found in this world in systematized catalogs, based on which these passages themselves are structured.

These catalogs, especially where we have them as literary genres, are examples of the process by which simple-level truth-telling is transcended; the simple facts are compiled in telling the truth with rising levels of complexity, and the order of their relationship appears. These catalogs reflect the complexity of the reality of related facts rather than revealing systems of abstraction about this reality.

But, whether in the form of catalogs or series or lists of items, there is evidence for the presence of the sciences—of course, in a state appropriate to the time—of anatomy, botany, zoology, metallurgy, and medicine, though less developed. Also available were the sciences of cosmology, astronomy, astrology, state administration, management, census-taking, architecture, construction, warfare, and more.

The deity in fact is seen as a "scientist," especially with regard to "plans" and "designs." Thoughts, plans, ideas, and especially concepts may be, but are usually not, "abstractions." They belong to the planning stage of all sorts of organized operations and represent the basis for the execution of these operations. They are real and operative in many compositions of the literary works of the Bible.

As far as the literary works are concerned, I know of no biblical text that is not based on and controlled by a planned concept in which both thought and story inseparably complement each other. Furthermore, "systems" can but need not involve abstract concepts. The cosmos of heaven and earth is experienced as a systemic order, even though there are chaotic elements throughout it. Does this telling of order or ordering of reality—naming and classifying verified facts—have anything to do with truth at either the simple or the complex level of truth and truth-telling? What does it have to do with metaphysics or even the deity?

I want to refer to the science of law, specifically, which is embodied in the legal corpora of the TaNaK. This type of science is especially relevant to the subject of truth-telling. Individual legal cases can be analyzed according to the complexity of the relationship among the various levels involved, because the legal corpora are embedded in the reality of the life of the society and institutionally aimed at keeping it from falling out of balance.

In the so-called case of prescriptive laws, the "if . . . then" laws, verdicts, and sentences are determined on the basis of establishing facts, whereby the weight of a sentence is perceived to be commensurate with the severity of the infraction (for example, a crime, violation, or accident for which a person is or is not responsible). Legal corpora are compositions of these laws, which presuppose that there are differences among cases and types of cases, dependent on the gravity of violations and the corresponding judgments on them. The complexity of the cases is addressed by arranging them in compositions according to different levels or groups of laws, whereby the individual laws in each group are even coordinated in a particular order.

Furthermore, in biblical texts the process of truth-telling itself is complex, be it in the form of "responsive" contributions by members of a council or in the circumspective accounting of the many-faceted aspects of an individual.

Types of Truth-Telling in the TaNaK

There are four more types of truth-telling that need to be mentioned. They are (1) the "naming" activities of human beings, (2) the so-called "better sayings," (3) modes of speaking (and thinking), both synchronically and diachronically, and (4) the structure of both large and small literary texts in the TaNaK itself.

On Naming

As human beings, we are distinguished by our names. Our name is given to us by others, and it is pronounced by others. It is not included in our biological condition. The word *God* is a generic term that signals the distinction between deity and world, especially humanity. However, the word did not indicate in ancient times, nor does it today, which God is meant among the gods in the polytheistic arena.

Thus, both Yahweh and Baal are deities, but they are identified and distinguished by their names. Now, a name is always pronounced, or spoken, because naming is always a language event. "The man gave names to all [domestic] cattle, the birds of the air, and to every [wild] beast of the field," which is a reference to three classified *types* of animals and their place in the cosmos.

The identification, differentiation, stratification, and ordering of living beings or material items through acts of language, by naming and classifying them—all belong to the fundamental set of truth-telling, precisely because of the complexity of the relationships.

On the Better Sayings

The Bible, influenced by ancient wisdom, uses a particular procedure for addressing and answering complex situations. The results of these procedures are contained in the genre of the so-called better sayings.

"A good name is to be chosen rather than riches, and favor is better than silver and gold" (Prov 22:1). In a thousand cases and types of cases, one does not know the truth in advance. One must search for it. Telling the truth requires a heuristic process through which options are compared, and "what is better" is discovered. The better result is a value judgment, virtually always derived from the conditions of real experience. It is relative, not absolute, but relational and in no way irrelevant.

On the Complexity of Reality

There are quantitatively different dimensions of reality, and they are embedded within the complexity of their interrelations. There are different perspectives on cosmic, terrestrial, territorial, and local reality—with additional aspects in between—and these perspectives range from human ethnicities and nations to communities of tribes, clans, families, and human beings as individuals (as distinguished by the names given them). Each of these views is distinct, none of them unrelated to the other. The biblical texts show in manifold ways how the place and value of these individual perspectives is, and/or should be, understood.

Of particular interest is the biblical text's clear recognition of the types of diachronic and synchronic perspectives to which these complex factors are related. Considered *synchronically*, the persons, groups, nations, and human generations of today are not isolated. How they are said to be related in the texts is—inevitably—for us to discover by bringing the varying biblical perspectives into a "responsive" dialogue. By critically comparing the varying positions juxtaposed in the so-called canon, the dialogue continues, even if the discussion was not carried forward to us canonically.

The presently existing entities—persons, groups, nations, and generations of today—are also known *diachronically*. The evidence is vast and multifaceted. Consider the genealogies of the human species, of Israel's tribes, of families. Here the "responsive" dialogue is inevitably confronted with the conflict between the historical verifiability of many of these genealogies and the ideological intentionality of the groups who own and control their functions as well as their selective compositions. Today it is of critical, world-historical importance that we consider what we affirm when hearing the truth claim that both Jews and Arabs are united by the same father: Abraham. Let us for the sake of argument—an argument not confirmed historically—assume that Abraham was the father of both Ishmael and Isaac. Despite the fact that the texts link them biologically together through their father, the texts overwhelmingly emphasize how the two sons and their respective offspring are separate; they have different mothers and are given different kinds of blessing and different countries for possession. One is considered elect from among the nations, and, in one sense, the other is not. What really happened genealogically is disputable, but the Israel-centric and Israel-based ideological perspective of the story of Abraham and his two sons is indisputable.

Of course, universally pervasive within diachronic perception, certainly in the TaNaK, is the history of traditions. This fact is well known among people of sufficient biblical education. The study of the history of traditions and their transmission concerns not only the study of the traditions themselves but also the way that the traditions live and function in the texts. What is manifest thereby is primarily how the concepts or conceptual patterns of traditions remain consistent throughout generations and how their conceptual identity is retained, even in modifications or adjustments caused by changing circumstances.

What is not equally registered is the fact that established traditions were in the course of transmission sometimes not just adapted to changing circumstances but abolished and replaced by new ones; or at least it was contested as being the only viable principle through the juxtaposition of an alternative or higher principle. For example, the emphasis in Jer 31:30 and Ezek 18:4, 20 on the liberation of the individual from the consequences of the sins of the fathers (Exod 20:5) so that the individual is responsible only for her/his own sins is one case in point. On occasion, Israel's deity, Yahweh, exhibits a change of mind, if not from one principle to a new one, then from one principle to a better one. Note Abraham's intercession in Gen 18 and Yahweh's repentance in the Jonah novella and in Hos 11:1–9. Most importantly, it is evident that the concept of the suffering of Jesus comes from the concept of the suffering servant in the TaNaK. However, it is also evident that Jesus is said to have suffered for the sins of the world, whereas any servant in the TaNaK only suffered for the sins of Israel.

In a "responsive" dialogue of this sort, the role of conceptual continuity and discontinuity in the history of traditions within the biblical literature shows that, when it comes to truth-telling, it is neither continuity nor discontinuity that would be a self-evident criterion for finding truth. Instead, telling the truth depends on other criteria, to which both continuity and discontinuity are subjected.

Thus far, what has been said applies also to the study of the kind of ontology that plays a particular role in the TaNaK. The origin of this study is especially clear in the work of Klaus Koch and the *Tatsphäre* ontology. It speaks about the indissoluble connection between the typical nature of an act or behavior and the way in which an act of this sort fulfills itself, by virtue of the autonomously progressing dynamic of natural processes. It is especially found in the arguments of proverbial wisdom (Ps 1). The observation of this kind of coherent process, beginning with an act and fulfilling itself in the fateful end of the act applies to individuals, communities, and all humanity.

Even so, as much as this kind of ontology rests on real experience, it too has been relativized by experience based on alternative, even opposite experiences. Broad evidence is especially found in the books of Job, Psalms, Proverbs, and Ecclesiastes. Thus, the biblical literature evidences what we call ontological thinking, but we also find evidence there for ontological varieties. Taken all together, one cannot say that its real interests are based on, let alone require, one and the same ontological perception of reality.

On Compositions and Structures in the Biblical Literature

The many aspects of truth-telling with their complex interrelations on different levels are brought together for the sake of ordered truth-telling; it is an *ordered* telling and also a universal property of biblical literature, including the TaNaK. There is no text, large or small, that is not organized. Thus, the understanding of texts, especially written texts, requires attention to the conditions that move texts beyond the etymology and semantics of words and beyond the grammar and syntax of sentences toward conceptualized units that employ the service of words and sentences. And the more the texts grow from the smallest identifiable unit to larger and larger units, the greater the complexity of the relationship between all the units. The final form of the text is the result of structuring, through which these units appear to be stratified in ever descending, narrower levels, with each level part of its higher level, and with all levels part of the whole inter-existing, pyramid-like system. The commentary The Forms of the Old Testament Literature[3] is especially designed to study and show the systemic nature of the structural complexity of the texts of the TaNaK.

---

3. See the multivolume series of commentaries, entitled The Forms of the Old Testament Literature (ed. Rolf P. Knierim, Gene M. Tucker, and Marvin A. Sweeney; Grand Rapids: Eerdmans, 1981–).

Our discussion of the four aspects of truth-telling attests the fact that the biblical literature is well aware of different levels of reality and complexity. They should be taken as sufficient evidence for the comparability or compatibility of the biblical state of affairs regarding the recognition and ordering of the various levels and their complexity in truth-telling.

Indeed, it can safely be said that biblical scholars who have become cognizant of the biblical aspects discussed above have learned about them from their study of the biblical texts, whether they were informed by the Whiteheadian ontological method or not. We must recognize that, in both arenas of study, the type of *Geistesbeschäftigung* (= activity or occupation of the mind) is similar or the same. The process of truth-finding and truth-telling is through determining "simple" facts or through determining complex situations via "responsive" pondering of the arguments.

In sum, the biblical literature gives us nothing but cases. However, it is not only case oriented, it is case based; it reveals how it moves from case to case, telling the truth in its own views by relating and comparing the various aspects of a case or complex of cases. And it does so without having developed an all-inclusive theoretical system.

The contact of the biblical literature with reality through its telling of real cases is direct, even at the cost of a unified ontology. Contact via a theoretical system is no better than an indirect system, and a theoretical system of this sort should serve real cases. It is not a goal or end in itself. If it were, it would truly be an abstraction—a replacement for real cases.

One may debate whether or not ontology, especially one particular ontology, is indispensable as a basis for truth-telling. As long as a debate of this sort is inconclusive, we may proceed with what inevitably confronts us: the real, even pressing cases and their complexity. And we may apply the mechanisms for truth-telling through "responsive" processes or the mechanisms for affirming "better sayings," as far as the complex conditions require these mechanisms from case to case.

Responsive Inquiry and the Study of Cases

I proceed now to apply the method of "responsive" inquiry, the presupposition behind truth-telling in the form of "better sayings"—some even in the form of a "best saying"—to the study of cases in biblical literature, basically in the TaNaK. It has already been said that *quantitative* aspects (such as cosmic, terrestrial, territorial, and local aspects) and aspects about all humanity (such as nations, including Israel, tribes, clans, families and individuals) must be accounted for in the truth-telling of complex cases. What has not yet been addressed is the *qualitative aspect of each case*. This aspect pervades all biblical literature and its cases. It is constitutive of it as well as of the biblical picture of the "truth" on the quantifiable side of the cases.

Expressed generally, the qualitative aspect is the contrast between what is good and bad, constructive and destructive. Cases about truth, order, justice, peace, communal solidarity, love in and of family and neighbor are found everywhere, just as much as cases about primordial chaos or the breakdown of order (injustice, violence, and war) and the breakdown of community (hate, untruth, and falsehood).

Equally involved in these cases is the difference in the texts before us between lower and higher levels of gravity concerning what is good or bad, constructive or destructive. There is the order of the created world compared with the postcreation order on earth, the order of societies, communities, and families. There is peace on the level of the family, the community, the nation, among nations, and on earth. Peace among all human beings is much more than peace in one's community or in one's family and life.

There is love of neighbor and love of enemy and so on. Likewise, destructive factors are weighted differently. An evil thought is bad but not as bad as an evil word, and both are not as bad as a murder, which itself is much worse than a theft. A murder of one person is less destructive than the annihilation of a community or than genocide. Violence in the family is bad, violence in a community and between communities is worse, and violence filling the earth is grounds for a flood that extinguishes all life on earth.

I refer to the area of hamartiological studies (studies of "sin") because this topic was part of my original work on the Hebrew Bible.[4] The study of the vast amount of material on the subject of "sin" throughout the entire TaNaK shows that there is scarcely any text where the subject is absent, terminologically or conceptually, explicitly or implicitly. The study of this subject alone reveals not only the distinguished types of "sin" and the different levels of gravity of each in its relation to others; it also points out the different levels of gravity within each type itself.

What is observed in the area of "sin" is also observed in the area of proposed punishment or in the carrying out of punishment according to what the TaNaK recounts. It is abundantly clear that—as far as punishment and other

---

4. Decades later I was privileged to contribute an essay on sin in the TaNaK to an interdisciplinary work by Prof. Suchocki and members of the Heidelberg faculty that was published as *Sünde: Ein Unverständlich Gewordenes Thema* (ed. Marjorie Suchocki, Sigrid Brandt, and Michael Welker; Neukirchen-Vluyn: Neukirchener Verlag, 1997). The last of my contributions on sin is "Sünde II, Altes Testament," in *TRE* 32.365–72.

kinds of retributive responsibility are concerned—there are clearly distinguished levels of more or less severe punishment, as well as different types of punishment and different kinds within certain types.

Anyone who wants (e.g., the United States) to have the Bible (which is also the Bible of the Jewish people) institutionalized as the basis for the law of the land will have to see to it that the more than twenty types of violation that fall under the law of capital punishment in the TaNaK are considered mandatory and to be obeyed in our public law! Only in this way will we be able to avoid violating the unfailing biblical truth of the instructions and laws of God.[5]

Especially important is the fact that the many terms for sin (just as the terms for punishment, judgment, justice, love, peace, war, and so on) are basically conceptual terms. Their nominal forms are called "abstract nouns," which is at least an ambivalent if not a misleading definition.

It is true that concepts can belong to a type of thought that refers to a world abstracted from the world of our real experience. But the "abstract nouns" in the Hebrew Bible have nothing to do with such a world. On the contrary, they express the type of experience that is grounded in reality. They express a particular act formally rather than substantively (based on the way that a society arranges its thinking by classifying different kinds of acts). All this is intrinsic to the experience of societal reality. It has nothing to do with abstraction of it. And it may be better to call conceptual nouns of this sort "typologizing nouns" rather than "abstract nouns." Most importantly, typologizing nouns are used for denoting typical conditions of reality itself. Words such as justice, peace, love, goodness, liberation, falsehood, violence, crime, "sin," and so on refer to the experience of the most important typical conditions in real affairs. They point to the presence and role of the qualitative side of values and anti-values in the experience of complex reality and its levels. Without these terms and their function in the biblical texts, an entire dimension of discerned differences and contrasts in the value-oriented side of the world view of the Hebrew Bible would be missed.

Throughout all biblical cases, truth-telling happens through the confrontation and separation of values and antivalues, through the comparison and gradation of the weight of good and constructive cases and of bad and destructive cases; truth-telling also happens through the assessment and appraisal of the different weights of value or antivalue within the cases themselves.

---

5. For the main study of this issue, see Rodney R. Hutton, *Declaratory Formulae: Forms of Authoritative Pronouncement in Ancient Israel* (Ph.D. diss., Claremont Graduate School, 1983). See also my "Strafe/Altes Testament," *TRE* 32.199–201; and idem, "Zum alttestamentlichen Verständnis von Strafe," in *Vielseitigkeit des Alten Testaments* (Wiener Alttestamentliche Studien 1; ed. James Alfred Loder and Hans Volker Kieweler; Frankfurt/Main: Peter Lang, 1999) 103–20.

Concepts play a particular, even constitutive role in the composition of works in the TaNaK. They signal the distinctive identity of the parts within a work as well as the identity of the whole. Therefore, it is important that all conceptually distinguishable parts on the surface of a work inevitably line up in sequential order, even when this sequential order reflects not only the concept of the sequence of the narrated events but also the relationship of the concepts of the parts to each other. The relationship between the conceptualized parts cannot be determined by their listing in successive numbers, such as 1, 2, 3, and so on. It can only be determined by showing how parts are related in super- and subordinated order, in a system of stratified levels with their sublevels.

An Example of Truth-Telling in the Torah

The Torah, the so-called Pentateuch, the most important part of the three-fold TaNaK is a central case in point. I must confine my argument to the most basic perspectives and to the dialogically "responsive" questions rather than to the answers.

It must be said that there is not only no proof that this work would represent the course of real history; there is even evidence that our knowledge of real history provides a different picture from the image provided by the biblical text. This does not mean, however, that this work is not a historical work. It belongs to the category of the history of Israel's ideology about its origins. We read the Torah as an ideological concept, which does not mean that it is not truthful, as might be assumed from the popular notion that ideology is always about falsehood. Whether or not any ideology tells the truth depends on whether it reflects reality as truth.

The major concepts by which the larger blocks of the Torah have been identified are known. The Torah in the biblical text before us is a unified literary work of history that stretches from the creation of the world—in the pattern of the seven-day Sabbath week, a pattern not found anywhere else but in Israel and Judaism—to the death of Moses in the plains of Moab. Considered structurally, not according to its division into five books, this work consists of two parts: (1) the history from creation to the movement of Jacob's family to Egypt (Genesis) and (2) the migration of the population of the Israelite tribes from Egypt to the plains of Moab under the leadership of Moses (Exodus through Deuteronomy).

What is the truth-telling of this work? What is the relationship of its two parts, of their unity in one concept? What is the connection between the Israelites' conquest of the land and their settlement within it? What is the importance of Moses for Israel's existence in the land after his death outside that land? Whatever the answers are, it is clear that these questions point to the conceptual complexity of the work and to the inevitability that its different aspects point to different levels of meaning within the whole and to the criteria by which it claims to tell truth.

One distinguishes the blocks in Genesis as the creation (Genesis 1–2), the primeval human history (with its own subsections of the periods before and after the flood and the periods from universal humanity to the Noahic humanity, Gen 3–11), the history of the patriarchs from Abraham's call by Yahweh to leave his home and family and move to not "a" but "the" land that Yahweh will show him, to the arrival of Jacob's family in Egypt (Genesis 12–50).

How is this kind of creation related to the course of human history? Is creation meant to be the category of reality before and the presupposition for all history, or is it meant to be the beginning of universal history itself? Or does the debate about the relationship between creation and universal history in Genesis 1–2 and 3ff. miss the primary conceptual point of this narrative in the first place? Does not its structure point to the concept that the historical narrations of both the creation and the universal beginning of history prepare for the history and existence of Israel—a preparation according to which Israel's existence is already embedded in nothing less than the fullness of creation? Indeed, Gerhard von Rad already said that "the creation belongs to the Etiology of Israel."[6]

How, then, are the conceptual levels of creation, human history, and Israel's story related? What is the order of the stratification of these concepts? Also, why does the primeval human history end in the history of the patriarchs rather than in the presentation of the genealogies of all its ongoing human families, at least the families from the Noahic time on? Or is the primeval history, at least the Noahic human history meant not to have ended at all with the conclusion of the book of Genesis but to exist forever? While this may not belong to the goal of the work, it is implied. Which concept guides the structure of this kind of history-telling? What is the truth-telling of this ideology of history?

The large story of Moses consists of the blocks about the Israelites' exodus from Egypt (Exodus 1–15), their migration toward nothing less than the promised land in two stages: migration to Sinai (Exod 16–18) and their stay at Sinai (the longest block, Exod 19–Num 10:10); and migration from Sinai to the plains of Moab (Num 10:11–21:35) and their stay in those fields (Num 22–36), ending with the testament of the dying Moses (Deut 1–34), which is meant to amend the Sinai instructions, not to replace them.

---

6. Gerhard von Rad, *Theologie des Alten Testaments*, vol. 1: *Die Theologie der geschichtlichen Überlieferungen Israels* (Munich: Chr. Kaiser, 1957) translated from the German, p. 143.

Why did the Israelites have to leave Egypt? Because they were oppressed or because they had to return to the land promised to the patriarchs? Were they liberated from oppression because they were the chosen people of Yahweh, their God, or because Yahweh was understood as the liberator of his people—as well as the deity who liberates all the oppressed in the world—and took them from the land of oppression to a land belonging to other people, which he gave them as their own? Is the liberation theology of the Israelite exodus from Egypt the paradigm for a theology of a God of universal liberation of all oppressed? What is the truth-telling of this story in light of truth-telling about God's relationship to all nations?

The way of the Israelites in the desert, prolonged by the Israelites' own murmuring—including their materialistic, idolatrous yearning for the flesh pots in Egypt compared with the precarious availability of bread and water in the desert—is anything but a wandering or journey. Before and after Sinai, it is a goal-oriented march through the countries of foreign nations based on the claim that the origin and goal of this march supersede the self-interests of these nations, and is carried through with divine support by essentially radical military action. Indeed, Israel's march from Sinai is conceptualized as the transmigratory, holy-war campaign of the holy sanctuary and all its personnel, accompanied and protected by the organization of the twelve tribes of the Israelites as a militia (Num 1–11), starting out under epiphanic events.

What is the place of the concept of the symbiotic unity of cultic, military, and national factors? What about the right of all of these factors to be employed against other nations' claims to their own rights in the process of truth-telling? Truth-telling involves complexity at multiple levels and also the acceptability or nonacceptability of some or all aspects. Is there a starting point anywhere that would be accepted by all? Is there a point when concepts that are in the interest of one party would be true for all parties simply because the one party says what it says and thinks what it thinks?

The story of Sinai tells about the establishment of Israel as Yahweh's "treasured possession," taken out of "all the peoples," as a "priestly kingdom" and a "holy nation" (Exod 19:4–6). The story is based on Yahweh's liberation of the Israelites from the Egyptians and his care of them on the way to Sinai on condition of their loyalty to Yahweh and the covenant.

Thus, Israel's organization begins with the laws introduced by the Decalogue (Exod 20–23; 24); the establishment of the one sanctuary (Exod 25–40; note the length of this block); then, in Leviticus, the organization of, first, the cult (1–16) and, second, predominantly the social order of the community (17–27). It ends with the preparations for campaigning toward Moab (Num 1:1–10:10). The concept of the Sinai narrative is clear: Sinai created the conceptual structure for Israel's permanent existence in the land. The same is also true for the Testament of Moses, the genre of the extant book of Deuteronomy.

The Decalogue, whether in the Exod 20:1–17 version or the Deut 5:6–21 version, is eminently tied to the identity of Israel. In neither case can it be separated from the presupposition expressed in its introduction (Israel's liberation [not from sin but] from Egypt by Yahweh, its God). For one thing, the Sabbath command is exclusively Israelite and, next to the circumcision of Israelite males, one of the two tenets that are exclusively constitutive for the identity of the Israelite community throughout all times. Christianity has adopted the pattern of the seven-day week but replaced the keeping of the seventh day with keeping the first day of the week, the day celebrating the resurrection of Jesus Christ, which is a break with the concept of Israel's Sabbath. However the validity of the Decalogue is recognized within the framework of Christianity, it is part of what Christians hold true, but it is neither genuinely Christian, nor is it the basis of Christian ethos or identity.

The laws and instructions for the sanctuary, cult, and social life are instructions for Israel's existence. And it is the prerogative of the Israeli-Jewish community to speak about the validity of these traditions for them today. However, these laws are neither meant to be the foundation for laws and ethical instructions for all humanity, nor were they ever validated by other communities, cultures, and religions as their own foundation.

Finally, why did the story of the life and work of Moses become so extensive and fundamental for Israel's life in the "land of Israel"? And why did the Testament of Moses reinforce the covenant under Moses at Sinai, outside the land, before Israel's possession of the land and before all other covenants between Yahweh and Israel and its representatives after Moses? Is not the concept of the Torah based on Israel's existence as a unity of one people under the one God of creation and of all nations, and in the one land given it by divine decree? Was not the land decree established through the life and work of Moses as the fulfillment of the history of the world from the week of creation on? Is it not true that Moses is the most important person in world history? And does not the work of Jesus Christ for the salvation of the whole world mean that Jesus Christ is the antitype of Moses? Does not the TaNaK—especially its Torah—also belong to the Bible of the Christians but only as the Old Testament?

Conclusion

Clearly, the telling of truth happens in statements of incontestable fact, be they good or bad. Mostly these statements recognize degrees of quantity and, especially, degrees of qualitative situational levels. Truth-telling also happens in statements regarding case decisions in which the comparison of factors is inconclusive and therefore subject to "better sayings," which result from the experience of more and less general values. In particular, truth-telling pertains to the entire arena of truth or falsehood in ideologies, to the level of typical factors in reality, and to the role of concepts in thinking, speaking, and acting. The subject of truth-telling is large and never ending. After each statement about it, truth demands that I be "more true," as a friend of mine has said.

I conclude with four points. First, from the biblical perspective, the issue of telling truth (insofar as it is taken up thematically) is inseparably connected with the assumption of God's relationship to God's world and of God's presence in God's world everywhere in all of its complexity and on all of its levels and at all times. What this assumption means metaphysically is subject to discussion, although this discussion is not a distinct focus of the biblical texts. What is distinct, however, is the fact that God is understood to be real but never as a part of this world. God is related to and present in the world but always vis-à-vis the world. There are many implications of this understanding; two may be highlighted.

One implication has to do with truth. Although truth cannot be understood as separate from God, it exists just as much vis-à-vis us as God. We face both as beings who are faced by them. They are not our property. But we cannot escape being confronted by them (Ps 139:1–18).

The other implication has to do with monotheism and the kinds of relationship in the three monotheistic religions. The concept of the oneness of God and the oneness of the world, vis-à-vis forms of polytheism, is at least defensible. But Israel/Judaism, Christianity, and Islam have in the course of history developed as three separate monotheistic religions, whose relations are often more about juxta-existence than co-existence. Not that any one of them alone would have in the course of its history facilitated the unity of humanity in terms of an all-inclusive, equitable form of peace and justice. But this is due more to their virtually polytheistic pattern of competitiveness than to their claims to let peace break out on earth. They are just as much a threat to the human race as they may be a help—and more so today than ever before. In what sense is truth revealed through the relationship of the three monotheistic religions? And what is the level of significance of this relationship in the complex reality of our world?

Second, since the rise of the nuclear age, the existence of our globe—a part of the cosmos—and human history have in their totality entered a second eon. Never before was it possible, or thinkable (least of all by any of the biblical generations) for humans to annihilate not the cosmos but all life on earth, and also the earth itself. This is now, and will from now on, forever be possible. The history of humanity stands from now on permanently at its abyss. This actual possibility was throughout the ages excluded from the faith systems of the religions (or those of the Bibles), as well as from philosophical systems. We can destroy the created earth, if we choose to do so, and there is nothing God can do to prevent it. This new fact of human history is a reality, and no theology or philosophy of truth-telling will be connected with the new reality of the world if it does not account for this threatening reality at its outset.

Third, in the movie *A Beautiful Mind*, Nash speaks in his acceptance speech about what is real in his and his wife's experience: what is real is that "the equation of reason is love." In the love of his wife, who has incomprehensibly stayed with him, he has experienced the wondrous in the misery of both. And Iris, with clear reference to her husband's love in his companionship with her into her fading Alzheimer's darkness, says to the audience: "You must speak about the reality of love as if you are an atheist." And then, as if the light of her life is going out, she prays to God, reciting words of Ps 139. Speak the truth of love like an atheist and turn around praying the truth to God—as if we are inescapable from the presence of God in any of our realities.

Of course, she could have referred to words found only in the NT, such as Rom 8:31–39: nothing in all creation "will be able to separate us from the love of God"—the triune God—"in Christ Jesus our Lord." Or, 1 John 4:16: "God is love, and those who abide in love abide in God, and God abides in them." Or, 1 Cor 13 or Matt 5:38–48. That the atheist knows about truth as love or love as the truth confirms what has been known for a long time: that the truth of all truths for all is love, which is the love of God through Jesus Christ precisely because it is, like God, not subject to the truths of our loves.

Fourth, the German writer Christa Wolf, born in 1929, from the former (East) German Democratic Republic, says semibiographically in her book, *Leibhaftig*[7] that she has been driven "to the point where the red-hot core of truth coincides with the core of lie," and "everything I say or write is adulterated by what I do not say and write."

Telling the truth? Telling it all? Knowing it all? Being silent about what I do not want to say, cannot say? Hiding it for self-protection or repressing it to prevent greater damage to many? And do we not experience in our time how the telling of the red-hot core of truth is subverted by the core of lie?

Does no minister ever feel the conflict between what he/she should say in the name of the truth of God and Jesus Christ and what he/she cannot afford to say, because of the need to keep "the peace" in the congregation or to prevent the membership and the contributions from falling?

---

7. Christa Wolf, *Leibhaftig* (Munich: Luchterhand Literaturverlag, 2002) 138, 159 (my translation).

Is it truthful if we speak about truth as if watching it in a movie, without it becoming the reality of our own lives? What is the price that I am prepared to pay—literally—when I speak out, even and especially in the name of theology? What distinguishes the truth in any of our tellings and not tellings? Are we ever even seeking the truth? Is not the truth ever seeking us, especially when we do not seek and tell it? Are we, can we ever be true? Are we not always at least compromising the truth?

Is it not more than conventional faith rhetoric to say: I am never *really* true? And, thus, I can say: may God, for the sake of God's better justice, have mercy on me and pardon me so that my violation of truth does not deny my right to life and the call to be more truthful. Is not this condition basic to truth itself in the reality of my life? Is any human being exempt from this condition?

PART 2
Aligning God's People with God's Call for Justice

Yahweh, Justice, and Religious Pluralism in the Old Testament

ELMER A. MARTENS
President and Professor of Old Testament, Emeritus
Mennonite Brethren Biblical Seminary
Fresno, California

Religious pluralism, the competing claims to truth of rival religions, is hardly a new phenomenon. The Bible knows this reality well. In leaving Ur of the Chaldeans, Abraham left a Babylonian religion characterized by multiple deities. In Egypt, to which Abraham's descendants later moved, the religious environment was replete with gods such as Osiris and Isis. The Exodus took Israel to Canaan where, as we now know from archaeology, the pantheon of El, including Baal and Astarte, held sway. During Israel's monarchy era Baalism was a rival religion, as Elijah's contest at Mt. Carmel illustrated. Later, Israel in exile was tossed back into the Chaldean cauldron of religious beliefs. Upon returning to the homeland, Israel was soon confronted and affronted by the Hellenizing Antiochus Epiphanes, who challenged the worship of one God by desecrating Jerusalem's temple. Still later, as a NT scholar notes, "The world in which the epistles were written was a world steeped in religious pluralism."[1]

Religious pluralism is biblical agenda. This essay investigates the OT in order to delineate its position on the issue of dealing with a plurality of religions. I begin by identifying the point of entry for this study: namely, the notion of biblical justice. Next, I elaborate on God's stance toward other so-called deities, toward other faith systems, and toward adherents of these faith

Author's note: The substance of this essay was presented at a consultation held at Eastern Mennonite University, Harrisonburg, Virginia, March 1998. It was published as "God, Justice, and Religious Pluralism in the Old Testament," in *Practicing Truth: Confident Witness in Our Pluralistic World* (ed. David W. Shenk and Linford Stutzman; Scottdale, PA: Herald, 1999) 46–63 and is reproduced here with permission from the publisher and with some revisions and bibliographic updating.

1. D. A. Carson, *The Gagging of God: Christianity Confronts Pluralism* (Grand Rapids: Zondervan, 1996) 272. For Carson's definitions of pluralism, see pp. 13–22.

123

systems. Finally, I comment on Israel's interaction with other faiths. The purpose of this study is to offer orientation to the twenty-first century church, which is sharply challenged in its mission.[2]

A Controlling Viewpoint: Justice

Scholars have followed different methods, mostly methods of a historical cast, in examining the OT for its teaching on pluralism.[3] This essay takes the approach of looking for a "control belief." The term is used by John Sanders to indicate the "givens" for an argument.[4]

One possible candidate for such a controlling viewpoint is the kingdom of God. This term is a major component in the NT material, and some scholars have also oriented the OT around it.[5] This position poses a number of problems, however, including the relatively rare occurrence of the expression in the OT.[6]

By contrast, the term "justice," along with its synonym "righteousness," is pervasive throughout the OT. _Mišpāṭ_ 'justice' appears more than 425 times in the OT. Its importance as a major motif has been championed by R. P.

---

2. The nature of the challenge and the reason for a new awareness is discussed by Daniel B. Clendenin, _Many Gods, Many Lords: Christianity Encounters World Religion_ (Grand Rapids: Baker, 1995) 11–34.

3. D. Clendenin traces texts according to the "history of salvation" schema ("Old Testament Faith and the World Religions" [chap. 5], in _Many Gods, Many Lords_). A historical schema is also followed by John E. Goldingay and C. J. H. Wright, "'Yahweh Our God Yahweh One': The Old Testament and Religious Pluralism," in _One God, One Lord in a World of Religious Pluralism_ (ed. A. D. Clarke and B. W. Winter; Cambridge: Tyndale, 1991) 34–52. A canonical schema is adopted in _Christianity and the Religions: A Biblical Theology of World Religions_ (Evangelical Missiological Society, Series 2; ed. E. Rommen and H. Netland; Pasadena, CA: William Carey Library, 1995). In this book, Ed Mathew deals with texts in the Pentateuch, Michael Pocock with Wisdom literature, and Robert B. Chisholm Jr. with prophetic literature. D. A. Carson stresses the plotline of the entire biblical story in _The Gagging of God_, 193–314.

4. John Sanders, _No Other Name: An Investigation into the Destiny of the Unevangelized_ (Grand Rapids: Eerdmans, 1992) 32.

5. See John Bright, _The Kingdom of God_ (Nashville: Abingdon, 1953); J. L. Mays, _The Lord Reigns_ (Louisville, KY: Westminster/John Knox, 1994); M. Z. Brettler, _God Is King: Understanding an Israelite Metaphor_ (JSOTSup 76; Sheffield: JSOT Press, 1989); George Ladd, _Jesus and the Kingdom_ (New York: Harper & Row, 1964); J. Gray, _The Biblical Doctrine of the Reign of God_ (Edinburgh: T. & T. Clark, 1979); and John Driver, "The Kingdom of God: Goal of Messianic Mission," in _The Transfiguration of Mission. Biblical, Theological & Historical Foundations_ (ed. Wilbert Shenk; Scottdale, PA: Herald, 1993) 83–105.

6. In addition to its infrequent use, the term is problematic because of its reference to monarchy, which is not now a predominant political system; because of its gender identification, objectionable to some; and because of the secular definition of a kingdom as spatial.

Knierim.[7] The argument presented here is that a concentrated look at "justice" goes a long way in determining the stance of the OT toward issues of religious pluralism.

The Hebrew word *mišpāṭ* 'justice' is a noun that derives from the verb *šāpaṭ*, which means 'to decide', 'to govern'. The word *mišpāṭ* has a legal, court-room setting (Deut 1:16–18). However, decisions are part of everyday behavior, certainly within the family. It is at least of interest that the first canonical mention of *mišpāṭ* 'justice' (along with *ṣedeq* 'righteousness') is in connection with Abraham's family and the "way of Yahweh" (Gen 18:19a). Decisions are not only made in court but at the level of relationships. How do ethnic groups relate to one another? How do those who govern related to the governed? How do members within a society which includes aliens and orphaned relate to each other? How do the rich relate to the poor? How is one to relate to parents, to children, to employers, and to employees? To think of justice biblically is to think of Yahweh-approved actions within these and other relationships. A short-hand way of conceptualizing "justice" is "honorable relations divinely defined." Traditions and culture may specify, for example, how men and women are to relate, but *mišpāṭ* obtains only when these relationships accord, not with culture as the benchmark, but with the divine instruction.

The semantic field of the term *mišpāṭ* is wide-ranging, from architectural specifications (1 Kgs 6:38) to judicial proceedings (Num 27:1–23; note *mišpāṭ* 'case', v. 5). Within this span the term *mišpāṭ* is heavily concentrated on actions that would be considered ethical (Mic 6:8). Richard Schultz puts it perceptively: "In the light of the usage of the corresponding vb., neither a narrowly juridical nor a narrow ethical emphasis is appropriate."[8] This claim that *mišpāṭ* has a moral and not only a forensic component can be illustrated from several passages in the OT. In his two-point temple sermon the prophet Jeremiah calls for people to "truly act justly one with another" (Jer 7:5).[9] At once he explains in negative terms what is meant by "acting justly": "if you do not oppress the

7. R. P. Knierim, *The Task of Old Testament Theology* (Grand Rapids: Eerdmans, 1995) 120, esp. pp. 14, 17. See J. Krašovec, *La justice (ṣĕdāqâ) de Dieu dans la Bible hébraïque et l'interprétation juive et chrétienne* (OBO 76; Göttingen: Vandenhoeck & Ruprecht, 1988); and H. G. Reventlow and Y. Hoffman, eds., *Justice and Righteousness: Biblical Themes and Their Influence. Festschrift for Benjamin Uffenheimer* (JSOTSup 137; Sheffield: JSOT Press, 1992).

8. Richard Schultz, "Justice," *NIDOTTE* 4.838. See his extensive bibliography. See also Thomas L. LeClerc who distinguishes three aspects of meaning: political/social; theological and moral; and legal (*Yahweh Is Exalted in Justice: Solidarity and Conflict in Isaiah* [Minneapolis: Fortress, 2001] 9–14). Temba L. J. Mafico stresses the judicial aspects concluding that "judges," even Yahweh, had the function of a deputy (*Yahweh's Emergence as "Judge" among the Gods: A Study of the Hebrew Root ŠPṬ* [Lewiston, NY: Edwin Mellen, 2006]).

9. All Scripture references unless otherwise indicated are from the NRSV.

alien, the orphan, and the widow, or shed innocent blood in this place, and if you do not go after other gods to your own hurt" (7:6). The relationships here are horizontal, to the marginalized, and vertical, the human-God relationship. When the same prophet exhorts kings to "act with justice and righteousness," he again specifies, among other matters, "deliver from the hand of the oppressor anyone who has been robbed" (Jer 22:3). So also Isaiah not only urges "seek justice," but at once elaborates along social ethical lines: "rescue the oppressed, defend the orphan, plead for the widow" (Isa 1:17). In another context, acting honorably has to do with avoiding land monopolies (Isa 5:7–8). Injustice is failure to be honorable in financial transactions such as compensating the laborer (Jer 22:13). Justice, "honorable relations," is a matter of ethical behavior outside the court-room as well as inside it.

Justice has both a retributive and a compassionate edge. God's righteousness has to do with "return[ing] your deeds upon your head" (Ezek 16:38–43; Jer 12:1, 14–17). The punitive aspect of judgment is also stressed in Isa 30:1–17, but in a significant bridge statement Isaiah declares: "Therefore, YHWH waits to be gracious to you; and therefore he is lifted up to be compassionate to you; for a God of justice is YHWH [$k\hat{\imath}$ $\dot{e}l\bar{o}h\hat{e}$ $mi\check{s}p\bar{a}t$ YHWH]; blessed are all who wait for him" (30:18).

Calling attention to the section about "salvation" on the far side (30:19–26) of this "hinge verse," LeClerc states: "The verse as a whole, which describes the divine advent in graciousness and compassion, provides the first context for understanding $mi\check{s}p\bar{a}t$ as more than 'the right thing'."[10] Isaiah 30:18 asserts that "God is gracious and compassionate because [$k\hat{\imath}$] he is a God of justice."[11] As also noted above, to act justly is to move in compassion towards the needy. Justice, so defined, has a tender edge to it and should not be conceptualized only (or chiefly as in Western thought) as enforcing the law, bringing punishment on the guilty. So understood, the expression "acting honorably in keeping with divine standards" helps in understanding what justice is about.[12] For

---

10. LeClerc, *Yahweh is Exalted in Justice,"* 78.

11. Ibid., 168. The translation of Isa 30:18 is LeClerc's. Noting that $mi\check{s}p\bar{a}t$ and $\dot{s}\check{e}d\bar{a}q\hat{a}$ are sometimes parallel with *ḥesed* and *ʾĕmet*, and *ḥesed* occasionally is associated with *raḥămîm*, Enrique Nardoni states, "These connections underline, in the terms $mi\check{s}p\bar{a}t$, $\dot{s}edeq$, and $\dot{s}\check{e}d\bar{a}q\hat{a}$, the meaning of a compassionate, generous, reliable and faithful goodness, always ready to serve the needs of others and to foster their well-being" (*Rise Up, O Judge: A Study of Justice in the Biblical World* [trans. Seán Charles Martin; Peabody, MA: Hendrickson, 2004] 102).

12. David Shenk cites Samuel Kibicho of Africa who has noted that "in Bantu languages the root word for justice is also the root for truth, wisdom, empowerment, win, or victory. All these gifts undergird the peace which sustains life" (*Global Gods: Exploring the Role of Religions in Modern Societies* [Scottdale, PA: Herald, 1995] 79). Shenk footnotes his source: Samuel C. Kibicho, *The Gikuyu Conception of God: His Continuity into the Christian Era and the Question It*

the transgressor, just action may entail punishment. For the person who is down and out, just action requires a helping hand. Both kinds of action would fall under the biblical rubric of justice.

Scripture leaves no doubt as to Yahweh's stance on the subject of justice. The declaration is so succinct that it cannot be misconstrued: "For I the LORD love justice" (Isa 61:8). The Psalmist echoes this conviction: "For the LORD loves justice" (Ps 37:28; see also Pss 33:5; 99:4). The word *'āhab* 'love' is the key verb in all four texts. If "love" has to do with "a passion for" then to paraphrase, Yahweh has a passion for justice. Yahweh, as Jeremiah notes, delights in justice and righteousness (Jer 9:24; Heb 9:23). The two, righteousness and justice "are the foundation of your [Yahweh's] throne" (Ps 89:14).[13] God is committed to justice (Deut 32:4), a point that Abraham pressed when he asked, "Shall not the Judge of all the earth do what is just?" (Gen 18:25b). Yahweh is so intentional about justice that in the ranking of priorities justice is put above worship (Isa 1:17). Yahweh is not interested in sacrifices and solemn assemblies when his people fail to honor Yahweh's priority. "Seek justice" is the demand put before the worshipers.

In the view popular in the West, justice stands for fairness. The guilty are punished, the innocent are set free, and the good are rewarded. The vocabulary of justice is legal, court-related. True, this view of justice, with its legal connotations of impartiality, is represented in the OT (Deut 1:17). But the point emphasized here is that the biblical notion of justice reaches beyond the tribunal and the court to every conceivable human activity. Table 1 can clarify.

It is this "control belief" of justice that offers a window into the vexed question of religious pluralism. Among competing beliefs about the deities, the justice dimension associated with Yahwism forms part of a compelling argument for setting Yahwism apart.

Raises for the Christian Idea of Revelation (Ph.D. diss., Vanderbilt University, 1972) 33. Might there be convergences between Bantu and Hebrew on the meaning and importance of justice?

13. Oversimplified, justice describes correct overt behavior; righteousness is the inner disposition to do the right. "Doing justice," the Hebrew idiom, is the implementation of divine norms, a "hands-on" righteousness. The emphasis on justice is an emphasis on conduct, behind which is the standard of righteousness. Thus, "*ṣĕdāqâ* is the quality of life displayed by those who live up to the norms inherent in a given relationship and thereby do right by the other person or persons involved." This quotation from James L. Mays is noted in a first-rate article on the subject by David Reimer in *NIDOTTE* 3.744–69. The quotation appears on p. 763. LeClerc (*Yahweh Is Exalted in Justice,* 10 and passim) adopts the explanation given by Moshe Weinfeld that the two terms *mišpāṭ* and *ṣĕdāqâ* are to be treated as a hendiadys with the meaning: "social justice" (*Social Justice in Ancient Israel and in the Ancient Near East* [Minneapolis: Fortress, 1995] 25–44).

Table 1. Conceptualizing Justice in the Bible and in Western Culture	
Old Testament	*Western Culture*
God-related	Statute-related
"Do Justice"	"Get Justice"
Honorable Relations	Fairness
Soft edge/compassion	Hard edge/retribution
Goal: Shalom	Goal: Order
Social, Religious, Legal, Economic	Courts
Central concern	Restricted concern
(Everyday; everywhere)	(Law enforcement)

The God of Justice Trumps Other Deities

In the OT, religious pluralism took the form of polytheism. In the ancient Near East environment, the claim that there is but one true God was challenged. Prophets and poets met this challenge by asserting that Yahweh was the true God and by offering evidence, also along the lines of justice, to support that claim.

Yahweh as Sole Deity

To set the context: verification for the claim of Yahweh as the exclusively sovereign deity turned on several issues including power, divine engagement in history, and prediction. The Exodus event figures large in Yahweh's power encounters (Exod 7:5, 17; 8:10, 22; 9:14; 10:2; 12:12; 14:4, 18; 16:12). God's sovereignty is also argued from his engagement in history. Ezekiel's book, in which this is a key point, is distinguished by the so-called recognition formula, "And they/you shall know that I am Yahweh," an expression which occurs more than 80 times. Walter Zimmerli observed that it is not by speculation or philosophical reasoning that people will be persuaded about Yahweh, but because of what has happened in history.[14] Further, Isaiah, quite possibly in response to the polytheism encountered by the exiles in Babylon, focused on the apologetic of prediction and fulfillment. In contrast to other deities, it is Yahweh who "has announced from of old the things to come" (44:7; see 46:8–11; 48:5; 41:21–24).

---

14. W. Zimmerli, "Knowledge of God according to the Book of Ezekiel," in *I Am Yahweh* (ed. W. Brueggemann; trans. D. W. Stott; Atlanta: John Knox, 1982).

Earlier assertions about God's uniqueness and incomparability were also based on considerations other than justice. Following the drama of the Exodus, Israel asked, "Who is like you, O LORD, among the gods?" and answered by confessing Yahweh's twin attributes of holiness and power (Exod 15:11). The prophet Isaiah answers with an apologetic drawn from God's creative activity (Isa 40:25–26; 48:12–13; 43:15; 44:24). Labuschagne has demonstrated that the force of this question is not only to place Yahweh as the topmost figure in a hierarchical ranking, but is idiomatic for placing Israel's God outside the category of "regular" deities altogether.[15] Yahweh, by reason of his power, holiness, and creative action is in a class by himself. Isaiah is intransigent on the absoluteness of Yahwistic faith: "Thus says the LORD . . . I am the first and I am the last; besides me there is no god" (Isa 44:6; see 44:8). "Before me no god was formed, nor shall there be any after me" (Isa 43:10c). "I am God, and there is no other" (46:9b). It is to this belief about monotheism that Paul is heir when he states: "For there is one God" (1 Tim 2:5).

Such assertions about God's incomparability fit logically with the assertion made at Sinai: Yahweh alone is God. It is a monotheistic claim that Israel hears in Moses' *Shemaꜥ*: "The LORD is our God, the LORD alone" (Deut 6:4). Translators and interpreters give various renderings, such as "The LORD is one," for the final half of the confession.[16] Possibly both unity and uniqueness are intended in the *Shemaꜥ*, but however nuanced, monotheism is implicit in the assertion.[17]

Some still claim that Israel never fully arrived at monotheism.[18] From the approach of a history of religion, that claim might be substantiated, but from the scriptural testimony there is no doubt about Israel's insistence on monotheism. Others have registered reservations that such a claim leads to intolerance, and that intolerance can lead to violence. But blame for violence cannot rightly be attributed to a belief in monotheism, for how one deals with

---

15. C. J. Labuschagne, *The Incomparability of Yahweh in the Old Testament* (Leiden: Brill, 1966) 89–123, esp. p. 90.

16. So J. G. Janzen, "On the Most Important Word in the Shema," *VT* 37 (1987) 280–300. See R. W. L. Moberly, "Yahweh Is One: The Translation of the Shema," in *Studies in the Pentateuch* (ed. J. A. Emerton; VTSup 41; Leiden: Brill, 1990) 209–15. Patrick Miller holds that the ambiguity is irresolvable (*Deuteronomy: Interpretation: A Bible Commentary for Teaching and Preaching* [Louisville, KY: John Knox, 1990] 99). The NT quotation in Mark 12:32, "He (God) is one, and besides him there is no other," allows for both unity and exclusiveness.

17. D. Christensen, *Deuteronomy 1–11* (WBC; Waco, TX: Word, 1991) 145. Contrast Daniel I. Block, "How Many Is God? An Investigation into the Meaning of Deuteronomy 6:4–5," *JETS* 47 (2004) 193–212. Block does not consider the *Shemaꜥ* to be so much a confession of monotheism as it is an identifying mark for the Israelites.

18. See, for example, James A. Sanders, "Adaptable for Life," in *From Sacred Text to Sacred Story: Canon as Paradigm* (Philadelphia: Fortress, 1987) 9–39.

competing claims or differences of viewpoints is a matter quite separate from the ideology at issue. To say that monotheistic belief contributes to world violence is to confuse cause and effect.[19]

Nevertheless, in the climate of postmodernism, the claim for monotheism is not always palatable. Regina M. Schwartz, for example, connects monotheism with notions of scarcity. She asks why God was stingy with his favors, so that only Abel's offering was acceptable. With the scarcity of divine favor, she claims, came murder and violence, and because of the emphasis on one God, one people, and one land, polarities and adversarial stances arose.[20]

In response, several points may be made. The first is to note that violence exists also where a plurality of gods are worshiped. Further, Schwartz's thesis is reductionistic. Violence, a complex phenomenon, has many sources—for example, greed and jealousy—so that an examination of human nature and fallibility might be more germane to her topic than the ideology of monotheism. More important still, her thesis quite overlooks and therefore fails to appreciate the nature of God's holiness as presented in the Bible. It is precisely God's righteousness and passion for justice which work against the negativity Schwartz attributes to the God of the Bible.

Who Is like Yahweh . . . a God of Justice?

The question of God's incomparability is asked at various junctures in Israel's history, not least during the monarchy period with its contact and altercation with the Canaanite baal religion. Who is like God? (Pss 35:10; 71:18–19; 113:5–9). The question is answered in the statement, "Righteousness and justice are the foundation of your throne" (Ps 89:6, 14).

The topic of justice as a defining quality of Yahweh which trumps the claims of other so-called deities is graphically developed by means of a pictorial scenario in Ps 82. This psalm draws on a mythology of divine councils and establishes the uniqueness of Yahweh as the sole divinity. Hypothetically, so one is to read the psalm, a plurality of deities take their place in the divine council over which Yahweh holds court. At issue at once is the question of their administration of justice. "How long will you judge unjustly?" the gods are asked (82:2). The directive is clear-cut and expresses the passion of Yahweh:

---

19. There are other analyses of violence, for example, "Human history is the relentless chronicle of violence that it is because when cultures fall apart they fall into violence, and when they revive themselves they do so violently" (Gil Bailie, *Violence Unveiled: Humanity at the Crossroads* [New York: Crossroad, 1995] 6).

20. Regina M. Schwartz, *The Curse of Cain: The Violent Legacy of Monotheism* (Chicago: University of Chicago Press, 1997). Her book should be compared with Gil Bailie, *Violence Unveiled*. Bailie, leaning on the work of René Girard, shows how the biblical tradition, especially in the Gospels, undermines systems of sacred violence.

"Give justice to the weak and the orphan; maintain the right of the lowly and the destitute. Rescue the weak and the needy; deliver them from the hand of the wicked" (82:3–4). The gods are summarily deposed and cast to the earth as mortals. Thus God, so committed to justice, is to be feared in the councils of deities (Ps 89:7, 14).[21] Psalm 82 ends on a note of triumph with the supremacy of Yahweh clearly established, "Rise up, O God, judge the earth; for all the nations belong to you!" (82:8). It is by the criterion of justice that polytheism, a subset of pluralism, is to be addressed: "Justice, just rule, is that central activity by which God is God."[22]

Visions provide another apologetic for Yahweh's greatness and justice. Especially graphic and detailed is Ezekiel's vision (1:4–2:2). The scene of a chariot platform, wheels and the brilliance surrounding the one seated on the throne above the platform is spectacular. A summarizing word is *kābôd* 'glory', 'impressive', 'incredible', that quality that elicits worship. It is this God whom Ezekiel hears say: "I will feed them [Israel] with justice" (Ezek 34:16). It is this God who adjudicates Israel according to the practice of honorable relations (Ezek 22:1–29; *šāpaṭ*, v. 2; *mišpāṭ*, v. 29). This extraordinary vision of God's glory bears on religious pluralism, as the further vision at the Jerusalem temple makes clear.

At the Jerusalem temple, where the *kābôd* appears again, Ezekiel encounters a variety of other religious belief systems and practices (Ezek 8–10). There in the temple is the image that provokes to jealousy—likely an asherah, a wooden pole representing the deity Astarte, dominant in Canaanite worship (8:5).[23] In the temple inside a dark room are seventy Israelite leaders worshiping creatures, apparently according to the practices in Egypt (8:7–12). In the temple are worshipers of Tammuz, the dying and rising god of Assyria, with his counterpart Baal in Phoenecia (8:14). In the courtyard at the door of the temple are twenty-five males worshiping the solar deities, as was the custom in the ancient Near East generally (8:16). Talk about pluralism!

In the space of several hundred square yards in the temple court, Ezekiel is confronted with multiple religions. Inside this space there is also visible the

---

21. W. Brueggemann concludes that the main force of the Mosaic revolution, "a theological *novum*," is "to establish justice as the core focus of Yahweh's life in the world and Israel's life with Yahweh" (*Old Testament Theology* [Minneapolis: Fortress, 1997] 735).

22. Patrick D. Miller Jr., *Interpreting the Psalms* (Philadelphia: Fortress, 1986) 124.

23. See R. Hess, "Yahweh and His Asherah? Epigraphic Evidence for Religious Pluralism in Old Testament Times," in *One God, One Lord in a World of Religious Pluralism*, 533. Hess clarifies that for some Israelite rulers as well as for the populace at times, syncretism, along with a propensity toward the embrace of other religions, existed. My interest, however, is not in a history of religions approach, but in a biblical theology approach where the canonical view, as represented by the prophets, is definitive.

glory of God, as Ezekiel had seen it in the inaugural vision (8:4). In the presence of Yahweh's awesome might and majesty, there is no need to debate the merits of these alternate deities and worship systems. Their illegitimacy is self-evident. No attempt is made to evaluate "from below" (from an anthropological stance) the rightness or wrongness of "other" religions. Seen "from above" (from a Yahwistic theology), the contrast is stark: all other religious preferences are a parody, a travesty.[24]

In summary, the OT claim is that Yahweh, who is the God of Abraham, Isaac, and Israel, is also the God of the cosmos. He is so because, among other reasons, he is the God of justice. All rival claims are empty, without warrant, weight, or ultimacy, because all other so-called gods are unjust (Ps 82). Hence, claims by any other religion are met confrontationally with the verdict: "I am God, and there is no other" (Isa 46:9b). When it comes to pluralistic religions, it is not tolerance but truth that is the issue. Christians confess in confidence that Yahweh, the God of Israel and the Father of Jesus Christ, is the sole deity and the only legitimate object of devotion and worship. There is no other god.[25]

Yahweh's Justice and Other Belief Systems

One conclusion about the OT and religious pluralism is that Yahweh's claim to be God, uniquely and exclusively, is categorical. Yet it does not follow that the OT takes an exclusive posture about other belief systems in the sense of judging them valueless.

The OT allows for common ground between Yahwism and other religions, even if that common ground is not very extensive. Just as the effects of sin, though they touch every area in life, do not dictate that every dimension of life is altogether depraved, so also in the sphere of religions, while all claims to ultimacy stand under God's truth, not all that is related to other religions is thereby condemned. Moral and religious tenets in non-biblical faith systems may in some instances be acceptable.

Three lines of investigation—from the prophets, from wisdom literature, and from the Torah—will show that there can be common ground between a

---

24. Further elaboration is given in my essay, "Ezekiel's Contribution to a Biblical Theology of Mission," in *Die Mission der Theologie: Festschrift für Hans Kasdorf zum 70 Geburtstag* (ed. Stephan Holthaus and Klaus W. Mueller; Bonn: Verlag für Kultur und Wissenschaft, 1998) 46–57.

25. D. A. Carson, in discussing the topic, "God is transcendent, sovereign, and personal," observes that "in the rising press of religious pluralism, this understanding of God [as transcendent, sovereign, and personal] is never allowed" (*The Gagging of God*, 223).

non-Israelite religion and Yahwism. The nature of this common ground is important for our understanding of the OT stance toward religious pluralism.

Amos is a prophetic book, the subject of which is often justice (see especially chapter 5). The opening eightfold woe against as many nations must be analyzed with the subject of justice in mind. Damascus is held accountable for cruelty to a neighboring population (1:3). Gaza is indicted for slave trade (1:6). Tyre is doubly accused, first for trafficking in the trade of human beings and secondly for treaty-breaking (1:9). Edom stands accused before Yahweh for its unrelenting hostility to its "brother," Israel (1:11). The people of Ammon in their craze to extend their borders committed gross evil by ripping open pregnant women (1:13). Moab is guilty for its insulting behavior in desecrating burial places (2:1).

Judah and Israel are also listed and indicted, but on a different basis: namely, their rejection of the divinely given Torah and their breach of covenant with God (Amos 2:4). Neither of these criteria is apropos to the pagan nations. On what grounds then are these others accountable? On the grounds of common human decency. There are moral values such as honesty and civility that are considered a given. Excessive cruelty, breaking of faith, and trading in human flesh are offensive and wrong. Rudimentary ethical requirements are inbuilt, as it were. Amos would claim that an understanding of the basic requirements of justice, honorable relations, exists among other peoples. Human beings are accountable to God quite apart from any specific revelation and will be judged by what they know, as Paul also makes clear when he speaks about Gentiles having a law to themselves: "They [the Gentiles] show that what the law requires is written on their hearts, to which their own conscience also bears witness" (Rom 2:15a).

The example from Amos 1–2 shows there are moral values in other cultures that can be affirmed as right. Moreover, while moral accountability is certainly heightened where there is knowledge of divine revelation, pleas for exemption from accountability because of an absence of specific divine revelation will not hold on the Day of the Big Audit. On the basis of Amos' prophetic text, one may extrapolate to say that there are positive moral and religious values in other cultures which can be affirmed from the standpoint of Yahwism.[26] One can also agree that "if as Master of the universe Yahweh

---

26. Terry C. Muck, "Is There Common Ground among Religions?" *JETS* 40 (1997) 99–112. He proceeds theologically to identify a threefold common ground: *logos spermatikos* (seed of wisdom), to which I would connect the Amos passage; *divinitatis sensum* (sense of the divine); and *imago Dei* (image of God).

holds exclusive rights to judge all nations . . . then the possibility of divine mercy is open to all who repent."[27]

That non-biblical religions are not hopelessly depraved but incorporate convictions that correlate with Yahwism is demonstrated by the book of Proverbs. This book is about wisdom and the conduct of the wise; it sorts through behaviors, some of which are right and some wrong. These proverbs include sayings from regions outside Israel. For example, the words of non-Hebrews Agur and Lemuel, both from Massa in Northern Arabia, are found in Proverbs 30 and 31. A section of the Proverbs (22:17–24:22) contains material echoing proverbs from the Egyptian collection attributed to the Pharaoh Amenemopet.[28] One example must suffice. From Egypt comes the proverb: "Do not associate to thyself the heated man, nor visit him for conversation" (XI, 13F). The Bible states: "Make no friends with those given to anger, and do not associate with hotheads" (Prov 22:24). Proverbs is written so that readers will gain "instruction in wise dealing, righteousness, justice, and equity" (1:3). Wisdom announces: "I walk in the way of righteousness, along the paths of justice" (Prov 8:20). Certain Egyptian precepts help define these "paths of justice."

Truth is not limited to what is divinely revealed; truth also derives from experience and from intuitive knowledge and so is not limited to Israel's religious book. Thus, there is no warrant for a wholesale disparagement of religious systems on the ground that they are not rooted in Yahwism.[29]

From the Torah section of the OT come further examples of overlaps between revealed faith and non-biblical religions. Israel's judiciary system derives from Jethro, the Midianite (Exod 18:19–27). Similarities exist between the so-called covenant code (Exod 20:22–23:19) and the ancient Near East. Millard Lind notes these but points also to the different orientation which marks the covenant code.[30] Yet the similarity in content is not easily dismissed.

---

27. R. Bryan Widbin, "Salvation for People outside Israel's Covenant," in *Through No Fault of Their Own?* (ed. W. V. Crockett and J. G. Sigountos; Grand Rapids: Baker, 1991) 78.

28. The dating of the Egyptian papyrus manuscript is 7th–6th century, according to some. The proverbs themselves are almost certainly earlier. For a summary of the literary relationship between Egypt and the biblical Proverbs, see John Ruffle, "The Teaching of Amenemope and Its Connection with the Book of Proverbs," *Tyndale Bulletin* 28 (1977) 29–68. Ruffle proposes a dependence, though indirect, of the biblical material on Egypt.

29. Further examples and discussion may be found in Andrew E. Hill and John H. Walton, *A Survey of the Old Testament* (Grand Rapids: Zondervan, 1991). See John H. Walton, *Ancient Israelite Literature in Its Cultural Context: A Survey of Parallels between Biblical and Ancient Near Eastern Texts* (Library of Biblical Interpretation; Grand Rapids: Zondervan, 1989). Michael Pocock acknowledges that literary forms from Israel and the ancient Near East are similar, and that even some content is similar, but insists on retaining an exclusivist stance ("Selected Perspectives on World Religions from Wisdom Literature," in *Christianity and the Religions*, 45–55).

30. Millard Lind, "Law in the Old Testament," in *Monotheism, Power, Justice: Collected Old Testament Essays* (Text Reader 3; Elkhart, IN: Institute of Mennonite Studies, 1990) 61–81.

I cite these examples, not to argue that Mosaic legislation was necessarily dependent on other law codes,[31] though that conclusion is not implausible, but to underscore the claim that biblically legitimate legislation is found in non-biblical religions. Whatever the reason for this overlap (whether a memory of an earlier divine revelation,[32] or an inbuilt sense of the right, or the pervasive ministry of the Spirit of God in the world, or literary dependency of some sort), it follows that other belief systems cannot be condemned wholesale. There is that in other cultures which persons committed to the truth of the biblical material can affirm and to which they can give approval.

But if divine justice will be the measure of what is legitimate, then it is soon clear that many of the religious beliefs and practices of peoples surrounding Israel come under divine judgment. A position statement is given in Leviticus: "You shall not do as they do in the land of Egypt, where you lived, and you shall not do as they do in the land of Canaan, to which I am bringing you" (18:3). The chapter continues with prohibitions of incest, homosexuality, bestiality, and adultery, as well as child sacrifice. "Do not defile yourself in any of these ways, for by all these practices the nations I am casting out before you have defiled themselves" (Lev 18:24).

That there is a fundamental clash of worldviews between Israel and pagan religions, and that this is largely over what constitutes justice, is illustrated in the Ahab-Naboth incident (1 Kgs 21:1–27). Ahab, king of Israel, wanted a choice vineyard which belonged to Naboth and offered to buy it. Naboth refused because land in Israel was not to be sold, since in his tradition all land belonged to Yahweh, who had apportioned it to families. Jezebel, Ahab's wife, believed that the king had an absolute right both to distribute and to appropriate land. In the clash of these two worldviews, Naboth lost both his land and his life. Elijah insisted that Jezebel's actions were unjust.

In sum, where divine justice is the criterion, some beliefs and practices in other religions may accord with Yahwism, but others, perhaps most, will not. The prescriptions for conduct are not arbitrary but are determined by a Yahweh kind of justice.

Yahweh's Justice and Non-Yahwists

Our investigation so far has led us to two conclusions. (1) Because God is without equal, he stands in judgment over any and all other claimants to deity.

---

31. See H. J. Boecker, *Law and the Administration of Justice in the Old Testament and the Ancient East* (trans. Jerry Moiser; Minneapolis: Augsburg, 1980) 15–19. See now Nardoni, *Rise Up, O Judge*, 1–41 for a review of the role of social justice in ancient Mesopotamia and Egypt.

32. A claim made by Richard D. Patterson, "The Widow, the Orphan, and the Poor in the Old Testament and the Extra-Biblical Literature," *BSac* 130 (1973) 233.

(2) Some values in belief systems outside Israel can be affirmed as legitimate, in accord with Yahweh's standard of justice, whereas others cannot.

These two conclusions still leave open the question of how God is disposed toward persons who live in the orbits of these non-Yahwistic faiths. Can these be saved, and if so, on what basis?[33]

The answers, we must humbly admit, are largely inferential. As Christopher Seitz notes, "How God might deal with the nations in their own religious systems lies beyond the horizon of the Old Testament, precisely because of its understanding of the specificity of God's disclosure."[34]

God's election of Israel, to judge from the narratives, does not preclude the acceptance into his favor of persons from other faiths. Melchizedek, Jethro, Balaam, Job, and Rahab are God-fearers; none are Israelites. One could say that Jethro and Rahab had received witness to God through Israel (Exod 18:1–12; Josh 2:1–11). There is no indication of any such witness to Melchizedek, Balaam, or Job. All of them, however, appear in Scripture as receiving divine favor and acceptance. The questions then are: What is involved in being acceptable in God's sight? By what means are persons justified before God?

By posing the questions in this way, we have once again landed on the category of justice.

An answer which may at first seem oblique may be formulated by tracing in brief the OT understanding of the means to salvation. The short answer is that persons are "saved" by embracing God. The longer answer entails recognition of several realities. (1) God is intent on reconciliation with humankind (Isa 45:22). (2) God is Spirit; hence, "embracing God" is problematic. (3) God makes himself available through his gifts. (4) Specifically, these gifts are at least his promises, his Torah, and the person of Jesus. (5) As persons embrace these gifts by faith, God counts them righteous. (6) A faith response includes a behavioral change and entails a disposition of heart longing for purity.

Comment here must be limited to only a few of these assertions. God's gifts, a crucial component for human salvation, are wide-ranging. That the embrace of God's promise is the means to righteousness is stated forthrightly: "And he [Abraham] believed the LORD; and the LORD reckoned it to him as righteousness" (Gen 15:6).

---

33. Lesslie Newbigin states that to ask the question this way is to fatally flaw the debate (*The Gospel in a Pluralist Society* [Grand Rapids: Eerdmans / Geneva: WCC Publications, 1989] 176). Salvation (and mission) includes other dimensions, such as community considerations and the glory of God, as he rightly states. But at some point the question of individual salvation does crystallize the issue of religious pluralism.

34. Christopher Seitz, *Word without End: The Old Testament as Abiding Theological Witness* (Grand Rapids: Eerdmans, 1998) 23.

More controversial is the assertion that an embrace of the law in faith was sufficient before God to be counted by him as righteous.[35] Yet Moses (Lev 18:5), Ezekiel (Ezek 18:5–9), Jesus (Luke 10:28), and Paul (Rom 9:31–10:5) all affirm that eternal life is made possible through an embrace of the law, God's gift of grace (John 1:16–17). The greatest gift of all is Jesus Christ; to embrace him in faith is to have eternal life (John 5:24). Through these three stages—promise, law, Jesus Christ—shines God's justice, a justice which remains consistent. Persons who respond to his gifts, whether promise (as Abraham), law including the sacrificial system (as Israel), or Jesus (as in the current dispensation), are counted righteous in God's sight.

This conclusion means that persons in the OT are not condemned for not knowing about Jesus. Nor could the patriarchs be condemned for not embracing the Torah about which they were ignorant. It follows logically that persons living before Abraham or outside God's specific revelation could not in justice be held responsible for what they did not know (i.e., Sinaitic law). But this does not mean that they were not responsible, nor that they were without some access to God.

Abel offered a sacrifice that God accepted (Gen 4:4). Noah is described as righteous: "[He] walked with God" (Gen 6:9). The NT book of Hebrews declares that Abel "received approval as righteous" and that, by faith, Noah "became an heir to the righteousness that is in accordance with faith" (Heb 11:4, 7). These two were not without a gift from God to embrace. The gift before them, we may infer, was the created world, a gift which pointed them to a Creator. Our inference is substantiated as correct by Paul: "What can be known about God is plain to them, because God has shown it to them. Ever since the creation of the world his eternal power and divine nature, invisible though they are, have been understood and seen through the things he has made" (Rom 1:19–20; see Ps 19).

Daniel Clendenin proposes three characteristics of persons who know God: orthodoxy, orthopraxis, and orthokardia.[36] Orthodoxy, right belief, is exemplified by Abraham (Gen 15:6; Rom 4:3). Orthopraxis, right action, is illustrated by the pre-Abrahamic Abel. Orthokardia, a right heart (Deut 6:4–5; 10:16), which the prophets described as a "circumcised" heart (Jer 4:4; see Joel 2:12–13) and the Psalmist as a "contrite heart" (Ps 51:16–17), is exemplified in pre-Abrahamic times by Enoch, who like Noah, walked with God (Gen 5:24). All three characteristics are explicitly asserted of Job. As for orthodoxy, Job believed God (Job 19:25); as for orthopraxy, he practiced justice

---

35. For a more extended discussion, see my essay, "Embracing the Law: A Biblical Theological Perspective," *BBR* 2 (1992) 128, also reproduced in this volume (see pp. 3–27).

36. D. Clendenin, *Many Gods, Many Lords*, 137–39.

(Job 31); and as for orthokardia, he was "blameless and upright, and one who feared God and shunned evil" (Job 1:1).

It is not our task to decide the eternal fate of persons outside Yahweh's direct revelation. The tilt of OT precedents, together with examination of God's *modus operandi* of justice, warrants concluding that persons could at least potentially respond in faith for salvation apart from special revelation (Scripture and Jesus Christ). In the NT, the Roman Cornelius may be cited as an example (Acts 10).[37]

It remains true that ontologically speaking, salvation is through Jesus Christ alone (John 14:6; Acts 4:12). Epistemologically speaking, however, persons apart from Jesus have at least the disclosure of creation and conscience. In short, persons have access to God through faith apart from knowledge about Jesus Christ.

On this issue of the eternal fate of persons in the orbit of other religions, our answer is that given by Abraham: "Shall not the Judge of all the earth do what is just?" (Gen 18:25b; see Zeph 3:5). The God of the OT is a God of justice who will not act in caprice but in righteousness. Moreover, the eschatological scenarios include that of Egypt having an altar to the LORD in the center of its lands (Isa 19:19). This elegant Isaiah text is described by Andre Feuillet as "the religious zenith of the Old Testament."[38] However, this passage should be compared to other texts that speak of the glorious prospect of nations coming to the light (Isa 60:3; 45:23; Zeph 3:9).

Justice, Israel, and the Nations

In summary, the God of Abraham, Isaac, and Israel is alone the true God. Peoples of different faiths have some knowledge of God, even if only minimal, which means that some of their beliefs and aspirations are to be affirmed. The God of justice will deal in righteousness with the eternal destiny of persons who live in the orbit of these religions. They cannot be censured or condemned for what they did not know; they, like we, will be justified if they wholeheartedly embrace the gift of God known to them. The more that is known about God, the more compelling is the call to embrace God.

Several passages from Isaiah, where "justice" and "nations" are prominent topics, point specifically to the way Israel was to function as God's agent. In Isa 49 the opening address is to the coastlands and "you peoples from far

---

37. William J. Larkin Jr. is among those who hold that Cornelius "is not an appropriate model for today's non-Christian religions" ("The Contribution of the Gospels and Acts to a Biblical Theology of Religions," in *Christianity and the Religions*, 72–91; the quote is from p. 81). So also D. A. Carson, *The Gagging of God*, 30–67.

38. Quoted in Lucien LeGrand, *Unity and Plurality: Mission in the Bible* (trans. R. R. Barr; Maryknoll, NY: Orbis, 1990) 23.

away" (49:1, 17). The servant, here specified as Israel (49:3), has a mission both to (apostate) Israel and beyond. She is given "as a light to the nations, that my salvation may reach to the end of the earth" (49:6).

R. Norman Whybray believes that "light" means enlightenment, but D. W. Van Winkle, drawing on the research of others, argues that the light is a figure for salvation (see Isa 42:6, 16; 45:7; 49:6; 51:4).[39] The metaphor of light evokes images of a presence; one is not to think of evangelism, NT style. What should be noted in connection with our "controlling belief" is the mention of justice in the phrasing: "A teaching will go out from me, and my justice for a light to the peoples" (Isa 51:4).[40]

Another passage, Isa 2:1–4, offers a complementary scenario to the "light" passages of 49:6 and 51:4. Again the world's people are in view. They are streaming up the mountain where the LORD's house is established, "the house of the God of Jacob," and they come for the purpose of being taught the ways of God. It is from Jerusalem that the word of the LORD will be given. It will be a radical word, given by one who "shall judge [exercise justice] between the nations" (2:4).

The three passages (Isa 49:6; 51:4; and 2:1–5) depict a scene in which Israel is an agent, but in the nature of an exhibit to which nations are drawn, though Israel shares the teaching of God when requested. In other words, Israel is to remain magnet-like, a trophy in "whom I [God] will be glorified" (49:3). While some scholars hold that there is little if any of a missionary "go structure" in Isaiah, Paul uses the Isaiah "light" texts as argument for his aggressive evangelizing of the Gentiles (Acts 13:47).[41]

---

39. D. W. Van Winkle, "The Relationship of the Nations to Yahweh and to Israel in Isaiah 40–55," *VT* 35 (1985) 446–58. See R. E. Clements, "A Light to the Nations: A Central Theme of the Book of Isaiah," in *Forming Prophetic Literature: Essays on Isaiah and the Twelve in Honor of John D. W. Watts* (JSOTSup 235; ed. J. W. Watts and Paul R. House; Sheffield: Sheffield Academic Press, 1996) 57–69. Clements, who examines three passages, Isa 9:2; 2:6; and 60:13, sees them in conjunction with the royal Zion motif. R. F. Melugin observes that in Isa 40–55 Israel was chosen for the sake of the world and that justice for Gentiles is central to God's purpose, but he thinks that these points are more forcefully made in Genesis ("Israel and the Nations in Isaiah 40–55," in *Problems in Biblical Theology: Essays in Honor of Rolf Knierim* [ed. Henry T. C. Sun, Keith L. Eades, J. M. Robinson, and G. I. Moller; Grand Rapids: Eerdmans, 1997] 246–64). On mission in the OT, see Walter C. Kaiser Jr., *Mission in the Old Testament: Israel as a Light to the Nations* (Grand Rapids: Baker, 2000); Eckhard J. Schnabel, "Israel, the People of God, and the Nations," *JETS* 45 (2002) 35–57; and idem, *Jesus and the Twelve* (vol. 1 of *Early Christian Mission*; Downers Grove, IL: InterVarsity, 2004); and especially Christopher J. H. Wright, *The Mission of God* (Downers Grove, IL: InterVarsity, 2006).

40. See LeClerc, *Yahweh Is Exalted in Justice*, 118–23, who considers that here *mišpāṭ*, should be construed as God's sovereignty.

41. See my "Impulses to Mission in Isaiah: An Intertextual Exploration," *BBR* 17 (2007) 215–39.

If these three passages (Isa 49:6; 51:4; and 2:1–5) are primarily about an Israel in the mode of *being*, Isa 42:1–4, by contrast, depicts a mode of *doing*. Questions about the servant's identity miss the message of the text, which is to highlight the function, mode, and motive of an anonymous but ideal servant.

The nub points of the passage can be summarized as follows. The activities of the servant swirl around bringing justice (the word *mišpāṭ* is mentioned three times in four verses). The goal is to persevere in this mission till justice reaches all the earth, even the coastlands (distant places). The mission is characterized by proclamation but not of the bombastic or self-advertising kind (42:2).

Moreover, the mode of mission is gentleness. The servant takes care not to snuff out the flickering wick or to break the bruised reed. God's servant is tender, yet also persistent and tough. The servant is highly motivated, for the servant is divinely endowed by an empowering Spirit.

To the extent that Israel qualifies as God's servant, her mission is unambiguous. It is to bring justice to the ends of the earth. Israel has a missionary responsibility to the nations, and that in two modes. In a largely passive mode, she is the showcase for what God's justice entails. In an active mode, she brings justice through proclamation.[42]

Concluding Theses

The foregoing discussion leads to the following conclusions about the OT's word on pluralism, which in turn informs a believer's stance:

(1) Viewed from the biblical perspective of God's justice, the phenomenon of polytheism (a subset of religious pluralism) is both evil and false. God grounds his exclusivity in the passion for and exercise of justice. There is no god but Yahweh; that is, there is no other god that is just. Concerning the claim to monotheism, the believer is firm and uncompromising.

(2) Adjudicated on the basis of God's justice, other religions may include elements of moral truth. The fact that notions of justice in other religions are sometimes commensurate with God's revelation requires from the believer a respectful attitude toward other faiths and makes possible points of contact in inter-religious dialogue.

---

42. "It is the task of the witnesses not only to attest the facts but also to convince the opposite side of the truth of them ([Isa] 41:21–24, 26; 43:9; 51:22; cf. Gen. 38:24–26)" (A. A. Trites, The New Testament Concept of Witness [Cambridge: Cambridge University Press, 1977] 46). John Oswalt's comment is puzzling: "Israel's function is that of witness as opposed to proselytizer" ("The Mission of Israel to the Nations," in *Through No Fault of Their Own?* [ed. W. V. Crockett and J. G. Sigountos; Grand Rapids: Baker, 1991] 85–95; the quotation is from pp. 94–95).

(3) As to the possibility of salvation for adherents of other faiths who are without knowledge of special revelation, the answer is best left to God, who proceeds justly. There is reason to hold, however, that non-Yahwists have access to God sufficient for their salvation apart from knowledge of salvation history and Jesus Christ. In God's economy it is the redemption by Jesus Christ on the cross that makes salvation possible at all for anyone. Epistemologically, however, knowledge of this event or other God-events in history, while compelling persons towards a faith commitment to God, is not "necessary." A faith commitment to God can be made, though perhaps is made only rarely, apart from knowledge of Christ's life and death. Believers do well to look and listen to discover how God is working.

(4) God's people, Israel and the church, are called to be exhibits of grace to the glory of God and proclaimers of God's justice. God's passion in bringing justice to the world far exceeds ours. Believers have reason to be bold and confident in this active witness to God's truth, irrespective of competing voices.

Creation and Peace:
Creator and Creature in Genesis 1–11

BEN C. OLLENBURGER
Professor of Biblical Theology
Associated Mennonite Biblical Seminary
Elkhart, Indiana

Creation, as a topic in OT theology, has received considerable attention over the past half-century. Concern for the earth and about the continuing and deepening environmental crises has generated some part of that attention recently. Particularly welcome, then, is the stress that recent work has placed on the moral dimensions of OT creation theology. William P. Brown, for example, pointed to a new urgency in relating creation theology and ethics.[1] This urgency, evident in Brown's own work, also appeared prominently in the writings of J. Richard Middleton and Terence E. Fretheim.[2] While I share their urgency and applaud their work, my focus in this essay will be narrower, of course, and also somewhat different. I will focus on creation and peace in Gen 1–11.

Associations between creation and peace remain underdeveloped in OT theology.[3] Yet, both creation and peace have to do with order—with things as they should be, as God intends them to be—even when God acts as creator against a false peace and a distorted order.[4] "Peace is, in fact, the order of

---

1. William P. Brown, *The Ethos of the Cosmos: The Genesis of Moral Imagination in the Bible* (Grand Rapids: Eerdmans, 1999) 17–18.

2. J. Richard Middleton, *The Liberating Image: The Imago Dei in Genesis 1* (Grand Rapids: Brazos, 2005); and Terence E. Fretheim, *God and World in the Old Testament: A Relational Theology of Creation* (Nashville: Abingdon, 2005).

3. Middleton refers to "God's cosmic, creational intent for peace" but does not expand on the statement ("Is Creation Theology Inherently Conservative? A Dialogue with Walter Brueggemann," *HTR* 87 [1994] 270).

4. See Stefan Paas, *Creation and Judgment: Creation Texts in Some Eighth Century Prophets* (Leiden: Brill, 2003) 184–85, 434–35. Earlier, H. H. Schmid drew associations between creation (and peace) and order, in *Gerechtigkeit als Weltordnung* (BHT 40; Tübingen: Mohr, 1968).

creation," as Joseph P. Healey wrote.[5] We may consider it constituent in "Divine Design," the title that Elmer A. Martens first attached to his then incipient book on OT theology, when I was his teaching assistant at the Mennonite Brethren Biblical Seminary. I recall fondly our many conversations about his proposal, long since published and twice revised as *God's Design*.[6] To Prof. Martens, an exemplary teacher and mentor, and both a colleague and friend, I offer this essay in grateful tribute.

That Genesis 1 has something to do with order should be obvious. I will claim that it has also to do with peace, though the claim will be oblique. Moreover, Gen 2–11 has to do in various ways with creation and threats to it, and with peace. These chapters narrate the progression from a created order that God declares to be very good (Gen 1:31) to God's estrangement from the world. At the beginning, of course, only God acts (1:1, 3). But in the course of these chapters, God acquires a narrative character; God interacts with and responds to the world and its creatures—especially, but not only, with its people. Indeed, the world becomes increasingly complex, and so does the narrative, as other actors come to exert their own freedom to act, to act independently of God, and even to rival God. Genesis 1, or the Priestly account, stands apart from this narrative development, serving as its prologue.[7]

Genesis 1

The creation account in Gen 1 is structured poetically on two patterns, liturgical and spatial. Encompassing both of these is a temporal progression through creation's six days, which forms a part of both the liturgical and the spatial pattern. God's—Elohim's—speaking dominates the former, which is marked by refrains: "God saw that it was good"; "there was evening and there was morning, the . . . day." These two refrains appear together, the first in expanded form, in 1:31—"God saw all that he had made, and assuredly, it was very good."[8] The Hebrew word *ṭôb* 'good' conveys a range of meanings, in-

---

5. Joseph P. Healey, "Peace: Old Testament," *ABD* 5.206. Healey refers, in context, to Gerhard von Rad.

6. Elmer A. Martens, *God's Design: A Focus on Old Testament Theology* (3rd ed.; N. Richland Hills, TX: Bibal, 1998). Martens stressed God's purpose in creation (pp. 21–22), as I shall do here.

7. Scholars almost universally assign Gen 1:1–2:4 (or 4a) to P, the Priestly source or tradition. On the character of Gen 1 as prologue, see Richard J. Clifford, "The Hebrew Scriptures and the Theology of Creation," *TS* 46 (1985) 507–23.

8. Translations are my own, unless otherwise noted. On the presentative *hinnēh*, here translated 'assuredly', see Paul Joüon and T. Muraoka, *A Grammar of Biblical Hebrew* (Rome: Pontifical Biblical Institute, 1996) #164a.

cluding "fitting" and "in order." Genesis 1 reflects this order, both in its composition and in the creation of the heavens and the earth it describes.

The second pattern offers another perspective on creation's order, arranging the daily sequence spatially into complementary pairs or panels.[9]

First panel: Day 1, light → Day 4, lights in the sky
(Gen 1:3–5)   (1:14–19)
Second panel: Day 2, sky dividing the waters → Day 5, sea creatures and birds
(Gen 1:6–8)   (1:20–23)
Third panel: Day 3, dry land and vegetation → Day 6, land animals and people
(Gen 1:9–13)   (1:24–30)

This complementary arrangement of panels displays a purposeful order, as does their sequence. Thus, the first panel concerns itself with light: first with its creation on day 1, and then on day 4 with the luminaries that will illumine the earth (vv. 3, 14–18). Further, dividing the waters in the second panel (vv. 6–8) provides place for both sea creatures and birds on the fifth day (vv. 20–21). This act of division or separation (*hibdîl*) also prepares for the appearance of dry land (vv. 9–13), whose vegetation will be necessary to sustain land animals and people (vv. 24–28). The artistry of this spatial pattern coheres with that of the liturgical pattern within the encompassing temporal progression of Gen 1:3–31—all of these together underlining both the effective power of "God said" ("and it was so") and the purposeful order that God's speaking and fashioning, creating and dividing brought about.

While God alone acts as creator in this artistic and liturgical account, the objects of God's creation themselves become subjects, actively participating in the emergence of a well-ordered world. For example, rather than simply speaking animals into existence, God assigns this function to the earth: 'Let the earth bring forth' (*tôṣē' hā'āreṣ*, v. 24). This assignment does not compromise God's singular status as the creator. As first to the earth, so God also speaks to the waters: "Let the waters swarm with swarms of living creatures" (v. 20)—but God then creates (*bārā'*) those very creatures (v. 21). The earth and the waters do not cocreate with God but, rather, respond to God's initiative. Creation is alive to God's purposes and responds immediately to them. Similarly,

9. Here I follow Bernhard W. Anderson, "A Stylistic Study of the Priestly Creation Story," in *Canon and Authority* (ed. G. W. Coats and B. O. Long; Philadelphia: Fortress, 1977) 148–62. For another, more recent analysis, see Ute Neumann-Gorsolke, *Herrschen in den Grenzen der Schöpfung: Ein Beitrag zur alttestamentlichen Anthropologie am Beispiel von Psalm 8, Genesis 1 und verwandten Texten* (WMANT 101; Neukirchen-Vluyn: Neukirchener Verlag, 2004) 154–61.

with respect to the luminaries, lights appear in the dome of the sky or the heavens (vv. 14–18). They are by no means themselves the source of light, which God had already created by verbal fiat (v. 3). But they function purposefully within the ordered creation, dividing day from night and the light from the darkness, serving the (festival) calendar and illumining the earth. Moreover, God assigns the sun and the moon to rule or exercise dominion (*lĕmemšelet*) over the day and the night (v. 16). They do have dominion, but their specific and limited dominion is delegated by the creator who made them.

Dominion or rule figures prominently in the final and climactic act of Gen 1, the creation of humankind, *ʾādām* (vv. 26–28). Here, the text expresses purpose both syntactically and semantically. The intra-divine deliberation ("and God said, 'Let us make humankind [*naʿăśeh ʾādām*],'" v. 26) sets the creation of humankind apart from the preceding acts and distinguishes humankind from the land animals, the sea creatures, and the birds. In the emergence of these creatures, the earth and the waters acted as created agents; not so with humankind.[10] Further, the syntax of God's deliberation expresses purpose and function, which is then elaborated:

Let us make humankind in [as] our image, according to our likeness,
so that they may rule (*wĕyirdû*)
the fish . . . , birds . . . , cattle . . . , in the whole earth,
and all creeping things that creep on the earth. (v. 26)[11]

Humanity's creation in (or as) the image of God and on the model of God's likeness has as its purpose the designated responsibility for human beings to rule or to exercise governance over or among the other creatures. The language here, as with the luminaries in v. 16, is royal. To cite but one example, the verb *rādâ* (v. 26) is used of the king in Ps 72:8—"May he rule from sea to sea."[12] The image and likeness of God, the *imago dei*, serves to distinguish and empower humankind as God's icon, God's royal representative in the world of God's creation, a view echoed (or anticipated) in Ps 8. This empowerment and its attendant assignment are described further by Gen 1:28. There God's blessing—thus God's empowerment of humankind—and God's correla-

---

10. Graeme Auld, "*Imago dei* in Genesis: Speaking in the Image of God," *ExpTim* 116 (2005) 259–62.

11. The (energic) *yiqtol* verb ('they may rule'), following a cohortative ('let us . . .'), is here a final or purpose clause (Joüon-Muraoka #116; Gordon J. Wenham, *Genesis 1–15* [WBC; Waco, TX: Word, 1987] 3–4). See the discussion, with further references, in Middleton, *Liberating Image*, 50–55.

12. Further illustrative examples can be found in Ezek 29:15 and Neh 9:28. See Neumann-Gorsolke, *Herrschen in den Grenzen*, 206–35.

tive command to multiply and fill the earth precede a further command to "subdue the earth" (NRSV); that is, to possess the earth, or to bring it under control, or to domesticate it (*wĕkibšūhā*).[13] The following verses (29–30) stipulate, with an introductory presentative (*hinnēh*), that God has given the earth's vegetation to humanity and to the animals for food. In other words, subduing the earth, possessing it, domesticating it serves to benefit human beings, who are to fill—and now have filled—the same earth. The blessing also extends benefits to the creatures that humanity is to rule. The command to "subdue the earth" amounts to a command to commit agriculture, for which God has prepared the earth; and agriculture requires some governance of animals.[14] At the same time, God has also given the earth's vegetation to all the living creatures, including those that fly or creep (v. 30). Among these, humanity is singled out; created as the image of God and according to God's likeness, humanity serves as God's royal representative.

The creation of human beings as God's image, on the model of God's likeness, reiterates a motif common in the ancient world. But in other ancient texts, the king himself, and only the king, is the divine image and likeness—sometimes represented by a statue—authenticating his sovereignty over peoples and lands.[15] Genesis 1 subverts and redefines royal theology (or ideology) by democratizing it, distributing royalty universally, and limiting it severely. No political terrain and no other human beings come within the scope of humankind's representatively royal dominion. No conquest will be necessary. Both rule and possession ("subduing") are with respect to what God has already accomplished, not a charge to conquer and exploit. God's own concluding estimation, upon inspection of everything created, is "very good" (v. 31). So God could rest and God did rest on the seventh day, sanctifying it (Gen 2:1–4a). The world, the cosmos, is in order, corresponding to God's intention. God has created a world at peace—thereby creating peace—with a royal representative designated to keep it, not to achieve it, which God had already done.

---

13. At 2 Chr 28:10, the LXX translates *kābaš* as 'gain possession of'. For discussion of the term, beyond the commentaries, see Norbert Lohfink, *Theology of the Pentateuch: Themes of the Priestly Narrative and Deuteronomy* (Minneapolis: Fortress, 1994) 8–13; Odil Hannes Steck, *World and Environment* (Nashville: Abingdon, 1980) 196–98; and the extensive discussion in Neumann-Gorsolke, *Herrschen in den Grenzen*, 274–97. She translates *kibšūhā* in Gen 1:28 as 'take it [the earth] into possession' (*Herrschen in den Grenzen*, 140, 297).

14. Middleton, *Liberating Image*, 59–60.

15. A. R. Millard and P. Bordreuil, "A Statue from Syria with Assyrian and Aramaic Inscriptions," *BA* 45 (1982) 135–41; Peter Machinist, "Literature as Politics: The Tukulti-Ninurta Epic and the Bible," *CBQ* 38 (1976) 455–82; and W. Randall Garr, "'Image' and 'Likeness' in the Inscription from Tell Fakhariyeh," *IEJ* 50 (2000) 227–34. In general, see Mark G. Brett, *Genesis: Procreation and the Politics of Identity* (London: Routledge, 2000) 27–28.

I have previously drawn attention to the spatial pattern in Gen 1. In its pairing of creation's days in three panels, the chapter also progresses from heaven (days 1 and 4), through water (days 2 and 5), to earth (days 3 and 6).[16] As a consequence, the chapter evinces a progressive distinction between heaven and earth. Indeed, distinctions figure prominently in Genesis 1. God separated or distinguished (*hibdîl*) between the light and the darkness (1:4); the dome or sky ("firmament," KJV) distinguished the waters from the waters (vv. 6–7); the luminaries distinguished day from night and light from darkness (vv. 14, 18).[17] Creation consists, to a significant degree, of imposing distinctions. When God began to create, the earth was *tōhû wābōhû* 'an indiscriminate mess'; darkness was over the face of the deep and there were but waters (v. 2). This was a world, a non-world, in which everything was indistinct, a "no-thing." In six days of creation, God brought things into being, imposed distinctions, assigned distinguishing and productive functions, and thereby created heaven and earth—the cosmos.[18]

Most important among the distinctions that creation entails is the distinction between God and everything that God has created. In the order of creation, *ʾādām* comes last . . . and also first. Last among all that God created, but first and distinct among the creatures of days 5 and 6 (Gen 1:20–30). Created as God's image, assigned by God thereby a delegated rule—a stewardship—*ʾādām* remains a creature, distinct from the creator that they, male and female, represent and serve.[19] Confusion on the point could only threaten creation and peace. According to the chapters of Genesis that follow, this is precisely what happened.

Genesis 2–3

Details of the many differences between Gen 1 and 2 need not detain us. The most significant difference, for our purposes, concerns *ʾādām*. While in

---

16. Anderson, "A Stylistic Study," 148–62. Middleton follows Anderson, with some modification (*The Liberating Image*, 74–77).

17. Middleton points out that medieval commentators referred to days 1–3 as "God's work of separation" (*The Liberating Image*, 76 n. 89).

18. I follow Michaela Banks in concluding that the phrase "heaven and earth" in Gen 1 refers to the entire cosmos (*Die Welt am Anfang: Zum Verhältnis von Vorwelt und Weltentstehung in Gen 1 und in der altorientalischen Literatur* [WMANT 74; Neukirchen-Vluyn: Neukirchener Verlag, 1997] 108).

19. Stewardship as a biblical, theological, and environmental category has come under debate, as in *Environmental Stewardship: Environmental Perspectives—Past and Present* (ed. R. J. Berry; London: T. & T. Clark, 2006). See the review by Celia Deane-Drummond, in *International Journal of Systematic Theology* 9 (2007) 375–78.

Gen 1 Elohim creates *'ādām*, humankind, male and female; in Gen 2 Yhwh Elohim molds a man, *'ādām*, from the dust of the ground or soil, the *ădāmâ* (2:7). The man is assigned to work and keep the garden that the Lord God, Yhwh Elohim, plants in Eden (2:15). Two features of the ensuing narrative demand attention. First, Yhwh Elohim issues a twofold instruction, granting permission to eat of the garden's trees but prohibiting eating from the tree of the knowledge of good and bad, on threat of death ("you will surely die," 2:16–17).

Second, God observes that "it is not good for the man to be alone" (2:18) and sets about providing a help.[20] To this end, God molds other creatures from the soil (*'ādāmâ*), just as he had done with the man. And just as the man is designated a "living being" (2:7), so are the creatures Yhwh Elohim molds as potential helpers (2:19). None of these, all of whom the man named, was found to be a helper corresponding to the man (*kĕnegdô*, 2:20). Finally, Yhwh Elohim forms a creature, not from the *ădāmâ*, but from the *'ādām* himself (2:21–23). This creature the man recognizes as being of his own flesh and bone; and he calls her *'iššâ* 'woman', because she was taken from *'îš* 'man'.

Among the living beings that were molded of soil, like the man, was the serpent—also a candidate to be the man's help. The serpent was unique among the creature-candidates, known as the most astute (*'ārûm*)—a virtue or vice that he proceeds to demonstrate (3:1).[21] In the conversation he initiates with the woman, he poses a question to her that expresses disbelief: "God [Elohim] did not really say, did he?"[22] After both he and the woman misquote the prohibition of 2:17, issued when neither of them yet existed, the serpent offers a revisionist interpretation of Yhwh Elohim's prohibition and threat. The serpent says: "You [plural] will surely not die, for Elohim knows that when you eat of it, you [plural] will be like Elohim who know[s] good and bad" (3:5).[23] While the serpent's "you-will-surely-not-die" directly contradicts Yhwh Elohim's "you-will-surely-die," the serpent appears to have it right. After eating

---

20. Both Brown and Fretheim see "is not good" in Gen 2:18 as a contrast with the repeated "it was good" of Gen 1 (Brown, *Ethos of the Cosmos*, 140; Fretheim, *God and World*, 40).

21. In Proverbs, *'ārûm* has a positive sense as in 'prudent'; it is a virtue (e.g., Prov 12:16). In Job, by contrast, it has a negative sense as in 'crafty' (e.g., Job 5:12). Brett (*Genesis*, 33) comments on associations between Gen 3 and Proverbs.

22. On the syntax, see Ronald J. Williams, *Hebrew Syntax: An Outline* (2nd ed.; Toronto: University of Toronto Press, 1976) #385.

23. Grammatically, the first instance of Elohim is singular ("God"), in agreement with the singular participle, while the second instance may be plural—"gods" or "divine beings"—preceding a plural participle.

fruit from the tree, the woman and "her man" (3:6) did not die.[24] Moreover, Yhwh Elohim subsequently acknowledges that "the man has become like one of us, knowing good and bad" (3:22).

The serpent's revisionist interpretation of Gen 2:17 seems to associate knowledge with perpetual life: God knows . . . you will not die . . . you will become like gods, who know.[25] However, the narrative dissociates this episode from a quest for immortality in two ways. The speech of Yhwh Elohim in 3:22 makes perpetual human life a threat still to be prevented, even after 'ādām has become "like one of us" with respect to knowledge. And the woman's own reasons for eating from the prohibited tree had nothing to do with immortality or with becoming godlike. Instead, according to the narrator, she saw that the tree was good for eating, that it was desirable, and that it was good for gaining insight or acting wisely (lĕhaśkîl; see Prov 34). That the serpent deceived her, she later makes explicit (Gen 3:13).

Even prior to the man and woman eating, the woman exercises a godlike act of discrimination: "she saw that it was good." This clause echoes God's repeated evaluation in Gen 1: God "saw that it was good." Her gaze was not only discriminating, it was also, if generously, acquisitive: "The woman saw that it was good . . . , she took . . . and ate . . . ; and she gave to her man . . . , and he ate." Both the serpent and the woman receive Yhwh Elohim's judgment for their acts, as does the man (3:13–19), but only the man's eating—his act of disobedience to the prohibition of 2:17—expressly poses a threat. In this act, the 'ādām acquired unlimited knowledge, a discriminating knowledge of the whole. This is precisely what Yhwh Elohim had forbidden him, a discriminating knowledge that is godlike.[26] The man's act of eating, regardless of his or of the woman's motivations or intentions, breeched a divine-human distinction that Yhwh Elohim makes explicit: "the 'ādām has become like one of us" (3:22).

For the second time, but not the last within Gen 1–11, God speaks in the first-person plural. On most contemporary interpretations, God's first-person plural speech reflects the setting of a royal court: in this case, a divine counsel or heavenly royal court in which God speaks to and with his courtiers.[27] In

---

24. The man names the woman Eve in Gen 3:20, while the man does not acquire the name Adam until 4:25.

25. See Ellen van Wolde, *Words Become Worlds: Semantic Studies of Genesis 1–11* (BIS 6; Leiden: Brill, 1994) 39–42. She also takes note of the striking absence of *yhwh* in the conversation between the serpent and the woman, who mention only *'elohim*.

26. Ibid., 36–37. The following verse suggests that Gen 3:22 has only the man in view.

27. 1 Kings 22 and Isa 6 provide other biblical examples. For comprehensive studies, see E. Theodore Mullen, *The Divine Council in Canaanite and Early Hebrew Literature* (HSM 24;

Gen 1:26–28, God's deliberative "let us" has to do with the creation of *ʾādām* as God's image: a royal image, as I have suggested, for a representative, iconic, and royal function.[28] The deliberation itself expresses a fundamental distinction between divine and human—between the divine "us" and *ʾādām*—consistent with the content of Gen 1 and its stress on distinctions. The divine deliberation in 3:22 first acknowledges the breech of this most basic distinction and then considers, in an elliptical construction, another one: "and now the man might stretch out his hand and take also from the tree of life, eat, and live forever."[29] Expulsion from the garden, which ensues (3:23–24), counts as punishment to be sure, but Yhwh Elohim takes this action in defense of creation. Unlimited human powers of discrimination, "the knowledge of good and bad," have already brought creation under threat. Unlimited human life would constitute a further threat to creation and to peace by further assaulting the distinction between divine and human.[30]

Lyle Eslinger, accurately in my view, described the divine first-person plurals in Genesis as "contrastive plurals." They mark a contrast between God and humanity. "The first person plurals schematize 'we', 'the gods', versus 'them', 'the humans'." The "common rhetorical purpose" of these contrastive plurals "is to mark out the ontological boundaries between gods and humans." With respect to Gen 3, having attained knowledge, "the humans have climbed the ontological ladder and it seems only a single step, immortality, stands between them and divine parity (iii 22)."[31] As Silviu N. Bunta put it, while Gen 1 "subtly bestows on humanity . . . divine form and iconic function," both chap. 1 and Gen 2–11 refuse "divine ontology" to humanity.[32] Parity with God, to use Eslinger's terms, would mean rivalry with God, a rivalry already initiated with—perhaps instantiated in—the transactions between the serpent and the woman, and between the woman and the man.

Missoula, MT: Scholars Press, 1980); Lowell K. Handy, *Among the Host of Heaven: The Syro-Palestinian Pantheon as Bureaucracy* (Winona Lake, IN: Eisenbrauns, 1994). Middleton comments specifically on Genesis in *The Liberating Image*, 55–60.

28. Silviu N. Bunta describes *ʾādām* as theomorphic and iconic but not isothetic ("Yhwh's Cultic Statue after 597/586 B.C.E.: A Linguistic and Theological Reinterpretation of Ezekiel 28:12," *CBQ* 69 [2007] 222–41).

29. On the elliptical construction with *pen*, see Bill T. Arnold and John H. Choi, *A Guide to Hebrew Syntax* (Cambridge: Cambridge University Press, 2003) 140; Williams, *Hebrew Syntax*, #461; and Joüon and Muraoka, *Grammar of Biblical Hebrew*, #169g.

30. David M. Carr, *Reading the Fractures of Genesis: Historical and Literary Approaches* (Louisville, KY: Westminster/John Knox, 1996) 237–38.

31. Lyle Eslinger, "The Enigmatic Plurals like "One of Us" (Gensis I 26, III 22, and XI 7) in Hyperchronic Perspective," *VT* 56 (2006) 171–84, quoting from pp. 174, 173, 177.

32. Bunta, "Yhwh's Cultic Statue," 241.

Genesis 4–11

Rivalry or resentment directed toward the woman or toward God may have motivated the serpent in his role as trickster.[33] Just as the serpent promised, upon their eating the fruit, the woman and the man had their eyes opened, and they knew. They knew that they were naked. The wordplay between the serpent's shrewdness (he was *ʿārûm*) and the couple's knowledge of their nakedness (they were *ʿārûmmîm*) is obvious. This initial exercise of discriminating knowledge fractured the communion of God and humanity, and of man and woman (Gen 3:7–8); it further established the conditions, announced by Yhwh Elohim, for rivalry between the couple (3:12–17; note there the man's repeated first-person references [3:12] distinguishing himself from the woman, in stark contrast with 2:23).

The narrative turns to lethal rivalry with the introduction of the couple's sons, Cain and Abel. Why God (Yhwh) had regard for—looked upon (*wayyîšaʿ*)—Abel's offering but not Cain's remains obscure.[34] Regardless, God's act of discrimination preceded and provoked rivalry and resentment that produced murder, fratricide. Outside the garden, without God's initiation and apart from any nonhuman provocation, history's first acts were of procreation (Gen 4:1–2); the next was of lethal violence. But the narrative exhibits verbal and moral continuities between what transpired in the garden and the murderous rivalry outside it.[35] The "desire" that will afflict the woman's relationship with her man (3:16) also describes sin's desire for Cain (4:7). God's questions to Cain, "Where is Abel, your brother?" and "What have you done?" (4:9–10), echo and conflate God's question to the man, "Where are you?" (3:9) and to the woman, "What is this you have done?" (3:13). Cain's question, "Am I my brother's keeper?" (4:9) echoes his father's self-exculpatory "the woman you gave me" (3:12). The culpable acts of the woman and the man in the garden, rendering them naked to each other and

---

33. On the trickster motif, see Ruthann Knechel Johansen, *The Narrative Secret of Flannery O'Connor: The Trickster as Interpreter* (Tuscaloosa, AL: University of Alabama Press, 1994).

34. Frank Spina suggested that Cain's offering from the cursed ground (Gen 3:17) rendered it unacceptable ("The 'Ground' for Cain's Rejection: *Adamah* in the Context of Gen 1–11," *ZAW* 104 [1992] 319–32). This seems the most likely explanation. See also Gary A. Herion, "Why God Rejected Cain's Offering: The Obvious Answer," in *Fortunate the Eyes That See: Essays in Honor of David Noel Freedman* (ed. Astrid B. Beck et al.; Grand Rapids: Eerdmans, 1995) 52–65. Lyle Eslinger's contention that Cain and Abel both intended to "placate an angered god" has no foundation ("Prehistory in the Call to Abraham," *BibInt* 14 [2006] 189–208; quotation from p. 192).

35. I draw on Reuven Kimmelman, "The Seduction of Eve and Feminist Readings of the Garden of Eden,"in *Women in Judaism: A Multidisciplinary Journal* 1 (1998), n.p. Online: http://jps.library.utoronto.ca/index.php/wjudaism/article/view/170/281 (accessed June 4, 2007).

before God, led them to hide themselves (3:9–10). Their attempt was as futile as was Cain's; Abel's blood cried out from the ground, from the *ʾădāmâ*. As punishment, God pronounced Cain "cursed from the ground"—from the *ʾădāmâ* of which the *ʾādām* and the serpent had been formed, from the *ʾădāmâ* God had cursed in 3:17. The transactions in the garden thus had lethal and peace-destroying consequences beyond it. Unlimited discriminatory knowledge—the godlike power to determine good and bad—came to humanity by an act of disobedience that assaulted the distinction between divine and human and threatened creation. Human godlike power to discriminate between good and evil did not carry with it the will to choose the good. Cain's act, by which he made himself lord over life and death, introduced lethal violence into the world beyond the garden; it violently disturbed the peace.

In response to Cain's fears of lethal retribution, God imposes a sevenfold vengeance on anyone who kills Cain (4:15). Subsequently, humanity makes itself the author and subject of the world's story. God nowhere appears in the creation of culture (4:17–22), as humanity takes vengeance into its own hands, multiplying it. If vengeance entailed killing a boy for wounding a man, and if a man required seventy-sevenfold vengeance (4:23–24), violence would soon fill the world. And it did. "The earth was corrupted before God and the earth was filled with violence. God saw the earth, and assuredly, it was corrupted, for all flesh had corrupted its way on the earth" (6:11–12). "God saw . . . was corrupted" echoes and reverses "God saw . . . it was good."[36] Humanity has brought about this reversal. Filling the earth with violence, humanity has rendered the earth distorted and disordered. God determines to meet this historical and social corruption with corruption of cosmic proportions (6:13; 7:11), bringing creation to the verge of chaos—to the verge of Gen 1:2.[37] With the flood, God acts once more as creator, though it is in an act of anti-creation that the world's story is reclaimed.

Intervening between the history of violence in Gen 4 and the flood narrative, Gen 6:1–4 narrates another assault on the divine-human/heaven-earth distinction, another threat to creation. Here, the actors are the mysterious "sons of God," figures unanticipated in Genesis but known elsewhere in the Bible (Job 1:6; 2:1; 38:7; Pss 29:1; 89:7; and see Ps 82:6).[38] As the woman

---

36. Ronald S. Hendel, "Tangled Plots in Genesis," in *Fortunate the Eyes That See: Essays in Honor of David Noel Freedman* (ed. Astrid B. Beck et al.; Grand Rapids: Eerdmans, 1995) 46. Hendel observes that only Gen 1:31 and Exod 39:43 share the "unusual" syntax of Gen 6:12a.

37. The Hebrew verb for "corrupted" in 6:11–12 is the same as the verb describing God's action in v. 13.

38. Walter Klaiber, *Schöpfung: Urgeschichte und Gegenwart* (Göttingen: Vandenhoeck & Ruprecht, 2005) 127–28.

did in the garden (Gen 3:6), these sons of God "looked and saw that . . . good" (6:2). They have cast a godlike discriminating gaze on women and discerned that they are good.[39] Moreover, their gaze is acquisitive; they *took* for themselves women they had seen and chosen. The woman's gaze in the garden was acquisitive; she *took* what she deemed good. But her taking, while also godlike and discriminating, and culpable, was for an intended mutual, human benefit; she shared with the man what she took.

The sons of God, however, act against humankind; the women are their victims. They also act against creation. In commenting on the first-person plurals in Gen 1:26 and 3:22 above, I followed Eslinger in noting their function with respect to the boundaries between divine and human. Those texts reflect the notion of a divine counsel or heavenly court in which God speaks with his courtiers. The sons of God in 6:2 represent members of that court. Their illicit union with humans breached the ontological boundary between divine and human. It threatened to circumvent the measure God took in Gen 3:22, where Yhwh prevented access to the tree of life and thus to life without any temporal limits. In this case, God imposes on human life a specific limit of 120 years (6:3). As Walter Klaiber remarked, "Here, clearly, a significant boundary is drawn between the divine and the human."[40]

God's imposition of a rather generous limit on human life does not amount to a punishment. The women of Gen 6:1–3 did nothing wrong; they were *taken*. Rather, God's imposition of a limit further *humanizes* human life and preserves a crucial distinction between embodied human existence that is life in the flesh and God's own divine spirit (6:3) that is life-giving. Once again, Yhwh thwarts a potential human-divine rivalry and asserts God's own prerogative and disposition over life and the created order.

The union of the sons of God with women also produced what the text (6:4) apparently regards as semidivine beings, the nephilim and "mighty men, renowned men [literally, men of the name]."[41] The nephilim appear elsewhere only in Num 13:33, which stresses their vast and frightening size. But this text also identifies the nephilim as the "sons of Anaq," whom Deut 9:1–2, echoing

---

39. The NRSV translates "fair," while other versions render it "beautiful," and so on. But the word is *ṭôb*, the same as in Gen 1:4, 12, 18, where "God saw that it was good." Lyle Eslinger noted the correspondence between Gen 3:6 and 6:2 ("A Contextual Identification of the *bene ha'elohim* and *benot ha'adam* in Genesis 6:1–4," *JSOT* 13 [1979] 67), but his identification of the *bene ha'elohim* as "Cainites" requires "sons of God" here to have an ironic sense (p. 71). This strikes me as special pleading.

40. Klaiber, *Schöpfung*, 129.

41. See van Wolde, *Words Become Worlds*, 66–67. The LXX translates both terms *gigantes* 'giants'.

Deut 1:28, identifies with the inhabitants of Canaan. This is a people greater (or more numerous) and stronger than Israel, with cities whose fortifications reach to the heavens or to the sky. The "sons of Anaq" were proverbial in Israel for their strength: "Who can resist the sons of Anaq?" (Deut 9:2). This association of the nephilim with the sons of Anaq helps in understanding the identification in Gen 6:4 of the nephilim with the 'mighty men' (*gibbōrîm*) or 'warriors'. In turn, this identification helps to explain the position of Gen 6:1– 4 between the preceding narrative—Gen 4 and its story of escalating violence—and the flood narrative that follows immediately. Thus, "the earth was filled with violence." Creation and peace had become disjunctive.

Genesis 11:1–9 concludes the primeval history. For the last time in the Pentateuch, God relates to universal humankind. And in this brief narrative, all humankind are united, speaking a common language and gathered on the plain of Shinar (11:1–2). There they embark on a common project: to build a city and a tower with its top in the heavens or in the sky. The purpose of this project is to "make a name for ourselves, lest we be scattered across the entire earth" (v. 4). The narrator's (on most accounts, the Yahwist's) description of this project and its motivation already echoes previous passages in Genesis. The people's desire to avoid being scattered seems to echo and to contradict God's command to "multiply and fill the earth," issued in 1:26 and repeated in 9:1.[42] On the other hand, the desire to "make a name" echoes the "men of the name"—the renowned men, the nephilim and warriors (Gen 6:4). These were, according to Num 13:33, descended from the offspring of Anaq, whose cities had fortifications reaching to the sky.[43] Further, the Bible reserves to God the making of a name for oneself (e.g., Jer 32:20; Dan 9:15; Neh 9:10). Finally, the plural cohortatives ("let us") in Gen 11:3 mimic the divine first-person plurals of Gen 1:26 and 3:22, not to mention 11:7.

Whatever may have been the motivations behind the Shinar project, which Gen 11:1–4 may leave ambiguous or even irrelevant, the project itself attracts God's attention. The description of this attention in 11:5 is itself suggestive:

---

42. Theodore Hiebert, in a comprehensive study of Gen 11:1–9, takes as the text's principal issue the people's desire to remain one people in one place with one language and culture ("The Tower of Babel and the Origin of the World's Cultures," *JBL* 126 [2007] 29–58). For an earlier, similar view, see van Wolde, *Words Become Worlds*, 84–109; and P. J. Harland, "Vertical or Horizontal: The Sin of Babel," *VT* 48 (1998) 515–33.

43. Both Gen 11:4 and Deut 9:1 have *baššāmayim* 'in[to] the sky'. I cannot here explore the possibility that the people on Shinar's plain were constructing a fortification. Brett points to links between Nimrod, the city builder, empire builder, and "tyrant" of Gen 10, and the city builders of Gen 11; the texts locate both at Shinar (Brett, *Genesis*, 46).

"Yhwh came down to see."[44] This marks the first time that God has had to "come down" to inspect the world or its creatures' activities (the next instance is Gen 18:21, with reference to Sodom and Gomorrah), and it contrasts dramatically with Yhwh Elohim's walking in the garden's evening breeze (3:8). Here, in Gen 11, God intrudes into the narrative and into a world from which he is alienated. And God offers an interpretation of the human project at Shinar. Because they have one language and the same vocabulary, this city and tower, this construction project is but the beginning of their projects. They will not be prevented from doing anything they may propose to do (11:6). This interpretation precedes the third and last divine, first-person plural ("let us"), deliberative speech in Genesis. Following Gen 1:26 and 3:22, this divine, first-person, deliberative plural marks the final insistence on the divine–human distinction on behalf of creation. The vocabulary and syntax of Gen 11:6b have their counterparts in Job 42:2b:

> You [Yhwh] can do all things. . . . No plan of yours will be thwarted. (Job 42:4b)

> This is the beginning of their doings. Now, nothing they plan to do will be thwarted. (Gen 11:6b)[45]

To thwart this god-rivaling power, God *babbled* their language so that they could not understand one another. This intervention was a means of (or for) the purpose of—contrary to their own plan—scattering them "over the face of the whole earth" (11:7–8). Naturally, having been universally scattered, they ceased building the city named Babel (11:9): that is, Babylon.

Theodore Hiebert and Ellen van Wolde are surely correct in interpreting Gen 11:1–9 in terms of God's desire that humans fill the earth and cultivate it on behalf of the earth (van Wolde) and in terms of God's desire for "linguistic and geographical diversity" (Hiebert).[46] As they and others have pointed out, this text does not exhibit a pattern of sin and judgment. God's response to the project (vv. 7–9) makes no mention of the people's motives. Further, their dispersal and diversity can be taken as a further act of humanizing for the benefit of both humans and the earth. In this regard, Gen 11 compares with

---

44. Hiebert connects this descent with "the Yahwist's conventional language of theophany" ("The Tower of Babel," 42), referring to Gen 18:21 as an example.

45. Hiebert insists that the last clause of 11:6 refers only to the building project (ibid., 43–46). However, the syntax of 11:6 exactly matches Gen 3:22—an initial *hēn* 'see!' followed by *wĕ῾attâ* 'and now', introducing a subsequent action with a verb in the *yiqtol* or imperfect.

46. Hiebert, ibid., 56. Bernhard W. Anderson argued somewhat similarly in "The Tower of Babel: Unity and Diversity in God's Creation," *CurTM* 5 (1978) 69–81. Hiebert ("The Tower of Babel," 30 n. 4) credits Anderson.

6:1–4. The women of that passage committed no sin; and the humanizing of human life by limiting it cannot be understood as punishment. However, in both events, the intentions of humans aside, creation came under threat because the distinction of human from divine came under threat: namely, the threat of rivalry. The woman in Gen 3, later named Eve, expressed no intention that her act should be one of divine human rivalry; but according to God, this is what it was.

Commenting on Gen 11:1–9, William P. Brown remarked:

> The issue [*sic*] of power and apotheosis once again come to the fore, as they had with the tree of life in the garden. . . . In both cases, the reach of human grasp is at stake . . . the end result is diversity by default. For the Yahwist, multiculturalism is a divine check on collective pride as much as the divinely ordained age limit in the antediluvian period was intended to arrest the growth of heroic power (Gen 6:1–4).[47]

Conclusion

From the beginning, creation involved imposing or granting distinctions. Beginning from Gen 1:2 and its *tōhû wābōhû*, everything indistinct and "no-thing," God brought about distinctions. Rather than eliminating darkness, God made the light distinct from it. Rather than eliminating one order of waters in favor the other, God imposed distinctions. God also made and empowered instruments to sustain these distinctions, even to rule them. Separately, God created animals and humankind; the latter God also commanded and empowered to rule—to exercise a custodial, stewardship role, as God's royal representative. Repeatedly, in the primeval history, in the story of creation, God responded to threats against the most fundamental of distinctions: between heaven and earth, between divine and human, between God and humankind. In Gen 2, unlimited human knowledge; in Gen 3, unlimited human life; in Gen 4, lethal human violence; in Gen 6, unlimited human life and semidivine power, spiraling violence, and corruption of the earth; in Gen 11, unlimited human power—to all of these, God responded in defense of creation and peace. As the final act of creation within the primeval history, God imposed distinctions among people, distinctions of language and geography.

This final divine act embodied within itself consequences not articulated in the narrative. Distinctions of language and geography inhere in ethnicity and in nationality. God's action as narrated in Gen 11:8–9 created the possibility of

---

47. Brown, *The Ethos of the Cosmos*, 183–84.

nations and, thus, the possibility of war. Violence the earth had known since Cain murdered Abel, but war became possible—not inevitable, but possible—only after Gen 11.[48] This possibility has been realized beyond reckoning. Still today, the blood of Abel cries out from the ground. Still today, regardless of their intentions, human beings—all in the image of God, all together God's royal representative, all together created and blessed, all entrusted with and empowered for stewardship of the earth on its and our creator's behalf—fall prey to rivalry with God and to lethal rivalry with one another.

Creation and peace, like justice and peace, kiss each other (Ps 85:11[10]). God is their creator in and from the beginning. Moreover, the product of righteousness/justice will be peace; and this labor consists above all and necessarily in quietness and trust (Isa 32:17; 30:15), whose object and source and norm is God the creator. In this light, perhaps what God did on the seventh day, when God rested, counts as the decisive act of creation. The Sabbath, as Reuven Kimmelman put it, "serves as an armistice. . . . Without the Sabbath, there would be no experience of the restraint of power."[49] Typically, we reserve for the dead the epithet: *requiescat in pace* or 'rest in peace'. We should recover the epithet for the living also, as a commendation of faith—vigorous faith and trust in God the Creator—for the love of God, for the benefit of the earth, and for each other.

---

48. Carl von Clausewitz famously defined war as a political affair between or among nations and as "the continuation of political intercourse by other means": namely, by means of "bloodshed" (*On War* [Princeton: Princeton University Press, 1976] 605–10; the first German edition was published in 1833).

49. Kimmelman, "The Seduction of Eve."

Jethro in the Structure of the Book of Exodus

WALDEMAR JANZEN
Professor of Old Testament, Emeritus
Canadian Mennonite University
Winnipeg, Manitoba

Early in my work on the Exodus volume in the Believers Church Bible Commentary,[1] Prof. Elmer Martens (the competent and always helpful OT editor of that commentary series) made one of his simple but wise suggestions to me: "When you consider what to write, ask yourself what questions your readers might wish to have answered." This question was often a helpful guide for me. And because an author is also the first reader of his or her work, I asked Elmer's question of myself: "What puzzles me about the composition and structure of Exodus?" What leaped out at me was this: "What is Jethro/ Reuel doing in the book? Why is he there?"[2] The search for an answer led me to the form with which I eventually structured my commentary. In the present essay, I will develop my conclusions regarding this structure. My focus will be the book of Exodus, and I will assume, rather than argue, its integrity as a literary unit in its final form.[3]

Reflections on Structure

The term *structure*, when applied to literary works, can have diverse meanings. In this study, my concern will be with "surface structures" discernible in the final text, not with the "deep structures" posited by Structuralists. S. Bar-Efrat's succinct definition offers a helpful starting point: "Structure can be

---

1. Waldemar Janzen, *Exodus* (Believers Church Bible Commentary; Scottdale, PA: Herald, 2000).

2. The priest of Midian, soon to become Moses' father-in-law, is called "Reuel" in Exod 2:18, and "Jethro" in all other occurrences in Exodus (but "Reuel" in Num 10:29). Because the same person is clearly meant, the various theories for this apparent duplication of name do not affect the thrust of this essay. I will use "Jethro" from here on.

3. Needless to say, Exodus is also a part of larger narratives, preeminently the Tetrateuch but also Genesis–Exodus, the Pentateuch, and even Genesis–2 Kings (thus Cornelis Houtman, *Exodus* [trans. Johan Rebel and Sierd Woudstra; 3 vols.; Kampen: Kok, 1993–2000] 1.1).

defined as the network of relations among the parts of an object or a unit."[4]
Bar-Efrat links the delimitation of the appropriate unit of investigation to the
concerns of the literary critic.[5] This raises the question of the basis of structure. Is it to be found in the author's intention; in the text itself, whether or
not the author intended it; or in the reader's effort to "make sense" of the text?
All three viewpoints and various combinations of them have their advocates.

Interpreters employing the "historical-critical method," dominant throughout much of the 19th and 20th centuries, have emphasized the empirical study
of the text, governed mainly by historical interest in the recovery of the earliest
layers of authorial or editorial intention and excluding as much as possible the
role of the reader's or interpreter's creative contribution to the construction of
meaning. Martin Noth succinctly summarizes this interest. Having stated the
general aim of interpretation—in this case, of Exodus—as being concerned
with the final form,[6] he describes the way to its understanding as a meticulous
unraveling of its history of composition and tradition:

> In its present state the book is as it were a fabric, skillfully woven from a
> series of threads, and the only satisfactory way of analyzing a fabric is to
> keep firmly in sight the threads of which it is made up and the material of
> which the threads themselves are composed. Each thread belongs to the
> pattern of the whole, and none is without its own importance.[7]

Because the end structure is to be the result of purely empirical descriptive
analysis, this process should ideally lead to at least a semblance of consensus in
understanding this final *Gewebe* (fabric).

A significant change in scholarly perspective was programmatically called
for by Brevard S. Childs in the introduction to his now classic commentary,
The Book of Exodus:

> The author does not share the hermeneutical position of those who suggest
> that biblical exegesis is an objective, descriptive enterprise, controlled solely
> by scientific criticism, to which the Christian theologian can at best add a
> few homiletical reflections for piety's sake.[8]

Childs did not reject empirical study in the mode of historical criticism by
any means, but he challenged "the *rigid separation* between the descriptive and

---

4. S. Bar-Efrat, "Some Observations on the Analysis of Structure in Biblical Narrative,"
VT 30 (1980) 155.
5. Ibid.
6. "Exegesis of the book is concerned with its final form" (Martin Noth, *Exodus: A Commentary* [trans. J. S. Bowden; OTL; Philadelphia: Westminster, 1962] 18).
7. Ibid.
8. Brevard S. Childs, *The Book of Exodus: A Critical, Theological Commentary* (OTL; Philadelphia: Westminster, 1974) xiii.

the constructive elements of exegesis."[9] Many have followed his lead, demonstrated with exemplary thoroughness in his commentary, or have taken their own paths of combining empirical study of the text with constructive reader participation. Childs himself devoted his creativity to constructive *theological* interpretation and was reticent to draw on strictly literary disciplines. Others, whether theologically or aesthetically motivated, became increasingly open to abandoning or deemphasizing the dominant *historical* methodologies in favor of the newer *literary* approaches emerging in the middle of the 20th century.[10]

Authors and Readers

Both theologically/canonically and literarily motivated interpreters of Scripture—often combined in the same scholar—wrestle seriously today with the question of the respective roles of author(s), text, and reader(s) in determining the meaning of a text. Many purely literarily motivated and most theologically motivated literary scholars have, however, upheld the view that the author (or the "implied author") and the text must control the meaning of the text communicated to the reader (or the "implied reader"), although most agree that the reader's creative contribution to the communicative process, or to "making sense" of the text, is significant.

This shift in emphasis throws new light on the astoundingly varied structuring[11] of Exodus that is often proposed in commentaries and other works in more recent times. While strictly empirical structuring must regard divergence in scholarly proposals in this respect as evidence of the unfinished task, or even as failure to find *the* true structure, the combination of empirical research with a creative role of the reader/interpreter allows for seeing the great diversity of structuring literary texts as part of the (legitimate) creativity of Exodus interpretation.

In addition to interpretorial creativity, the variety and richness of potential "structural markers" embedded in the book itself contribute to the amazing diversity in structuring Exodus that is found in commentaries. Should one, for example, subdivide Exodus on the basis of geography (Egypt, wilderness, Sinai)? Or of divine-human interaction (liberation/salvation/grace followed by covenant/commitment/law)? Or of textual formulations and key words? Should one mix these categories of structuring? Or privilege some over others? Bar-Efrat has proposed ordering the "elements upon which structural analysis

---

9. Ibid.; italics added.

10. A helpful overview of these developments in literary theory can be found in Gary Yamasaki, *John the Baptist in Life and Death: Audience-Oriented Criticism of Matthew's Narrative* (JSNTSup 167; Sheffield: Sheffield Academic Press, 1998) 33–63.

11. In view of this greater recognition of the reader's and interpreter's creative participation, I will often (not always) use the verbal noun *structuring* instead of the more static noun *structure*.

may be based," or "structural markers" as I call them, into four groups or levels: "(1) the verbal level; (2) the level of narrative critique; (3) the level of the narrative world; (4) the level of the conceptual content."[12]

A complex question for a commentary writer relates to the implied reader, and this is true in a twofold sense. First, whom is the biblical author[13] addressing as his or her implied reader/hearer? Every work has its "first-time readers," who read the narrative sequentially and know it only up to the point they have reached in their reading. The biblical author of Exodus, however, does not stop there, I believe. In view are readers familiar with much of the Exodus material and, beyond this, at least with Genesis, if not with the whole Pentateuch and further, through stories and cultic practices handed on in Israel over the centuries. I call these readers "repeat-readers."

Second, a commentary writer must determine his or her own implied reader(s). Yamasaki has developed a reading strategy that attends consistently to first-time (sequential) readers. These readers could, strictly speaking, never be guided by the overall structure of a longer text because they could not, for example, recognize a segment of text as part 1 of a tripartite whole, given that they could not know that parts 2 and 3 would follow.[14] The commentary writer does well to take his or her reader through the refreshing exercise of reading Exodus through the eyes of a first-time reader. At the same time, this modern author knows that his or her real readers will be, for the most part, repeat-readers—that is, readers who minimally have some knowledge of the Exodus story, together with its pentateuchal context. Because the biblical author of Exodus also primarily addresses repeat-readers, the modern commentator should do no less. In sum, the commentary author needs to take his or her readers through both reading experiences simultaneously, as it were.

Let me illustrate from Exodus 2. A first-time reader arriving at this chapter and knowing the pharaoh's threats and Israel's danger (chap. 1) will see Moses' flight to Midian as the bare escape of a hunted murderer to a desolate desert refuge. For such a reader, the proper interpretation of Moses' son's name, "Gershom," may well be 'I am [now] an alien in a foreign land [= Midian]'. A repeat-reader, on the other hand (having been helped by the commentator to know that 'basket' translates a Hebrew word also meaning 'ark'), may recognize that a child floating in an "ark" upon the death-bringing waters can only be, like Noah, a child saved by God's special election. Further, this reader may recognize the whole incident told in vv. 11–15 (note this delimitation) as

---

12. Bar-Efrat, "Some Observations," 157; developed on pp. 157–72.

13. *Author* will be used for the final major shaper(s) of the canonical text, whatever the number of authors or the precise nature of the process.

14. Yamasaki, *John the Baptist*, 65–66, 74–75.

a "mini-exodus," foreshadowing through the escape of Moses the eventual God-initiated triumphal exodus of Israel from Pharaoh's realm to its desert relatives in the wilderness.[15] For this repeat-reader, Moses becomes the "firstfruits" of those saved (1 Cor 15:20). His son's name can now be read more properly as: 'I have been an alien in a foreign land [= Egypt]'. But what about the rest of the Israelites? On the human level, not even a change to a new pharaoh can bring them relief. But for the first time, the narrator lets the reader but not the participants in the story know that God has not forgotten Israel or God's covenant with Abraham (vv. 23–25). While God seems virtually absent from the lives of the participants, the repeat-reader recognizes that the salvation of *one* Israelite prepares the salvation of the rest.[16] The commentary writer need not expound the text from the vantage point of both the first-time reader and the repeat-reader at every point but should draw both perspectives to the attention of the real reader when significant insights would be lost if one sort of reader were neglected.[17]

Jethro's Role in Exodus

In Jethro, in the role of a host in chaps. 2–4 and then again in chap. 18, I discovered the key markers for generating the structure of Exodus in my commentary.[18] The first story in the earlier Jethro material (2:16–22) has been identified by Robert Alter as a "type-scene"—that is, a story governed by a literary convention in which archetypal experiences (in this case, betrothal and marriage) are narrated by arranging specific components in a specific order. Other biblical "betrothal type-scenes" are found in Gen 24:10–61, 29:1–20; and Acts 4. Although some scholars see variations between type-scenes as merely being the inevitable result of telling and retelling an originally oral story, Alter plausibly proposes that any change or suppression of a key component in the convention must be taken as conveying an important, specific message.[19]

I consider the deviations from the expected pattern that are particularly relevant for our purposes to be the following: (1) Zipporah is not singled out

---

15. According to Gen 25:1–4, the Midianites were descendants of Abraham by his wife Keturah.

16. I prefer "salvation" to "escape," for it emphasizes God's agency, while "escape" seems to be the result of human success.

17. See my *Exodus* for my attempt to do justice to this task.

18. In Bar-Efrat's four levels of elements on which structural analysis may be based, characters and events belong to level three: "The narrative world" (Bar-Efrat, "Some Observations," 161–70).

19. Robert Alter, *The Art of Biblical Narrative* (New York: Basic, 1981) 47–62.

in the initial encounter as particularly beautiful, helpful, or otherwise out-
standing; she remains an unnamed sister among the seven. She does not appear
as a future bride, as do Rebekah and Rachel in Gen 24 and 29, respectively.
(2) Unlike Rebekah and Rachel, the seven daughters neglect the expected extension of hospitality to the stranger. Perhaps their mistaking Moses for an
Egyptian, which contrasts sharply with the recognition of kinship in Gen 24
and 29, accounts for this. (3) Reuel curtly orders his daughters to return and
make up for the neglected offer of hospitality. Could it be that he somehow
recognizes the mistake of characterizing Moses as an Egyptian? The narration
is too spare to confirm this possibility. In any case, the practice of hospitality,
expected to begin at the well but neglected by the daughters, is fully shifted to
Reuel. (4) Engagement, marriage, and the birth of a son follow, but they are
underemphasized in comparison with the Genesis stories. The summarizing
theme sentence places the emphasis unambiguously on one point: "I [Moses]
have been an alien in a foreign land, [and now I am no longer an alien but have
come home]" (2:22). Jethro is emphatically being characterized, based on all
the variations of this type-story, as the welcoming host—not only offering a
fugitive temporary accommodation but inviting him into permanent association as a resident alien.[20]

   In what sense could Midian be home to Moses? Several lines of thought
converge to make a cumulative case: (1) Even if one does not subscribe to
Alter's view of divergences in type-scenes, one must concede, with Gordon F.
Davies, that—on the basis of simple repetition—Moses' action "is significant
because he reenacts [in Exod 2] the histories of Jacob [Gen 29] and the servant
of Abraham [Gen 24]."[21] Even the first-time reader can be expected to recognize this element of reenactment. (2) A first-time reader would also surely
remember Joseph, who is singled out from the other sons of Israel as having
preceded his father and brothers to Egypt (in an involuntary move that, however, saved his life and later the life of his family, Exod 1:5) and having been
raised to high position at Pharaoh's court. The reversal of theme in Moses'
flight from Pharaoh's court to the nomads of the wilderness could hardly be
missed. But Moses could not have fled to his own people, Israel, for they
were—at least in the story world, if not in external history—all still in Egypt.
The Midianites, represented by Jethro, the model host, not only represent the
shepherd life of the wilderness to which Moses' ancestors had belonged in a

---

20. A comparison of the wording of 2:21 with Judg 17:11 confirms that a longer stay is
anticipated. We see Moses in this role in Exod 3:1.
   21. Gordon F. Davies, *Israel in Egypt: Reading Exodus 1–2* (JSOTSup 135; Sheffield: Sheffield Academic Press, 1992) 148; see also pp. 142–64.

general way but also figure as Abraham's descendants from his wife Keturah (Gen 25:1) and thus as Moses' and Israel's kinfolk.[22]

As indicated already, the appearance of Reuel/Jethro in Exod 2–4 and then his only reappearance, in chap. 18, attracted my attention when I was designing my Exodus commentary. What is his role in these two places? Minor characters in a narrative generally function with reference to the main protagonist(s), in this case, Moses and Israel.[23] We have now seen Jethro's role with respect to Moses to be the host par excellence who welcomes home an escaped stranger (yet on closer look, a returning kinsman). Yamasaki advocates an interpretation that allows characters to develop, if they do develop. This is the only way first-time readers can experience them.[24] Without privileging the first-time reader as he does, I consider this to be a worthwhile heuristic reading strategy.

Let us first ask whether Jethro develops as a character in the first context (chaps. 2–4). Jethro is introduced as "the priest of Midian." By reference to his daughters and his flocks, he is also shown to be a father and head of a household (2:16) who practices model hospitality. His role as host to Moses expands of course, due to the marriage of his daughter Zipporah to Moses, to become Moses' "father-in-law . . . the priest of Midian" (3:1). No character development is implied here. Next, Jethro as Moses' "father-in-law" grants Moses leave to visit his kindred in Egypt with the words "Go in peace!" (4:18). Jethro's familial role takes precedence over his priestly role, but no development of character is evident. Nothing indicates that Moses has told Jethro of his theophany at the burning bush.

We hear of Jethro again when he meets Israel, delivered now from Egyptian bondage, at the "mountain of God" (chap. 18). He is introduced as "Jethro, the priest of Midian, Moses' father-in-law," just as in chaps. 2–4. Although chap. 18 contains two main scenes set on consecutive days (vv. 1–12

---

22. John I. Durham proposes that the theological motivation for the unification of all the descendants of Abraham, including both the nomadic desert side (Midian, the descendants of Keturah) and the settled farming side (Israel, the descendants of Sarah) before the momentous covenant at Sinai accounts for the introduction of Jethro and the Midianites into Exodus at this point. This must remain hypothetical, but the point that the fleeing Moses was received by "his own," through Jethro, finds support in Durham's view (Durham, *Exodus* [WBC 3; Waco, TX: Word, 1987] 246; see also pp. 238–46).

23. Literary studies of this functioning of biblical characters treated relatively briefly or in scattered references are not plentiful; for examples, see the study of Michal in relation to David, in Alter, *The Art of Biblical Narrative*, 114–27; and the treatment of John the Baptist in Matthew's Gospel, in Yamasaki, *John the Baptist*, 77–148.

24. Ibid., 49–51; according to John A. Darr, "*character is cumulative*" (emphasis original) (*On Character Building: The Reader and the Rhetoric of Characterization in Luke–Acts* [Louisville: Westminster/John Knox, 1992] 42).

and 13–27, respectively; the first is divided into two subscenes, vv. 1–7 and 8–12), interpreters widely agree on the narrative unity of the chapter. After the turbulent experiences in Israel's past, culminating in the aborted attack of the Amalekites (17:8–16), Israel has arrived in the "friendly territory" of the (kindred) Midianites, and more specifically, at the "mountain of God" (v. 5). Peace and tranquility pervade this chapter.

Jethro wastes no time in coming to welcome Moses and his people, just as he had energetically taken up the duties of hospitality neglected by his daughters on Moses' earlier arrival (2:20). The fact that Jethro "came into the wilderness" (v. 5), that is, traversed some distance, does not make him the guest or Moses the host; the mountain of God is still in the roaming realm of Jethro's pasturing tribe (3:1), while the Israelites have come from afar. At the mention of the mountain of God, even the first-time reader may recall God's words to Moses at the burning bush (3:12) and realize that a significant sequence of events has come to its conclusion now, in keeping with God's promise there.

After an explanation of the presence of Moses' wife, Zipporah, and their two sons, a tradition-guided but warm and family-centered greeting scene ensues (vv. 1–7). A more formal reception follows in "the tent" (vv. 8–12).[25] Here, Moses gives a personal report to Jethro of God's deliverance of Israel, a story that Jethro had only heard second-hand (v. 1). Jethro rejoices at this good news (vv. 8–9). This leads to a more formal praise and affirmation of the LORD (Yahweh) by Jethro, which are followed by a sacrificial meal. Jethro presides, being the older patriarch in the family and the welcoming host, and Moses, Aaron, and the elders of Israel partake as guests (vv. 10–12). But in this section, Jethro is identified twice as Moses' father-in-law, not as priest. That he presides at a sacrificial banquet, bringing "a burnt offering and sacrifices," places him in a role similar to the patriarchs of Genesis (see Gen 8:20; 31:54; 46:1; see also Exod 10:25) and has no necessary connection to the priesthood to be introduced later at Sinai.[26] Just as Jethro had ordered his daughters, "Invite him [Moses], to break bread!" (Exod 2:20), Jethro's guests assemble "to

---

25. Moses' tent? Equally plausibly, "Jethro's desert home, or . . . his desert shrine," as suggested by J. Gerald Janzen, *Exodus* (Westminster Bible Companion; Louisville: Westminster/ John Knox, 1997) 127. It was certainly not the "tent of meeting," in anticipation of the Tent of Meeting fully developed in chaps. 25–31, as claimed by Eugene E. Carpenter ("Exodus 18: Its Structure, Style, Motifs and Function in the Book of Exodus," in *A Biblical Itinerary: In Search of Method, Form and Content—Essays in Honor of George W. Coats* [ed. Eugene E. Carpenter; JSOTSup 240; Sheffield: Sheffield Academic Press, 1997] 105).

26. See J. G. Janzen (*Exodus,* 126–27) for a description of the role of such a "priest" in the kinship context of nomadic shepherds.

eat bread with Moses' father-in-law in the presence of God" (Exod 18:12).[27] Jethro is again, or still, the host.

On the next day (18:13–27), Jethro watches his son-in-law wearing himself out by adjudicating cases brought before him "from morning until evening" (vv. 13–14). Being experienced in overseeing tribal affairs, he recognizes the burdensome inefficiency of this procedure and offers his advice: 'I will give you counsel' (*ʾîʿāṣĕkā*, v. 19). Moses should conserve his strength by limiting himself: "represent the people before God," "bring their [difficult] cases [*dĕbārîm*] before God," "teach them the statutes [*ḥuqqîm*] and instructions [*tôrōt*]," and "make known to them the way [*derek*] they are to go" (vv. 16, 20). To deal with lighter cases, he should select 'heads' (*roʾšîm*, v. 25) over the people, and 'officers' (*śārîm*, vv. 21, 25, NRSV; 'chiefs', NJPSV) over thousands, hundreds, fifties, and tens from among the people, "able" men, "who fear God," are "trustworthy," and "hate dishonest gain." Moses listens to his father-in-law and follows his advice. The advice is given out of Jethro's experience-based wisdom.[28] Then they part and Jethro sets out for his home.[29]

Throughout chap. 18, Jethro's character has not developed beyond what we saw in chaps. 2–4. He is the priestly patriarch of the region, he is the welcoming host for Israel as he was earlier for Moses, and he draws on his experience to initiate Moses into sustainable ways of leading a people in its new circumstances, just as we can imagine him initiating the former princeling Moses (earlier) into the art of "keeping the flock" (3:1). In both Midian sections, chaps. 2–4 and chap. 18, Jethro functions as welcoming host and as a facilitator to settling down to traditional wilderness life after a turbulent escape. There is no development in Jethro's character or role; he is what modern narratologists call a *flat character*, "whose traits are all consistent and predictable," in contrast to "*round characters*, who possess a variety of potentially conflicting traits." He may even be considered a "*stock character . . .* with a single

---

27. In the story world of the final text, vv. 8–12 imply no conversion of Jethro to Yahweh or "Kenite Hypothesis" or covenant conclusion ceremony.

28. The fact that Jethro adds "if you do this, and God so commands you" (v. 23) is not a foreshadowing of God's lawgiving at Sinai. Wisdom in Israel was viewed as God-given, and this clause means something such as: "If you follow my advice, God opening your mind to recognize it as wisdom. . . ."

29. Several tensions are evident in this passage. Is Jethro's advice simply meant to reduce Moses' workload, or is he to focus on communicating God's will to the people rather than adjudicating their disputes? How are the references to judicial activity to be related to the designation of "officers" and the apparently military divisions suggested by Jethro? How is this tradition related to Deut 1:9–18, a similar passage (but without Jethro, and placed at the end of the Sinai period), and to later royal, judicial, and military structures in Israel? All these questions point to a long and complex textual tradition but cannot concern us here.

trait who perform[s] a perfunctory role in the story." This trait, for Jethro, is hospitality.[30]

My Proposal for Structuring Exodus

Important to the structure of Exodus is the question how Exod 18 functions in its present Exodus context. Several interpreters—correctly, I believe—have recognized a significant break in the Exodus text between chaps. 18 and 19 but for differing reasons. Historical-critical scholars posit here the seam between originally separate exodus and Sinai traditions. Others, guided by a tripartite geographical structure (Egypt, wilderness wandering, Sinai), see here the (temporary) end of Israel's wandering stage. Of special interest with respect to my proposal is the assumption, expressed by some interpreters, that chap. 18 is the midpoint of Exodus, summarizing Israel's preceding exodus story and also anticipating the following theophany, law proclamation, and covenant conclusion at Sinai.

Eugene E. Carpenter proposes that Exod 18 "is a major transitional chapter that serves both as an epilogue (vv. 1–12) to the first half of Exodus (chs. 2–17) and as a prologue (vv. 13–27) to the second half of Exodus (chs. 10–40)."[31] In a detailed analysis of vocabulary distribution and other structural and stylistic features, he argues—correctly, in my opinion—for the narrative unity of this chapter, the close links between the two Jethro sections (chaps. 2–4 and 18), and the function of 18:1–12 as a concluding summary of Exod 5–17.

My portrayal of Jethro as a flat character representing the host par excellence makes it impossible for me to accept Carpenter's view that "the hospitality of Jethro in chapters 2–4 is returned by Moses in 18:6–7."[32] It is Jethro who is the host in both situations, receiving first Moses, and then, in a parallel fashion that will be discussed further, Moses and his people Israel. Where Carpenter sees reciprocity, I see continuity of character and role.

I part ways with Carpenter also when he argues for an anticipatory and preparatory role of 18:13–27 in regard to the following chapters, 19–40. In his words: "The administrative structure necessary to execute the total judicial/cultic/jurisprudence program of Israel needed to be presented before the content of that program. . . . And, to keep from breaking the tightly knit narrative that follows in chapters 19–40, the writer has placed it here."[33] In other words,

---

30. Quotations from Mark Allan Powell, *What Is Narrative Criticism?* (Minneapolis: Fortress, 1990) 55.
31. Carpenter, "Exodus 18," 107; see his argumentation throughout the article, pp. 91–108.
32. Ibid., 100; similarly, p. 106.
33. Ibid., 105.

Carpenter claims that Jethro's counsel provides Moses in advance with the structure for administering the law yet to be given by God at Mount Sinai.

To me, Carpenter's claim is unconvincing. Jethro counsels Moses how to deal with *existing* problems of maintaining justice; his counsel does not anticipate problems that might arise after God's covenant law has been promulgated at Sinai. The measures for administering the covenant law that are later introduced at Sinai will take a very different form. They will revolve around Aaron and his priesthood, qualified by descent and consecration, or possibly by endowment with the Spirit (Num 11:14–17), rather than around men chosen from among all the people on the basis of personal qualities of character. Further, nothing in the Sinai law requires grouping the people into thousands, hundreds, fifties, and tens. A first-time reader expecting a future for Israel along the lines of Jethro's counsel would be ill prepared for what actually follows at Sinai. A repeat-reader also will recognize that a radical turn of events separates chaps. 18 and 19, rather than thinking that a transition is being anticipated and prepared for in 18:13–27. The theophany at Sinai will break into Israel's anticipated future as projected by Jethro's counsel with just the same irresistible and radically upsetting surprise as the theophany at the burning bush broke into Moses' settled life in Midian and set him on a totally unanticipated course.[34]

In sum, there is an inescapable narrative parallelism between Moses' experiences and Israel's: flight, welcome by Jethro, settling down in Jethro's world, unexpected theophany, election and commission, and setting out under God's orders toward an unanticipated task. This parallelism became the key to my structuring of Exodus. It led me, first, to a bipartite division:

Section 1: Anticipation: Focus on Moses (1:1–7:7)
Section 2: Realization: Focus on Israel (7:8–40:38)

---

34. Space prevents me from engaging Carpenter's supports for his proposal in detail; I must limit myself to a few examples: (1) In 18:7 already, Carpenter interprets "the tent" to which Jethro and the others withdraw after the first greeting as the "tent of meeting," viewing this tent as an anticipation of the Tent of Meeting (= tabernacle) of chaps. 19–40, without any textual or other basis. (2) I cannot see how, for example, a common root such as *špṭ*, which occurs 6× in 18:13–27, points forward to chaps. 19–40, where it occurs 9×, if it also occurs 6× in chaps. 1–17 (and ca. 180× in the OT!). For further distribution figures of common words (in most cases, similarly unconvincing to me), see the table in Carpenter, "Exodus 18," 104. (3) Particularly unconvincing to me is the claim that the 10 occurrences of *dābār* in 18:13–27 (9 singular forms and 1 plural form) "indicate the ten 'words' given at Sinai (Exod 20:1)" (ibid.). Neither the NRSV nor the NJPSV translates any of these 10 as 'word' but always with more extended meanings, such as 'thing', 'matter', and even 'dispute'. (4) The only features reminiscent of the law to come are the references to 'statutes' (*ḥuqqîm*) and 'instructions' (*tôrōt*) in v. 16; see also v. 20. Their usage is not exclusive to the Sinai legislation, however, and the context suggests that their use here was within traditional case law.

The assumption here is that Moses, in section 1, is not only prepared by God for his task related to Israel but that he "pre-lives" Israel's future experiences in which he is to be instrumentally engaged as God's chosen instrument.[35] Next, each section parallels the other in its sharp, bipartite division:

SECTION 1
    Part 1: Salvation of Moses (1:1–2:25)
    Part 2: Commissioning of Moses (3:1–7:7)
SECTION 2
    Part 3: Salvation of Israel (7:8–18:27)
    Part 4: Commissioning of Israel (19:1–40:38 [and beyond])

This division of each section into two formally parallel parts was indicated to me by the identical role of Jethro as welcoming host for Moses and Israel, respectively. He not only welcomes a fugitive/fugitives from Pharaoh temporarily but opens up a settled and traditional long-range future (3:1; 18:13–27) for him/them. This humanly anticipated future is then dramatically interrupted and redirected into different paths through a totally unexpected theophany in each case, followed by a commissioning of Moses and Israel, respectively, to God-set tasks: for Moses, to lead Israel out of Egypt; and for Israel, to be for God "a priestly kingdom and a holy nation" (19:6), modeling a God-directed life for the nations of the world, a life centering around God's dwelling in its midst (40:34–38, and beyond).[36] Further, this division into salvation-commissioning, both in the Moses section and in the Israel section, can best be summarized as a *change of masters*, which then becomes my formulation for the overarching theme of the book of Exodus.[37]

To my knowledge, the parallelism marked by Jethro's two appearances has generally not been recognized, although the association of the burning bush with Sinai has often been made. I believe that my interpretation of Jethro strongly undergirds the importance of the pattern just described. The abrupt changes from hospitality/settling down (Jethro settings) to theophany/com-

---

35. Similarly, Mark S. Smith asserts that "his [Moses'] own commission and mission anticipate the mission and identity of Israel as Yahweh's servant" ("The Literary Arrangement of the Priestly Redaction of Exodus: A Preliminary Investigation," *CBQ* 58 [1996] 25–50; quotation from p. 40). Smith, however, focuses on the P source and does not take cognizance of Jethro's role as a structure marker. His conclusions regarding the structure of Exodus differ from mine (see below). See also the fuller study by Smith (with contributions by Elisabeth M. Bloch-Smith), *The Pilgrimage Pattern in Exodus* (JSOTSup 239; Sheffield: Sheffield Academic Press, 1997).

36. See my article, "Tabernacle," *NIDB* (in preparation).

37. On the appropriateness of this, see also Jon D. Levenson, *The Hebrew Bible, the Old Testament, and Historical Criticism: Jews and Christians in Biblical Studies* (Louisville: Westminster/John Knox, 1993) 127–59.

missioning (burning bush/Sinai), discussed here on Bar-Efrat's story-world level, are supported by a number of structural markers on the levels of the narrative world and the conceptual content. Significant support could also be adduced on the verbal level. For space reasons, I can only point out three features: (1) There is general assonance between 'bush' (*sĕneh*) and the name 'Sinai' (*sînay*). (2) The root *qdš* ('holy') appears for the first time in the burning bush context (Exod 3:5), is associated with fire and God's speaking voice, and figures prominently in a similar way but on a grand scale in the Sinai theophany. In each setting, the proper human approach is called for. It is expressed to Moses in God's order to remove his sandals, and it is assumed for Israel in the Sinai prescriptions for the priesthood by the absence of provision for footwear. (3) The appearance and the summarizing of the name(s) of Moses' son(s) in each Jethro context is significant.

Can Diverse Structuring Proposals Coexist?

How can major structuring proposals coexist without invalidating each other? One example of this possibility must suffice. Many interpreters consider the "Sea Event" to be *the* major structural marker. Some understand it to be a sharp division point between Exod 1:1–15:21 and 15:22–40:38. Some (with Mark Smith)[38] consider the Song of the Sea (15:1–21) to be separating yet holding together what lies before it and what comes after it. Privileging the Sea marker over other structural markers inevitably leads to a basically bipartite Exodus structure (however, the two parts may be subdivided further, if only on account of their length). One could characterize the two parts generically as "Israel in Egypt/Israel under Pharaoh" and "Israel in the wilderness/Israel under God."[39]

My proposal, with the overarching theme of "Change of Masters" is compatible, I believe, with this perspective. The difference in specifics lies, first, in according a more distinct profile to the "pre-living" or modeling role of Moses;[40] and second, in seeing the change of masters as a process in which God's twofold commission to Moses (*from* serving Pharaoh *to* worshiping God, 3:10–12) is *gradually* coming to fruition with Moses' departure from Jethro's world and the mountain of theophany and Israel's arrival in Jethro's world and at the same mountain. The loosening grip of Pharaoh, evidenced by the stages

---

38. See works by Smith listed in n. 35.

39. Idem, "The Literary Arrangement," 38–39; also William H. C. Propp, *Exodus 1–18: A New Translation with Introduction and Commentary* (AB 2; New York: Doubleday, 1999) 38; Propp, however, reflects extensively on various possibilities of structuring Exodus (pp. 32–38).

40. Smith also acknowledges this; see quotation in n. 35.

of Israel's departure (12:37; 13:17; 15:22), and the increasing "takeover" by God worked through signs of grace in the wilderness are, from one perspective, sharply separated by the Sea event. Seen from another perspective, they constitute a continuing process, with the Jethro theophany scenes as bookends. These two aspects are suitably comprehended by God's self-introduction formula with its two addressees: "Pharaoh/the Egyptians shall know // you/Israel shall know that I am Yahweh" (7:5, 17; 14:4, 18 // 6:7; 10:2; 16:12). The Sea marker retains its *centrality* in the panorama of Israel's change of masters but is embedded—helpfully, I believe—in the *process* as characterized in my structuring proposal.

The Case of the Venus Flytrap:
The Argument of the Book of Job

PIERRE GILBERT
Associate Professor of Biblical Studies and Theology
Canadian Mennonite University
Winnipeg, Manitoba
Mennonite Brethren Biblical Seminary
Fresno, California

The argument of the book of Job has long represented a perplexing problem for scholars. In spite of the enormous amount of attention devoted to this wisdom masterpiece, there is still little unanimity in regard to the purpose of the book.

Any "successful" articulation of the argument of Job should first take into account the wisdom character of the book. This factor is generally not afforded sufficient attention. Second, it should reflect its canonical shape. And third, it should seek to integrate its long list of peculiar features: the declarations relative to Job's absolute moral integrity in the prologue, the unusual and unexpected wagers between God and the Satan, the extreme degree of suffering experienced by Job, the absurd ideological reductionism of the friends' discourse as well as their growing and intense hostility toward Job, Job's dogged uncompromising insistence on his innocence, the seemingly out-of-context Hymn to Wisdom in chap. 28, the unexpected appearance of a fourth proponent (Elihu), the apparent irrelevance of the Yahweh speeches, the odd omission of any reference to Elihu in Yahweh's concluding address, and Job's remarkable restoration at the end of the book.

Author's note: Prof. Elmer Martens's contribution to OT studies and particularly to the difficult field of biblical theology cannot be overestimated. His book *God's Design* still represents in my opinion one of the most brilliant, helpful, and dynamic proposals to highlight the OT's basic organizing principle and its unity. I no longer keep track of the number of times I have referred to his book in courses, workshops, and sermons over the last twenty years. The central thesis of *God's Design* has in fact become a core component of many of my students' theological discourses. It is an honor and privilege to be counted among Prof. Martens's friends and colleagues. I dedicate this essay on Job to this great scholar.

In this essay, I will seek to demonstrate that the primary purpose of the book of Job, in conformity with the fundamental intent of wisdom literature, is to draw attention to the dangers of idolatry: the innate tendency to reduce spiritual reality, including God himself, to simplistic ideological mantras.

Survey of Positions

Determining the overall argument of the book of Job is a notoriously difficult enterprise. Although commentators write at length about the substance of the arguments found in the various speeches, and while there is an enormous corpus of detailed investigations on a multitude of Job-related topics, exegetes have shown a remarkable degree of equivocation in regard to the purpose of the book as a whole.[1]

Most readers view the book of Job as a response to the problem of undeserved pain.[2] Job is therefore often characterized as a theodicy. Few scholars, however, suggest that the book is in fact proposing a comprehensive solution to this most unpleasant dimension of human life. As a cursory reading of the book demonstrates, it proposes no obvious answer to the problem of suffering. Let me rephrase that. There is an answer: Job's suffering is portrayed as the outcome of a wager between God and the Satan! Be that as it may, few consider this to be an adequate response for individuals who are in the throes of suffering!

Moreover, as David Clines notes, if Job is intended to be an answer to the problem of suffering, then the lesson of the book can be stated roughly in this manner:

> By all means let Job the patient be your model so long as that is possible for you: but when equanimity fails, let the grief and anger of Job the impatient direct itself and yourself toward God, for only in encounter with him will the tension of suffering be resolved.[3]

But as Clines rightly observes, even within this framework, the book does not provide a concrete solution. At best, Job offers a model of how one should deal with suffering. This latter approach has in fact proven to be the most enduring view of the book's argument. Marvin Pope succinctly summarizes

---

1. For a review of earlier positions, see C. Kuhl, "Neuere Literarkritik des Buches Hiob," *TRu* 21 (1953) 163–205, 257–317; H. H. Rowley, "The Book of Job and Its Meaning," *BJRL* 41 (1959) 167–207; and James Barr, "The Book of Job and Its Modern Interpreters," *BJRL* 54 (1971–72) 28–46. For a thorough review of earlier as well as more recent works on the book as a whole, see David J. A. Clines, *Job 1–20* (WBC 17; Dallas: Word, 1989) lxxxiv–xci; and James L. Crenshaw, "Job, Book of," *ABD* 3.866–67.

2. See Marvin H. Pope, *Job* (AB 15; Garden City, NY: Doubleday, 1965) lxviii.

3. Clines, *Job 1–20*, xxxix.

the position: "The transition from fear and hatred to trust and even love of this One—from God the Enemy to God the Friend and Companion—is the pilgrimage of every man of faith. Job's journey from despair to faith is the way each mortal must go."[4] August H. Konkel, in his recent commentary on Job, states that while the book does not provide an intellectual solution to the problem of suffering, it does speak, through the example of its main character, to the necessity to think and respond to inexplicable suffering in reference to God. "The fundamental issue is Job's relationship to God."[5]

In a slightly different vein, John Gibson suggests that the book is offered as an exploration, if not a solution, to the vexing problem of unmerited suffering.[6] This question, more than any other, represents a profound challenge to the moral integrity of God.[7]

Others have expressed some doubt about the centrality of suffering as the book's major theme. They tend to view Job as a work that addresses basic theological issues or is intended to challenge false world views.[8]

---

4. Pope, *Job*, lxxvii. Rowley, who proposes that the book is written to explain that the cause of undeserved suffering is ultimately a mystery, echoes this sentiment. While there is no intellectual solution that is offered, Job's experience teaches that people who suffer will wrest "profit from the suffering through the enrichment of the fellowship of God" ("The Book of Job and Its Meaning," 207). In a similar vein, see Robert Gordis, *The Book of Job* (New York: Jewish Theological Seminary, 1978) xxxi.

5. August H. Konkel, "Job," in *Job, Ecclesiastes, Song of Solomon* (Cornerstone Biblical Commentary 6; Carol Stream, IL: Tyndale, 2006) 4.

6. John C. L. Gibson, *Job* (Daily Bible Study; Philadelphia: Westminster, 1985) 3.

7. C. Hassell Bullock, *An Introduction to the Old Testament Poetic Books* (Chicago: Moody, 1988) 65–66.

8. James Barr, for instance, surmises somewhat tentatively that the purpose of the book may be to challenge the traditional concept of divine retribution ("The Book of Job," 44–45). In this respect, Rowley rightly observes that what some call the "traditional" view of divine retribution is not, strictly speaking, true to the OT but is a distorted view of that doctrine ("The Book of Job and Its Meaning," 195–97). J. Gerald Janzen suggests that the book of Job constitutes a critique of Israel's world view, particularly as it pertains to its understanding of creation, covenant, and history. He writes: "What does it mean to be . . . an earthling, made from dust? What does it mean to be the divine image, and therein a royal figure in the earth? What does it mean to affirm at one and the same time that to be human is to be dust and the royal image of God? Can these two metaphors be sustained together?" (*A Bible Commentary for Teaching and Preaching: Job* [Interpretation; Atlanta: John Knox, 1985] 13). David Wolfers argues that the book of Job is composed as "a politico-historical allegory . . . and that it seeks to justify God's assumed role in certain historical reversals (such as the apparently arbitrary destruction of Judah at the hands of Sennacherib in the time of Hezekiah) which are symbolized by the catastrophes of Job" (*Deep Things out of Darkness* [Grand Rapids: Eerdmans, 1995] 69). In the same vein, Samuel R. Driver and George B. Gray contend that the book is not about solving the problem of suffering. The book seeks to vindicate "God and the latent worth of human nature against the conclusions drawn from a partial observation of life" (*The Book of Job* [ICC; Edinburgh: T. & T. Clark, 1921] li).

This survey highlights at least two difficulties. First, most of the proposals tend to focus on Job, the character, and not the entire book. Job is seen as the focus of the book and his steadfastness as the key to its interpretation. Second, in cases where the commentators attempt to provide a comprehensive argument, the suggestions tend to be too vague or general. For instance, it seems rather improbable that the main objective of such a complex and elaborate piece of literature is to teach that ultimate reality is opaque and beyond the human intellect and that we must therefore be faithful in spite of our inability to make sense of the world. Moreover, I suggest that a major shortcoming of most of the proposals is the insufficient degree of attention paid to the wisdom character of the book.

Toward a Comprehensive Hypothesis:
Preliminary Matters

Literary Genre

The necessity of interpreting biblical texts with regard for their literary distinctiveness is a most basic hermeneutical principle.[9] The book of Job is characterized as a wisdom book.[10] The formulation of its argument must therefore be articulated within the broader frame of reference represented by Israelite wisdom literature. James L. Crenshaw defines biblical wisdom as the exposition of the basic order in the universe.[11] Wisdom can also be described as the art of discernment. Its ultimate purpose is to put in evidence that which favors life or, conversely, that which leads to death and chaos.[12]

Biblical wisdom exhibits an apologetic and polemic agenda. The Israelites were subject to powerful and competing religious constructs. And like all human beings, they also had an innate tendency to resist the living God and to project themselves into the realm of the divine.[13] The role of wisdom writers was to persuade their audience of the legitimacy and superiority of faith in Yahweh and the folly of the alternatives.[14] The goal of Hebrew wisdom was to expose and subvert idolatry, using the entire range of rhetorical devices at its disposal. It is a grave error, therefore, to view Job as a tame essay on the mysteries of life. If Job is indeed a wisdom book, our challenge is to

---

9. Grant Osborne, *The Hermeneutical Spiral* (Downers Grove, IL: InterVarsity, 1991) 149–51.

10. See for instance, Roland E. Murphy, *The Tree of Life* (2nd ed.; Grand Rapids: Eerdmans, 1996) 33–34; and Konkel, *Job*, 3.

11. James L. Crenshaw, *Old Testament Wisdom: An Introduction* (Atlanta: John Knox, 1981) 66.

12. Jean-Noël Aletti, ed., *Aux racines de la sagesse* (Cahier Evangile 28; Paris: Cerf, 1979) 6–7.

13. See, for instance, Paul's comment to that effect in Rom 1:21–22.

14. This theme is particularly well portrayed in the book of Ecclesiastes.

discern as precisely as possible, using the literary clues offered by the text itself, the method used by the author to meet this objective.[15]

It Is All about the Reader

The book of Job is not primarily about the person of Job but about the reader.[16] First, the purpose of Israelite wisdom literature is to promote faith in Yahweh, and it, therefore, reflects an agenda that targets the immediate audience. Second, the text itself draws attention to the readers by providing privileged information in the prologue that is accessible only to them. Third, the author invites the reader to be an active participant in a debate that will unfold throughout the book.

At the center of the disputation is Job and whether or not he is blameless. The three friends and Elihu categorically and mercilessly put forward the thesis that Job's misfortune is the consequence of his sins. Job, on the other hand, unequivocally defends his absolute integrity. There is no compromise possible and no midway position allowable. Either Job is a sinner or he is blameless. The reader is expected to take part in this debate and to adopt a position in regard to both Job's character and, by extension, the justice of God. But the reader is not expected to side with or against Job simply on the strength of the arguments proposed in the speeches. He or she must judge the validity of the opinions put forward by the various speakers on the basis of the information provided in the prologue as well. In other words, the reader is, right from the outset, conditioned to embark on this journey with a positive bias toward Job.

However, the author does not assume the reader's ability to maintain a consistent position only on the basis of the information provided in the prologue. The book is designed in such a way as to *compel* the reader to identify with Job. It uses a variety of literary techniques that ensure that the reader will not

---

15. As appealing as it may be to read the book of Job as a simple historical narrative, it is preferable, particularly because of its wisdom character, to view the book in terms of a work that may in fact be using a real incident as a starting point but expanding it into a full-fledged literary masterpiece, in order to provide a platform to reflect on a critical aspect of life. Job may well have been a historical character, but the story of his misfortunes was integrated into a much broader wisdom literary framework (see Konkel, *Job*, 30–31). Many of the difficulties that readers experience when reading the book of Job are related to an attempt to situate what is happening to Job within a historical framework. It is, however, virtually impossible from a strictly historical point of view to make sense of the bizarre wager between God and the Satan, Job's moral perfection, the intensity and unfairness of Job's suffering, the burlesque-like portrayal of Job's opponents, and the trivialization of the children's fate. The issue is not to rationalize these unusual elements but to discern how they contribute to the overall literary purpose of the book.

16. David J. A. Clines examines at length the question of the book's impact on the reader in "Why Is There a Book of Job and What Does It Do to You if You Read It?" in *The Book of Job* (BETL 64; Leuven: Leuven University Press, 1994) 13–20.

only opt to maintain his or her belief in Job's integrity but to identify fully with Job in his plight against his human (and divine!) opponents. The purpose of the various elements of the book of Job, from the prologue to the Elihu speeches, is to bring the reader into a state of full identification, emotionally and intellectually, with Job. The author's strategy is to elicit such a close sense of solidarity between the reader and Job that, when God finally speaks, Job is no longer the sole or the central target of these speeches: the reader is! The book of Job is a *Venus Flytrap*. How do the various features of the book contribute to this narrative goal?

The Argument in a Nutshell

The book of Job is not a response to the problem of undeserved pain. The fact that the issue, after being at the forefront throughout the book, is so elegantly, dramatically, and unexpectedly sidestepped in the Yahweh speeches unmistakably speaks to a different agenda. Job's extreme suffering is more likely a "hook" that is intended to draw the reader into a deeper reflection on the more fundamental issue of idolatry. The prologue, the friends' brutal speeches, the intriguing and seemingly out of place Hymn to Wisdom, the arrogant Elihu, the mystifying Yahweh speeches, and the final restoration of Job serve the overall purpose of the book, which is to challenge the reader's innate tendency to reduce the complexity of God and the universe to death-generating formulas.

A Journey into the Book of Job

The Prologue (1:1–2:13)

The prologue provides the information needed to navigate the rest of the book. It begins by an assessment of Job's character. "There was once a man in the land of Uz whose name was Job. That man was blameless and upright, one who feared God and turned away from evil" (Job 1:1).[17] Job is portrayed as a paragon of moral perfection. As Pope so succinctly states: "Taken together, they [the adjectives] indicate the peak of moral perfection."[18] The appraisal of Job's character is further supported by an appeal to Job's behavior (1:2–3), God's own attestation (1:8; 2:3), and Job's submissive response to his afflictions (1:22; 2:10).[19]

---

17. Unless otherwise noted, all citations are from the NRSV.

18. See Pope, *Job*, 7.

19. In spite of the extraordinary lengths to which the author goes to qualify the impeccability of Job's character, historically Job's readers have sought to mitigate this portrait. James L. Cren-

But this is not the only view of Job. The Satan (hereafter referred to as the *Adversary*) provides an alternative position. The Adversary does not dispute the basic facts of the case. He chooses rather to focus on motives. Job is faithful to God because it serves his personal interests. However, the Adversary is well aware of the difficulties inherent in judging motives, so he proposes a wager to determine whether Job is a man of integrity or an opportunist. God gives the Adversary permission to strip Job of his wealth. His children are killed and his livestock is destroyed (Job 1:13–17).[20]

God is vindicated; Job is devastated, but he refuses to turn against the Almighty. This should have been the end of it, but in the course of a second encounter with God, the Adversary sets up the terms of a second wager. The stakes are presumably not high enough. Job will show his true character if the Adversary is allowed to ruin his health (2:1–8).

At this point, there are a number of elements that need to be highlighted. First, the whole exercise seems meaningless. There is no reason to question Job's integrity. In fact, we have every reason to believe, based on the author's and God's own testimonies, two actors who have a unique insight into Job's motives, that Job is truly a man of integrity. Second, while it is customary to vilify the Adversary for causing so much trouble for Job, it should be noted that it is Yahweh who draws attention to Job. Third, this whole affair should have been resolved after Job's successful handling of the first trial. But the Adversary presents himself a second time to God, who eagerly takes this opportunity to zoom in on Job again, thus setting the stage for another devastating wager. As stunning at this may sound, the prologue portrays Yahweh, not the Adversary, as the "bad guy." God is the ultimate cause of Job's misery. This literary strategy is very deliberate. It raises the question of God's goodness and good judgment and portrays Job as the ultimate underdog.

The purpose of the prologue is to capture the reader's attention; something that is imperative in a polemical piece. It is designed to arouse intense sympathy for Job. The declarations of personal integrity, the two quasi-comic

---

shaw writes: "Unlike the Epistle of James (5:11), early opinions about Job's character did not always emphasize his patient endurance. The *Abot de Rabbi-Nathan* accuses Job of sinning with his heart and in this way defends divine justice. Rashi faults Job for talking too much. According to Glatzer (1966), later interpreters went beyond calling Job a saint or an imperfectly pious man to quite different categories: a rebel (Ibn Ezra, Nachmanides), a dualist (Sforno), a pious man searching for truth (Saadia Gaon), one who lacked the love of God (Maimonides), an Aristotelian denier of providence (Gersonides), one who confused the work of God and Satan (Simeon ben Semah Duran), a determinist (Joseph Albo), . . ." ("Job, Book of," *ABD* 3.866).

20. Livestock and children were the measure of a man's wealth in the patriarchal period (Gen 12:16).

encounters between God and the Adversary,[21] the death of Job's children, the loss of his wealth and his health (which in this case signals a terrifying skin ailment), the loss of his social status, the abandonment of his wife, and finally his own stoic acceptance are elements that taken together compel the reader to feel sorry for Job and take a position in the debate that unfolds in the rest of the book.

Job's Lamentation (3:1–26)

As we should have expected from the lofty portrayal of Job's character in the prologue, the man remains firm. This resolve should not come as a surprise, for one should rightly expect a man of Job's caliber to stand firm in the face of abject adversity. But in chap. 3, something unexpected occurs. This chapter reflects a thoroughly negative assessment of Job's entire life and the crass unveiling of the indescribable pain that now afflicts him. We are exposed to the raw struggle of a man who faces the collapse of his world.[22]

This chapter provides a first opportunity for the reader to test his or her resolve to identify with Job. At first blush, Job's pronouncements reflect an utterly irrational response, compelling the reader to question whether Job is justified in making such a negative assessment of his existence, especially in the light of the long and prosperous life he has had until now. This question is legitimate, for Job's response seems to contradict the submissive attitude attested in 1:20–21 and 2:10. From a narrative perspective, this chapter offers a clever transition into the dialogue section. The author provides a catalyst for the debate to begin and a rationale for the friends' hostile attitude.

The Dialogue (4:1–27:23)

Before we actually get into the dialogue, four comments are in order.[23] First, the speakers do not necessarily respond to each other in a rigorous, logical, and orderly fashion.[24] The purpose of the dialogue is not to report

---

21. On the book of Job as comedy, see J. William Whedbee, "The Comedy of Job," *Semeia* 7 (1977) 1–39; and *The Bible and the Comic Vision* (Cambridge: Cambridge University Press, 1998) 221–62.

22. An excellent example of this can be found in C. S. Lewis, *A Grief Observed* (Norwalk, CT: Easton, 2002 [1961]).

23. Although I have adopted the conventional grouping of the speeches into three "cycles," there is no scholarly unanimity on whether this is the best way to articulate the structure of the dialogue. While Clines presents the dialogue within a three-cycle framework, the overall organization differs from the traditional divisions (see for instance John E. Hartley, *The Book of Job* [NICOT; Grand Rapids: Eerdmans, 1988] 50–56). Other scholars such as Konkel (*Job*, 24–26) and R. A. F. MacKenzie and Roland E. Murphy ("Job," *NJBC*, 468–69) avoid it altogether.

24. See C. Hassell Bullock, *An Introduction to the Old Testament Poetic Books* (Chicago: Moody, 1979) 90; and Solomon Freehoff, *The Book of Job* (Jewish Commentary for Bible Readers; New York: Union of American Hebrew Congregations, 1958) 120.

a conversation verbatim but to draw the reader into the issue of Job's guilt or innocence. Second, the tone of the speeches increasingly worsens. Though we detect a hint of sympathy in the early stages of the conversation, the friends' discourse rapidly degenerates into a series of virulent, personal, and unsubstantiated attacks on Job.[25] Third, I will not attempt to examine each cycle in detail. I will highlight the basic argument offered by the three friends and present a brief survey of Job's responses. Fourth, I will focus most of my attention on the first cycle, because the other two cycles mostly repeat the positions expounded in chaps. 4–14.

The first cycle (4:1–14:22) opens with Eliphaz (4:1–5:27). The basic thesis is remarkably simple but is conspicuous for the weakness of its argument. For Eliphaz, the universe functions strictly according to a principle of cause and effect (4:7–11). The innocent are saved, but the wicked are destroyed. One harvests what one sows (4:7–11). Eliphaz's argument is fatally undermined by the claim that the innocent never face destruction (4:7), and those who "plow iniquity" are consistently destroyed (4:8). This statement is patently absurd and obviously false. The accumulation of contrived and bizarre rhetorical devices[26] further weakens the overall thesis.

Eliphaz, however, proposes a secondary point that mitigates to a certain extent the bluntness of the basic premise. He asserts that suffering is also used by God to correct and discipline (5:17). The strict application of the law of retribution would normally leave no hope for the transgressor. Because Job's suffering clearly marks him as a sinner deserving of punishment, there should be no exit for Job but death. But there is hope in the disciplining action of God and his mercy. Consequently, if Job discerns the real significance of his suffering, he will be restored (5:18–27).

How should the reader react to this first assault against Job? Eliphaz's thesis—that one reaps what one sows—is reasonable, but his desperate allusion to dreams and visions as a way of bolstering his position underlines its weakness. The appeal to God's discipline and potential restoration if Job repents would normally have some degree of validity, but the prologue is still too fresh in the reader's mind. He or she knows that Job is *not* being disciplined, because he was described as a man of unimpeachable integrity. At this stage, the reader's sympathies must remain with Job.

Job's first response is brutal and disheartening (6:1–7:21). In 6:2–3, he seeks to rationalize the excessiveness of his earlier comments. They were motivated

---

25. See Norman C. Habel, *Job* (Knox Preaching Guides; Atlanta: John Knox, 1981) 8.

26. In 4:12–16, Eliphaz claims special revelation as the source of his understanding. In 5:2–6, he alludes to a historical precedent that is strangely similar to Job's situation: the case of a "fool" who experienced God's curse. The circular argument could not be more obvious. Since Job's plight is similar to the punishment suffered by the "fool," Job must indeed be a "fool."

by hopelessness and despair (7:1–11). But Job refuses to play the victim, thus antagonizing his friends even more. He challenges them to give it "their best shot." To declare that Job has sinned is simple enough, but proving it is another matter altogether. If there was any trace of sympathy from the three friends, it will now vanish like ice on hot pavement (6:24–30). In the last section of his speech (7:17–21), there is a first hint of the critical issue that is at the very heart of the book—God's moral integrity. In this section, Job challenges God to divulge the sins he has committed.

Bildad (8:1–22) adopts a firmer stance than his predecessor, but before he gets to the heart of the matter, he indulges in a personal attack on Job: "How long will you say these things, and the words of your mouth be a great wind?" (8:2). His thesis is remarkably similar to Eliphaz's. God is righteous and he operates according to an immutable principle of justice. The wicked are punished and the just are blessed. At this point, Bildad cannot be bothered with the usual niceties one expects from friends in this kind of situation. He goes for the jugular. The proof of what Bildad puts forward is the very death of Job's children, who perished as punishment for their sins (8:4). If Job is just, as he pretends to be, he will surely be blessed and the wicked will be destroyed (8:20–22).

In his response to Bildad (9:1–10:22), Job concedes the point his opponent makes about the righteousness of God and the general fate of the righteous and the wicked (9:2). But if Job concedes the validity of the general principle, he refuses to accept a judgment of culpability on himself. For Job, the issue is not that he may have sinned. The real problem is inherent to God himself, who is so powerful and mighty, no force in the universe can resist him (9:3–10). Might indeed makes right (9:11–20).

In this chapter, Job's anger toward God reaches new heights. He characterizes God as a heartless dictator who destroys those who oppose him (9:2–20). In 9:21–10:22, he attacks God's moral integrity. There is no justice in the person of God: "It is all one; therefore I say, he destroys both the blameless and the wicked" (9:22). God is an immoral despot (9:22–23). In the remaining section of his complaint, Job expresses the utter futility of defending his integrity. Regardless of what Job may do or say, nothing can change God's judgment against him. Even if Job were to obtain a hearing in court, God would bring false witnesses to testify against him (10:17). Job finally ends by asking why God is so cruel toward him. Did God allow Job to live simply to torture him (10:19–22)?

At this point, the reader may begin to experience mixed feelings about Job. On the one hand, he or she may still entertain strong feelings of sympathy on account of the intensity of his sufferings, the insensitivity of his imbecile friends, and his utter and absolute isolation. On the other hand, though the reader may also wonder about God's unwillingness to put an end to Job's torture, he or she may not be completely ready to follow Job in accusing God of being a heartless despot who derives perverse satisfaction from torturing an innocent and defenseless creature.

Zophar (11:1–20) expresses the outrage some of the readers may now begin to feel toward Job. How dare he pit his limited perspective against the infinite wisdom of God? For Zophar, Job's guilt is undeniable. He is guilty of *some* sin. Rather than rail against God, Job should be thankful that God, in his great mercy, is not holding all of Job's sins against him (11:6). Hope is within reach but only if Job will appeal to God and let go of his sin (11:13–20).

Job's final response (12:1–14:22) in this first cycle is peppered with razor-sharp sarcasm and a steely resolve not to be intimidated by the three friends' accusations against him: "No doubt you are the people, and wisdom will die with you. But I have understanding as well as you; I am not inferior to you. Who does not know such things as these?" (12:1–3). Job's antagonists have said nothing new, and the thesis they have put forward is not supported by the facts. Job is after all an innocent man, but he will be unable to persuade them of his innocence. Their reductionistic moral formulas will not allow an alternative reading.

Job knows there is no greater authority to appeal to than God (12:7–25). His only hope is to argue his case before the Almighty (13:3). Job requests that God put an end to his torment and that he prove his case against him. The burden of proof is now squarely on God's shoulders (13:20–28). At this point, the reader might be tempted to distance himself from Job. How does he dare accuse God of being a cruel tormentor? But the final words of Job's soliloquy, in which he gives us an insight into the real impact of the friends' words on him, win the sympathy of the readers: "But the mountain falls and crumbles away, and the rock is removed from its place; the waters wear away the stones; the torrents wash away the soil of the earth; so you destroy the hope of mortals" (14:18–19).

As the reader considers Job's intense and unjust treatment, the corrosive impact of the friends' words, and his complete isolation and despair, he or she cannot but feel growing sympathy for Job, renewed anger toward the three friends, and an increased sense of frustration with a God who could and should put an end to this charade but stubbornly refuses to do so.

The second cycle (15:1–21:34) repeats the pattern of the first. The three friends renew their relentless attacks on Job's character but add a new sin to the list: his raging arrogance toward the Almighty himself. The friends are on a holy crusade to demonstrate that Job is guilty. This endeavor becomes a compelling quest, for to fail would mean the utter ruin of reality itself. But Job refuses to admit his guilt. While he fires a few angry and sarcastic shots across the bow of his adversaries (16:1–5; 17:12; 19:1–5; 21:1–3), his ultimate target is God. The main theme of his accusation against God is simple and heart wrenching; Job holds God wholly responsible for what is happening to him. There is absolutely no justifiable reason behind God's vicious assault on Job (16:17; 19:6–13). The author paints a most pathetic picture of Job (19:14–20) who, in the end, is reduced to pleading for mercy (19:21–22).

Job's final response to Zophar punches a devastating hole in the friends' moral equation. He reminds them that the wicked do not always suffer judgment. Sometimes, they live on, and their children are established (21:4–13). In fact, in some cases, the wicked prosper even in spite of their blatant rejection of God (21:14–34). The argument is devastatingly simple. If some wicked men can prosper, perhaps some righteous men can unjustly suffer. The second cycle brings the real issue into sharp focus. This is no longer a debate between Job and his friends but between Job and God himself.

The author's intent is to sharpen Job's portrait as the ultimate underdog in order to compel the reader to identify deeply with Job, even in his accusations against God. But some readers may begin to waver in this respect. The prologue is by now but a distant memory. The purpose of the next cycle is to firm up the reader's contempt for the friends and to bring the degree of identification with and sympathy for Job to a climax.

In the third cycle (22:1–27:23),[27] the friends reiterate their simplistic moral theory and use increasingly more preposterous arguments to make their point. A few observations about Eliphaz will suffice to illustrate the overall direction of their attacks. The argument is simple: What would God have to gain by condemning an innocent man? Eliphaz cannot imagine any scenario in which God would be motivated to inflict suffering on a righteous individual (22:1–3). Eliphaz is done with trying to demonstrate the validity of his moral axiom. The proof is intrinsic to Job's condition: the man's wickedness is great, his sins are endless. Eliphaz provides a detailed list of sins allegedly committed by Job. The fact that there is no proof to support these accusations is irrelevant. Eliphaz resorts to fabricating evidence in order to preserve his view of reality (22:4–20)!

If some readers have until now maintained sympathy for the friends' position, it vanishes with Eliphaz's last statement. Eliphaz is lying. The principle he constantly alludes to may have a degree of legitimacy, but the creation of

---

27. The third cycle (22:1–27:23) presents structural difficulties that have been the object of much scholarly discussion. For a summary of the issues, see Gordis, *The Book of Job,* 530–31; and *The Book of God and Man* (Chicago: University of Chicago Press, 1965) 93–103.

false evidence against Job is unconscionable and the reader has therefore no choice but to side with Job.

As for Bildad (25:1–6; 26:5–14) and Zophar (27:13–23), they, like mindless sheep, bleat away at their mantra: God rewards the righteous and judges the wicked. In response, Job vows to maintain his integrity and blatantly accuses God of injustice (26:1–4; 27:1–12).

Hymn to Wisdom (28)

Prior to Job's closing statement, which incidentally parallels his opening speech in chap. 3, we find what is generally known as the Hymn to Wisdom.[28]

The author of the book wishes to engage the reader in a legitimate process of reflection. For the exercise to be successful, the reader must thoughtfully, willfully, and completely embrace Job. Ultimately, the reader must become one with Job in his angry challenge to God. In this perspective, the most likely explanation for the presence of this puzzling and seemingly out-of-context hymn is to allow some "breathing space" for the reader to reflect on everything that has been said and to clarify his or her stance toward Job before heading for the surprising conclusion of the book.

The poem also provides a hint regarding the ultimate interpretation of the book. This innocuous chapter essentially states, contrary to what the friends have been suggesting, that wisdom is not a commodity that is readily available. As the search for precious metals requires sustained effort, so does the quest for wisdom. In fact, as v. 29 reminds the reader, true wisdom can only be derived from a very careful consideration of the person of God (28:29). Getting an insight into ultimate reality may not be as easy as the friends or even Job contend.

Job's Closing Comments (29:1–31:39)

Just as Job opened with a soliloquy, the dialogue cycles end with Job taking the stand to make a final plea. Chapters 29–31, like chap. 3, are an extended lament that ends with a demand that God answer Job. These chapters are designed to elicit the complete and utter sympathy of the reader by confronting us with the utter wretchedness of Job's condition.

Chapter 31 anticipates an unavoidable question. While there may be no doubt about the exceptional quality of Job's character, the inquisitive reader will ask whether anyone can literally be without sin. Could not the character statements offered in the prologue just be hyperbole? Even the most upright

---

28. Scholars have puzzled over the insertion of this poem at this juncture of the book. For a brief discussion, see Gordis, *The Book of Job*, 536–38; and H. H. Rowley, *Job* (Century Bible; Nashville: Thomas Nelson, 1970) 13–14.

occasionally sin: a sin of omission perhaps, an occasional lustful glance. Job must be guilty of *some* sin. Because the prologue is by now distant memory, it is critical that the reader be reminded of Job's absolute integrity. Job himself states his innocence in the strongest terms possible—by using a series of self-imprecations. Job is so confident of his innocence that he demands an answer from God (31:35–37)!

Elihu (32:1–37:24)

If this book followed a strictly linear plot line, God would now appear and answer Job, but instead, the author introduces a new character: Elihu.[29] The function of the Elihu speeches is fourfold. First, he demonstrates the vacuousness of the friends' thesis. Despite his claims to originality and special divine insight (32:11–12, 14), Elihu offers nothing new (32:15). His thesis is but a repetition of the three friends' discourse (33:11–12, 34–37). Elihu's irrelevance is so glaring that he does not even earn the benefit of a mention in the Yahweh speeches. He who summarily dismisses Job and the three friends (32:2–3) is himself completely ignored later on. Second, his arrogance (32:8, 18) and callousness (32:2) are calculated to create intense empathy for Job. Elihu's speech reinforces the painful reality of Job as the victim, thus compelling the reader to consider seriously the legitimacy of the hypothesis that Job vigorously defends: that God is indeed unjust. And fourth, he presents himself as God's defender. By the time he is finished, God has no choice but to appear and set the record straight.[30] The introduction of Elihu represents the author's final and ultimate strategy to get the reader to side with Job against the friends and even against God.

Yahweh and Job (38:1–42:6)

The time for learned abstractions has come to an end. The living God will now settle the issue. Job has defended himself well. His character has been vindicated. He has endured unspeakable suffering without compromising his integrity. It would have been easy for Job to agree with his protagonists and be done with it, but Job would not take the easy road. He is, as the prologue states, a man of unimpeachable integrity.

By the time Elihu ends his soliloquy, it has become glaringly apparent that the friends' simplistic and reductionistic moral formulas are utterly inadequate

---

29. The authenticity and role of the Elihu speeches have been forcefully debated by commentators. For more details, see for instance Hartley, *The Book of Job*, 28–29; and Gordis, *The Book of Job*, xxxi–xxxii, 358.

30. See idem, *The Book of God and Man*, 115–16.

to describe reality. By now, this painfully long dialogue should have accomplished its goal, which is to bring the reader to identify fully with Job. Job's accusations against God are not only his own; they are now the reader's. The author's strategy is to ensure that, when God responds, it is not only to Job that he will speak but also to the reader who shares Job's outrage. As I noted at the beginning of this essay, this wisdom book is not about Job but about the reader. The real target of the Yahweh speeches is the reader. Job is simply an accessory.

Let us review Job's thesis before we survey God's speeches. Job has maintained his complete and absolute innocence throughout the entire ordeal. Nonetheless, Job is being afflicted like no other person ever has been. According to the law of retribution, God rewards the righteous but punishes the wicked. Job's condition is, within the parameters of that formula, the proof that he has sinned. But because Job did not sin, he leaps to the only possible conclusion: God is unjust and cruel. In one seemingly unassailable logical swoop, Job has now redefined God and the premises of ultimate reality itself. He has reached a stage of absolute understanding and ultimate enlightenment. And the reader has no choice but to identify with Job.

At this point, we are anxiously awaiting God's response. We expect God to sit in the dock and shamefully admit his guilt. Instead, God goes on the offensive. He subjects Job to a series of speeches that essentially represent a grueling examination. No surprise here. Job has made an extraordinary claim. Not only does he possess the key to the most complex moral issues of the universe, he alleges a thorough understanding of the moral principles that govern God's actions. That God would want to test the extent of Job's newfound and astonishing expertise is only to be expected (38:2–3; 40:2, 7).

In this section, Yahweh draws ever-tightening circles around Job. He begins by questioning him about the process inherent to the creation of the world (38:4–11). God then moves to an exploration of the mechanisms that govern the operation of the universe (38:12–38). On both counts, Job remains silent. God then shifts to an easier field of inquiry, something Job has some experience with: the animal kingdom (38:39–39:30). But again, Job is found wanting (40:4–5).

Evidently, these are not fair questions. Consequently, God moves to something even closer to him: the human species. God challenges Job to bring his deep understanding of reality to human affairs and asks whether he has a comprehensive solution to the problems plaguing human society (40:10–14). Again, Job remains silent.

Human psychology turns out to be just on the perimeter of Job's vast field of expertise. So Yahweh proposes simpler beasts for him to consider: the hippopotamus (40:15–24) and the crocodile (41:1–34).[31] Surely Job, who has claimed to have infallible insights into the very person of God, should at least be able to explain the behavior of these seemingly simple beasts. But Job remains utterly powerless to do so.

What is the significance of Yahweh's speeches? First, we need to consider carefully the oversimplified moral theory proposed by Job's dialogue partners. It is too obvious to ignore. Though they make a partially valid point, it is taken to absurd lengths. It is so absurd and reductionistic that the reader cannot avoid postulating the hypothesis that, whenever God speaks, he will surely address the incongruity of the moral framework put forward so uniformly by the friends. The Hymn to Wisdom in chap. 28 provides an important hint with regard to the meaning of these speeches. The essence of this hymn goes against the grain of everything said by all the actors, including Job and Elihu. Contrary to what the speakers have so confidently stated throughout their speeches, figuring out where wisdom lies is no simple matter. Ultimate reality is not as easily accessible as they have claimed. It stubbornly resists any attempt to reduce it to a simple formula.

Yahweh's response reminds the reader that the universe is not anthropocentric but theocentric. Job had come to see himself as the center of the universe and called on God to take the stand like a vulgar criminal. Yahweh assumes instead the role of the inquisitor: "Gird up your loins like a man; I will question you, and you shall declare to me" (38:3). God's categorical refusal to play the role of the accused clarifies his status. He is the creator and we are creatures. The Yahweh speeches expand on the epistemological hint offered in the Hymn to Wisdom (especially 28:28). In order to gain real insight into the human condition, men and women must first position themselves appropriately with regard to God. In other words, human beings must recognize their intrinsic epistemological limitation. God's answer implies that Job needs much more than a rational response; he needs a new perspective. And this leads us into the second point.

Job is utterly unable to answer any of the questions that God puts to him. The implication is glaring. If Job cannot explain the mechanisms that govern the created order, how can he pretend to provide a comprehensive explanation of moral reality and the creator himself? Job, his three friends, and Elihu all suffer from the same epistemological malaise. They all believe that the most basic moral laws of the universe are transparent. The Yahweh speeches make the point that, if the relatively simple laws of the physical universe are not

---

31. On the precise identity of "Behemoth" and "Leviathan," see Konkel, *Job*, 230–33; and David Wolfers, *Deep Things out of Darkness*, 161–93.

transparent, how much less the spiritual laws that govern the moral universe. Relative to the first, the latter represents an exponential leap. If we entertain any hope of gaining real insights into the great enigmas that plague humanity, we must first cultivate an accurate awareness of our limits.

C. S. Lewis expressed a similar idea in *Mere Christianity*:

> It is no good asking for a simple religion. After all, real things are not simple. They look simple, but they are not. . . . A child saying a child's prayer looks simple. And if you are content to stop there, well and good. But if you are not—and the modern world usually is not—if you want to go on and ask what is really happening—then you must be prepared for something difficult. If we ask for something more than simplicity, it is silly then to complain that the something more is not simple.[32]

The primary purpose of the Yahweh speeches is to force Job and, by association, the reader to reflect on their status in the universe. Are we creatures or are we gods? Are we contingent or autonomous?

Idolatry represents one of the major themes found in biblical wisdom literature. This is also the issue that drives the book of Job. But what is idolatry? Our definition is often too rudimentary. Idolatry is most commonly defined as the outward worship of the physical representation of one or more deities. We know that the practice is abhorrent to God, but the exact reasons often elude us. Cynics attribute God's displeasure to the small-minded pettiness of a god who cannot stand to have any competition. However, the perniciousness of idolatry extends far beyond the mere act of bowing down before a cultic object. At the very core of idolatry, there is a set of ideas and values, a world view that essentially negates life and promotes dehumanization and oppression. God hates idolatry because idolatry always generates death and chaos.

The problem of undeserved suffering is *not* the book of Job's real concern; it is simply a pretext. The real issue is idolatry. At its most basic level, idolatry constitutes a process of reduction that ultimately collapses the majestic complexity of reality and of God. Idolatry is ultimately a process that turns God into our own image.[33] In the book of Job, everyone, including Job, reduces reality, truth, and God to a simple formula.

In order to address the problem of the reader's idolatry, the author engineers the book in such a way as to force the reader to identify fully with Job. The most insidious aspect of idolatry is that we are not naturally aware of it. It is akin to pride, which a person can harbor for a long time without realizing

---

32. C. S. Lewis, *Mere Christianity* (New York: HarperSanFrancisco, 2001) 40.
33. See Rom 1:18–23.

it has infected every aspect of his or her personality. And as with pride, only a metaphorical slap in the face can make people aware of idolatry's hold.

Because of the insidious nature of idolatry and its opaqueness in our own lives, the book of Job adopts a two-pronged strategy. First, it lures the reader into fully identifying with Job. Throughout the book, it becomes clear that the three friends and Elihu are blindly committed to an ideological mantra. They do not really care about truth. They obsessively and narcissistically worship the Formula—the unified theory that infuses their world with meaning. But ironically, Job also worships the Formula. He even admits as much. In his final response to God (42:1–6), Job concedes that he did not have all the data at his disposal to arrive at such sure conclusions. He also recognizes that his understanding of God was more akin to a caricature than reality: "I had heard of you by the hearing of the ear, but now my eye sees you" (42:5). Job was basing his entire understanding of ultimate reality on hearsay, not facts. He too had become guilty of reducing his understanding of reality and God to a simple formula. But here is the surprise ending. As we the readers recognize the reductionism of Job's formula (it is always easier to recognize idolatry in others), it simultaneously dawns on us that we too are guilty of the same, for we have become one with Job!

Conclusion: Beware of Idolatrous Mantras

The book of Job does not intend to provide a response to the problem of undeserved pain, for the text provides no clear solution to this vexing question. Job's desperate condition and the quasi-comical process that leads him there are designed to capture the reader's attention and to compel him or her to identify fully with Job against everyone else, even God. Until the Yahweh speeches, the reader's sympathy for Job is maintained and nurtured by a clever series of literary devices.

The primary intent of the book of Job is to uncover humanity's intrinsic and nearly overwhelming tendency to define God and reality in terms of re-ductionistic constructs, which, in turn, become ideological grids through which we evaluate human experience. This process is so inherent to human nature in origin (Gen 3) and overwhelming in its implementation that we are virtually blind to it. It is only when we are somehow caught "red-handed" or rhetori-cally "trapped" that it becomes transparent. David's affair with Bathsheba and eventually taking responsibility for his sin are an excellent example of this principle. It is only when Nathan "reports" on the outrageous and unjust be-havior of a rich man toward a poor peasant and David realizes that he in fact is the man that the enormity of his sin finally dawns on him. His transgression only becomes transparent to him when he is indirectly "trapped" by Nathan's parable (2 Sam 12).

Similarly, the intent of the book of Job is to "catch" the unwary reader and thus to precipitate an acute awareness of the reductionistic constructs he or she may have come to embrace. Most men and women are extraordinarily predisposed to retreat into the illusionary safety of ideological mantras when facing complex issues. Of course, some may wonder where the harm is in all of this. The fact is that we live and die by the ideas we hold to be true. Any form of reductionism that distorts our perception of truth or impedes our ability to face reality, whether it applies to the nature of God or to other aspects of our lives, always entails some degree of harm. The more reductionistic and pervasive the mantra proves to be, the more chaos it will generate.

How can one discern this sort of ideological reductionism? While this discussion could be the object of another essay, three hints will suffice for now. First, those who embrace ideological mantras are often willing to sacrifice human lives, either by commission or by omission, to demonstrate the validity of their ideology. Second, an ideological mantra is sometimes recognizable by its ability to be reduced to an aphorism, a catchphrase, a rallying cry, or a slogan. Third, those who embrace ideological mantras often resort to the systematic creation of straw men to characterize the alternatives.

An Afterthought? The Epilogue (42:7–17)

If the book of Job were a mediocre piece of literature, it would end with Job's act of repentance in 42:6. But it is a masterpiece. As there was a prologue, so there is an epilogue.[34] Contrary to what many have proposed, the epilogue is a critical component of the book of Job. First, God offers a final verdict on the participants' positions. Eliphaz and his two friends are rebuked for what they said. Interestingly, Elihu is not mentioned. Scholars either puzzle over this omission or ignore it altogether.[35] The omission is extremely significant, for it denotes Elihu's complete and utter irrelevance. The astute reader will not miss the irony. He who claimed to possess the truth and hold the key

---

34. The literary integrity and the purpose of the epilogue have been debated at length by scholars. For a brief discussion of the issues, see Rowley, *Job*, 8–12, 15–18; Carol A. Newsom, "The Book of Job," in *1 and 2 Maccabees, Introduction to Hebrew Poetry, Job, Psalms* (NIB 4; Nashville: Abingdon, 1996) 634–37; Barbara Green, "Recasting a Classic: A Reconsideration of Meaning in the Book of Job," *New Blackfriars* 74/870 (April 1993) 213–22; Gordis, *The Book of Job*, 575–76; and Geevarughese Mathew, *The Role of the Epilogue in the Book of Job* (Ann Arbor, MI: Tyndale, 1997).

35. See, for example, Hartley, *The Book of Job*, 538; Janzen, *Job*, 262–67; and Konkel, *Job*, 239–40.

that would finally unlock Job's dilemma finds himself not only silenced but, what is worse, completely ignored. To be ignored is the ultimate affront. The omission signals that Elihu's position does not deserve any consideration whatsoever. Individuals who worship reductionistic formulas will also be deemed insignificant.

As for Job, God affirms his integrity and restores him. He is also ushered into a more enviable position than the one he enjoyed before his ordeal. But does not this new development signal an endorsement of the law of retribution? Is the point of the book then to reaffirm that old principle? This apparent inconsistency needs some explanation.

First, as I have attempted to demonstrate throughout this essay, the real issue of contention is not the law of retribution but the human tendency to embrace reductionistic moral formulas. Second, the principle of the law of retribution is not invalidated. While the friends and Elihu take it to absurd lengths, we need not throw out the baby with the bathwater. There is validity to the notion of integrity and justice as the basic components of a long and prosperous life, and to deception and wickedness as the portents of a short and miserable existence.[36] This axiom *usually* holds true, even if sometimes a righteous person gets a raw deal or a wicked person prospers. Third, the principle that links happiness to ethics is generally true, because there is a personal God who has imposed a moral order in the world and who ensures that this order is not unduly violated.[37] Job's restoration is a necessary component in confirming Yahweh's moral character.

In the ancient Near Eastern world, there was no intrinsic link between divine power and morality. The originality of the Hebrew faith was to propose a God who was both all-powerful and intrinsically moral.[38] It is thus extremely important that Job be restored in order to maintain the notion of a moral and ethical God. By reestablishing Job to his former position, the author affirms that there is in fact a common and universal understanding of justice and righteousness. We do not know everything about God, but what we know we can trust. God is not just the utterly Other who cannot be meaningfully described. There is a bridge linking the God of the universe and humanity, a bridge we can safely cross, thus enabling us to live with confidence.

---

36. This principle is well attested in the deuteronomic tradition, the book of Proverbs, the Psalms, and the prophetic literature.

37. See, for instance, Pss 37 and 73.

38. C. S. Lewis discusses this idea in *The Problem of Pain* (New York: HarperSanFrancisco, 1940) 1–15.

Church of Justice

ALFRED NEUFELD
Professor of Systematic Theology
Universidad Evangélica del Paraguay
Asunción, Paraguay

Alix Losano, a Colombian Mennonite theologian, presented her concept of local churches functioning as "sanctuaries of peace" at a symposium of historic peace churches. The meetings were held at the Theological Seminary in Bienenberg, near Basel, Switzerland. Here a group of theologians explored the peace witness of the church within the wider society. The concept of "sanctuaries of peace" grew out of the Colombian experience of violence and civil war over a period of several decades. Ricardo Esquivia, a black Colombian Mennonite lawyer, developed the idea from the OT law of Israel's "cities of refuge." Ricardo, founder of the *Institute Justa Paz* in Bogotá, proposed that every local church should become a refuge of peace and a place where enemies can talk to each other, exploring possibilities of reconciliation.[1]

The question I started pondering after these meetings was how local churches could become "sanctuaries of justice." Of course—to proclaim justice, to prophetically denounce injustice, and to pursue peace as the fruit of justice—these ideas had already been part of my thinking as part of the agenda of the historic peace churches. But to be "a church of justice," like "a sanctuary of peace," seemed to me something even more radical. It would imply that the church, especially the local church, as representative of God's new humanity would be a community of justice, providing models of justice and exploring new and innovative ways of establishing and administrating justice.

I am no OT theologian and only had some NT studies as part of the *Theologiegeschichte* in my doctoral study program in the field of mission theology at the *Staatsunabhängige Theologische Hochschule* in Basel, Switzerland. But OT theologians such as Profs. Elmer Martens and Waldemar Janzen have been esteemed teachers and also dear friends to me. Both have always complained

---

1. Alix Losano, "Being a Peace Church in the Colombian Context," in *Seeking Cultures of Peace* (Telford, PA: Cascadia, 2004) 147–54; and Alfred Neufeld, *Vivir desde el futuro de Dios* (Buenos Aires: Kairós, 2006) 459–60.

that Anabaptist Mennonite theology seems to have forgotten the OT, the Bible of Jesus. Waldemar Janzen went as far as to say that, when he introduces himself at various meetings as a Mennonite theologian, some of his colleagues wonder if there is any difference between a Marcionite and a Mennonite!

Elmer Martens's outline of a fourfold design in OT theology[2] greatly influenced me when I sat in his classes back in 1982. He was well respected by students but was also known to generate some fear because of his exacting demands. There was never discussion about Elmer's motivation, however. He was a fair professor and·a seminary president with a high sense of justice and responsibility. His magnificent book *God's Design* served me in Latin America as a main text for the college-level classes that I taught in Asunción. We actually produced an unauthorized Spanish translation of his textbook that my colleagues continue to use to this day!

When I began to explore the NT idea of the "church of justice," I realized right away that everything on this topic leads to the OT, to the idea of the people of God, to Elmer's four basic concepts of OT theology: (1) deliverance and liberation, (2) covenant community and alternative society, (3) knowledge of God, the God of justice, and (4) shalom and the new order of life within the "promised land," present and future.

Jesus and the Community of Justice

There is no doubt that justice and righteousness are very prominent topics in the life and teaching of Jesus. The preaching ministry of John the Baptist already focused mainly on doing justice, on making the ways straight, and on repenting from injustice (Matt 3:1–12; Luke 3:1–20). His sermon on justice challenged King Herod so severely that he sent John to prison and had him killed later on. Now it is important to realize that the ministry of John the Baptist is closely linked to the coming of 'the kingdom of heaven' (*basileia tōn ouranōn*, Matt 3:2).

Jesus begins his ministry by picking up the message of John the Baptist on repentance and the closeness of the kingdom (Matt 4:17). The first major instruction Jesus gives his community of disciples in the Sermon on the Mount focuses on justice and on the kingdom. At least three beatitudes cover the topic: the spiritually poor will inherit the kingdom (Matt 5:3); blessed are those who hunger and thirst for justice (5:6); and blessed are those who are persecuted for the sake of righteousness (5:10). In v. 20, he sums up his teaching in

---

2. Elmer Martens, *God's Design: A Focus on Old Testament Theology* (Grand Rapids: Baker, 1981).

contrast to the Scribes and Pharisees, stating that only "a better righteousness" will enable his disciples to enter the kingdom.

In the Lord's Prayer, the disciples are taught to pray wholeheartedly for the coming of the kingdom and to pray for the Lord's will to be done on earth as it is in heaven. This is nothing other than striving for righteousness on earth, as righteousness and justice is done in heaven, where God's rule is complete. And this is precisely what Jesus wants his disciples to set their minds on, instead of worrying about food and drink and clothes: "Seek first the kingdom of God and his righteousness" (Matt 6:33).[3]

The Sermon on the Mount ends with a call to do the will of God and to move beyond the rhetorical or liturgical realm (Matt 7:21). "Evildoers" have no part in the kingdom. Their houses will be destroyed by the floods because, although they know justice, they do not do justice (Matt 7:21–27). And in the last judgment, the doers of righteousness will be the blessed ones who inherit the kingdom, because what they did to the needy, they did to Jesus. This is why they are labeled righteous, in contrast to the condemned, who did not practice what is right (Matt 25:31–46).

The kingdom of heaven—the kingdom of God and his righteousness—"is a comprehensive symbol," including humanity's relationship with God but also the many relationships within humanity. "Indeed, it encompasses creation as a whole. It has a *future* dimension, necessarily so because this world is presently still deeply in need of mending. It also implies a strong *present* expression of God's reign and rule whenever the power of God comes to expression."[4]

Tim Geddert, analyzing the kingdom of God language in the Gospels, notes that the meaning of "your kingdom come" in the Lord's Prayer is given in the next line of the prayer: "your will be done on earth as it is in heaven" (Matt 6:10). In other words, "God's kingdom is in the process of coming as God's purposes are accomplished in the world, particularly in and through God's people."[5] Furthermore, according to Mark's Gospel, "God's reign is established as Jesus does the works of God, calls disciples, works in them and through them, and leads them in the way of the cross, and so on. It involves living by God's values rather than human values."[6]

But what kind of justice are we talking about? In his essay on righteousness within the groundbreaking work of his commentary on Paul's letter to the

---

3. Translations of biblical texts are my own, unless otherwise noted.

4. Tom Yoder Neufeld, *Recovering Jesus: The Witness of the New Testament* (Grand Rapids: Brazos, 2007) 137–38.

5. Timothy J. Geddert, *Mark* (Believers Church Bible Commentary; Scottdale, PA: Herald, 2001) 423.

6. Ibid., 423.

Romans, John E. Toews states: "The background to righteousness in Paul is Hebrew (*tsedeq/tsedaqah*) and the Greek (*dikaiosynē*), not Latin. In the ancient world righteousness language generally was relational, ethical language. The basic meaning was the right ordering of things. It was associated with the ancient Near Eastern concept of cosmic and/or social order."[7] Thus, righteousness in the OT is about faithfulness within the demands of relationship, either with God or with fellow human beings. Actions or behaviors are righteous if they build the relationship and support the social order of which they are a part.

The community of disciples and believers that Jesus gathered and instructed was to become the future church and the community of justice. Karl Barth concludes that the church as a community is highly interested in justice because God is not a God of disorder but of peace (1 Cor 14:33). "Wie könnte die Kirche vom Staat Recht erwarten und sich zugleich dem Recht selber verschliessen? . . . Kirchliche Autorität ist geistliche, d.h. mit dem Zeugnis des Heiligen Geistes rechnende Autorität. Ist sie darum weniger strenge, ist sie nicht gerade so die strengste Autorität?"[8] And he sustains a model, claiming that the light from the heavenly city falls on the earthly *ekklesia* and from there reflects itself in the earthly polis: "Das von der himmlischen Polis auf die irdische Ecclesia herabfallende reflektiert sich in einem von der irdischen Ecclesia auf die irdische Polis hinüberfallenden Licht."[9]

Acts: The Holy Spirit and the Church of Justice

Acts is the story of the newly founded apostolic church in the power of the Spirit. It is the community of the new covenant, where the new Spirit takes away the "heart of stone" and provides a heart that walks in the laws of the Lord and keeps his commandments (Ezek 36:26–27). The new covenant consists of the writing of God's law into the hearts and minds of God's people, so that they walk in the knowledge of God (Jer 31:33–34). With the coming of the Spirit comes a new willingness and enablement to live and pursue justice. Individuals who walk according to the Spirit fulfill the righteousness required by the law (Rom 8:4). Peter's first Spirit-filled message, in Acts 2, ends with an assertion similar to the one made by John the Baptist: "Repent, and be baptized," and "save yourselves from this corrupt generation" (Acts 2:38, 40, NIV). In their defense before the Jewish authorities, Peter and John appeal to their

---

7. John E. Toews, *Romans* (Believers Church Bible Commentary; Scottdale, PA: Herald, 2004) 401.

8. Karl Barth, *Rechtfertigung und Recht: Christengemeinde und Bürgergemeinde* (4th ed.; Zurich: Theologischer Verlag, 1989) 33–34.

9. Ibid., 35.

sense of justice and righteousness: "Is it right in the sight of God to obey you more than to obey God?" (Acts 4:19).

The new Spirit-filled community had a new sense of social justice. Interest in private property was subordinated to the needs of the community. No one was to suffer need; lying to God and the community, as Ananias and Sapphira did, was severely punished by divine justice (Acts 5:1–16). Peter understood the lesson well and told the high priest: "It is more important to obey God than to obey men" (5:29), and "the Holy Spirit is given to those who are willing to obey God" (5:32).

It is also necessary to place the genesis of diaconal theology and diaconal practice in the context of social justice. The reason for selecting deacons was to deal with the injustice and unrest within the community due to the unfair treatment of Greek widows compared with Hebrew widows (Acts 6:1). The apostles appealed to the need for establishing justice within the community. They also recognized that it was not right for them to neglect the preaching of God's word in order to do table service. The three conditions in choosing deacons were: good testimony, wisdom, and fullness of the Holy Spirit. All three can be related to a lifestyle of justice.

The whole story of Peter and Cornelius has to do with cross-cultural communication and with overcoming unjust ethnocentrism and cultural arrogance. Through this experience, Peter probably learned more about justice than Cornelius: "Now I realize truthfully that God does not show partiality, but all people that fear him and do right [*ergazomenos dikaiosynēn*] are accepted by him" (Acts 10:34–35). Again, the criterion for being part of God's covenant community is doing what is right or just.

The Apostolic Council in Acts 15 must also be seen as the struggle of the early church to become a community of justice. It would not be right to put a heavy yoke on the new Gentile believers that the Jewish believers were not able to bear themselves (15:11). The wise and very Jewish James sees the need to 'judge' (*krinō*) within the community and to establish a rule that the Gentile Christians should not be "bothered" by the Jewish Christians anymore on matters of Jewish tradition or religious culture (15:19).

The final imprisonment of Paul in Jerusalem and his deportation to Rome are also concerned with matters of justice. In order to have him arrested, the crowd accused him of taking Trophimus of Ephesus into the temple. Although this was a false accusation, Paul did not defend himself. Surely he was convinced that an authentic follower of the Messiah Jesus such as Trophimus had every right to step into the temple of Israel (Acts 21:27–30). When Paul was again in prison, Felix enjoyed listening to him. Paul did not hesitate in instructing Felix about "justice, self-control, and the coming judgment" (Acts 24:25).

Although Felix gave very clear signs that Paul's freedom could be bought with money, the apostle was unwilling to bribe him. Not only would a bribe have given him freedom to preach the gospel, but it was probably very common in the culture of his time.

Corinthians: Conflicts and the Need for Christian Judges

Moisés Mayordomo once called the church of Corinth a "conflict factory."[10] There were disputing parties who championed their identities by appealing to founding figures such as Peter, Paul, and Apollos (1 Cor 1:10–13; 3:5–9). There were believers who tried to "resolve" their conflicts by going to the secular courts (6:1–7). However, actions of this sort were highly problematic because lawsuits tended to favor the rich. More conflict emerged among the so-called weak and strong (1 Cor 8–10). Conflict erupted over the symbolic representation of gender roles in worship (11:2–16). Still another conflict, having to do with differences between the rich and poor, manifested itself during the Lord's Supper (11:18–34). There were arguments about the value of the more spectacular charismatic gifts (1 Cor 12–14) and the future resurrection of Christians (1 Cor 15). The entire letter of 1 Corinthians seems to be a call for the exercise of fair judgment within the community of believers, where mediation is the tool to resolve conflicts.

The precondition for a "church of justice" is that it must have "the mind of Christ" (1 Cor 2:16). Jesus himself is the place where believers find their identity in the newly reconfigured people of God; they are *en Christō*. Thus, we participate in his 'wisdom' (*sophia*), 'justice' (*dikaiosynē*), 'sanctification' (*hagiasmos*), and 'redemption' (*apolytrōsis*; 1 Cor 1:30). These four qualities of Jesus and of the Christian seem to belong together.

The 'spiritual person' (*pneumatikos*) 'judges all things' (*anakrinei panta*), but no one is able to judge him or her (1 Cor 2:15). It is evident that Paul is not speaking of highly sophisticated spiritual leaders in the church but of common people within the church membership. Of course, there are leaders with a very poor capacity to judge (1 Cor 3:1–4; 3:3–4), and it is also important to be modest and not to judge things too hastily (1 Cor 4:5).

Even the work of church leaders will be judged by "fire." And church leaders who have not used durable materials to build up their congregation will see that their work is not "fire proof." They will be saved "as out of fire," but their work will not resist the "proof of fire" (1 Cor 3:9–18).[11]

---

10. Moisés Mayordomo, "Paul as Mediator in Seeking Cultures of Peace," in *Seeking Cultures of Peace* (Telford, PA: Cascadia, 2004) 173.

11. See also Neufeld, *Vivir desde el futuro de Dios*, 361–73.

Paul makes it very clear that the local church is something like a community of judges and a society of justice:

If any of you has a dispute with another, dare he take it before the ungodly for judgment instead of before the saints? Do you not know that the saints will judge the world? And if you are to judge the world, are you not competent to judge trivial cases? Do you not know that we will judge angels? How much more the things of this life! . . . I say this to shame you. Is it possible that there is nobody among you wise enough to judge a dispute between believers? (1 Cor 6:1–3, 5, NIV).

The call to resist going to worldly courts carries with it a positive injunction: bring cases of community conflict to the church and its saints, because they will one day judge the world and the angels. What a shame it is if in a local congregation there is no one able to discern justice between sisters and brothers of the congregation!

The strong assertion of the Apostle Paul, that there ought to be judges within the local congregation, has an important limitation. Judgment within the congregation has a completely different character from judgment outside the congregation. "What reason would I have to judge those that are outside? Do you not judge those that are inside? Because those that are outside, God will judge" (1 Cor 5:9–13). In all three cases, the crucial and critical word *krinō* is used for our words 'critique' and 'judgment'.

The topic of justice is central to the community of believers and can be found in all the rest of Pauline literature. In 2 Corinthians, Paul describes his whole ministry as a ministry that preaches justice (2 Cor 3:9). And as ambassadors of Christ, we preach justice that is valid in the eyes of God (2 Cor 5:21). The Christian battle is waged with "weapons of justice" (2 Cor 6:7). Christians protect themselves with the "breast plate of justice" (Eph 6:14). The new human is created in the image of God, with "justice and holiness" (Eph 4:24). And the Christian church will be full of the "fruit of justice" for the day of Christ's return (Phil 1:11). The young Timothy is urged to flee all desires of materialism and instead to pursue "righteousness" (1 Tim 6:11).

Romans: Justification and a Life of Justice

There can be no question that righteousness and "the justice that is valid in the eyes of God" are the central topics in Romans. However, the forensic justice by which Luther claims to have rediscovered the gospel does not deal adequately with the biblical text. John E. Toews claims that justice and righteousness in Romans ought to be defined in a more coherent way—a way more true to its OT roots. According to Toews, the "protestant paradigm" may be summarized as follows: (1) God is perfectly righteous. (2) Righteous-ness is a requirement for personal salvation. (3) Humanity is unable to be righ-teous. (4) Humanity can only stand in God's merciful declaration of legal right standing. (5) God declares human beings righteous by a legal declaration (a forensic act).[12] However, Toews claims that this "protestant paradigm" must be challenged in order to recover the "covenant language" that is "concerned with right relationships within the covenant community."[13]

It is true that righteousness is often associated with "judgment," such as when the "rightness" of a relationship was determined "at the village gate," a place of legal judgment in ancient Israel. So, in one sense, righteousness is a legal term. The person who is righteous is judged to be in the right; and what is right is what meets the demands of relationship in community. "The func-tion of the judge is to maintain the community, and to restore the right to those from whom it has been taken. Thus righteousness as legal language is not concerned with an impartial legal decision between two people but rather with protecting and restoring relationships in community."[14]

Toews makes the case that the Jewish understanding of righteousness—as concern for social-ethical relations within the faith community—was identical to the old Greek idea held by Aristotle. "The same fundamental meaning is also apparent in *Aristotle*, the key definer of the term in Greek literature. Righteousness concerns behavior that is right and good for the city state (*polis*), the basic political association of Greek civilization. The concern is the right ordering and well-being of the community as a whole."[15]

However, a shift in the meaning of righteousness came with Augustine and with the translation of ecclesial language into Latin. "His discussion of righteousness is the first significant exposition in the early church, and it estab-lishes the framework for future discussions. The language in Augustine shifts from Hebrew and Greek to Latin. That transference results in a fundamental alteration in the concept of righteousness, from a theologically centered under-standing to a human centered one."[16]

According to Toews, Luther's understanding of righteousness in Romans has brought more damage than good to the biblical understanding of the con-cept: "The shift introduced by Augustine becomes a landslide with Martin Luther. The basic meaning of righteousness becomes a legal (forensic) dec-laration that a person has right status with God, or is acceptable before God."[17]

---

12. Toews, *Romans*, 404.
13. Ibid., 404.
14. Ibid., 401.
15. Ibid., 402.
16. Ibid.
17. Ibid., 403.

Thus, "the righteousness of God" describes God's gift of right status given to sinful human beings. In other words, righteousness involves a change of status, not a transformation of being or nature. "To be made righteous is an act of God external to humanity; the alien toward humanity, not an act of God within human beings. The wicked are not made righteous, as in Augustine, but only proclaimed righteous."[18]

Luther's interpretation of the gospel message is a completely new development. He embraces the human-centered half of Augustine but not the ethical-political half. Luther transforms the social-political-ethical language of the gospel into the psychological-salvation language of the Enlightenment. Thus, "righteousness has nothing to do with relationships in the believing community or with the ordering of the world. Being made righteous is something that happens to an individual believer when in faith he or she accepts Christ's atonement on the cross."[19]

In my personal opinion, the forensic dimension is definitely present in NT language about justice, justification, and righteousness. However, since the 16th-century Reformation, it has been tremendously overemphasized, to the determent of the Greek-Hebrew idea of restoration of right social relationships. In my view, there is a dialectical dynamic and tension between "imputed justification" and "realized justification" in the sense of effective transformation toward the life of justice in right relationships. And this must be seen within the biblical dynamics of a life of sanctification, fullness of the Holy Spirit, and surrender to the lordship of Christ.

James: Justification and a Life of Justice

Anabaptist theology has always claimed that righteousness in Romans and righteousness in James are not contradictory, as Luther sometimes seems to suggest. Of course, any attempt to hold both Paul and James together is impossible within a forensic understanding of righteousness. Only a more holistic Greek-Jewish idea of right relationships has the capacity to do this.

I suggest that the clue to this perspective is found in the key verse of James: "For as the body without the spirit is dead, so also faith without works is dead" (2:26). The *soma-pneuma* image actually is a powerful metaphor of the interrelatedness of faith and life. Spirits without bodies are as unrealistic and as useless as bodies without spirits. Actually, our very existence as "psychosomatic" beings makes it clear that *pistis* and *erga* combine in a living organism of body and spirit. Where there is separation of body and spirit, there is death.

---

18. Ibid.
19. Ibid.

James abounds in works of the spirit and works of faith; where they are present, there is 'divine righteousness' (*dikaiosynē theou*, 1:20–22). This is why hearing and doing grow out of a life rooted in the "perfect law of freedom" (1:22–25). And this life results in pure church service, which consists of doing justice for widows and orphans (1:26–27).

It is not coherent with the justice of faith to discriminate against persons within the congregation (2:1–9). This is not right and is rooted in wrong judgment (2:4). What is right and lawful is a life lived according to the law of love (2:8). The fruit of justice has to do with wisdom, because the wisdom "from above" results in the fruit of righteousness and peace (3:13–18).

To judge a brother or sister by way of condemnation is unjust, because whoever does this puts himself/herself above God and above the law (4:11–12). What is needed is closeness to God (4:8), resistance to the devil (4:7), a humble walk before God (4:10), a life of subordination and dependence to the will of God (4:15), and an attitude predisposed to doing good (4:17).

Wealthy people in the congregation who do not pay fair salaries to their employees will face God's judgment (5:4–6). God listens to the cry of individuals who are suffering injustice. If church members complain against each other, they will face judgment, because the judge is at the door (5:9).

Honest relationships and the integrity of a person's "yes" and "no" are crucial within the congregation. The brothers and sisters who swear oaths but do not follow through on their "yes" and their "no" are entitled to divine judgment (5:12).

A strong sense of communal justice is also present in the last verses of James (5:13–20). There is communal prayer in suffering, communal Psalm-singing on good days, calling of elders and anointing with oil in cases of sickness, communal confession of sins, and intercessory prayers for healing. "The prayer of the just [*dikaiou*] is powerful, if it is sincere" (5:16).

Justice for James seems to be linked very closely to 'truth' (*alētheia*) and walking on the right path (5:19–20). In this sense, even brothers and sisters in the congregation need to 'convert' (*epistrephō*), if they get onto a 'wrong path' (*planē hodou*). To bring them back onto the right path (that is to walk again in truth and justice) means saving them 'from death' (*ek thanatou*).

Hebrews: Backsliding and Persevering in the Community of Justice

Definitely the most Jewish book in the NT along with the Gospel of Matthew is the Letter to the Hebrews. It starts with an OT vision of the Messiah (Ps 45:7–8), who rules with justice and who loves justice and hates injustice (Heb 1:8–9). And it puts the Messiah into an eschatological context where heaven and earth will vanish, but the Messiah and his justice will prevail (1:10–12).

But then, again and again, Hebrews covers the topic of backsliding, of not reaching the goal, or of taking the wrong direction. Jesus was faithful. That is why we too ought to be faithful (3:2–6), because we have become part of Christ (3:14). And disobedience makes it impossible to reach the goal and enter divine rest (3:18). This is why we must be eager not to leave anyone behind (4:1) because everything is open to the eyes of God, to whom we are accountable (4:13). This is why our high priest, Jesus, can identify with our weakness, and we can trust him (4:15–16).

Backsliding or staying immature is extremely dangerous and can even become fatal (6:1–9). But God is not unjust and will not forget our works and our love (6:10). The new covenant with the high priest Messiah Jesus is actualized as God's law is inscribed on the minds and hearts of the new covenant community (8:10). And the new tabernacle is already the new creation of God (9:11). This is why he has been able to make atonement once and for all, the atonement valid for the last judgment (9:27).

The result of this divine intervention is the cleansing of heart and body, deliverance from a bad conscience (10:22). It remains necessary, however, to watch over each other, to grow in love and good works, and not to sin anymore (10:24–26). Willful sinning is a terribly dangerous thing and will not escape God's judgment (10:31). Backsliding is very destructive to the church, because it compromises the church's identity as representatives of the new society of life and justice.

The heroes of faith and the cloud of witnesses (Heb 11) had a common characteristic—they persevered in obedience. This is why we are called to rid ourselves of sins and burdens and to run with patience, keeping our eyes on Jesus, the initiator and completer of our faith (12:2). The community of believers arrives at Mount Zion, the heavenly Jerusalem (12:22). It is the gathering of the 'spirits of the just ones, those that have attained the goal' (*kai pneumasi dikaiōn teteleiōmenōn*, 12:23).

The whole exhortation in the last chapter encourages a life of familial love (13:1). This life is inspired by joining the one "who suffered outside the camp" (13:13). We have no permanent city here but seek the future city (13:14). Jesus, our good shepherd, enables us through the blood of his covenant to do "everything good," creating in us things that please him (13:21).

Teachers and pastors are accountable for the lives of the community of believers. This is why it is necessary to attend to the leadership of these elders, that they may do this ministry with joy and without complaint (13:17).

The strong admonitions in Hebrews against backsliding and the promotion of faithfulness as modeled by Jesus bear clear testimony to the idea of the church as a community of faithful followers of Jesus, the righteous high priest and "senior pastor" (13:20).

The Coming of the End
and the Justice of the Kingdom of God

Helmut Isaak has done us a great favor by publishing what was meant to be his doctoral dissertation, before his mentor died. The title of his book is *Menno Simons and the New Jerusalem.*[20] Helmut makes the case that, for the ethics of Menno Simons and his Anabaptist church, the image of the New Jerusalem was crucial. Christians have abandoned Babylon and have set their eyes on the Lord and now walk toward Jerusalem. Thus, their social order is now marked by the will of God and the power of his new creation. This view of the church is rooted clearly in biblical eschatology and has strong implications for the idea of justice within the community of believers.

My own theological journey has found great merit in beginning any discussion of Christian theology with eschatology. The college-level introduction to Christian theology that I have written, *Vivir desde el futuro de Dios,* does just this. In the book, I make the case that the church lives more from the future than from the past, more from the coming eon of the presence of the kingdom than from the vanishing eon of the powers of evil.

2 Peter 3:13 bluntly says that, according to the Lord's promise, we have our attention set on a new heaven and a new earth, 'in which justice dwells' (*en hois dikaiosynē katoikei*). The eschatological dimension of the church is crucial, but it is not only futuristic. The end-time age begins with the coming of the Spirit and the birth of the church and ends when Christ returns in glory. The precise chronology of events may continue to be debated. For me, it was very liberating to realize that time ceases once Christ returns. And where there is no time, there is no chronology—only realized eternity.

But the concept of time concerns us a great deal as we try to achieve clarity about the eschatological character of the church. There is agreement that the last judgment will be something in real time. It begins in Rev 19:11, where Christ appears on the white horse as King of Kings and Lord of Lords (19:16); his name is faithfulness and truthfulness, and 'with justice he judges and makes war' (*en dikaiosynē krinei kai polemei*, 19:11). All those found in the Book of Life are judged according to their works and the rest condemned (Rev 20:11–15).

---

20. Helmut Isaak, *Menno Simons and the New Jerusalem* (Kitchener, ON: Pandora, 2006).

But how shall we understand the matter of the New Jerusalem? It seems to be a reality that is present and future. The old earth and the old heaven flee from the face of the one sitting on the big white throne; they are not to be found anymore (20:11). But then the new heaven and new earth are suddenly visible, and the New Jerusalem descends from heaven (21:2). When did it start to descend from heaven? Did it not start with the coming of the Holy Spirit? And when did God begin to "tabernacle" among humanity (21:3)? Was it not when Jesus lived among us and we saw his glory, the glory of the father (John 1:14)? At least, in both cases the same word, 'tabernacle' (*skēnē*) and 'tabernacling' (*eskēnōsen*) among us is used. Is not the Holy Spirit the presence of the triune God on earth? And is not the church the tabernacle of God? The well-known covenant formula—"they will be his people and he will be their God" (Rev 21:3)—does not begin to be reality once this world comes to an end; rather, it begins at the very genesis of the people of God, a people gathered now around Jesus.

So, the question of new heaven and new earth as well as the coming down of the New Jerusalem is an eschatological phenomenon but not just a futuristic phenomenon. The whole project of the church actually is to bring down heaven onto earth. The whole project of the kingdom of God is to anticipate and extend what is yet to be realized perfectly: God's reign without any restrictions. Tom Yoder Neufeld is right when he says:

> Jesus believed God to be king already *now*, a loving sovereign whose rule has always shown itself in sustaining normal everyday life—a daily miracle brought about by the love of a creator, of a divine parent, of a father—*Abba*, as Jesus repeatedly calls God. That creator's love and care comes to expression in, for example, Jesus' healings and exorcisms, but also when people forgive each other, when they do not retaliate when abused, when they love their enemies—in short, when they exercise God's will in everyday social and economic relationships.[21]

When we look at the eschatological character of the church, we see two powerful topics that dominate the future but have implications for the present: the last judgment and the coming of the New Jerusalem. Actually, these two topics should inform the everyday agenda of the global and local church. Both carry on the decisive dimensions of justice: justice will be done in the last judgment, and the New Jerusalem is marked by justice. This allows and obligates us to make the case that the church must be a community of justice. Justice, with its concern for the inner life and for external witness, must rank high on the agenda of the church.

---

21. Yoder Neufeld, *Recovering Jesus*, 137–38.

Concluding Reflections

Two of my friends did their doctoral dissertations on the topic of bribing and corruption. The title of Paul Kleiner's project was *Bestechung: Eine theologisch-ethische Untersuchung*, and Karl Rennstich's title was *Korruption: Eine Herausforderung für Gesellschaft und Kirche.*[22] Both were missionaries, and both struggled with the question of what the church does and says in societies where corruption and bribing are part of the social system within which the church finds itself. An ecclesiology that focuses heavily on the church as the community of justice will have clear and convincing things to say on the topic to a wider society as well.

I was born and live in a country that has the largest split between rich and poor in all of Latin America. At the same time, more and more members of the faith community are active in public life. They pursue dimensions of social justice within their economic enterprises and take part in the political and economical leadership of the country. What frame of reference does the local church provide for these kinds of ministries?

Crime continues to be an issue that brings much anxiety to populations in the North and in the South. There is no question that crime violates human rights and diminishes the quality of life for the rest of population. But what is a redemptive way of dealing with criminals? And to what extent does a local church help to provide fair judgments, restorative justice, and social reintegration for former criminals and prison inmates?

Globalization brings new forces to the global economy and to global security. Fair trade policies are suspect in a global order dominated by a mix of free market, national interests, and domestic subsidies. One of the favorite expressions of the president of my country is: "It is better to be a cow in Europe than to be poor in the South." European governments spend more subsidy money on a cow each day than it takes for one person to make a living in Paraguay! The church of Christ is also a global church. Why is it unable to speak on behalf of global justice, if it is the one body of Christ, with voices from all parts of the globe?

History has not been fair. Relationships among various nations have not been marked by justice. As a matter of fact, there are many painful memories between fraternal nations. History textbooks teach our school children very different perspectives on the topic of justice. Paraguay is still suffering from the memories of a terrible war with Brazil, Argentina, and Uruguay 140 years ago.

---

22. Paul Kleiner, *Bestechung: Eine theologisch-ethische Untersuchung* (Bern: Peter Lang, 1992); and Karl Rennstich, *Korruption: Eine Herausforderung für Gesellschaft und Kirche* (Stuttgart: Quellverlag, 1990).

The outcome of the 1870 war was a loss of half of the territory and most of the male population. For every seven women, one man survived. Today, there are shared hydroelectric projects with Argentina and Brazil, but the treaty arrangements are unjust and unfair from the Paraguayan perspective. Does the church of justice have any chance to mediate historic injustices such as these? Recently, the presidents of 21 Latin American members of the National Council of Churches met to call the church to serve as facilitators of justice in relation to the real needs of historical injustices such as these.

One of the most devastating tragedies in our society has to do with marital conflict and divorce. Many related behaviors such as adultery, abuse, betrayal, and lying are usually part of the trajectory that leads to separation and divorce. For the historic peace churches, matters related to divorce and the breakup of marriages may well be one of the biggest contemporary challenges to peace theology and to peacemaking values. The matter of justice is crucial in marital conflict. Before couples go to a lawyer, the local church needs to demonstrate that it is truly a community of justice and compassion.

There is a wonderful movement going through the churches, the World Evangelical Alliance, and many Christian service and mission agencies; it is called the Micah Challenge (see www.micahchallenge.org). It centers on the three requests that Micah made of Israel: do justice, love mercy, and walk humbly before God (Mic 6:8). The Micah Challenge movement calls followers of Jesus and local congregations to aim at holistic transformation by becoming communities of justice, mercy, and humility. The movement also aims to influence the wider society and whole nations, because what is good for the church is good for society.

Chances are that initiatives of this sort and all the above-mentioned social challenges will not be very successful in the light of dominating realpolitik. But if the church is convinced that it is the only organism that will prevail in history, and if the mark of the new and coming Jerusalem is justice, then it has a right to dream big dreams and to make large claims. Was this not precisely what Moses understood (and what Elmer impressed upon us) when God revealed his fourfold design in Exod 6:1–13?

Righteousness in Romans:
The Political Subtext of Paul's Letter

JOHN E. TOEWS
Academic Dean and Professor of New Testament, Emeritus
Mennonite Brethren Biblical Seminary
Fresno, California

In this essay, I want to make more explicit the case that I outlined in my commentary on Paul's Letter to the Romans.[1] There, I argued that the primary concern of Romans is the politics of the church. The root of the word *political* is the Greek word for 'city' (*polis*). *Politics* is the organized living together of numbers of people. Anything is political that deals with how people live together in organized ways. Paul's primary concern in Romans was political not soteriological, as in traditional Christian interpretation since Augustine, both Catholic and Protestant.

Paul is writing a letter to churches in the capital of the 1st-century Roman Empire. He is not writing a letter to outline the order of salvation for guilt-ridden Christians in the 16th or 21st centuries. He is writing a letter to churches at the center of imperial power and politics. And he is writing to these churches following the exile of some members for approximately five years because of the politics involved in the relationships between these churches and their parent communities, the Jewish synagogues in Rome.[2]

Author's note: Prof. Elmer Martens is a longtime friend (1961–), faculty and administrative colleague at Mennonite Brethren Biblical Seminary (1977–95), and intellectual interlocutor. As biblical scholars, Elmer and I have talked often about righteousness in the OT and in Paul. As an administrator Elmer was concerned about leading justly. It is a privilege to honor Elmer and to continue the extended conversation about "righteousness" in the Christian Bible and in the life of the church in the world.

1. John E. Toews, *Romans* (Believers Church Bible Commentary; Scottdale, PA: Herald, 2004).

2. For more details, see ibid., 20–29, 370–71.

A Political Manifesto

Paul opens the letter by asserting that he has been called by God to proclaim 'the gospel of God' (_euanggelion theou_), which concerns God's "Son, the one having descended from David according to the flesh, the one having been appointed Son of God in power according to the Spirit of holiness by the resurrection from the dead, Messiah Jesus our Lord" (Rom 1:3–4). He concludes the final argument of the letter by declaring that this Son came in order that "the nations might glorify God because of his mercy" (15:9), that this Son is the Messiah ("the root of Jesse") who will "rule the nations" and be the center of hope for the nations (15:12). Paul's mission, stated at the beginning and end of the letter, is to promote "the faithful obedience among all the nations" (1:5; 15:18; 16:26). Paul greets his readers "from God our father and the Lord Messiah Jesus" (1:7). His mission in Rome is 'to preach the good news' (_euanggelisasthai_), because "he is not ashamed of the good news [_euanggelion_], because it is the power of God to salvation to all the faithful ones, Jews first and also Gentiles, because the end-time, world-transforming righteousness of God is revealed in it from faithfulness to faithfulness, and because as it has been written, 'the righteous one will live out of faithfulness'" (1:16–17).[3]

These are "fighting words," a declaration of an _intifada_ against Caesar and Roman imperial power and religion. Romans, Jacob Taubes declares, is "a political declaration of war on the Caesar."[4] The language "screams (counter) empire," says Diana Swancutt.[5]

Every word, so rich in Christian theological interpretation, is also loaded with political meaning—gospel, son of God, Lord, power, glorify, mercy, faithful (or loyal) obedience among the nations, rule the nations, hope for the nations, faith, father, salvation, righteousness. The referent for this vocabulary is understood in Rome to be Augustus, the emperor. Paul asserts without qualification that the Romans have misunderstood; the God of the Jewish people and this God's Jewish Messiah, Jesus, are the referents.

The letter frame of Romans (the opening and closing) outlines a counter-imperial theology. Paul challenges the very center of Roman imperial ideology.

---

3. For the exegesis undergirding this translation, see ibid., 50–64; see also D. A. Campbell, "The Faithfulness of Jesus Christ in Romans and Galatians" (paper presented at the annual meeting of the SBL, San Diego, November 17–20, 2007), to be published in _The Deliverance of God: An Apocalyptic Rereading of Justification in Paul_ (Grand Rapids: Eerdmans, forthcoming).

4. Jacob Taubes, _The Political Theology of Paul_ (Palo Alto, CA: Stanford University Press, 2004) 16.

5. Diana M. Swancutt, "_Ho Dikaios Ek Pisteōs Zēsetai_ in Intercultural Translation: 'Living Justly' as Paul's Jewish Paideia to Roman Greeks" (paper presented at the annual meeting of the SBL, San Diego, November 17–20, 2007) 13.

He commits treason. No one understood this more clearly than Clement of Rome. He tells the churches of Corinth about 50 years after Paul's Letter to the Romans that the apostle was martyred because he 'preached righteousness' (*dikaiosynēn didaxas, 1 Clem.* 5:7). Was Paul executed because he preached the good news of God's salvation? Or might the language have meant something else to 1st-century Romans and Roman officials than it has meant to centuries of post-Roman Christian readers of Paul?

Early Clues

The *intifada* quality of the letter is intensified by three other features of Paul's introduction. Paul identifies himself in a most unusual way, "a slave of Messiah Jesus" (Rom 1:1). Except for Philippians and Philemon, Paul either introduces himself as "an apostle of Messiah Jesus" (so 1 and 2 Corinthians, Galatians, Ephesians, Colossians; so also 1 and 2 Timothy) or as a colleague of Silvanus and Timothy (so 1 and 2 Thessalonians). The "prisoner" identification in Philemon reflects Paul's actual legal-sociological status. Why the different self-identification as "slave of Messiah Jesus" in Romans and Philippians? Michael Brown has proposed that Paul intentionally identifies himself with the slaves of the *Familia Caesaris* in Rome and Philippi.[6] One of the governing innovations of Julius Caesar and Octavian was the creation of an imperial slave-class bureaucracy of 5–6,000 people to govern the empire in place of the senatorial elite who had been responsible for the affairs of state during the republic. The majority of these imperial slaves were located in Rome and in the imperial colonies (e.g., Corinth, Philippi). Many of the names identified in Romans 16 are slave names—many of whom were likely slaves of the emperor, as Brown proposes. A significant number of the imperial slaves had enormous power because they governed in the name of the emperor himself; when they delivered a message to a province, a city, or a member of the senatorial class, they spoke on behalf of the emperor, and their words carried the authority of the emperor. Paul introduces himself as "the slave of Messiah Jesus." Before Paul says that he is "an apostle set apart for the good news of God," he claims that he is a slave of the emperor, in this case Messiah Jesus rather than Caesar Augustus. He writes the letter to the Roman churches with the authority of King Jesus.

Second, what Paul writes is defined as 'the good news of God' (*euanggelion theou*). "Good news" has both a Jewish and a Roman political meaning.[7] It is

---

6. Michael J. Brown, "Paul's Use of *Doulos Christou Iēsou* in Romans 1.1," *JBL* 120 (2001) 723–37.

7. For a summary of the OT/Jewish background, see my *Romans*, 45–48.

the Roman meaning that concerns us here. Graham Stanton makes the case that "good news" language was introduced into the early Christian vocabulary in the mid-50s C.E. to tell "a counter-story to the story associated with the imperial cult."[8] Christians, he argues, borrowed "good news" terminology from the imperial cult and filled it with new content at precisely the time that the Emperor Gaius was trying to erect a statue of himself in the Jerusalem temple. "Good news" language had been associated with the imperial cult from the time of Octavian, renamed Caesar Augustus (Caesar, the divine one). It narrated the stories of victory or special events (e.g., birth of a son to the emperor), which were celebrated in Rome and throughout the empire with public sacrifices, festivals, and the erection of temples to the emperor. This worship of the emperor as good news was the most important type of worship in the empire from the time of Octavian (1st century B.C.E./C.E.) until Constantine (early 4th century). It honored the emperor in the eschatological and soteriological language that the early Christians ascribed to Messiah Jesus—savior, Lord, divine, son of god, bringer of peace, righteousness, the new age. But, strikingly, as Stanton points out, the "good news" in Roman and Jewish writers describing the worship of the emperor in the imperial cult is always used in the plural. In contrast, the early Christians, including Paul in Romans, use only the singular. The "good news" (plural) of the emperor's many benefactions is contrasted with the good news (singular) of Messiah Jesus—specifically, the good news of his death/resurrection. Stanton concludes that "gospel proclamation did not take place in isolation from the social, political, and religious culture of the time; it was regularly heard against the backdrop of the imperial cult . . . what is clear is that there were rival gospels."[9] The linguistic pattern of the singular gospel, in contrast to the plural gospels, "was honed in the teeth of the rival 'gospels' of imperial propaganda."[10]

Third, when Paul greets the believers in Rome "from God our father and our Lord Messiah Jesus," he is using explicitly political language. 'Father' (Latin: *pater*) was a common form of address to rulers in Greco-Roman political culture. The identification of god and ruler with "father" is routine in Hellenistic and Roman political literature. The Roman Senate, itself made up of fathers of large and prominent families, passed a decree labeling Augustus the *pater patriae*, the 'father of the homeland'. Roman emperors from Augustus on were called 'father' (*pater patriae*). "'Father'," Bruno Blumenfeld claims, "is a politically charged word, and it is meant to be understood politically."[11] Add

---

8. Graham Stanton, *Jesus and Gospel* (Cambridge: Cambridge University Press, 2004) 25.

9. Ibid., 34–35.

10. Ibid., 51.

11. Bruno Blumenfeld, *The Political Paul: Justice, Democracy and Kingship in a Hellenistic Framework* (JSNTSup 210; Sheffield: Sheffield Academic Press, 2001) 363.

the designation of Jesus as 'Lord' (Greek: *kyrios*), the title of the Roman emperor, and it is clear that Paul is making political claims from the outset of the letter. There is a Father and a Lord of the Christian house churches in Rome who is different from Caesar.

The Central Claim

The central claim Paul makes in Romans is that the good news of Messiah Jesus discloses the righteousness of God in the world and that this disclosure effects end-time, world-transforming righteousness in the world (Rom 1:17; 3:21–22). This revelation of divine, eschatological righteousness puts people, specifically Jews and Gentiles, and ultimately all creation in right relationship with God and each other.[12]

The claim that the gospel reveals the righteousness of God is a special claim in Romans. Righteousness language is much more dominant in Romans than in Galatians, the other Pauline letter that emphasizes the importance of righteousness. The noun 'righteousness' (*dikaiosynē*) is used 34 times in Romans compared with 7 times in Galatians; the verb usage (*dikaioō*) is 15 in Romans and 8 in Galatians, while the adjective (*dikaios*) ratio is 7 to 1. In addition, other words from this family are used only in Romans: *dikaiōma* (3 times), *dikaiōsis* (2 times), *dikaiokrisia* (1 time), *adikia* (7 times), *adikos* (1 time). The important phrase 'righteousness of God' (*dikaiosynē theou*) is used 8 times in Romans and not at all in Galatians (the only other appearances in Paul are 2 Cor 5:21; 9:9). The phrase 'the righteousness of faith' (*dikaiosynē tēs pisteōs*) is unique to Romans.

Why the focus on righteousness and the righteousness of God in Romans in contrast to the other letters of Paul? Is there a unique soteriological issue among Roman Christians that calls for this emphasis? Or, might there be a political context for Paul's concern about righteousness in Rome?

The Politics of Righteousness

Righteousness in Ancient Political Thought

Righteousness has a long history as a theological term in Judaism and Christianity. The primary focus of concern in the history of scholarship has been

---

12. For a more detailed discussion of this understanding of righteousness and the righteousness of God in Romans, see my *Romans*, 400–407; and D. A. Campbell, "The Meaning of *Dikaiosynē Theou* in Paul" (paper presented at the annual meeting of the SBL, San Diego, November 17–20, 2007) and to be published in *The Deliverance of God: An Apocalyptic Rereading of Justification in Paul* (Grand Rapids: Eerdmans, forthcoming).

the relationship of righteousness to salvation.[13] The agenda is shaped by Augustine and Luther.[14]

But *righteousness* has an equally long history in the Greco-Roman world as a political term. It is "the pre-eminent political arete [virtue] in all Classical and Hellenistic political tracts."[15] 'Righteousness' (*dikaiosynē*), 'unrighteousness' (*adikia*), and 'sin' (*hamartia*) belong to a vast political semantic field that is concerned with the nature and structures of society, including its statutes, roles, norms, and institutions. Plato's *Republic* is a complex essay on *dikaiosynē*; righteousness is the supreme political virtue that is concerned with doing it right. *Dikaiosynē* is the perfect virtue for Aristotle, and it cannot be understood outside politics. The political domain is the only proper context for the discussion of justice. It is righteousness alone that makes possible the common good for the *polis*.[16]

Righteousness determines and defines the nature of political society. It gives unity to the individual and the *polis*. It harmonizes the state and the cosmos. Righteousness is the common good for both the ruler and the ruled. Further, righteousness has a divine or quasi-divine quality. It can derive only from a transcendent source. The administrator of righteousness is consistently accorded superhuman powers.[17]

---

13. For a few recent examples, see David E. Aune, *Reading Paul Together: Protestant and Catholic Perspectives on Justification* (Grand Rapids: Baker Academic, 2006); C. Brown and H. Seebass, "Righteousness, Justification," *NIDNTT* 3.352–77; James D. G. Dunn and Alan M. Suggate, *The Justice of God* (Grand Rapids: Eerdmans, 1993); David Hill, *Greek and Hebrew Meanings: Studies in the Semantics of Soteriological Terms* (Cambridge: Cambridge University Press, 1967) 82–162; Gottfried Nebe, "Righteousness in Paul," in *Justice and Righteousness* (ed. Henning Graf Reventlow and Yair Hoffman; JSOTSup 137; Sheffield: Sheffield Academic Press, 1992); John Reumann, *Righteousness in the New Testament* (Philadelphia: Fortress, 1982); Gottlob Schrenk, "*dikē, dikaiosynē*," *TDNT* 2.175–225; and J. A. Ziesler, *The Meaning of Righteousness in Paul* (Cambridge: Cambridge University Press, 1972).

14. For a more recent move to broaden the understanding of "righteousness" language in Paul to include the social dimension, see A. Katherine Grieb, "'So That in Him We Might Become the Righteousness of God' (2 Cor. 5.21): Some Theological Reflections on the Church Becoming Justice," *Ex Auditu* 22 (2006) 58–80; Helmut Koester, "Paul's Proclamation of God's Justice in the Nations," *Theology Digest* 51 (2004) 303–14; Christopher D. Marshall, *Beyond Retribution: A New Testament Vision for Justice, Crime, and Punishment* (Grand Rapids: Eerdmans, 2001) 35–53; Willard M. Swartley, "The Relation of Justice/Righteousness to *Shalom/Eirēnē*" (paper presented to the 2006 Symposium on the Theological Interpretation of Scripture, North Park Theological Seminary; published in *Ex Auditu* 22 [2006] 29–53; does not contain the Pauline materials); and Campbell, "The Meaning of *Dikaiosynē Theou*."

15. Blumenfeld, *The Political Paul*, 419.

16. For a helpful analysis of Plato's and Aristotle's thoughts on "righteousness," see ibid., 36–79.

17. For a more extended discussion of righteousness as a political term in the Hellenistic world, see ibid., 36–274.

Adikia is the opposite of *dikaiosynē*. It is that which harms the order of the cosmos and the *polis*. It describes civil war among the parts of the whole, whether the soul, the family, the city, the army, or the state. *Adikia* usually appears in the singular, which means it is not focused on the act(s) of individuals but on the whole phenomenon of unrighteousness (injustice). It is often paired with *asebeia* 'impiety, irreligious' to include rebellion against the gods and thus cosmic discord. *Adikia* and *asebeia* combine to fracture community and the cosmos.[18] *Hamartia* belongs within this semantic field; it is the opposite of righteousness and means doing it wrong. Sin is more a conceptual error than a moral fault; it reflects a mental incapacity to correctly perceive reality.[19]

Righteousness and unrighteousness are core and pervasive political categories in the ancient world. Rome is the center of the political world when Paul writes his letter to the Roman churches. One of the earliest historians of the empire, Dionysius of Halicarnassus (60–67 B.C.E.), claims that 'righteousness' (*dikaiosynē*), 'just rule' is the reason Rome was granted its worldwide *imperium* 'rule' (*Roman Antiquities* 1.3.5). Could it be that Paul chooses *righteousness* as the central theme of his letter because he is addressing one of the central ideas in his world: how the world and community is structured and shaped? Could it be that Paul is challenging a fundamental conviction of his time, that the embodiment and bringer of righteousness is the Roman emperor and the empire?

Righteousness and the Roman Emperor

Three characteristics of Roman religion are critical to understanding Roman imperial theology and ideology in the 1st century. First, religion is political, and politics is religious. Roman reality is a mono religiopolitical reality: all reality is one, and it is simultaneously religious and political. The emperor is the political (*imperator*, *Augustus* = *Sebastos*) and the religious leader (*pontifex maximus*) of the empire and the people of the empire.[20] The modern, Western notion of the separation of religion and state is unfathomable in 1st-century Rome. Second, Roman religion is about cult practice, not belief. The proper

---

18. See ibid., 84, 327; W. Günther, "*adikia*," *NIDNTT* 3.573–76; and Gottlob Schrenk, "*adikios*," *TDNT* 1.150–51.

19. Blumenfeld, *The Political Paul*, 39–40.

20. See J. Rufus Fears, "Rome: The Ideology of Imperial Power," *Thought* 55 (1980) 98–109; idem, "Ruler Worship," *Civilization of the Ancient Mediterranean* (ed. Michael Grant and Rachel Kitzinger; 3 vols.; New York: Scribners, 1988) 2.1009–25; S. R. F. Price, *Rituals and Power: The Roman Imperial Cult in Asia Minor* (Cambridge: Cambridge University Press, 1984); and Paul Zanker, *The Power of Images in the Age of Augustus* (Ann Arbor: University of Michigan Press, 1990).

observance of cult—sacrifices, prayers, offerings—are critical to the *pax deorum* (the peace and goodwill of the gods). One can/does/should participate in cult observance to many gods to maintain the *pax deorum*. Third, 1st-century Roman religion is centered in the worship of the emperor. He is a divine figure in one form or another who is willed by the gods to rule the world.[21] The worship of the emperor in a wide variety of daily cultic practices and contexts is almost universal. The various media of the empire consistently proclaim the divinity of the emperor: temples, public buildings, statues, altars, sacrifices, prayers, festivals, inscriptions, coins, offerings, proclamations, and literature encourage the honor and cultic worship of him.[22]

One important component of the religious phenomenon of Greco-Roman religious reality was the deification of Virtues, sometimes called personifications of the king or emperor. A condition or quality is recognized and worshiped as a characteristic of divine power, which in turn produces the condition or quality that it embodies (e.g., *Concordia* is the godhead that establishes *concordia* 'harmony'; *Pax* is the godhead that establishes *pax* 'peace'). Virtues possess all the trappings of cult: temples, altars, feast days, sacrifices, prayers. The Virtues are objects of profound and sincere religious piety. One of the deepest fears of the Roman people is the disturbance or fracturing of the peace of the gods (*pax deorum*) through impiety. The proper worship of the emperor and the Virtues associated with the emperor are necessary to secure the blessing and the peace of the gods. The ruler who embodies and manifests the Virtues is the *sōtēr* 'savior' and *euergetēs* 'benefactor' of the empire and the people; he is the source of supernatural benefits to the people. The Virtues of the emperor mirror the divine; the well-ordered and prosperous condition of the empire flows directly from his Virtues. The Virtues of *Homonoia* 'harmony', *Dēmokratia* 'democracy', *Eirēnē* 'peace', *Dikē* 'righteousness', *Eusebeia* 'religious piety', *Eleutheria* 'freedom', and *Pistis* 'faith/faithfulness/loyalty' are adopted by the Romans from a rich Greek tradition as the slogans of political activity and the goals of the social order. Initially these Virtues are the characteristics of the Roman republic and people. But in the late republic, the Virtues become bound to the person of a charismatic leader and are used to proclaim the superhuman achievements of this person and the blessings he brings to the people. The Virtues now work through the beneficent influence of the charismatic leader—that is, the emperor.[23]

---

21. See Fears, "Rome"; idem, "Ruler Worship."

22. See Price, *Rituals and Power*; Zanker, *The Power of Images*.

23. See J. Rufus Fears, "The Theology of Victory at Rome: Approaches and Problems," *Aufstieg und Niedergang der Roemischen Welt* 17.2 (Berlin: de Gruyter, 1981) 736–826; and idem, "The Cult of Virtues and Roman Imperial Ideology," in ibid., 827–948.

In 45 B.C.E., the Senate decreed a temple to *Concordia* in honor of Julius Caesar's end of the civil wars in the empire. This was followed by the erection of statues to *eusebeia* 'religious piety', *dikaiosynē* 'righteousness', and *agathia* 'goodness' in Caesar's honor and the dedication of a temple to *Clementia* 'clemency' Caesar (44 B.C.E.). *Pax* 'peace' appeared on Roman coinage together with the image of Caesar. In 27 B.C.E., Augustus placed a golden shield in the Senate house (the curia) honoring his *Clementia*, *Iustitia* 'righteousness', and *Pietas* 'religious piety'. An altar to *Pax Augusta* was established in Rome to celebrate the peace that Augustus brought to the Roman state and to the entire human race. Augustus was credited with restoring the peace of the gods (*pax deorum*). On January 8, 13 C.E., Augustus established a temple to the goddess *Iustitia* in Rome and returned the goddess to Rome, from which she together with *Pax* 'peace' and *Fides* 'faith' fled during the civil war between Caesar and Pompey. The linkage of *Augusta* to *Pax*, *Iustitia*, *Concordia*, and *Providentia* expressed the fundamental requirement for the maintenance of proper relations with the divine order. The *Pax Augusta* or the *Iustitia Augusta* proclaimed that Augustus together with the divine power produced peace or righteousness within the sphere of Augustus's person and activity. *Victoria*, *Pax*, *Fortuna*, *Virtus*, *Clementia*, *Iustitia*, and *Pietas* were established as central to the imagery of the principate under Augustus. They defined the character of the emperor and of his politics; Augustus is the emperor of righteousness in Roman imperial ideology and politics. Tiberius, Augustus's successor, dedicated a statue to *Iustitia Augusta* early in his reign, and in 22–23 C.E. issued coinage proclaiming *Iustitia* and *Salus Augusta* 'the righteousness and salvation of Augustus'. The same year, he also issued coinage that recognized the *Clementia*, *Moderatio*, *Iustitia*, and *Salus* of Tiberius 'the clemency, moderation, righteousness, and salvation of Tiberius' and the *Pietas* of his son Drusus. Nero in 56/7 and 57/8 issued coins proclaiming the *Dikaiosynē* 'righteousness', *Eirēnē* 'peace', and *Pronoia* 'providence or forethought' of his rule.[24]

Through the worship of the Virtues of the emperor, the Roman worshipers invoke the specific power whose benefit they seek rather than invoking a deity like Jupiter, Apollo, or Venus. Worshipers name the god from whom they desire benefits and celebrate the emperor who can bestow these benefits through his politics. The Virtues most worshiped in the Roman west are *Victoria* 'victory', *Fortuna* 'good fortune', and *Pietas* 'religious piety'. In contrast, *Dikaiosynē* 'righteousness' is the most popular Virtue in the Greek east. Cults in numerous cities of the east nurture the worship of *Dikaiosynē Augusta*.[25]

---

24. See idem, "The Theology of Victory"; idem, "The Cult of Virtues."
25. See idem, "The Theology of Victory"; idem, "The Cult of Virtues."

The Greek east is the context of the Pauline mission and the venue from which he writes the letter to the Roman churches. He lives and evangelizes in a world that worships the emperor as divine and worships *Dikaiosynē Augusta* as the embodiment and giver of righteousness to all people; and he is writing a letter to the capital of the empire where the *Dikaiosynē Augusta* lives and from which he practices the politics of righteousness throughout the empire.

The Politics of Romans 1

Imagine gathering with a small group of people in the house of a friend to hear a communication from a distant and controversial church leader by the name of Paul. The opening greeting and introduction are startling; they proclaim an anti-imperial message. But then imagine listening to the *propositio*, the thesis statement of the letter. The anti-imperial good news that Paul is proclaiming concerns *dikaiosynē*. It announces that a righteous divine being, God, is revealing righteousness in the world and that this God is doing so through the faithfulness of a "righteous one" who is God's son. Paul's announcement that the revelation of the righteousness of God through the good news of Messiah Jesus reveals the true *Iustitia*—that it puts people and creation right—is shocking; it is nothing short of seditious. His claim is a direct challenge to imperial ideology and pretension. Paul is turning Roman ideology on its head. The good news of salvation and righteousness is not the Roman emperor or empire but Messiah Jesus and his small band of followers who preach and incarnate the gospel. The good news moves from the bottom up, not from the top down.

It is hard for us even to begin to imagine the boldness of Paul's thesis after two millennia of Christian history. Paul wrote the Letter to the Romans early in the reign of Nero, the last of the Julio-Caesarean emperors and the only emperor declared a public enemy by the Senate. Nero sought to imitate Augustus by picturing himself widely with the gods Apollo and Sun. He believed that he was "the mind of the empire," that he was the bond who held the empire together, and that the prosperity of the world depended on his benevolent and righteous leadership. The rightness and inevitability of his reign was proclaimed in every public corner of Rome. Nero was a megalomaniac and paranoid emperor who tolerated no rivals. He murdered his own son, Britannicus, early in 55 C.E., around the time that Paul wrote Romans. Nero was worried about his son's advancing maturity and the support that he found in his mother, Agrippina. A few years later he murdered Agrippina.[26]

---

26. For biographies of Nero, see Miriam T. Griffin, *Nero: The End of a Dynasty* (New Haven, CT: Yale University Press, 1985); and Edward Champlin, *Nero* (Cambridge: Harvard University

Without "shame" or fear, Paul proclaims that Jesus is the embodiment and bearer of the righteousness of God; Nero is not. Paul writes Romans to proclaim an alternative politics to the politics of the Roman emperor and empire.

Arguing the Politics of Righteousness

The central claim of Paul's thesis in Romans is elaborated in a series of arguments that are theopolitical in nature and that further criticize the politics of Roman imperial righteousness.

First, the righteousness of God revealed in Messiah Jesus is designed to overcome the problem of 'unrighteousness' (*adikia*), 'godlessness' (*asebeia*), and 'those who suppress the truth in unrighteousness' (*tōn tēn alētheian en adikia katechontōn*, Rom 1:18, 29), which is manifest in different ways by Romans and Jews—that is, by all people (1:18–3:20). The politics of Rome and Jerusalem are the problem; these are politics that are centered in the worship of false gods, politics that encourage wrong behavior in people who know better, and politics that divide people. The language Paul uses is political—the power of righteousness overcomes the power of unrighteousness, godlessness, and untruth that fractures community and the empire.

Second, the God revealed in Messiah Jesus is genuinely righteous, faithful, and true. God manifests this righteousness in the world in two ways: (1) God judges all *hamartia* 'sin' of all people equally. The righteousness of God is impartial in judgment in contrast to Roman and Jewish partiality in judgment (Rom 1:18–3:20). (2) God reveals end-time, world-transforming righteousness through the faithfulness of one person, Messiah Jesus (*pisteōs Iēsou Christou* is understood as a subjective genitive).[27] The faithfulness of Jesus to the purposes of God demonstrates that God is righteous and that God makes righteous all people without distinction as a gift of divine benefaction (by grace, Rom 3:21–26).

The problem in the world is the politics of *hamartia* 'sin', the wrong perception of reality and power; this is what destroys relationships, community, and empire. The remedy is a righteous and faithful Jewish Messiah rather than a "righteous" and "faithful" Caesar. The categories of thought and language are political.

Press, 2003); and for an outline of the official propaganda of Nero's regime, see D. A. Campbell, "'Blasphemed among the Nations': Pursuing an Anti-imperial 'Intertextuality' in Romans" (paper presented at the annual meeting of the SBL, San Diego, November 17–20, 2007) 5–9, to be published in *The Deliverance of God: An Apocalyptic Rereading of Justification in Paul* (Grand Rapids: Eerdmans, forthcoming).

27. For the rationale for the subjective genitive interpretation, see my *Romans*, 99–113.

Third, God makes righteous all people, Gentiles and Jews, who place faith in God on the model of Jesus and Abraham. The righteousness of God 'according to grace' (*kata charin*) is a 'righteousness by faith' (*dikaiosynē pistei*) or 'righteousness through faith' (*dikaiosynē pisteōs*), not a righteousness 'through works of law' (*ex ergōn nomou*) or 'through works' (*ex ergōn*). Because it is righteousness through faith, it is equally accessible to all people in the world. Jesus and Abraham are the paradigms of faith, not Caesar (Rom 3:27–4:25). Loyalty to Messiah Jesus, not Caesar as in imperial ideology, is salvific.

Fourth, the righteousness of God makes people right and establishes peace in the world because one man, Messiah Jesus, overcame the *hamartia* 'sin' of one man, Adam. The ones receiving righteousness by grace are empowered to overcome the power of *hamartia* and are made kings with Messiah Jesus. People are now faced with a choice, be slaves of 'unrighteousness' (*adikia*) or slaves to 'righteousness' (*dikaiosynē*, Rom 5:1–6:23). In one bold move right at the center of the letter, Paul takes on the Roman myth of the Golden Age, in which Caesar Augustus is pictured as the savior who overcomes the problem of *scelus* (= *hamartia*) and establishes righteousness and peace in the world. Jesus, not Caesar, is the answer to the problem of the power of 'sin' (*hamartia*) and 'unrighteousness' (*adikia* = *scelus* in Latin).[28] It is Messiah Jesus who introduces the new eschatological age rather than Caesar, as in Roman imperial propaganda.[29]

Fifth, Messiah Jesus is the way to righteousness for all people of faith. This way to righteousness stands in contrast to all ideologies and practices that attempt to achieve righteousness by law or by a group's "own seeking" (Rom 9:30–10:10).

Sixth, the gift of righteousness leads to a life of transformed thinking ("to be transformed by the renewal of the mind in order to demonstrate what is the will of God, the good, acceptable and complete," Rom 12:2), 'reasonable thinking' (*sōphronein* rather than *hyperphronein*), and 'love' (*agapē*) that builds the common good and tolerates differences between different peoples and their ethnic traditions (Rom 12:1–16:27). Except for "love," the description of the "righteous" life uses the language of Greco-Roman politics: transformed thinking and reasonable thinking (often translated as "sober-mindedness") are the goals of good politics.[30]

---

28. See Virgil's fourth Ecologue for the literary articulation of this myth, and for a scholarly analysis, see Andrew Wallace-Hadrill, "The Golden Age and Sin in Augustan Ideology," *Past and Present* 95 (1982) 19–36.

29. J. R. Harrison, "Paul, Eschatology and the Augustan Age of Grace," *Tyndale Bulletin* 50 (1999) 79–92.

30. See my *Romans*, 302–9; Blumenfeld, *The Political Paul*, 381–82; and H. North, *Sōphrosynē: Self-Knowledge and Self-Restraint in Greek Literature* (Ithaca, NY: Cornell University Press, 1966).

The Politics of Righteousness Again

All of Paul's letters are political tracts. He writes letters to build communities of followers of Messiah Jesus. The letters are designed to foster a distinctive identity and communal unity that is faithful to the gospel of Messiah Jesus. They propose theological centers, draw boundaries, create structures, organize small house churches, exhort appropriate patterns of relationships and behavior, while proscribing inappropriate relationships and behaviors. They are con-summate political statements that are intended to build and nurture alternative communities within major urban centers in the Roman Empire. To organize a group of sociopolitically disparate people into a unified community is a pro-foundly political activity. To organize these people in the capital of the Roman Empire into an alternative society that valorizes a crucified Jewish man, that proclaims a lord other than Caesar, that offers a righteousness other than Caesar's is a profoundly subversive activity.

Romans is a superb example of the politics of Paul. He writes to congrega-tions of mixed ethnic composition who have clear differences in ideologies and practices. He grounds his politics in one of the central ideologies of the Roman Empire, 'righteousness' (*dikaiosynē, iustitia*). Transcendent righteous-ness is revealed and demonstrated in the world through Messiah Jesus, the son of God, not through Caesar Augustus. Righteousness is embodied in the world through Messiah Jesus, not through Caesar. Righteousness is accessible to all people equally as a gift ("by grace") through faith in Messiah Jesus, not by any ethnic or class privilege or any kind of works, Roman benefaction, or Jewish identity markers.

Romans is politically subversive. Paul challenges the center of Roman imperial ideology. He uses the language of the empire but then subverts it by giving the terms new meaning. Even more than that, Paul is radically subver-sive. The bearer and embodiment of righteousness is a crucified, Jewish savior, not the divine emperor of the Roman world. This savior turns the social and ethical values of the Roman world on their head—there is equality between all people in judgment and salvation; there are no elite because all people are slaves (either of *adikia/hamartia* or *dikaiosynē*). Therefore, the people at the top of the highly stratified Roman sociopolitical pyramid or the elite ("the strong" in Romans) are to "lift up" the people at the bottom of the pyramid ("the weak" in Romans). The model of how to relate to people, including people who are different, is the crucified Messiah Jesus rather than the Roman emperor. The righteousness of God through Messiah Jesus erases the ethnic, social, and political binaries of the Roman world—Jew-Gentile, Greek-Barbarian, free-slave, elite–non-elite, ruler-ruled—to create one community in which every-one equally is gifted by grace and exhorted to build the common good.

Romans could not be written, heard, or read in 1st-century Rome as anything other than a direct challenge to the central ideology of the Roman Empire. It is a profoundly subversive political statement.

But Romans is also a profoundly theological statement. Paul not only uses Roman imperial language to challenge the ideology of Rome; he also uses Jewish scriptural language and tradition to shape the ideological and political meaning of Jesus for the churches in Rome. Messiah Jesus is the fulfillment of God's promises to Abraham and the Jewish people to bring righteousness to all people. Jesus is the righteousness of God for Jews and Gentiles. He is God's son, the Messianic seed of David, whom God has enthroned as Lord and Ruler of the nations through the end-time resurrection.

Romans is a theopolitical letter. It is a letter that addresses both theological and political issues.[31] Twenty-first-century Christians do a disservice to Paul to read Romans as exclusively political or theological. It is both/and. As Edward Champlin has argued, Roman people were extraordinarily sensitive to double entendre. James Scott has demonstrated that double-entendre reading and understanding is especially characteristic of marginalized and oppressed groups, which was the subtext of the small Christian house churches in 1st-century Rome and Paul's letter to them.[32]

---

31. For a similar conclusion, see N. T. Wright, "Paul and Caesar: A New Reading of Romans," in _A Royal Priesthood: The Use of the Bible Ethically and Politically_ (ed. C. Bartholemew; Carlisle: Paternoster, 2002) 173.

32. See James C. Scott, _Domination and the Arts of Resistance: Hidden Transcripts_ (New Haven, CT: Yale University Press, 1990); for the implications of Scott's thesis for Paul, see Neil Elliott, "Strategies of Resistance and Hidden Transcripts in the Pauline Communities," in _Hidden Transcripts and the Arts of Resistance_ (ed. Richard A. Horsley; Atlanta: Society of Biblical Literature, 2004) 97–122; and Richard A. Horsley, "Introduction—Jesus, Paul, and the 'Arts of Resistance': Leaves from the Notebook of James C. Scott," in ibid., 1–26.

PART 3

Addressing the Issue of Land in the Life of God's People

"O Land, Land, Land":
Reading the Earth Story in Both Testaments

ELMER A. MARTENS
President and Professor of Old Testament, Emeritus
Mennonite Brethren Biblical Seminary
Fresno, California

Jeremiah's cry "O land, land, land" follows God's judgment oracle against the kings of Judah, notably Jehoiachin (Jer 22:29). It is a cry of lament for what is imminent for a people long dismissive of God's instructions. The term *ʾereṣ* 'land' can refer, depending on context, to all the earth or to a specific region, such as the land of Israel, or to the inhabitants of a territory. In this essay, which deals with the theology of land, it is ground, territory, and acreage that are in view—Israel's land.

The threefold cry "land, land, land" highlights the frequent use of this term and its synonyms in the OT, as compared with scant mention of the subject in the NT. The term "land" is the fourth-most-frequent substantive in the OT (more than 2,700×), thus more ubiquitous than "covenant." In contrast, NT words such as *gē* 'land' and *chōra, chōrion* 'region' and *agros* 'field' are found in the NT some 325×. This huge disparity raises the question how to read the earth story, especially theologically considered, in the two testaments.[1]

For a Christian there lurks the hermeneutical-theological question: does this subject of land, so prominent in the OT, have any continuity in the NT? In part this question is a question of the unity of the Bible. In part the question is driven by the desire to have a wholistic understanding of the Scripture. In part the question is driven by the conviction that, while separate theologies of the OT and NT will no doubt continue to appear, it is time to emphasize that, for a Christian, theologies had better not focus on specializations but

---

1. The term "earth story" connects, but only on the level of vocabulary, with titles such as *The Earth Story in Genesis* (2000); *The Earth Story in the Psalms and in the Prophets* (2001); and *The Earth Story in Wisdom Tradition* (2001); all three of which Norman C. Habel, the director of the Earth Bible Project, is the editor. The Earth Bible series is published by Sheffield Academic Press.

be overarching and therefore include both testaments.[2] One readily echoes Walter Brueggemann, an OT scholar, who remarks, "I am compelled by my faith stance and my interpretative decisions to determine where land theology leads if it is understood as moving toward the New Testament."[3]

This essay probes the earth story in the two testaments via the hermeneutic of metaphor. First, this hermeneutic is described; then it is applied to the biblical category of land. Past approaches are acknowledged, but here my interest is rather narrow and turns on the question how has and how might land be treated in a whole-Bible theology?

The interest in land as a theological theme is relatively recent.[4] Legitimacy and impetus were given to the subject toward the end of the last century by W. D. Davies (NT) and W. Brueggemann (OT). Both cited G. von Rad's earlier article.[5] Other monographs that treat land theologically or ideologically include those by N. Habel and C. J. H. Wright.[6] Of OT theologies, only a few isolate the topic of land for significant treatment.[7]

---

2. On a whole-Bible theology, see Brevard S. Childs, *Biblical Theology of the Old and New Testaments: Theological Reflections on the Christian Bible* (Minneapolis: Fortress, 1992); Paul R. House, "Biblical Theology and the Wholeness of Scripture," in *Biblical Theology: Retrospect and Prospect* (ed. Scott J. Hafemann; Downers Grove, IL: InterVarsity, 2002) 267–79; Elmer A. Martens, "Reaching for a Biblical Theology of the Whole Bible," in *Reclaiming the Old Testament: Essays in Honour of Waldemar Janzen* (ed. Gordon Zerbe; Winnipeg, MB: Canadian Mennonite Bible College, 2001) 83–101; Craig Bartholomew, ed., *Out of Egypt: Biblical Theology and Biblical Interpretation* (Grand Rapids: Zondervan / Carlisle: Paternoster, 2004); and Scott J. Hafemann and Paul R. House, eds., *Central Themes in Biblical Theology: Mapping Unity in Diversity* (Nottingham: Apollos / Grand Rapids: Baker, 2007).

3. Walter Brueggemann, *The Land: Place as Gift, Promise, and Challenge in Biblical Faith* (2nd ed.; OBT; Minneapolis: Fortress, 2002) 158; Waldemar Janzen notes, "The paucity of theological material identifiable by the key word 'land' raises the question whether that theme, so ubiquitous in the OT, has lost its significance in the NT or whether it comes to expression in different ways" ("Land," *ABD* 4.151).

4. The four-volume dictionary, *Interpreter's Dictionary of the Bible* (1962), did not have an entry on the topic "land." By contrast, the theological dimension has large prominence in Janzen, "Land," 143–54. See C. J. H. Wright, "*'ereṣ*," *NIDOTTE* 1.518–24.

5. Brueggemann, *The Land*; William D. Davies, *The Gospel and the Land: Early Christianity and Jewish Territorial Doctrine* (Berkeley: University of California Press, 1974); G. von Rad, "The Promised Land and Yahweh's Land in the Hexateuch," *The Problem of the Hexateuch and Other Essays* (trans. E. W. T. Dicken; New York: McGraw-Hill, 1966) 79–93; repr. in *From Genesis to Chronicles: Explorations in Old Testament Theology* (ed. K. C. Hanson; Minneapolis: Fortress, 2005) 59–69.

6. Norman Habel, *The Land Is Mine: Six Biblical Land Ideologies* (Minneapolis: Fortress, 1995); and Christopher J. H. Wright, *God's People in God's Land: Family, Land, and Property in the Old Testament* (Grand Rapids: Eerdmans, 1990).

7. Walter C. Kaiser, *Towards an Old Testament Theology* (Grand Rapids: Zondervan, 1978) 122–42; Elmer A. Martens, *God's Design* (3rd ed.; N. Richland Hills, TX: Bibal, 1998) 113–37, 217–36, 299–331; John Goldingay, *Old Testament Theology, Volume One: Israel's Gospel* (Downers Grove, IL: InterVarsity, 2003) 451–528; idem, *Old Testament Theology, Volume Two: Israel's Faith*

Of works offering a whole-Bible theology, C. H. H. Scobie's book is note-worthy. Scobie approves of Davies's conclusion that there is a deliberate "re-placement of 'holy places' by the Person of Jesus."[8] However, Scobie favors a connection via paradigm or pattern. He highlights a pattern of movements between (1) landless and (2) land. In the OT the rhythm is essentially Israel's movement from landlessness to landedness. This rhythm was reversed in the NT, which begins with the story of Jesus and the early church rooted in a limited geographical place but ends with landlessness in the sense that the Christian witness is no longer attached to the land but extends to all lands. The movement is "from the land to the lands."[9] However, seldom if at all in these discussions is land as metaphor given consideration.

Exploring the Hermeneutic of Metaphor

The understanding of land within a whole-Bible theology rests largely on hermeneutical approaches. The traditional-critical methods have been great tools, but they have limitations. Literary approaches, such as metaphor, hold promise for biblical theology.[10]

Metaphor is a form of analogy with an initial appeal to the imagination. "Metaphor is that figure of speech whereby we speak about one thing in terms which are seen to be suggestive of another."[11] Analysts of the anatomy of

---

(Downers Grove, IL: InterVarsity 2006) 438–49; Horst D. Preuss, *Old Testament Theology* (2 vols.; trans. L. G. Perdue; Louisville: Westminster/John Knox, 1995) 1.117–28; and Rolf Rendtorff, *The Canonical Hebrew Bible: A Theology of the Old Testament* (trans. David E. Orton; Leiden: Deo, 2005) 220–25, 457–69. One might add Stephen Dempster, who tells the story in part around (1) geography and (2) genealogy (*Dominion and Dynasty: A Biblical Theology of the Hebrew Bible* [Downers Grove, IL: InterVarsity, 2003] 75–92, 117–23, 126–30, 163–67). Note-worthy, most recently, is Bruce Waltke, *An Old Testament Theology* (Grand Rapids: Zondervan, 2007), who devotes three chapters to the subject of land (pp. 512–87).

8. Charles Scobie, *The Ways of Our God: An Approach to Biblical Theology* (Grand Rapids: Eerdmans, 2005) 541–59.

9. Ibid., 556.

10. Ian Paul claims that metaphor "is one of the most crucial areas in the whole of herme-neutics since so much biblical theology hangs on metaphors" ("Metaphor," *Dictionary for Theological Interpretation of the Bible* [ed. Kevin Vanhoozer; Grand Rapids: Baker, 2005] 507). Illustrative of this claim is Samuel Terrien's article, "The Metaphor of the Rock in Biblical Theology," in *God in the Fray: A Tribute to Walter Brueggemann* (ed. Timothy K. Beal and Tod Linafelt; Minneapolis: Fortress, 1998) 157–71; J. Gordon McConville, "Metaphor, Symbol and the Interpretation of Deuteronomy," in *After Pentecost: Language and Biblical Interpretation* (ed. Craig G. Bartholomew et al.; Scripture and Hermeneutics 2; Grand Rapids: Zondervan / Carlisle: Paternoster, 2001) 329–51; William P. Brown, *Seeing the Psalms: A Theology of Metaphor* (Louisville: Westminster/John Knox, 2002); and Trevor Burke, *Adopted into God's Family: Exploring a Pauline Metaphor* (Downers Grove, IL: InterVarsity, 2006).

11. Janet M. Soskice, *Metaphor and Religious Language* (New York: Oxford University Press, 1985) 15. Leo G. Perdue explains, "A metaphor says that one thing is something else" (*The*

metaphor speak of the "one thing" as the tenor (subject) and the "another" as the vehicle.[12] Other terminology is the "source domain" and the "target domain."[13] In the standard example of metaphor, "man is a wolf," the subject (tenor) is "man" and the vehicle is "a wolf." In a comparison of this sort, as Ian Paul stresses, leaning on Paul Ricoeur, the "is" frames the comparison, but simultaneously the "is not" remains.[14] The metaphor evokes images of fierceness. At the same time the two remain quite distinct, for the one is a human being; the other is an animal.

George B. Caird, in a seminal book on biblical images, notes how metaphor systems were used by the biblical writers to characterize the exodus, the temple, and the law-court. Citing OT references to the exodus and noting Col 1:13, he writes: "Thus a whole language [about exodus] was ready-made for the early Christians as they strove to expound the significance of the life and death of Christ."[15] Might the metaphor system of land not also hold similar possibilities and so be another option for the exposition of NT realities? Already Davies, Brueggemann, and Janzen tapped into this methodology somewhat.[16] The proposal here is that previously offered conclusions about the theological interface of land in the OT and NT become more compelling by probing into land as a metaphor and as a metaphor system.[17]

Collapse of History: Reconstructing Old Testament Theology [OBT; Minneapolis: Fortress, 1994] 201). On metaphor generally, see Paul Ricoeur, *Interpretation Theory: Discourse and the Surplus of Meaning* (Fort Worth, TX: Texas Christian University Press, 1976); and idem, *The Rule of Metaphor: Multidisciplinary Studies of the Creation of Meaning in Language* (trans. Robert Czerny et al.; Toronto: University of Toronto Press, 1977). For metaphor in biblical studies, in addition to works cited in n. 10, see Stephen Bigger, "Symbol and Metaphor in the Hebrew Bible," in *Creating the Old Testament: The Emergence of the Hebrew Bible* (ed. Stephen Bigger; Oxford: Blackwell, 1989) 51–80; Gerald A. Klingbeil, "Metaphors and Pragmatics: An Introduction to the Hermeneutics of Metaphors in the Epistle to the Ephesians," *BBR* 16 (2006) 273–93 (esp. n. 3 and the bibliography there); Ian Paul, "Metaphor and Exegesis," in *After Pentecost* (Scripture and Hermeneutics 2; Grand Rapids: Zondervan / Carlisle: Paternoster, 2001) 387–402; and Perdue, *The Collapse of History*, especially the bibliography in n. 9 on p. 201. His section on metaphor and religious language (pp. 201–13) is repeated in *Reconstructing Old Testament Theology: After the Collapse of History* (OBT; Minneapolis: Fortress, 2005) 147–59.

12. The terminology is I. A. Richards's, according to Ricoeur, *Interpretation Theory*, 50.

13. George Lakoff and Mark Turner, *More Than Cool Reason: A Field Guide to Poetic Metaphor* (Chicago: University of Chicago Press, 1989) 63, 165, 196, 203.

14. Paul, "Metaphor," 507–8.

15. G. B. Caird, *The Language and Imagery of the Bible* (Philadelphia: Westminster, 1980) 156.

16. Davies, *Gospel and Land,* 162 n. 3; Brueggemann, *The Land,* 2; and Janzen, "Land," 152.

17. Metaphor has to do with comparison but of a more limited kind; metaphorical systems entail a larger cluster of meanings that gather around a concept and become the substance for comparison.

Leo Perdue describes how metaphors "work."[18] The first stage is destabilization. In the metaphor "man is a wolf," the disjunction between the two is at first dismaying, troublesome, and disconcerting. Perdue uses the example from Jeremiah: the metaphor of Judah and Jerusalem as a loincloth (Jer 13:1–11).[19] In a second stage, which Perdue labels mimesis, there is the "shock of recognition." There is some insight that makes the comparison meaningful; for instance, in the wolf metaphor, it is the characteristic of fierceness. Through reflection one enters the third stage, "transformation and restabilization." The metaphor makes for a changed, possibly enlarged, understanding of the subject. In our example, the listener is given an unflattering, starkly negative assessment of the male gender. However, in a fourth stage, tensions in the comparison remain; the analogy is only partial. The likeness must not be pressed (e.g., the intelligence of the two, man and wolf, is certainly unequal). While there is overlap between the two, there is not identity.

The Metaphor of Land in Romans

In several NT statements, metaphorical overtones of land can be detected, some more faintly and others quite marked. Paul's argument is about law and faith when he says, "For the promise that he would inherit the world [Greek: *kosmos*] did not come to Abraham or to his descendants through the law but through the righteousness of faith" (Rom 4:13). In this statement, Paul has given to land a meaning that differs from the literal promise of delimited territory to Abraham (Gen 15:18–21). The Apostle Paul's comment about land is more than a grandiose rhetorical flourish; he is employing land metaphorically. For Paul the land is "a great advance metaphor for the design of God that his people should eventually bring the whole world into submission to his healing reign."[20] Like the loincloth in Jeremiah, which is Judah and Jerusalem, so the Promised Land of Israel is metaphorically now the entire world; what is true of the Israelite land is in some sense true of the cosmos. With this statement, one has entered Perdue's stage one of understanding metaphor: destabilization. A small geographical region *is* and *is not* the cosmos. The other stages of reflection, transformation, and tension-recognition of this metaphor could be explored further, were it not for space constraints.

---

18. A more theoretical discussion of how metaphors work is found in Lakoff and Turner, *More Than Cool Reason*, esp. 60–67.

19. Perdue, *The Collapse of History*, 201–17.

20. N. T. Wright, quoted in Scobie, *The Ways of Our God*, 558. John E. Toews, who called my attention to Rom 4:13, says, "From the beginning both terms, promise and inheritance, meant the land (Gen 15:7), but over time they expanded to include 'the whole world' and even 'the world to come'" (*Romans* [Believers Church Bible Commentary; Scottdale, PA: Herald, 2004] 122).

Still another statement from the book of Romans launches one into the metaphor of discourse. Paul says: "We know that the whole creation has been groaning in labor pains until now" (Rom 8:22). Now while the whole creation may include more than the earth, it surely does include the earth. The metaphor, though larger than "land of Israel," is stark and shows that "land" is metaphorically part of salvation/redemption language. Creation (including land) groans as a woman in labor. There is also an intertextual echo from Jeremiah: "How long will the earth mourn [*'ābal*]?" (12:4; 12:11).[21]

To return to Perdue's analysis, language about the earth groaning/mourning is destabilizing; there is an "is/is not" relation. Reflection, the next stage of metaphor interpretation, focuses on the juxtaposition of tenor or subject (land) and the vehicle (a woman giving birth). Reflection of this sort yields comparisons and insights, as well as emotional reverberations. This leads in turn to a transformation with new insights about the subject, creation (earth/land). The earth is pained. Ricoeur's comment is apropos: "It [metaphor] has more than an emotive value because it offers new information. A metaphor, in short, tells us something new about reality."[22] Metaphor makes for a new mental mapping of reality. The concept of a pained earth is considerably enhanced by the image of a travailing female. Yet, in the end, the tension between subject and vehicle remains. Earth's "voice" differs from the human voice of a mother giving birth.

The Metaphor of Land in Hebrews

The book of Hebrews indulges in metaphoric speech about land in which the notion of rest in the land is analogous to salvation rest (Heb 4:5–9).[23]

One of the features of the Promised Land was that in it Israel would be at rest (Deut 25:19; Josh 1:13, 15; 23:1). For Israel the land was a permanent home. As John Oswalt explains, the components of this "rest" are permanence, security, freedom, and tranquility. "However long the people of God endure, just so long they have the land (1 Chr 23:25; Isa 32:18; Ezek 37:14)."[24] The land was associated with safety and security. Egypt was not a

---

21. The Earth Bible Team discusses the metaphor of earth as having a voice: shouting (Ps 65:12–13), rejoicing (Pss 96:11; 97:1), roaring (Ps 96:11), and singing (Ps 96:12). "The Voice of Earth: More Than Metaphor?" in *The Earth Story in the Psalms and the Prophets* (ed. Norman Habel; Sheffield: Sheffield Academic Press, 2001) 23–28.

22. Ricoeur, *Interpretation Theory*, 52–53.

23. For a treatment of the book of Hebrews as forerunner to biblical theology, see Andrew T. Lincoln, "Hebrews and Biblical Theology," in *Out of Egypt* (ed. C. Bartholomew; Grand Rapids: Zondervan / Carlisle: Paternoster, 2004) 313–38.

24. John Oswalt, "Rest," *NIDOTTE* 4.1133.

safe place; there Israel was subject to maltreatment by overlords who could (and did) become cruel and heartless. Nor was Israel at rest when wandering aimlessly in the wilderness. In its new habitat, however, it would not be readily vulnerable to the attacks of adversaries. Security lay in being shielded from enemies (Deut 12:10; 25:19; Josh 23:1). Moreover, in contrast to the land of Egypt, the land of Israel offered relief from taskmasters—hence, freedom (Ps 105:14; Isa 14:3). Thus, while the land as territory is all about turf, beyond the literal meaning, land comes to have associations of home, safety, peace, and freedom.

"Rest" is not ultimately contingent on physical life in a physical land. The exile experience put this feature of "rest" into another key; "rest" was transcendentalized, to use Davies's term.[25] "Rest is not to be found in a deed of ownership. Rather, it is to be found in the embrace of the God of the promise (Isa 28:12; 30:15)."[26] The psalmist could say, "My soul finds rest in God alone" (Ps 62:1 NIV; Isa 63:14). Rest is now not only the environment of peace in a physical land but part of the larger salvation. Occupancy of the land under Joshua was not the ultimate rest promised (Heb 4:8). Commenting on the way that Hebrews exegetes Scripture by using Ps 95 to speak about entering into God's rest, long after Joshua's time, when Israel was at rest, Caird concludes, "This rest, then, must be a spiritual rest of which the entry into Canaan was only a symbol."[27] Similarly, Oswalt states: "The land was a metaphor, God was the reality (Ps 61:1[2]; Jer 6:16)."[28] The earlier linkage between "land" and "rest" takes on additional connotations so that, much like a setup for a spike in volleyball, the metaphor strikes home.

With these three references to land in the NT—Rom 4:13; 8:22; and Heb 4:5–9—there is sufficient warrant for further exploration of land as a metaphor for the larger meaning of salvation, concretized sometimes in the kingdom of God and sometimes in the person of Christ.

Seeing Metaphor as Clue to the Theological Dimension of the Earth Story

The reader who encounters the notion that land may be a metaphor for NT salvation realities will no doubt experience an initial phase of destabilization, of "semantic impertinence."[29] The two entities, land and "kingdom salvation,"

---

25. Davies, *Gospel and Land,* 336.

26. Oswalt, "Rest," 1135.

27. G. B. Caird, "The Exegetical Method of the Epistle to the Hebrews," *Canadian Journal of Theology* 5 (1959) 48.

28. Oswalt, "Rest," 1135. Further material on "rest" can be found in Kaiser, *Toward an Old Testament Theology,* 127–30.

29. The phrase is Paul Ricoeur's, borrowed from Jean Cohen (Ricoeur, *Interpretation Theory,* 50).

seem too distant from one another. The first is physical, measurable, and particular. The second, God's kingdom, is more abstract, not measurable, and although not without aspects that are physical, is ever so much more than physical. The analogy borders on the strange, some would say absurd. But such is the nature of communication by metaphor. Soskice speaks of the "dissonance or tension in a living metaphor whereby the terms of the utterance used seem not strictly appropriate to the topic at hand."[30] Another stage in metaphor interpretation is reflection. Here one ponders questions such as: where are the commonalities? The following paragraphs surface reflections in response to this question. What does land, when not construed as turf, signify? How does land function as metaphor for spiritual realities, such as the theological complex of kingdom of God/salvation/Jesus Christ?

Ian Paul helpfully notes that, in the hermeneutic of metaphor, two contexts must be taken into account: the historical and the literary.[31] Here the historical context is not just any land but the land of Canaan. The literary context is the commentary in the OT about land. If something meaningful is to be conveyed about the subject (kingdom of God) by means of the vehicle (land), then an important step is to become especially familiar with the literary context of this vehicle. A sketch of this literary context follows.

Land as New Habitat, Home, Security, and Rest

For Israelites, the prospect of living in their land was altogether positive. For them, their land represented not only space but ample living space. It was space in which Israel took pleasure and delight. It was a 'glorious' land (*ṣĕbî*, Ezek 20:6, 15), or in God's own words, "a pleasant land, the most beautiful heritage [*naḥălâ*] of all the nations" (Jer 3:19).[32] En route to this land, Israel heard words of instruction from Moses in the context of anticipation: "When you enter the land of Canaan . . ." (Lev 14:34); or again, "When you enter the land I am giving you . . ." (Lev 23:10; cf. 25:2; Num 34:2; Deut 7:1; 11:29; 23:20; 30:16). The prospect held out to the Israelites was all about their living

---

30. Soskice, *Metaphor and Religious Language*, 73.

31. Ian Paul offers a compelling illustration of the historical (geological) context of Laodician hotsprings in understanding "hot, cold and lukewarm" ("Metaphor," 508).

32. The OT term rendered 'inheritance' connects with family and home, as in the story about levirate marriage in Ruth (Ruth 4:5, 10). However, "A *naḥălâ* in its primary meaning, is not something simply handed down from generation to generation but entitlement or rightful property of a party that is legitimated by a recognized social custom, legal process, or divine character" (Habel, *The Land Is Mine*, 35). See also C. J. H. Wright, "*naḥălâ*," *NIDOTTE* 3.77–81; and the excursus in R. Rendtorff, *The Canonical Hebrew Bible: A Theology of the Old Testament* (trans. David E. Orton; Leiden: Deo, 2005) 458–60, which explains that *naḥălâ* is a theological legal term.

"in the land," another frequent expression to identify their habitat, their home (Num 10:9; 34:12; Deut 5:33; 11:9; 32:47).

The allotment of land to all Israel meant bringing order out of chaos; it also meant security and rest (Deut 12:10; 25:19; 1 Kgs 8:56). The image of safety for Israel is of "all of them under their vines and fig trees" (Isa 36:16; 1 Kgs 4:25; Mic 4:4; Zech 3:10).

Reflection on these aspects of land—habitat, home, and security—brings the metaphor into focus. One reads in the NT of entering the kingdom (Matt 5:20; 19:23; Acts 14:22). There is talk of inheriting the kingdom reminiscent of 'allotment' (*naḥălâ*) language (1 Cor 6:9–10; Gal 5:21; Eph 1:11). Just as in the OT "in the land" is an oft-recurring expression, so in the NT "in Christ" is a formula of high frequency. By it the NT epistles indicate the believer's (and the church's) new habitat. George Ladd, noting that the expression "in Christ" is one of Paul's most characteristic formulations, concludes, "Therefore to be 'in Christ' means to be in the new sphere of salvation."[33] "In Christ" is the ambience for the believer; it is the space where the believer is at home. This is where he or she really lives. As E. Best notes, "Christ is the 'place' in whom believers are and in whom salvation is."[34] Davies put it similarly: "Life 'in Christ,' abiding in him, taking the yoke of the kingdom—these signify in the New Testament the fulfillment of the hope for that fullness of life in the land that Judaism had cherished."[35] It is not hard to detect a certain inter-textuality. The OT phrase "in the land" is echoed in the NT by the phrase "in Christ" but also by the broader reality of "in the kingdom." One might say that the two testaments are held together by the categories of space, conceptualized as land (OT) and kingdom/Christ (NT). Land functions in metaphor as a transposable concept.

Land as Abundance, and Satiation

In general, land and acreage as the source for vegetation and food are crucial for human existence. However, the biblical metaphor is not about land in general but about a specific land. Here in the land of Israel, one need not eke out an existence, for the land is a land of abundance. It is a land of plenty; witness the return of the spies with a large grape cluster (Num 13:23), and the ample

---

33. George E. Ladd, *A Theology of the New Testament* (rev. ed.; Grand Rapids: Eerdmans, 1993) 525; see his discussion on pp. 523–25 and bibliography.

34. Ernest Best, *One Body in Christ* (London: SPCK, 1955) 8. He cites previous studies observing that the formula "in Christ" occurs 164×. "'In Christ', answering to 'in the land', denotes a status and a relationship, a position of inclusion and security" (C. J. H. Wright, *God's People in God's Land*, 111).

35. Davies, *Gospel and Land*, 374.

water supply (Deut 8:7–9). The epithet "a land flowing with milk and honey" (Exod 3:8) may be an idiom for having all that is desirable. Neither milk nor honey is the result of human labor. "Milk and honey are 'free gifts' of animal and insect."[36] Whatever the more precise meaning of the idiom, one can agree that these "images combine to form a picture of total satisfaction."[37]

The unique abundance of the land of Canaan is highlighted by a comparison with Egypt. The land in Egypt requires intense labor and irrigation, but the land of Israel is land watered by rainfall. Furthermore, in Canaan rich resources of minerals and the like are to be found (Deut 11:10–12). The land is a good land, says Jeremiah, a jewel of a possession (Jer 3:19) and certainly a place of great fertility. Inhabitants will "be radiant over the goodness of the LORD, over the grain, the wine, and the oil . . . their life shall become like a watered garden and they shall never languish again" (Jer 31:12). God promises: "My people shall be satisfied with my bounty" (Jer 31:14). In Brueggemann's words: "Land is for satiation."[38]

With this association in mind, one can hear an intertextual (metaphorical) echo when Jesus in the NT announces that he came "that they might have life, and have it abundantly" (John 10:10). Using down-to-earth images of bread and water, both connected with land, Jesus presented himself as One in whom there is abundance and satiation. He is the bread from heaven who satisfies fully, for "whoever comes to me shall never be hungry" (John 6:35). He is the living water; those who avail themselves of his gift will never thirst. Even more, the water will become in them "a spring of water gushing up to eternal life" (John 4:10–14; see also 7:38). The eschatological portrait of salvation is of trees producing fruit each month (Rev 22:2). The Bible's picture of satiation echoes the picture of physical satiation described in Deuteronomy and by the prophets. The metaphor takes on color.

Paul's exposition of the believer's "place" in the heavenlies touches on the memory of the exodus (Eph 1:3, 7) but proceeds to deal more precisely with a spiritual inheritance, as with the allotment of land (1:11). The passage brims with language of abundance: "lavished" (1:8 NRSV); "riches of his glorious inheritance" (1:18). In Colossians it is about spiritual fruitfulness, echoing fruitfulness of the land (Col 1:6, 10; Hos 2:8).[39] Persons attuned to OT talk of land

---

36. Waldemar Janzen, *Exodus* (Believers Church Bible Commentary; Scottdale, PA: Herald, 2000) 61.

37. "Land of Milk and Honey," *Dictionary of Biblical Imagery* (ed. Leland Ryken, James C. Wilhoit, and Tremper Longman III; Downers Grove, IL: InterVarsity, 1998) 488.

38. Brueggemann, *The Land*, 46.

39. See Brian J. Walsh and Sylvia C. Keesmaat, *Colossians Remixed: Subverting the Empire* (Downers Grove, IL: InterVarsity, 2004) 71–75.

will hear these passages stereophonically and, given the associations of abundance with land, savor with additional insight and pleasure Paul's exposition of what salvation entails. The metaphor works!

Land as Promise

Secular history can be written around topics such as populations and land, but redemption history adds another subject—namely, God. Redemption history makes for a triad: God, people, and land.[40] God's call to Abraham included the promise of a land for him (Gen 12:1–3, 7; 15:7, 18; 17:8). This promise of land is reiterated to Isaac (Gen 26:3), to Jacob (Gen 28:13; 35:12), and to Moses (Exod 3:8, 17; 6:8; Deut 1:8). Like the promise of descendants, this promise is uneven in coming to fulfillment, for its fulfillment is endangered (e.g., Canaanites were in the land, Gen 12:6). Even though Joshua declares the promise fulfilled (Josh 21:45; 23:15), land is later lost at the time of the exile. However, the promise, though fulfilled, lies dormant, ready to take on a new life. The prophets Jeremiah and Ezekiel promise a return to the land, though for other motivations than that the initial promise requires it (Jer 16:15; 24:6; 30:3; 31:17; Ezek 11:14–21; 34:11–14; 37:1–14).[41]

H. D. Preuss notes that the divine promise of land is unique: "No texts of the religious environment of ancient Israel know of a promise of the land."[42] Biblical Hebrew, however, as has been pointed out, does not have a term that corresponds to the English "promise." Yet the promissory nature of God's statements about land are strongly worded, and that by oath. The land is the land 'sworn' (root *šbʿ*) by God himself to belong to the people Israel (Gen 26:3; Num 14:23, 32:11; Deut 6:10). The singularity of this conjunction of land and promise, unique in ancient Near Eastern literature, readily adds another layer of metaphorical meaning to land.[43]

"Promise" is part of the land metaphor system available for NT appropriation. Daniel anticipated: "And in the days of those kings the God of heaven will set up a kingdom that shall never be destroyed" (Dan 2:44). This kingdom was one that demonstrated God's victory over contrary powers. Fulfillment of the kingdom promise came in Jesus, who by triumphing over Satanic powers

---

40. C. J. H. Wright, *God's People in God's Land*, 3–114.

41. Elmer A. Martens, *Motivations for the Promise of Israel's Restoration to the Land in Jeremiah and Ezekiel* (Ph.D. diss., Claremont Graduate School, 1972).

42. Preuss, *Old Testament Theology*, 1.119.

43. For discussion of the land promise, see M. Weinfeld, *The Promise of the Land* (Berkeley, CA: University of California Press, 1993); Brueggemann, *The Land*, 1–26; Kaiser, *Toward an Old Testament Theology*, 122–42; Preuss, *Old Testament Theology*, 1.117–27; and Rendtorff, *The Canonical Hebrew Bible*, 457–69.

demonstrated that "the kingdom of God has come to you" (Matt 12:28–29).[44] Similarly, Christ in his person is the fulfillment of OT promises, as the fulfillment texts in the Gospels indicate (e.g., Matt 1:23; 2:5–6; 4:15–16). Davies's comment is apropos: "For Paul, Christ had gathered up the promise into the singularity of his own person. In this way, 'the territory' promised was transformed into and fulfilled by the life 'in Christ'."[45] If the span between the first promise for land and its fulfillment was a long one in the OT, so also was the span between the initial promise for a deliverer (some see it as early as Gen 3:15) and its fulfillment. Just as hopes for a land were pinned on the divine promise in the OT, so also hopes for a deliverer were fixated on the promised deliverer in the NT (Luke 24: 21). Just as the road to fulfillment of the Promised Land was marred by setbacks and detours, so also fulfillment of the promise of a Messiah took tortuous turns (e.g., the apparent ending of the Davidic Dynasty). Just as fulfillment of the land promise brought reassurance of God's faithfulness to his word, so the fulfillment of the Messiah promise confirmed God's commitment as uncompromising.

Land is a transposable concept corresponding in certain ways to God's kingdom. As in a novel, the connections between the early parts and the later are present but not explicitly identified, thus enhancing the pleasure of a reader who recognizes them, so the correspondences between land, a major topic in the OT, and the major topics of kingdom of God and Christ in the NT are not only present but enhance understanding of the whole.

Land as Gift

The book of Deuteronomy is noted for its repeated emphasis on the land as God's gift to a people (e.g., 1:8; 3:18, 20; 5:31; 9:6; 11:17; 26:9). It is not in Israel's power to take the land, but it can receive it as a gift. Brueggemann helpfully elaborates this principle via two histories, noting especially the sequence of events at Kadesh Barnea (Num 14) and the reflections at the boundary (Deuteronomy).[46] At Kadesh Barnea Israel learned through defeat that land could not be grasped; it was a gift. At the boundary, prepared to enter the land, Moses repeatedly emphasized the gift nature of Israel's possession; the word *nātan* 'give' occurs more than 30x in Deuteronomy. God has the prerogative as owner ("the land is mine," Lev 25:23) to parcel out the land as a gift. This is the literary context that Brueggemann enlarges to include the NT by offering the principle that those who grasp, trying to save their own life, lose.

---

44. See Ladd's discussion on "The Kingdom of God" in *Theology of the New Testament*, 54–67.
45. Davies, *Gospel and Land,* 179.
46. Brueggemann, *The Land,* 33–38, 45–50.

This ideology of "gift," the literary context, can be set alongside the historical context. The king's prerogative, according to ancient Near Eastern practice, was to allot the land at his pleasure to individuals he might choose.[47] In this way the land was a commodity of power. The story of Ahab and Naboth's vineyard operates with this sort of ideology. As Queen Jezebel announced: "I will give you the vineyard of Naboth the Jezreelite" (1 Kgs 21:7). By contrast, in Israel's understanding, Yahweh gave the land, not to an individual, but to a community. Land was not to be a commodity, the coinage of power, but instead it was a gift over which stewardship was to be exercised.[48] This entailed giving the land a sabbath. Its wealth-producing power was not to be exploited to the maximum. Every seven years and during the jubilee year, the land was to lie fallow (Lev 25:1–12). Stewardship also entailed bringing the firstfruits as an offering to Yahweh because Yahweh was the initial giver of the wealth-producing land (Exod 23:16, 19; Deut 26:2). Though land was a gift, certain demands of discipleship, to use NT language, were articulated.

Indeed, the NT counterpart of land theology is readily discernible. Jesus spoke of *giving* his little flock the kingdom (Luke 12:32). He said twice in the beatitudes that "theirs is the kingdom of God" (Matt 5:3, 10). G. E. Ladd puts it succinctly: "The Beatitudes view the kingdom as a gift."[49] Jesus Christ, the central figure in the kingdom of God, is God's indescribable gift (2 Cor 9:15), not to an ethnic group but to the world (John 3:16). The gift of a Savior, such as the gift of land, is not conditioned on merit. The gift of Jesus, as with God's gift of a land, is an expression of God's grace and benevolence (John 1:16). We speak of both land and the person of Jesus in superlative terms. Both represent a solution to a problem. As with land in the OT, where it was imperative that Israel claim the gift, so it is with Christ. A gift calls for acceptance on the part of the recipient. As with land, salvation cannot be grasped through effort; it must be received as a gift.

Here then, as with the features of rest and abundance, land by virtue of what it symbolizes becomes a transposable concept, a metaphor by which to appreciate the significance of God's kingdom, Jesus, and salvation—gifts, all three.

---

47. For examples from Ugarit of kings and their land grants, see William W. Hallo, ed., *The Context of Scripture* (3 vols.; Leiden: Brill, 2003) 3.108, 109. Scott Booth, to whom I owe this reference, also noted examples of royal land grants in the same source, *Context of Scripture*: from Egypt (1.38, 79), Old Aramaic (2.37), and Phoenician (3.55).

48. Note the subtitle, *Place as Gift*, for Brueggemann's monograph, *The Land*. There, see pp. 45–50, 157–64. See also P. D. Miller, "The Gift of God: The Deuteronomic Theology of the Land," *Int* 23 (1969) 240–51; Habel, *The Land Is Mine*, 39–41; and Janzen, "Land," 147–48.

49. Ladd, *A Theology of the New Testament*, 71; see the discussion, pp. 70–78.

Land as the Place of God's Presence

Israel's tabernacle and later the temple in Jerusalem were, in a manner of speaking, the locus for God's presence. The tabernacle was the deity's *miqdāš* 'dwelling' (Exod 25:8–9), an idea reinforced by the position of the ark of the covenant in the holy of holies. Moreover, the glory cloud signified God's presence in the tabernacle (Exod 40:34) and in the temple (1 Kgs 8:11–13). In Ezekiel the temple structure is designated 'Yahweh is there' (*YHWH šāmmâ*, Ezek 48:35). To put it this way was already to say that God was understood to be present in the land (Jer 7:3, 11).[50] God promised to dwell with Israel: "And I will walk among you" (Lev 26:11). The literary context, whether Pentateuch or Prophets, testifies to Yahweh's presence in the land. Yet there is also a disclaimer. In the phrase "the place that the LORD your God will choose . . . as his habitation to put his name there" (Deut 12:5), as McConville explains, there is a "theology of place and 'journey' that refuses to see any one place as having a final or supreme function in Israel's life."[51] On the one hand, "Heaven is my throne and the earth is my footstool" (Isa 66:1). On the other hand, as Ps 113 so wonderfully portrays, the God who inhabits eternity is at the same time present in the immediate situation of a mother and her child in a nursery. Even more, God is present with the individual who is of a contrite heart (Isa 66:2). No surprise! God who is present in the land is not present only in the land.

Within the historical context, Israel shared with its neighbors the notion that God took up residency in a locale. The Syrians, for example, distinguished between the gods of the hills and the gods of the plains (1 Kgs 20:23). However, quite different from the faith of its neighbors was Israel's understanding that Yahweh's primary relationship was to a people and then, only secondarily, to land.[52]

The NT incorporates both of these trajectories: God spatially localized and God present with (in) persons. John, resorting to spatial language, states, "And the Word became flesh and lived [Greek: *eskēnōsen* 'tabernacled'] among us" (John 1:14 NRSV; "made his dwelling [*eskēnōsen*] among us," TNIV), and again

---

50. A textual problem in Jeremiah's temple sermon centering on the pointing of *'tkm* is best resolved as in W. Holladay's proposal that for Jer 7:3 one should read, "and I will dwell with you [*'itĕkem*] in this place [*māqôm*]," meaning temple, but in 7:7, "I will let you dwell [*'etkem*] in this place [*māqôm*]," meaning land, "the land that I gave of old to your ancestors forever and ever." A few ancient MSS and the Vulgate, however, read for 7:7, "I will dwell with you [*'itĕkem*] in this place [*māqôm*], in the land that I gave of old to your ancestors forever and ever" (so the NRSV). See Holladay, *Jeremiah* (Philadelphia: Fortress, 1986) 235, 237.

51. McConville, "Metaphor, Symbol and the Interpretation of Deuteronomy," in 335.

52. D. I. Block, *The Gods of the Nations* (Grand Rapids: Baker, 2000) 21–33.

in the eschatological vision, "He [God] will dwell [*skēnōsei*] with them" (Rev 21:3). Paul resorts to incarnational language more directly: "God was in Christ" (2 Cor 5:19), and John individualizes God's presence within persons, "he [Christ] abides in them" (1 John 3:24). Once again the metaphor system about God's presence in the land is fertile ground for comprehending NT theological teachings.

Land as a Place of Righteousness

Probing further the analogy of "land" (OT) with "kingdom of God" (NT) puts one in touch with the subject of righteousness. Land, when regarded as other than turf, gathers to itself notions of right living. Prescriptions about life-style and ethics given to Israel are introduced with the phrase, "When you enter the land. . . ." These instructions have to do with rituals (Deut 12), but they also have to do with ethics: sexuality within the family (Lev 18), treatment of neighbor and the handicapped, business practices, judicial proceedings, integrity, and much else (Lev 19).[53] Israel's behavior in the land is to be of a different order than the behavior of people living in the land of Canaan or Egypt (Lev 18:2–4). The king in Israel, especially, is called to rule his dominion with righteousness (Ps 72:1–2). In an enlarged sphere, righteous rule would entail care of the land. Proscribed activities such as going after other gods pollute the land in Yahweh's sight (Jer 2:7–8; 16:18). Immoral behavior such as dishonesty, murder, and adultery affects the environment negatively and disastrously (Lev 18:24–28; Num 35:33; Jer 3:2). Indeed the prophets announce provocatively that morality (or its lack) affects the environment. Hosea declares that what transpires in the ecological world, the disappearance of fish and birds, is the result of moral transgressions such as murder, theft, and deceit (Hos 4:1–3). Amos declares that the rain is withheld because of Israel's rebellion (Amos 4; see also Jer 5:25). In short, ideally, land comes to have associated with it the notion of discreet, God-approved, righteous behavior.[54]

When one steps into the NT to listen to Jesus, one hears of kingdom and righteousness (Matt 5:20–48; 6:33). These terms go together, even as land and righteousness go together. Jesus spoke about the righteousness that belongs to the kingdom, explaining that, while formerly adultery was wrong (so the Israelite law), lust that precedes adultery is also wrong (Matt 5:20–26). The requirement of truth-telling is an everyday requirement and not limited to

---

53. For an analysis of Lev 19, see my "How Is the Christian to Construe Old Testament Law?" *BBR* 12 (2002) 199–216. For a discussion of ethics related to property, see C. J. H. Wright, *God's People in God's Land*, 119–80.

54. See von Rad, "The Promised Land," 90–91; Brueggemann, *The Land*, 56–62; Davies, *Gospel and Land*, 51–52; Habel, *The Land Is Mine*, 43–47; and my *God's Design*, 127–37.

formal proceedings (Matt 5:33–37). If under the old order, greed was severely censured (Josh 7:1–20) so, clearly, it is also by Jesus (Luke 12:15). Just as life in the land was to be of a high moral order, so life with Jesus in the kingdom is of a high moral order.

Paul, like Jesus, characterized the kingdom along the lines of righteousness: "For the kingdom of God is not food and drink but righteousness and peace and joy in the Holy Spirit" (Rom 14:17). Not unlike the OT, which proscribed certain activities associated with Canaan or Egypt—lands outside the land of Israel—so Paul lists behaviors common in the "world" but disapproved for kingdom people (e.g., Gal 5:16–21; Eph 4:25–32; Col 3:5–12) and enjoins ethical practices (Rom 12:9–21). Because somewhat parallel ethical standards are attached to both—living in the land (OT) and living in the kingdom (NT)—the metaphor carries major freight.

These six threads of land as a metaphor system for the kingdom of God are but briefly sketched here. My purpose is to point them out in order to highlight the bond between the two testaments. These connections are not in each instance made explicit but are evoked through metaphor.

To return to Perdue's process of working with metaphor, beyond the initial destabilization brought on with the analogy of land and kingdom of God, reflection will tease out "sets of association(s)."[55] The net result, then, is to garner fresh appreciation for the subject (kingdom of God) by contemplating the vehicle (land). In particular, the kingdom of God—given its connection with land as home, a place of rest—has about it a warmth, an invitational aspect. The kingdom of God gains in appeal with the realization that it, like the land of abundance, holds the promise of a fulfilled life for those who enter it.[56] Although the NT emphasizes propositionally that the kingdom is not available by works, the metaphor of land, clearly a gift, fleshes out the proposition through historical experiences. Critical to the kingdom of God is God as present; this abstraction was "earthed," so to speak, in the way God was present in the land. With this assertion, a range of analogous experiences come into view. If the NT discussion of the place of righteousness within kingdom-living tends toward generalizations, the metaphor of land and righteous living within it offers "body" to the instructions. Finally, the open-endedness of promise characteristic of the OT land promise serves the citizens of God's kingdom well, for anticipation marks their existence also.

---

55. The phrase is from Soskice, *Metaphor and Religious Language*, 49.

56. "'Land thus becomes inseparable from the Deuteronomic vision of a people keeping covenant, worshiping and enjoying blessing in the context of community, justice, peace and joy ([Deut] 16:13–15)" (McConville, "Metaphor, Symbol and the Interpretation of Deuteronomy," 337).

If this metaphorical system is so rich, why did the NT writers not capitalize on it? The answer is no doubt because at that time the land under Roman administration had too many political associations. The NT Christian message was not to be encumbered with provincial, geographical, or ethnic matters, because it was global in its import. Indeed, that message had for its context a "cosmic eschatology."[57] Furthermore, other symbolic systems such as temple and sacrifice were available for Jews, as for Gentiles. Quite possibly, for the apostles to exploit the land metaphor would not have resonated much with the Gentiles, who were soon in the majority. Centuries later, we as Christians, now somewhat loosed from these political encumbrances, can savor the richness of the land metaphor.

Yet, to follow Perdue, we must also note that the tension in the metaphor between kingdom of God and land remains. For example, the land of Israel has associations (e.g., warfare, loss of land) that are inimical to the kingdom. As with a parable, analogies cannot be pressed too far.

Concluding Observations

This essay has been an experimental exploration of land as a metaphorical system illuminates the subject, the kingdom of God. The points of departure come from the books of Romans and Hebrews, which use land metaphorically. The exercise engenders several reflections.

(1) Metaphor analysis is a useful tool for the exegete. Examining the text according to grammar, historical context, and the critical tools of form and redaction is customary and necessary. For forty years it has been my staple approach, a profitable and mostly satisfying approach. Nor will I dispense with it. But that approach does not exhaust the richness of biblical material; nor will attention to imagistic investigation, such as metaphor, be the magic key to unlock all the riches of Scripture. But attention to metaphor and metaphor systems, itself an exegetical method, is a supplement to the more traditional tools of word studies and other "scientific" approaches to assure objectivity.[58]

The use of literary tools such as simile, metaphor, and symbol is hardly new to interpretation. G. B. Caird argued a half-century ago that the author of Hebrews made his point about the "self-confessed inadequacy of the old order" by exegeting written texts (Pss 8, 95, 110, and Jer 31:31–34) in the customary mode. But then, as Caird astutely noted, beyond exegeting texts,

---

57. Davies cites this as an important reason (*Gospel and Land*, 370).

58. "It is this capacity of metaphor to go beyond itself and reveal the unknown, the latent, or the hidden that deserves recognition as we explore the text" (Habel, *The Earth Story in the Psalms and the Prophets*, 27).

the author of Hebrews discussed Aaron, Melchizedek, and sacrifices in order
to elaborate his claims about Jesus Christ further. Priesthood and sacrifices were
"shadow pictures" of other realities (Caird eschews language of "type"). By
means of familiar "picture language," listeners and readers were helped to
apprehend and more effectively convey the fuller scope of God's salvation.[59]

Much can be conveyed with propositions. As much, perhaps more, can
sometimes be conveyed with pictures, analogy, and metaphor. Metaphors are
evocative and suggestive rather than definitive in supplying meaning. They
invigorate and imaginatively invite listeners and readers into a new reality.
The standard approach to biblical theology via exegesis, of course, should not
be jettisoned. Rather, an aspect of this exegesis is to keep an eye open for
metaphor.[60]

(2) Metaphor enriches understanding. Analysts speak of metaphor as having
the ability to "*create* structure in our understanding of life."[61] To speak meaningfully of realities such as the kingdom of God or present and eschatological
salvation is not always easy. For this reason Jesus spoke in parables, a form of
analogy. Consequently, when discussion of salvation invokes land as a metaphor, several things happen. At once salvation has a this-wordly flavor about
it. It breathes, as does the longing for land, about necessities. Language about
the kingdom becomes language of home and security, along with emotions of
warmth and comfort. "Israel's faith is anything but a disembodied spirituality.
It is rooted in dirt and soil—*'ǎdāmâ.*"[62] As territory is an ambience for living
physically, so the kingdom of God is an ambience for all Christian living.
Living of this sort is characterized by abundance. The citizen of the kingdom,
like the inhabitant of the Promised Land, lacks no good thing. This "space"
in which the believer lives is a space where justice and righteousness are
not strangers or occasional guests but permanent and welcome companions.
Though the kingdom of God and the attendant meanings of salvation are concepts, they are also realities. Imagistic thinking via metaphor fosters an immediacy for these realities.

(3) Metaphor aids in recognizing the unity of the two testaments. The essay
began with the puzzle of relating the two testaments even though the OT
features land so prominently and the NT seems to ignore it.[63] This observa-

---

59. Caird, "The Exegetical Method of the Epistle to the Hebrews," 44–51.

60. As an example, see Brown, *Seeing the Psalms: A Theology of Metaphor*, n. 11; more generally, Lakoff and Turner, *More Than Cool Reason*.

61. Ibid., 62 (italics theirs).

62. Dempster, *Dominion and Dynasty*, 85.

63. "The trajectory of the Land motif into the New Testament, however, is the most difficult biblical motif to track" (Waltke, *An Old Testament Theology*, 559). His tracking method is
through redefinition and typology (p. 560).

tion holds true if the comparison centers on vocabulary. If, however, the investigation of the relationship between the two testaments is broadened to include imagistic aspects of communication, a link is offered. Some hold that the motif of land dead-ends in the OT. This is a superficial view, however, considering that the Bible presents its message on the large canvas of creation and re-creation. In a well-written novel, a motif introduced early on may be thought not to reappear later. However, the discerning reader may discover in a highly satisfying and instructive way that the matter has not been dropped but reappears, though in somewhat disguised form, toward the end of the book. Land as turf is an issue in Israel's story in the OT. Land as metaphor taps into that ancient story to enlarge the horizon against which the message of God's kingdom is given. Seeing land as metaphor, as the NT invites us to do, teases out fresh connections between the two testaments.

An exploration of land as a metaphor that links the two testaments is congenial to the current emphasis on the canonical approach to biblical interpretation.[64] The canonical approach invites consideration of links not only between discrete pericopes but between books and, ultimately, between parts of the entire canon. The canonical approach embraces both the critical analysis and the theological appropriation of texts. It is the theological appropriation to which the appreciation of metaphor points. Metaphoric exegesis provides one track by which a community can move to interpretation and appropriation.

This essay has focused on land as a theological datum with an emphasis on the bridging power of metaphor to connect the two testaments. A literary bridge such as metaphor has large, strong arches. For a full compass of a "theology" of land, other arches such as the ethical, eschatological, environmental, and economic should be investigated.

(4) Biblical theology is a discipline that, among other benefits, offers a service to the church. Andrew Lincoln asks: why bother with biblical theology? His answer, derived from the book of Hebrews, is pastoral. The book of Hebrews investigates Scripture in the light of the Christ event and the current situation.[65] A pastor has concern for the guidance of believers through teaching and exhortation. This teaching, often geared to a specific situation, requires wrestling with all of Scripture, not least to know where the continuities and discontinuities are.[66] In this enterprise, especially in a postmodern era with its visuals and icons, imagistic thinking resonates well. There are reasons to agree with Paul Avis, "Postmodernity privileges image over discourse, *eidos*

---

64. See the essays in *Canon and Biblical Interpretation* (ed. Craig G. Bartholomew et al.; Grand Rapids: Zondervan, 2006).

65. Lincoln, "Hebrews and Biblical Theology," 333.

66. Ibid., 331.

over *logos.*[67] Preachers who labor to instruct about God's kingdom, Christ's message, and salvation might clarify for their hearers and excite them with the use of the protracted metaphor of land.

---

67. Paul Avis, *God and the Creative Imagination: Metaphor, Symbol and Myth in Religion and Theology* (London: Routledge, 1999) 23, quoted in Stephen B. Chapman, "Imaginative Readings of Scripture and Theological Interpretation," in *Out of Egypt* (ed. C. Bartholomew; Grand Rapids: Zondervan / Carlisle: Paternoster, 2004) 482. On the topic of imagination, Chapman lists six problems and four constructive proposals.

Israel and Its Land in Biblical Perspective

WALTER C. KAISER JR.

President Emeritus
Gordon-Conwell Theological Seminary
Hamilton, Massachusetts

Few issues arouse more excitement or sharper divisions in the work of interpreting the Scriptures than the question of the future of Israel and the land of Israel. I too have taken pen in hand on a number of occasions to address this lingering debate.[1] However, this discussion will be followed by many more contributions, despite optimistic hope that a definitive word might be found as a result of our dialogue.

A Recent Case from an Exegetical Standpoint

In recent times, O. Palmer Robertson has made a very fine contribution to this debate with his *Israel of God: Yesterday, Today and Forever.*[2] Robertson first makes the point that "the arena of redemption has shifted from [OT] type to

---

Author's note: It is a special privilege to dedicate this article to Prof. Elmer A. Martens, whose friendship and professional stimulation over the years have been a special joy. A preliminary form of this essay was read at the November 2005 Philadelphia meeting of the Evangelical Theological Society. I want to give special recognition to Elmer's landmark dissertation written (on the same topic as this essay) under the direction of Prof. W. H. Brownlee entitled *Motivations for the Promise of Israel's Restoration to the Land in Jeremiah and Ezekiel* (Ph.D. diss., Claremont Graduate School, 1972).

1. For example, Walter C. Kaiser Jr., "The Promised Land: A Biblical-Historical View," *BSac* 138 (1981) 302–12; idem, *Toward Rediscovering the Old Testament* (Grand Rapids: Zondervan, 1987) 46–58; idem, "Israel as the People of God," in *The People of God: Essays on the Believer's Church* (ed. Paul Basden and David S. Dockery; Nashville: Broadman, 1991) 99–108; idem, "An Assessment of Replacement Theology: The Relationship between the Israel of the Abrahamic-Davidic Covenant and the Christian Church," *Mishkan* 21 (1994) 9–20; and idem, "The Land of Israel and the Future Return: Zechariah 10:6–12," in *Israel: The Land and the People* (ed. H. Wayne House; Grand Rapids: Kregel, 1998) 168–85.

2. O. Palmer Robertson, *The Israel of God: Yesterday, Today, and Forever* (Phillipsburg, NJ: Presbyterian and Reformed, 2000).

reality, from [OT] shadow to substance. The land which once was the specific place of God's redemptive work . . . has expanded to encompass the whole world."[3] For Robertson, the promise of the land is placed in the same category as the offerings and services of the tabernacle: all are types for which the new realities have transcended their older forms. Thus, the land was never an end in itself, nor was it as eternal as was the offer of the gospel or of the seed of Messiah mentioned in the same contexts.

His second argument is to view the nation Israel of today and of the future in terms of the phrase "the Israel of God" in Gal 6:16. This is followed by an excellent interpretation of Heb 7 on the worship of Israel today; he then ventures away from what the text says to make a third statement that, in light of the context, the writer of Heb 7 (see also Ps 110) "shows how futile it would be to rebuild the temple and reinstitute sacrifices and a priesthood."[4] A fourth claim is this: nowhere "is [there] evidence for a three-staged coming of the messianic kingdom outside of Revelation 20."[5] This leads Robertson to conclude that the reference to the thousand years in Rev 20 should be interpreted symbolically rather than introducing a new stage into the concept of the kingdom. Finally, and most importantly, the discussion comes round to Rom 11, where it must always finally focus in this discussion. The full cycle of movement in this text about the Jews takes place in the present age, begins Robertson. But then he decides that the statement "all Israel will be saved" refers not to all the elect Jews but to all the elect of God, Jew and Gentile.[6] Alas, Robertson disappointingly concludes that "nothing in this chapter [Rom 11] says anything about the restoration of an earthly Davidic kingdom, or of a return to the land of the Bible, or of a restoration of a national state of Israel."[7] His summary is found in proposition number five (of twelve propositions):

> Rather than understanding predictions about the "return" of "Israel" to the "land" in terms of a geo-political re-establishment of the state of Israel, these prophecies are more properly interpreted as finding consummate fulfillment at the "restoration of all things" that will accompany the resurrection of believers at the return of Christ (Acts 3:21; Rom 8:22–23).[8]

It is to these conclusions that we must now turn, hopefully to further the discussion of this central but elusive topic.

---

3. Ibid., 30–31.
4. Ibid., 82.
5. Ibid., 160.
6. Ibid., 187.
7. Ibid., 191.
8. Ibid., 194.

The Israel of God versus the People of God

The proper treatment of the identity of Israel, the Jews, the Church, and the "people of God" is central to the discussion.[9] Few dispute the fact that the roots of Christianity are firmly embedded in the promise/plan given to Eve, Shem, Abraham, Isaac, Jacob, and David. Unfortunately, this is as far as many can go.

The questions who are the "people of God" and what happened to the promise/plan of God given to the patriarchs and David receive quite different answers. In classical dispensationalism, Charles C. Ryrie supplies our first answer this way:

> What, then, is the *sine qua non* of dispensationalism? . . . A dispensationalist keeps Israel and the Church distinct. . . . This is probably the most basic theological test of whether or not a man is a dispensationalist, and it is undoubtedly the most practical and conclusive.[10]

A second answer is traditionally associated with covenant theologians, as exemplified by William E. Cox. His answer is this:

> The OT records two kinds of promises which God made to national Israel: national promises and spiritual promises. The spiritual promises encompassed every spiritual descendant of Abraham, and were not restricted to national Israel (Gen 12:3; 22:18; Rom 2:28–29; 4:17; Eph 2:11–16; 3:6–9; Phil 3:3; Col 2:11). The spiritual promises are still being fulfilled through the church today. Israel's national promises all have either been fulfilled or invalidated because of unbelief.[11]

A mediating position poses, in my estimation, a better solution to these problems. It agrees with dispensationalism that God is not finished with Israel yet and, therefore, the so-called national promises that are so deeply embedded in the spiritual promises are all part of God's purpose for the present and the future. But this mediating position also agrees with covenant theology that there has been and always will be only one "people of God." Rather than quoting from my own work, wherein I agree with the concept of the one "people of God," allow me to cite George E. Ladd:

> There is therefore but one people of God. This is not to say that the Old Testament saints belonged to the Church and that we must speak of the

---

9. See the contribution of Jacques B. Doukhan, *Israel and the Church* (Peabody, MA: Hendrickson, 2002).

10. Charles C. Ryrie, *Dispensationalism Today* (Chicago: Moody, 1965) 44–45.

11. William E. Cox, *Amillennialism Today* (Philadelphia: Presbyterian and Reformed, 1966) 34.

Church in the Old Testament. . . . The Church properly speaking had its birthday on the day of Pentecost, for the Church is composed of all those who by one Spirit have been baptized into one body (1 Cor 12:13), and this baptizing work of the Spirit began on the day of Pentecost. While we must therefore speak of Israel and the Church, we must speak of only one people of God.[12]

How then will this debate be resolved? For dispensationalists, I call attention to the fact that the term of continuity in both testaments is "people of God," which encompasses both "Israel" (e.g., Exod 5:22–6:8; Deut 7:6–8; 2 Sam 7:23–24) and the NT "Church" (Acts 15:14; 2 Cor 6:16; 1 Pet 2:9–10). Thus, the NT concept of peoplehood reflects its OT origins without making a second category for individuals who participate by faith.

For covenant theologians, I note that the NT, which for some is made the "coin of the realm" for final interpretation on all matters, employs the term "Israel" 73 times. Only one of these 73 uses, Gal 6:16, is uniformly appealed to as demonstrating that the Church equals Israel; none of the other 72 citations is contested as referring to anything but the national people of Israel.[13] Thus, the whole case for finding that the Church replaces Israel rests on this one verse, for none of the other 72 NT passages will demonstrate this alleged equation.

Galatians 6:16 teaches: "Peace and mercy to all who follow this rule, even to the Israel of God" (NIV). Actually, the Greek text reads: "And as many as walk by this rule, peace be upon them, and mercy, and upon the Israel of God." Surprisingly enough, the whole case for the equation of Israel and the Church rests on the conjunction "and," which the NIV took in its secondary and lesser meaning of "even." But this is doubtful from the context because, if Paul had wished to identify the Christian Church with Israel, the best way to have done this would have been to omit the Greek *kai* altogether and simply allow the phrase "Israel of God" to stand in apposition to the preceding clause! The Apostle Paul had just made his case in v. 15 against the Judaizers, who were demanding that Gentiles must obtain their salvation by adhering to the Law of Moses. Instead, Paul cites the "rule" that salvation comes by faith alone, faith in the cross of Jesus Christ (vv. 14–15). Paul pronounces a blessing on

---

12. George E. Ladd, *The Gospel of the Kingdom: Scriptural Studies in the Kingdom of God* (Grand Rapids: Eerdmans, 1959) 117.

13. Two other references sometimes appear in covenantal lists (Rom 9:6 and 11:26). But usually these texts are quickly conceded after a close exegetical examination. See my "Israel as the People of God," 100–102.

individuals who live according to "this rule."[14] Two groups are included in the blessing: (1) the "them" of v. 16, that is, the Gentile Christians; and (2) the "Israel of God," who in this context are the Jewish believers who have been justified by faith in the work of Christ on the cross. Consequently, it is impossible to call the Church a "spiritual Israel" or a "new Israel" that now replaces the Church in a supersessionistic way.

The Patriarchal Promises: Conditional or Unconditional?

In order to make the Church the inheritor of the promises made to the patriarchs and Israel, the Abrahamic promise must be shown to be either: (1) conditional and bilateral in nature, or (2) somehow possessing a meaning that is not the plain or natural meaning of what is said. This raises a troublesome problem for evangelicalism, because some individuals consider the Abrahamic promise to be part of a type of prophetic literature for which a special principle obtains. It is not that a secondary sense is added to the Scriptures, we are assured, but a "deeper meaning" is found; God, the primary author of the text intended this meaning, which is not the grammatical or syntactical meaning given to the text by the human writers of Scripture. Therefore, in this case, contrary to most other interpreting situations, the assertions of the text cannot be determined by following the usual grammatical-historical method of interpreting what the human authors of Scripture wrote.[15]

However, in Gen 15:17–21, only God himself passes between the divided pieces of the heifer, goat, and ram. God appears as a "smoking firepot with a blazing torch." Some have attempted to divide the imagery so that either the

---

14. In a paper delivered at the 1998 annual meeting of the Evangelical Theological Society ("The Old Testament Background of 'Peace and Mercy' in Galatians 6:15–16"), Greg Beale argued that the reversal of "peace" and "mercy" in Paul's blessing could not reflect the language of the Jewish prayer *Shemoneh Esreh* ("Grant peace, salvation, and blessing, grant favor, grace, and mercy to us and to all Israel, thy people"), for the prayer did not exist in this form in Paul's day, but Paul took it from Isa 54:10. Hans Dieter Betz, however, said otherwise: "There is no certainty how old this benediction is, but in all likelihood it is at least as old as the time of Paul" (*A Commentary on Paul's Letter to the Churches in Galatia* [Philadelphia: Fortress, 1979] 321–22).

15. Louis Berkhof famously adopted this "deeper meaning of Scripture" when he stated, "The real meaning of Scripture does not always lie on the surface. There is no truth in the assertion that the intent of the secondary authors [God being the primary author], determined by the grammatico-historical method, always exhausts the sense of Scripture, and represents in all its fullness the meaning of the Holy Spirit" (*Principles of Biblical Interpretation* [Grand Rapids: Baker, 1964] 59–60; see also pp. 133–66). This is an amazing statement that could potentially vitiate all that he holds true for Scripture and its authority.

smoking firepot or the blazing torch represents Abraham, who may then be represented as passing between the pieces along with the Almighty. Thus, this was a bilateral (or double-sided) covenant or a social contract; the whole thing defaulted if either party failed to keep its side of the covenant. However, this argument neglects the fact that the two items are not joined by the conjunction "and." The smoking firepot is dominant and has a blazing torch with it. Moreover, nowhere else in Scripture is a mere mortal represented as a blazing torch. Instead, fire is connected in both testaments with God himself (e.g., Exod 3:2; 19:18; Deut 1:33; Isa 66:15).

Oswald T. Allis, later joined by Ronald Youngblood, declared the Abrahamic and Davidic covenants to be conditioned on Israel's obedience.[16] But I argue, with Scripture, that the alleged conditional elements in the covenants with Abraham and David never constituted a threat to the intrinsic nature of these covenants, nor did they add stipulations to them. God never found fault with his own covenants but *only with the people.* Thus, individuals could *personally fail to participate* in the benefits of the covenant through disobedience, but they were often still called upon to *transmit* the benefits of God because these benefits were irrevocable.[17]

The Alleged Lack of Evidence for
Two Future Resurrections

Robertson argues that only Rev 20 provides any evidence of a three-staged coming of the messianic kingdom. But this is not so, for the Apostle Paul presents the three-staged view in 1 Cor 15:22–23. He declares that *all* are dying since the sin of Adam, but indeed *all* can be made alive in Christ. However, there is a sequence of resurrections: "each in his own order." The word for 'order' in Greek is *tagma*. Christ's resurrection, the first of the three resurrections, will lead the other orders. 'Afterward' (*epeita*), but not at the same time, a group "who belongs to him" will be resurrected. 'Finally' (*eita*), a third group is raised when the "end comes," when Christ "hands over the kingdom to God the Father after he has destroyed all dominion, authority and power" (v. 24). The Greek formulaic words "then . . . and then . . ." are always found paired, like "love and marriage," "horse and carriage," and they imply an unspecified time sequence between them. For example, note the time elapse shown by the

---

16. Oswald T. Allis, *God Spake by Moses* (Nutley, NJ: Presbyterian and Reformed, 1958) 72; and Ronald Youngblood, "The Abrahamic Covenant: Conditional or Unconditional?" in *The Living and Active Word of God: Studies in Honor of Samuel J. Schultz* (ed. Morris Inch and Ronald Youngblood; Winona Lake, IN: Eisenbrauns, 1983) 31–46.

17. For a fuller discussion, see my *Rediscovering the Old Testament,* 50–51, 149–55.

same Greek pair of words in "first the stalk, then [*eita*] the head, then [*eita*] the full kernel in the head" (Mark 4:28).

Another text supporting two future resurrections (in addition to Messiah's) is Dan 12:1–2. Almost all commentators agree that this text is eschatological and that it relates primarily to Israel. It reads in v. 2, "And many of those who sleep in the dust of the earth shall awake, some to everlasting life, and some to shame and everlasting contempt." The 'many' (*rabbîm*) 'from' (*min*) all the sleepers in the dust, a euphemism for the dead, will be raised along with the other believers. Another resurrection speaks to another order for those who are resurrectible but only to shame and everlasting contempt. According with this view are certain expressions in John 5:28 and 29. Thus, Rev 20 is not alone in setting forth the view of two future resurrections.

Was the Land an Everlasting Possession?

The promise of God to Israel was that possession of the land was to be "everlasting" or "eternal" in its scope. But some writers such as, relatively recently, Chris Wright admonish that "the expression 'for-ever' (Hebrew *lĕ-ʿōlām*) needs to be seen, not so much in terms of everlastingness in linear time, but rather as an intensive expression within the terms, conditions, and context of the promise concerned."[18] To demonstrate his point, Wright points to the Rechabites, who were promised descendants "forever" (Jer 35:19). If this is so, Wright asks, where are their descendants today? Unfortunately for Wright's argument, the word *lĕ-ʿōlām* does not appear in Jer 35:19, nor does it appear in a second reference to the Levites and the House of David that he cites Jer 33:17–22. Both passages use the expression "will never fail to have a man."

Whenever the word *lĕ-ʿōlām* is used of the Levites and of David, it has reference to the *office*, not primarily to the person(s) involved. To add to the enduring aspect of this promise of the land, the writer says that it lasts as long as the sun and moon last (Jer 31:35–40).

Finally, note that the word "forever" is not limited in all of its appearances, for the same word also describes God in some contexts. If someone does not notice that the promise of the land is found in the same covenant as the promise of the Messianic "seed" or the promise of the "gospel" (Gal 3:8) that "in your seed all the nations of the earth will be blessed," surely he or she will at least understand texts such as Gen 17:8 and 48:3–4 as promises that should be taken in linear terms, with qualities of eternality and enduring perpetuity.

---

18. Christopher Wright, "A Christian Approach to Old Testament Prophecy concerning Israel," in *Jerusalem Past and Present in the Purpose of God* (ed. P. W. L. Walker; Cambridge: Tyndale, 1992) 6.

The New Covenant

God never made a covenant with the Church as such! Certainly the new covenant was made with the "house of Israel and the house of Judah" (Jer 31:31b). This is not to say that the Church cannot share in this covenant, for God's purpose from Gen 12:3 on has been to gather the believing Gentiles into this one enduring promise/plan of God.

Without the roots of the promise to the patriarchs and the trunk of the Israelite tree, the Church would float in the air with no rootage, history, or grounding! So if we the Church are to have any grounds for our being, we must find them squarely in the Abrahamic-Davidic new covenant. No other covenant is mentioned in the NT. The first redemptive covenant was made with Abraham, Isaac, Jacob, David, Solomon, and his successors, just as the new covenant was made with the two houses of Israel. No one to my knowledge has attempted to equate either or both the house of Israel and the house of Judah with the Church. Thus, we must be careful about assuming that the older covenant with Abraham and David has been replaced and that the new covenant has now been signed over to the believing Gentiles in the Church.[19]

Romans 11:11, 29:
The Failure of Israel

"Because of Israel's disobedience, salvation has come to the Gentiles" (Rom 11:11). In the divine plan, rather than Israel's failure to obey sending a signal that it was all over for Israel as a nation—a nation now bankrupt of its national promises—the reverse was declared by the Apostle Paul. As Henrikus Berkhof observed, "She [Israel] is and remains the link between the Messiah and the nations. She could be this link through her obedience, but even now, in her *dis*obedience she still fulfils her function as a link."[20]

Paul gives us another argument along the same lines in Rom 11:15, where he argues, "If [Israel's] rejection means the reconciliation of the world [in that Gentiles are given an opportunity to come to Messiah as never before], what will [Israel's] acceptance mean but life from the dead?" Paul, rather than speaking spiritually here, appears to be picking up the same figure of speech found in Ezek 37:12 and 14 in the prophet's Valley of Dry Bones speech.

---

19. For a fuller development of the New Covenant, see my "Old Promise and the New Covenant," *JETS* 15 (1972) 11–23; repr. in *The Bible and Its Literary Milieu* (ed. John Maier and Vincent Tollers; Grand Rapids: Eerdmans, 1979) 106–20.

20. Hendrikus Berkhof, *Christ the Meaning of History* (trans. Lambertus Buurman; Richmond, VA: John Knox, 1966) 142.

Ezekiel hears God cry out, "O my people. I am going to open up your graves and bring you up from them: I will bring you back to the land of Israel. . . . I will put my Spirit in you and you will live, and I will settle you down in your own land." Although some have preferred to see in Ezekiel's text a reference to an individual's resurrection, the divine interpreter disallowed this sort of move in Ezek 37:11, where the Lord summarized the whole vision: "Then he said to me, 'Son of Man [= Ezekiel], these bones are *the whole house of Israel*'" (emphasis mine). Thus, the Apostle Paul was referring to the reestablishment of Israel in the land again, which would be accompanied by Israel's acceptance of its Messiah in the end times—an event that would be like coming back to "life from the dead."

How can we be so sure of this interpretation? There is just one reason: because Paul announces that God's "gifts and his call [are] irrevocable" (Rom 11:29). Although Israel may appear to have given a final answer to God's gift of the land and his call on their lives to be the spark that brings the Gentiles to the Lord, even in their failure the Israelites cannot get away from their intrinsic part in the divine plan of God. Thus, even Israel's spirit of stupor and rejection was calculated into the plan of God (Rom 11:8, using the informing theology of Deut 29:4 and Isa 29:10). However, when the "full number of the Gentiles has come in" (Rom 11:25), then the "full number" of Jewish believers will be completed.

Romans 11:25–26:
The Natural and Wild Olive Branches

If Rom 11 is the *crux interpretum* of this whole problem of the relationship of Israel and the Church, then vv. 25–26 are at the heart of the debate. This key chapter begins with the question: "I say then, did God reject his people?" (= Israel; see Rom 11:1). Paul thunders back, "By no means!" He then gives his pedigree as a distinguished member of the physical seed of Abraham. Just as God had reserved 7,000 in Elijah's day who had not bowed the knee to Baal, so even in Paul's day there was still a Jewish "remnant chosen by grace" (11:5).

What role then do the Jewish people and the nation of Israel play in the plan of God? As one Christian writer put it, is this hope tantamount to making Israel a co-redemptrix with Christ?[21] Others charge that inclusion of Israel in

---

21. So complained John R. Wilch ("The Land and State of Israel in Prophecy and Fulfillment," *Concordia Journal* 8 [1982] 173). He was provoked by my statements in "Must the Christian Include Israel and Her Land in a Contemporary Theology?" (*Rediscovering the Old Testament,* 46–58).

the plan of God is an act of introducing "Christian Zionism" and "Christian apartheid" into the Bible![22]

But Rom 11:25–26 will not agree with these rather harsh rebukes. It argues instead that "Israel has experienced a hardening in part until the full number of the Gentiles has come in. And so all Israel will be saved." To conclude that God is finished with Israel is to run counter to the biblical claim itself. Just as the whole soteriological case involved Jew and Gentile from the very beginning (Rom 1:16), so a balanced doctrine of eschatology and ecclesiology demands that the same 'full number' (*plēroma*) of Israelites will come to believe in their Messiah after the 'full number' (exactly the same word) of the Gentiles has been completed.

The late Anthony A. Hoekema raised two objections to the argument I have just set forth. First, Rom 11:26 does not say, "And *then* [implying the Greek word *tote* or *epeita* in a temporal sense] all Israel will be saved," but instead the Greek text reads, 'thus', 'so', or 'in this manner' [*kai houtōs*] all Israel will be saved.[23] As Hoekema would have it, the text did not teach the timing for the massive salvation of Israel, but instead it described the manner in which it would happen.

Hoekema's second objection was that to wait for this huge ingathering of Jews until the end times did injustice to Paul's word "all," for that generation would only be a fraction of the generations of Jews that had died in the meantime. So how could anyone possibly claim that "all Israel" would be redeemed?

Thirteen years before Hoekema wrote, however, another Dutch Reformed theologian by the name of Hendrikus Berkhof had already supplied an answer to Hoekema's first objection. He reasoned:

> We do not read "then" or "after this." But there is no reason to exclude the possibility that this "and so" is a future event. Paul is dealing with the historical order of God's activities, and only just before used the conjunction "until" (25). Yet, "and so" implies more than "until." However, it is less clear what the antecedent of "and so" is.[24]

Berkhof went on to suggest that the antecedent was probably the "full number of Gentiles" (meaning that, because the "full number" of Gentiles has come in, all Israel can now be saved; the first last and the last finally will be first).

---

22. Both of these charges come from Tom Wright ("Jerusalem in the New Testament," *Jerusalem, Past, and Present in the Purpose of God* [ed. P. W. L. Walker; Cambridge: Tyndale, 1992] 73–75).

23. Anthony A. Hoekema, *The Bible and the Future* (Grand Rapids: Eerdmans, 1979) 144–45.

24. Berkhof, *Christ the Meaning of History*, 145.

But I argue that what both Hoekema and Berkhof missed is that Rom 11:27 linked this "and so" with "this is my covenant with them when I take away their sins." Here is nothing less than a reference to the new covenant (Jer 31:31–34), given that much of the content of the new covenant is really an expansion of the promises made to Abraham and David—as much as 70 percent of the content of the new covenant.

Even the highly regarded Reformed theologian John Murray commented, after correctly noticing that Rom 11:26–27 contained citations from Isa 59:20–21 and Jer 31:34, that

> [t]here should be no question but Paul regards these Old Testament passages as applicable to the restoration of Israel. . . . We cannot dissociate this covenantal assurance from the proposition in support of which the text is adduced or from that which follows in verse 28 [on account of the patriarchs]. Thus the effect is that the future restoration of Israel is certified by nothing less than the certainty belonging to covenantal institution.[25]

Accordingly, I conclude with Berkhof, Murray, and the Apostle Paul that, even though the "and so" is debatable in its meaning, in its context it must be temporal, sequential, and consequential in that it ties together the promises made in the Abrahamic-Davidic new covenant, which argues for the "full number" as well as the full inclusion of Israel in that ancient but eternal promise.

With regard to Hoekema's second objection about missing too many previous Jewish generations for the "full number" of Jews to come to salvation in the end times, I can only point to where Paul and the prophets before him pointed: there always had been and will be a remnant of Jews who believed. But a "full number" awaits the final days, when the natural branches that had been lopped off will be regrafted into their own trunk once again to match the wild branches of the Gentiles that have been grafted into this same Israel trunk of the tree in the meantime.

Did Not the Return from the Babylonian Exile Fulfill the Land Promise?

Repeatedly the OT prophets depicted a return to the land of Israel as God had promised to the patriarchs and David. Not only would Israel return to the land, as Isa 10:20–30 promised, for example, but Israel would become prominent once again among the nations.

---

25. John Murray, *The Epistle of Romans* (2 vols.; Grand Rapids: Eerdmans, 1965) 2.99–100.

The return from the 70 years of captivity in Babylon did not completely fulfill what God had promised. If it had, then why was the prophet Zechariah (Zech 10:8–12) still predicting this return to the land once again as late as 518 B.C., some 18 years after the return from Babylon?[26] Well after the days when Judah had returned from the Babylonian captivity, the prophet Zechariah was still repeating this same ancient promise of God.

Conclusion

God has not cast off disobedient Israel and replaced it with the Christian Church for all time and eternity. The natural branches, meaning present-day Jewish people, must not be regarded as dead and finished as far as the promise/plan of God is concerned. Look for God to one day regraft believing natural branches back into the original tree and to fulfill his ancient promise. In the meantime, the wild branches, those of us who are Gentile believers, must not get on our high horses and become high and mighty about being the real tree that God has now chosen to replace Israel. God never made a separate covenant with the Church; the only covenant that is still operative is the covenant given to the patriarchs, David, and Jeremiah.

---

26. For a fuller development of this argument, see my "Land of Israel and the Future Return," 168–85.

God's Design and the Church

Timothy J. Geddert
Professor of New Testament
Mennonite Brethren Biblical Seminary
Fresno, California

It is with a particular set of lenses that I read OT theology books. These lenses are shaped by my own biblical, theological, and churchly priorities. As a NT scholar, I am inclined to read books such as Prof. Elmer Martens's *God's Design: A Focus on Old Testament Theology* with the following questions in the forefront: (1) How do the author's insights into the theology of the OT shed light on the theology of Scripture as a whole? (2) Did the author's way of reading the OT correspond to the way the NT writers seem to have read those Scriptures? (3) Has the author provided guidance for the reader in discerning the contemporary relevance of insights from OT theology for the church in our day?

Happily Martens's OT theology book explicitly addresses some of these matters. Fourteen chapters are devoted to exploring the theology of the OT. Then a final chapter entitled "Divine Design and the New Testament" probes Matthew's Gospel and Paul's Letter to the Romans "in order to see whether the pattern of God's design is exhibited in the New Testament."[1] Martens concludes his look at Matthew with these words: "The affinity between the facets of the divine design in the Old Testament and Jesus and his message of the kingdom in the New is a close one."[2] He concludes his look at Romans thus: "In broad outline Romans is a commentary on God's design: deliverance (chapters 1–5), experience of God (chapters 6–8), community (chapters 9–11), and blessing (land), including life-style (chapters 12–15)."[3] While one might quibble that the parallels are not quite as close as Martens claims (and perhaps that Rom 16 should not have been omitted), I have chosen to quibble about something else. I do so with great respect for my OT theology professor, his

---

1. Elmer Martens, *God's Design: A Focus on Old Testament Theology* (Grand Rapids: Baker, 1981) 249.

2. Ibid., 253.

3. Ibid., 260.

biblical scholarship, and his contributions to the church. I do so also with concern that parts of Martens's final chapter undercut the relevance of the first
14 chapters for the church.

My concern centers around one paragraph of *God's Design* in the middle
of Martens's discussion of "land" and its relevance for the "Israel" of the NT.
Before citing this paragraph, I make three disclaimers: (1) Martens's real views
on Israel's contemporary right to the land might have very little actual relevance
to the implications he wants to draw from *God's Design* for the NT church.
This is so because, even in the OT, the actual "meaning" of land centers more
heavily on the concepts of "the good life" and "life-style" than on mere real
estate. And Martens is clear that the symbolic meaning of land is what follows
through from the OT to the NT. (2) It may well be that Martens's views on
the issues I will address have changed since he published *God's Design*. There
is some evidence in his work on law in the NT that he now leans at least a little
toward the so-called "New Perspective." (3) It may well be that Martens's practice is better than his theory. Said another way, Martens proposes applications
for the church that seem valid to me but that I think depend on a different
theory from the theory he claims to espouse. That said, I quote a partial paragraph near the end of Martens's *God's Design* that provoked so many scribbles
in the margins of my well-used copy that I decided I needed to find another
venue for interacting with its claims. I chose this essay.

The context of this paragraph is Martens's tentative proposal that God's
fourfold design, so clearly portrayed in Exod 6 and reflected throughout the
OT, provides a helpful grid for reading the NT. In addressing the relevance of
land, Martens writes:

> There is reason to believe, judging from Paul's discussion of Israel in
> Romans 9–11, that the national history of Israel will indeed be resumed
> by God in salvation history. Whether such a position has credibility de-
> pends to some extent on whether the church is viewed as a distinct "new"
> people of God, or whether the church is the anticipated outgrowth of
> ethnic Israel, thus abrogating any further salvation significance for Israel.
> This writer holds to the position that the church does not supplant Israel.[4]

Here Martens proposes that interpreters of Scripture have a choice to make.
Either the church is (1) "a distinct 'new' people of God," or else it is (2) "the
anticipated outgrowth of ethnic Israel."

Martens clearly *denies* that the church "supplants Israel." By implication he
seems to *affirm* the view that "the national history of Israel will indeed be resumed by God in salvation history." He is less than crystal clear about whether

---

4. Ibid., 259.

this means he is opting for number 1 or number 2 above. I think the most natural reading is that Martens rejects the second and by implication accepts the first. He is saying: no, further salvation significance for Israel is *not abrogated* (which he associates with number 2). Therefore, the church is to be viewed as a distinct "new" people of God (number 1).

What is the problem with this? It is twofold. It sets up a false dichotomy and thus excludes the third option, now widely accepted by interpreters of both testaments. And it makes me wonder whether *God's Design* should really have been called *God's Design for Israel*. By what right (according to Martens's view) may we draw any valid lines that connect Martens's insights into OT theology with the church, the "distinct 'new' people of God" (Martens's words) that the NT addresses?

In the first part of this essay, I wish to do two things: (1) sketch the "third option" that Martens seems to have overlooked and (2) indicate why this third option should be chosen—not only in order to be faithful to the NT, but also in order to justify the conclusions that Martens himself proposes.

The second part of this essay will turn to Mark's Gospel and use it as a test case for examining "God's fourfold design" along the lines of the "third option." The goal here is to examine the shape of God's design as it applied to the Christian church that was Mark's first audience and as it applies to the contemporary church still reading this Gospel.

Part One: Israel and the Church

Martens does not use the usual label for the viewpoint he rejects, *supersessionism*. He is perhaps wise to avoid the label. Why invite all defenders of the view to protest with their nuanced qualifications of what they "really believe"? Why narrow or split one's readership by labeling two boxes and then casting a vote for only one of them. Yet supersessionism seems to be precisely what Martens rejects in the paragraph quoted above. Martens is concerned to deny that the church supersedes ("supplants" is Martens's word choice) Israel. He is concerned to deny that the advent of the church abrogates (Martens's word) "any further salvation significance for Israel."

If, in fact, Martens is casting a vote against supersessionism, he is in very good company. Most of his former students would do this as well, and many of them learned it from him. The problem is that he considers a vote against supersessionism to be a vote also against seeing any strong theological connections between Israel and the church. To put it baldly, he implies that, if one rejects supersessionism, one by definition views Israel and the church as two separate "peoples of God." In fact, in the paragraph quoted above, Israel appears to be characterized as the "old" and also "future" people of God, whereas the church appears to be the "distinct 'new' people of God"—apparently, God's second "people."

Now Martens also avoids labeling this option and may well want to deny that it should really be called *dispensationalism*. One can hardly deny, however, that this theological system most explicitly works out both the past and future implications of drawing a clear line separating Israel and the church.

The Excluded Third Option

It is crucial to recognize that there are various versions and degrees of supersessionism and dispensationalism. Yet no matter how carefully these two approaches are nuanced, they seem to allow no room for a third option—an option that Martens seems to leave out of consideration in the paragraph quoted above. The third option I want to propose is closely tied to a movement that has gained a strong following in the quarter-century since *God's Design* first appeared. I am referring to the so-called New Perspective on Paul that has gained a phenomenal following, if not in sheer numbers of scholars, then in the stature of the theologians who have affirmed its basic assertions (Krister Stendahl, E. P. Sanders, James D. G. Dunn, N. T. Wright, J. E. Toews, Luke T. Johnson, Richard B. Hays, etc.).

In this view, there is far more continuity between God's design for Israel and God's design for the church than either supersessionism or dispensationalism can make room for—and for very good reason. The church is the *continuation* of Israel. Jesus came to build the church but not to found it. He could not found it, for it had been founded millennia before his advent.[5] The church is the Israel of God, the end-time form of the renewed humanity that Israel was called to be and that Jesus called to be renewed.

The church is indeed (quoting some of Martens's words but not his meaning) "the anticipated outgrowth of . . . Israel." But by no means does the church (usually wrongly conceptualized as the *Gentile* church) "supersede" Israel. No Gentile olive tree ever replaces a Jewish one (Rom 11:17–24). Neither does a Gentile tree stand alongside a Jewish tree. Though both supersessionism and dispensationalism claim to be taking seriously Paul's discussion about Israel and the church in Rom 9–11, both systems, in different ways, reject precisely the image that Paul uses for the people of God. There is and can be only one olive tree because there is only one people of God. Branches may be broken off or grafted in, but the tree (the people of God) is one and continues to grow.

---

5. Gerhard Lohfink, *Jesus and Community* (Philadelphia: Fortress, 1984) xi.

The oft-made claim that "*Israel* rejected Jesus" is just plain false. Israel did not reject Jesus and therefore could not possibly be replaced or superseded by the church. Rather, Israel was *divided* in its response to Jesus, just as the Gentile world was divided in its response when the gospel was preached beyond the bounds of Israel. There is no Gentile church in the NT. There is only a Jewish church (at first) and then later a mixed church, after the church learned that one does not need to become a "naturalized Jew" in order to join the people of God. Put another way: one can become part of "God's Israel" without becoming either ethnically or nationally Jewish. The church learned what had always been true throughout the entire history of Israel. True Israel is neither an ethnic people nor a national people; it is a covenant people. God's intention was for the boundaries of ethnic and/or national Israel to line up with the boundaries of God's covenant people. In reality, covenant Israel was always a subset, sometimes a small subset, but always a faithful remnant of a larger ethnic or national people group. Thus, "ethnic Israel" and "covenant Israel" have always been by definition two different concepts (Matt 3:8–9; Rom 9:6).

I borrowed Martens's words in calling the church "the anticipated outgrowth of . . . Israel." But I also left out a key word. The church is not the anticipated outgrowth of *ethnic* Israel. Neither is it the anticipated outgrowth of *national* Israel. Martens uses both of these terms in the paragraph I quoted. The church is the anticipated outgrowth of *covenant* Israel. The burden of Jesus' ministry was to clarify what should have been clear from the Pentateuch and the Prophets: namely, God's covenant people may share a common ethnicity; they may justly or unjustly claim a land as their possession; they may form themselves into a nation; and they may do all the other things that an *ethnos* (nation/people group) might do. But Israel is God's people because it is a *laos*, a covenant partner with God. (Hebrew scholars are invited to substitute the *gōyîm* and God's *ʿām* for *ta ethnē* and *ho laos*.)

How else are we to read Stephen's speech in Acts 7 but as a claim that the part of Israel that confessed Jesus as Messiah is the true heir of the entire history of the patriarchs and of Israel? (They—that is, *we*—are the true Israel.) How else are we to read Acts 15 but as a polemic for an ethnically mixed church *as the rebuilt House of David*? How else are we to read Rom 11:17–24 but as a polemic against the forerunners of both supersessionism (where a Jewish tree is uprooted and replaced by a Gentile tree) and dispensationalism (where two separate trees grow in God's garden, though one will need to be raptured before the other can take its rightful place again). And how else are we to read the Gospels but as simultaneously Jesus' word to Israel and God's Word to the church? To deny that the church is the intended outgrowth of Israel is not only to cut us off from the OT; it cuts us off from the Gospels as well.

According to the NT, there is only one people of God. It is not "the Gentile church" for there is no such thing. It is "the anticipated outgrowth of . . . Israel." It is by definition both Jewish and Gentile, just as it is by definition Greek and Roman, Georgian and Gothic, German and Turk, Navajo and Telegu, Palestinian and Iraqi.

Does God's Design Apply to the Church?

Our fathers and mothers were slaves in Egypt. *Our* ancestors became God's covenant partners at the foot of Mt. Sinai. God intervened in *our history* when God rescued, delivered, and restored *us*, whether in the Promised Land or in the exile. God transformed *us* in new ways when God sent Jesus to inaugurate the age of God's already/not yet kingdom, when *we* became people of the resurrection, and when the Spirit was poured out on *us*. *Our* early church leaders discerned that *we* can all be members of God's true covenant people without becoming ethnically Jewish, as are many of *our* brothers and sisters. And along with Paul, *we* hope for the day when people with a Jewish ethnic or national identity who do not yet share a common faith in Messiah Jesus will be grafted back into the one people of God. This people neither stands beside covenant Israel nor takes covenant Israel's place but rather *is* covenant Israel, as God had designed from the start.

The excluded third option is the perspective that provides valid justification for reading the entire NT as a word to both Jewish and Gentile Christians. And it is the only one that justifies reading Martens's OT theology book as fully applicable to the church today. Only when we read the entire Bible as God's Word to "the one true people of God" can we find helpful guidance as we learn to interpret and apply Scripture, particularly the first three-quarters of the Bible that narrates the long part of *our* journey before God's Son became a traveler with us along the road.

Though Martens does not seem to have the third option in view as he writes the final two pages of his OT theology book, his final conclusions about the extension of God's design into the NT and beyond it toward eternity only needs slight rewording to be completely consistent with the third option. Indeed, the very fine concluding reflections seem, at least to me, to be the logical extension of this third option and not of the other two options, one of which Martens seemed to be defending. Perhaps before Martens's illustrious scholarly career ends, he will admit that he actually holds to this third option, though I vividly remember him arguing strongly against it when I sat in his OT theology class, way back when *God's Design* was still awaiting publication.

Part Two: Divine Design and the Gospel of Mark

Martens's opening claim in his focus on OT theology is that God's design was revealed most clearly to Moses in Exod 6:6–8 and that the four key elements of this design form a pattern reflected throughout the OT and on into the NT. God's design is to create a people who will experience God's salvation, who will be a covenant community, who will experience and know God, and who will experience abundance (i.e., dwell in the land). Where and how are these four themes reflected, refracted, or perhaps reframed in the Gospel of Mark?

Salvation/Deliverance

Before there can be any covenant community, any knowledge of God, and any abundant life, God must intervene to deliver and to save. That was Israel's experience at the exodus and it is Mark's assumption as he begins his narrative about Jesus. The first four disciples are "delivered" from the ordinariness of life. They are called out, called away (1:16–20) that they might later meet Jesus on the mountain and enter into a covenant relationship with Jesus as disciples and as apostles (3:13–15). Israel's story is being recapitulated.[6]

Jesus' first miracle in Mark is a miracle of deliverance, and most of his subsequent miracles expand on the theme. Jesus first delivers from demonic oppression (1:25–26; 5:9–13, etc.), then from illness (1:30–31, etc.), from uncleanness (1:41, etc.), from sin (2:5), from physical disabilities (2:11–12, etc.), from legalistic rules (2:25–28, 7:18–20, etc.), from storms at sea (4:39, etc.), from social exclusion (5:34), from physical death (5:41–42), and from hunger (6:42, etc.). And this is by no means a complete list. Where Jesus delivers, he also saves, whether this salvation takes the form of healing, of rescue, of forgiveness, of social integration, or of eternal life.

In the OT, the theme of salvation and deliverance for God's people is closely associated with images of God as "Divine Warrior" and as judge of the nations. In Mark the Divine Warrior disarms and defeats demonic powers (including the sea!), discredits and embarrasses unfaithful religious leaders, and stands courageously defiant in the face of political and military powers. But in the end, the Divine Warrior succumbs to the sword, the whip, the nails, and the cross, convinced that his death is a cup he was called to drink, a baptism he is commissioned to undergo (Mark 10:38–39). And when the Divine Warrior

---

6. Willard Swartley, *Israel's Scripture Traditions and the Synoptic Gospels: Story Shaping Story* (Peabody, MA: Hendrickson, 1994) 254; and Timothy J. Geddert, *Mark* (Believers Church Bible Commentary; Scottdale, PA: Herald, 2001) 234–36.

steps forth from the tomb, it is not as a roaring lion but as one who gives second chances to his faithless followers, inviting them to meet him once more in Galilee.[7] There they will learn to follow once more, carrying their crosses, bearing the message of salvation and deliverance to the ends of the earth.

Mark's Gospel was written to a persecuted minority church, ethnically diverse and learning from Jesus to carry its cross. That the church would one day become what Israel had often aimed to be—a powerful social group with national identity and armies to defend its causes—is something Mark could not have anticipated and would never have endorsed, any more than Jesus before him. In this respect they perhaps understood God's design for God's people better than many who aimed to speak for God's chosen people centuries and millennia earlier and later. God's design has not changed; it is increasingly clarified when we learn to follow more faithfully the one whose acts of deliverance and salvation are no guarantee that life will always be easy or that our enemies will always be defeated, at least not as long as God's kingdom remains a secretly growing seed or a slowly maturing mustard shrub.

Covenant Community

God's first order of business after rescuing Israel from Egyptian oppression was to create a covenant community. As Bernhard Ott writes of the Israelites camped at the foot of Sinai: "Lots had to happen before this bunch of runaway slaves could truly become a people. All the more so if this people group was to become a prototype of God's *Shalom* project."[8] And so it is in Mark. Jesus' first order of business after announcing the arrival of God's kingdom is to reassemble the kingdom community. Four men are called from their nets and their parental homes. Later Levi joins them, then others. Later "the twelve" are appointed, clearly a symbolic representation of covenant Israel. But saying "yes" to the initial call is almost the only thing they get right! Jesus' "followers" seem intent on diverting his journey, contradicting his teaching, and denying their allegiance to him.

As Israel journeys to the Promised Land, Israel is being taught to trust its Covenant Partner, the One who promised to be their guide, their security, and their provider. No Gospel more poignantly reminds us how hard it is to learn the lessons of discipleship (and how patient our true Leader is) than the Gospel of Mark. Nor is any Gospel as insistent as Mark that this covenant community is not based on bloodlines or family ties but on the call of God. In fact, natural family ties are all but obliterated in Mark. No earthly father of Jesus is

---

7. Ibid., 394–406.
8. Bernhard Ott, *God's Shalom Project* (Intercourse, PA: Good Books, 2004) 43.

ever alluded to in Mark. Jesus' earthly mother is barely considered Jesus' relative, for Jesus asks, "Who is my mother?" And Mark responds in kind, identifying Mary at the foot of the cross only obliquely as "the mother of James and Joseph." If Mark had not included an earlier reference in 6:3, the reader would not even know this was Jesus' own mother. Not only that, Jesus explicitly redefines family as believers who gather around Jesus and do God's will (3:34–35). And when he promises a hundredfold return for believers who give up their families, he explicitly cites a hundredfold return of brothers, sisters, mothers, and children. But he deliberately leaves "100 fathers" off the list. Truly Jesus' family transcends ethnic and blood connections to become a new spiritual family characterized by "motherliness, fraternity and childlikeness before God the Father."[9]

Mark's Gospel lacks some of the more explicit statements found in other Gospels that salvation is *not* linked to ethnicity. But Mark's Gospel is by no means unique in its subtle messages that "being Jewish" does not constitute "being the people of God." This is why John comes baptizing Jews, a ritual usually reserved for proselytes. What is the meaning? Jews are becoming "Jews" all over again! And this is why Jesus counsels his apostles to shake the dust off their feet when leaving towns that reject the kingdom message, a ritual usually reserved for reentry into the Promised Land after treading in Gentile places. Again, what is the meaning? A village can be ethnically Jewish and located in the Promised Land but yet be a pagan village.

Mark is saying with Jesus before him: those who hear and obey the word of God are the true Israel of God, the true family of Jesus. Those who imagine that the terms "ethnic Israel" or "national Israel" can be carelessly substituted for "the people of God" (i.e., *covenant* Israel) are misreading both testaments. The line separating individuals who are God's people from all others never did run between Jews and Gentiles. It ran through ethnic Israel prior to Pentecost. Today it runs right through every ethnic group on earth, Jewish and Gentile. And all too often it runs through the church as well.

Mark is not innovating here. He is speaking to the church and saying exactly the same thing that Jesus said to Israel, for the church is Israel. And both are saying exactly what we read over and over again in the OT: being ethnically Jewish never did and never will provide the basis for either God's salvation or membership in God's covenant community.

Knowledge/Experience of God

God (the Father) does not appear often as a character in the Markan narrative. God speaks the words of affirmation and commissioning to Jesus at his

---

9. Lohfink, *Jesus and Community*, 49.

baptism (1:11), addresses three disciples on the Mount of Transfiguration (9:7), and raises Jesus from death (16:6; 12:11).

However, a closer look suggests that God's involvement in the story goes much deeper. Jesus' repeated reference to what must happen (*dei*) clearly identifies the main events of Jesus' life and death as part of God's will, long before Jesus explicitly calls it God's will (14:36). Many passive verbs imply that God is the actor. Thus, when Jesus predicts that the stones of the temple "will be thrown down" (13:2), he is alluding to God's act of judgment on individuals who reject the Son.

But a still closer look reveals something even more profound. Over and over again Jesus is presented as the person who plays the roles only God can fill. Never is Jesus called God in Mark (and rarely if ever in the NT). But in Mark, Jesus forgives sin, something only God can do (2:7). He calms wind and waves, something only God can do (4:41; Ps 107:28–30). Jesus is "good," something that can be said only of God (10:18). Jesus commissions a healed demoniac to announce what *the Lord* has done for him; he goes out and reports what *Jesus* has done. Jesus identifies himself as *egō eimi* 'I Am' when his terrified disciples fail to recognize that he is repeating God's epiphany to Moses—passing by and announcing the Divine Name in their presence (Mark 6:48–50; see Exod 33:19). Jesus presents himself to his contemporaries and Mark presents Jesus to his readers as the one who is the elusive presence of the invisible God, if only we have eyes to see and ears to hear.

Mark's Gospel is all about knowing and experiencing God. Provocatively, Mark subtly directs the discerning reader to the primary means of doing this—by knowing and experiencing Jesus.

Land and the Good Life

Jesus promises his followers that if they give up land for him and the gospel, they will receive land back a hundredfold (with persecutions) *in this life*. There is a separate promise for the age to come. Clearly Mark is assuming that the hundredfold return was already being experienced by the community of disciples to which he was writing. They, the persecuted minority, were experiencing that God is faithful. In their earthly families, "brother betrayed brother to death and a father his child" (13:12a), but in the church they would be a family of "brothers and sisters and mothers." Children might turn against them (13:12b), but in the family of God they would find joy and security (the two things most closely associated with children in their world). They have given up homes and have hundreds now at their disposal. But how will God keep his promise to give them the land?

Land had never been more than *one of the signs* that God was faithful to Israel. OT prophets were at pains to insist that, even apart from the land, God was Israel's faithful God. The NT further develops this emphasis. Jesus in Nazareth and Stephen in Jerusalem both retell Israel's story so as to highlight how God frequently spoke to foreigners, or through them, or outside the boundaries of the land that Israel claimed as theirs (Luke 4:24–27; Acts 7:2–38). If Israel thought that possessing real estate in the Near East was the only way God could care for them or bless the covenant community, then they had not listened carefully to God or the individuals who spoke on God's behalf.

According to Mark, Jesus saw clearly that it is possible to live in a Jewish village in what they claimed as their Promised Land, and yet in reality be living on "pagan soil" (6:11). And Mark saw just as clearly that what really constitutes the good life (8:34–38) is meeting the risen Jesus in "Galilee" and following him on the road to "Jerusalem," to "Golgotha," and beyond it, out of the garden tomb, and into glory. And one can do this without ever setting foot in Palestine. It seems that Mark had listened carefully to Jesus, who had listened carefully to his heavenly Father, who had clarified the fine points of God's design that was once revealed most clearly to Moses but now has been revealed even more clearly to those of us who are learning to follow Jesus.

Biblical Perspectives on Biodiversity: A Conversation with E. O. Wilson

THEODORE HIEBERT
Francis A. McGaw Professor of Old Testament
McCormick Theological Seminary
Chicago, Illinois

E. O. Wilson, Pellegrino University Professor Emeritus at Harvard, a world expert on ants and a fervent advocate for the earth's endangered species, has recently written an appeal to religious people everywhere to join him and other scientists in the urgent task of protecting the earth's fragile biosphere from human assault. In his book *The Creation: An Appeal to Save Life on Earth*, Wilson lays out the scientific argument for saving the creation, and he invites faith communities to ally themselves with scientists by marshaling their own resources on behalf of creation. Wilson, once a Southern Baptist but now a secular humanist, reaches out to religious people because he believes that "religion and science are the two most powerful forces in the world today" and that "if religion and science could be united on the common ground of biological conservation, the problem would soon be solved."[1]

Wilson actually addresses his appeal to a fictional pastor from his own Southern Baptist heritage. While I am not a pastor but a professor of biblical studies, and while I am not a Southern Baptist but a Mennonite teaching in a Presbyterian seminary, I wish to respond as a member of the larger religious community to which Wilson appeals. Furthermore, I want to respond as a professor of biblical studies in particular, asking whether the Bible—the very foundation of the theology, ethics, and values of Judaism and Christianity— contains any warrant for taking E. O. Wilson seriously and, if so, what this

---

Author's note: My interest in the OT began in Prof. Martens's "Introduction to the OT" course at MB Biblical Seminary, my first seminary class. Under Elmer's instruction, the literary forms, historical and social settings, and theological themes of books such as Genesis, which I examine here, first caught my attention and provoked my imagination.

1. E. O. Wilson, *The Creation: An Appeal to Save Life on Earth* (New York: Norton, 2006) 5.

warrant might be. But to do so I will first have to argue that we need a new way of understanding the relation between the Bible, science, and the world of nature, because the major ways that Christians and Jews have come to understand this relationship simply do not work.

Before turning to the Bible, however, let me underline the urgency of Wilson's appeal. If the human race does not change its ways, Wilson argues, it will cause the extinction of a quarter of the species of plants and animals on land in the next 50 years. This will be a catastrophe comparable to the last great extinction spasm 65 million years ago when a meteorite hit the earth and wiped out the dinosaurs, putting an end to the age of reptiles. This extinction will be irreversible, at least for us, our children, and the human race as we know it. Extinction is forever. It will take 10 million years for nature to replicate any semblance of our contemporary biodiversity. All of the consequences of a mass extinction of this order are not known, but it is clear that the cost to life on earth will be catastrophic, not only to the life forms threatened with extinction, but to humanity itself, which depends for its health and well-being upon the ecosystem services that a healthy biosphere provides: breathable air, water management, pollution control, soil enrichment. Ours is a moment when, as Stephen Jay Gould, Wilson's former colleague at Harvard, put it, "salvation truly becomes a question of now or never."[2]

These sorts of crises have always sent religious people back to their sacred traditions to find their bearings. I want to explore the very beginning of these traditions in Scripture to see whether or not they provide a helpful orientation for this new and unprecedented challenge and whether they contain any warrant for answering Wilson's appeal. Wilson considers modern religious people—even in the very conservative form of his fictional Southern Baptist pastor—potential allies, because he believes they share his basic concern for the future of human welfare on this planet. But he is not as positive about their Scriptures. Wilson actually quotes the Bible at least twice in his book to support his scientific arguments (he is too much of a Southern Baptist not to do so), yet he is on the whole suspicious of it, if not downright critical.

The most obvious reason for his suspicion, of course, is that the Bible has been used by creationists (and more recently by advocates of Intelligent Design) against him to deny the very truth of the science—evolutionary biology —to which he has devoted his life.[3] Furthermore, Wilson believes that the Bible possesses such a fervent otherworldly orientation that it encourages its

---

2. Stephen Jay Gould, *The Hedgehog, the Fox, and the Magister's Pox: Mending the Gap between Science and the Humanities* (New York: Harmony, 2003) 141.

3. Wilson, *Creation*, 3, 9, 105, 165–68.

heirs to count as ultimately inconsequential the fate of life on earth.[4] Finally, Wilson views the Bible as "the sacred scripture of Iron Age desert kingdoms" and therefore pretty much out of date, bound to its own time and place with little direct value for ours.[5] This last concern was also that of the great environmentalist Thomas Berry, who considered the biblical story "dysfunctional" for contemporary believers and advocated a new creation story based on the latest findings of modern science.[6]

In this response to E. O. Wilson, I want to move beyond his appeal to shared contemporary values about human welfare—which is, of course, entirely valid in itself—to look at the roots of our values as religious people in our biblical traditions. In so doing, I will consider each of these problems that Wilson raises about the Bible as a resource for our age of environmental collapse by holding them up to the lens of an actual biblical text, the famous story of creation in Gen 1. The Bible, ultimately, must speak for itself. In order to let it speak authentically, however, I must argue for a new way of reading it—in particular, a new way of understanding its relation to science and to the natural world that is now under threat.

The traditional options for understanding the biblical view of the natural world and its origins fall into three major camps: the creationist option, the accommodationist option, and the theological option. Almost all of the Christians I know fit into one or another of these camps or some combination of them. But none of these options actually works, either to describe the real character of the Bible and of its authors' actual views or to provide an authentic starting point for understanding the relationship between the Bible and science today. Here is why these ways of reading the Bible do not work and why we need a fourth way.

The first and oldest option, creationism, claims that the world came into being just as it is described in Gen 1, in six calendar days by separate creative acts. This puts the Bible in direct contradiction with modern science, which regards the earth and its life forms as evolving over millennia. When this sort of contradiction occurs, creationists claim, the Bible must be taken as the true account of the way nature works, and modern evolutionary explanations must be dismissed as false. This is actually the perspective that Wilson attributes to the Southern Baptist pastor to whom he addresses the book: "You are a literalist interpreter of Christian Holy Scripture. You reject the conclusion of science that mankind evolved from lower forms."[7] Whether or not all Southern

---

4. Ibid., 3, 6, 13, 105.
5. Ibid., 28, 84.
6. Thomas Berry, *The Dream of the Earth* (San Francisco: Sierra Club, 1988) 123–37.
7. Wilson, *Creation*, 3.

Baptist pastors may be placed in this camp, as Wilson assumes, many vocal conservative Christians do fit here, including many who now support Intelligent Design, creationism's stepchild, and they have caused evolutionary biologists such as E. O. Wilson a great deal of grief.[8] In a Pew Research Center poll, almost two-thirds of Americans thought that creationism should be taught with evolution in public schools.[9]

The creationist option cannot be the way we read Scripture, and it cannot provide the starting point for a response to E. O. Wilson's appeal. This lesson was learned long ago. Creationism's view that the Bible can be successfully defended against newer scientific viewpoints was dealt a fatal blow at the beginning of the Scientific Revolution. When Galileo argued the Copernican theory that the sun was the center of the universe, church leaders moved to suppress his teaching, force his recantation, and put him under house arrest, because his view contradicted the clear witness of Scripture that the sun revolves around the earth. It took the church two hundred years to learn that it could not defend biblical views against newer and better scientific ones: two centuries after it condemned Galileo's work, the church finally removed his volume from the Index of Prohibited Books.

Even the most strident creationists today accept Galileo's heliocentric universe over the Bible's geocentric universe. But while they are willing to accept modern scientific viewpoints over the Bible's view in this regard, creationists now wish to renew this old battle, already lost in the 17th century, on a new evolutionary front. Creationism thus represents a classic case of the refusal to learn from history. This approach did not work in the heliocentric debate, and for the same reasons it cannot work in the evolutionary debate. At the same time, we must recognize one important insight in the creationist position. While creationism cannot be defended as a legitimate approach to Scripture, its proponents do recognize that biblical writers were, in a certain respect, "scientists" in their own time and that they were deeply interested in the origins of the natural world, a point to which we shall return below.

An alternative view of the relation between the Bible and science held by moderate and liberal Christians is the accommodationist option.[10] The members of this camp regard the biblical account of nature and its origins, if properly interpreted, as consistent with the modern evolutionary explanation of the world and its life forms. For example, if the days of creation in Gen 1—

---

8. Ibid., 165–68.

9. Laurie Goodstein, *The New York Times*, August 31, 2005.

10. See, for example, Bernard Ramm, *The Christian View of Science and Scripture* (Grand Rapids: Eerdmans, 1954); and Pattle P. T. Pun, *Evolution: Nature and Scripture in Conflict?* (Grand Rapids: Zondervan, 1982).

to take the most famous instance—are interpreted as ages rather than 24-hour days, the biblical story actually describes the gradual evolution of life in a way that would accommodate some of the major outlines of evolutionary science. Perhaps God even revealed this sort of design to ancient authors, who unknowingly anticipated the discoveries of modern science. This option has the great virtue of respecting both the biblical account of origins and modern scientific accounts, and it allows religious people to take both of them seriously, rather than rejecting one or the other, as creationists insist that we do.

But this approach has two major drawbacks. First, it misrepresents the aims and intentions of biblical authors. The author of Gen 1 *was* talking about 24-hour days: otherwise it would make no sense that God consecrated the seventh day (Gen 2:1–4a), thus establishing the seven-day week and the Sabbath at the beginning of time. Second, this approach does not actually "fit" the evolutionary model very well: the biblical sequence does not perfectly match the nature and order of the complex evolution of life that modern biologists have documented. Trying to accommodate the biblical and scientific accounts forces the reader constantly to tweak and twist the biblical story to align it with new discoveries. Moreover, this "make it fit" approach sometimes masks the creationist intention to claim absolute scientific truth for the Bible's picture of the origins of the universe, if we just interpret it correctly so that it matches new science. In spite of its failure to honor the Bible's actual intentions or to understand the proper relation between the Bible and modern science, this option does, like the creationist option, recognize the "scientific" interests of biblical writers. There is a better way, however, to understand these "scientific" interests.

The third option, the theological option, avoids some of the pitfalls of the first two options.[11] Like the accommodationist option, it makes space for both the Bible and science, and it allows religious people to take them both seriously. But it does so in just the opposite way: instead of artificially melding biblical and scientific accounts, it separates them completely. According to this approach, the Bible is about theology, not about science. Its real interest is God, not the physical processes by which the world and its life forms emerged. The Bible communicates spiritual truths, not scientific truths. Some who take this approach refer to the biblical accounts as poetic, lyrical, symbolic, or mythical, but their point is the same. Biblical writers had no interest in the hard facts of astronomy, geology, and biology. This is an apparently brilliant, clean solution to the problem. It allows the Bible's writers and its theological interpreters to do their thing, and it allows the scientists to do their thing, and

---

11. See, for example, Conrad Hyers, *The Meaning of Creation: Genesis and Modern Science* (Atlanta: John Knox, 1984); and Seán P. Kealy, *Science and the Bible* (Dublin: Columbia, 1987).

the two never conflict because they have nothing to do with one another. Both can be taken seriously in their own distinct and different worlds.

But alas, the drawbacks to this option are just as serious as those of the first and second options. This approach in its own way misrepresents the aims of biblical texts and the nature of their content. Biblical authors were not *just* theologians reflecting on God and God's ways; they *were* deeply interested in the natural world, its orders and its origins. This is obvious in Gen 1, where, as we shall see, major attention is given to describing the different forms of life, their specific species and environments, and their interrelationships. Furthermore, by divorcing the Bible and science, this option provides no real platform for modern conversations between religious people and scientists. It easily leads to the impression that spiritual questions alone are important to the Bible and its heirs, while the whole material world is no concern of theirs. This is an ineffective position from which to begin reflections on our role as humans in the ecosystem we inhabit. In fact, it is more than ineffective: it is dangerous. It creates a dichotomy that discourages the search for ways of understanding God and the world in the context of contemporary thought. It encourages a kind of schizophrenia that inhibits rather than supports our search for a religious faith that makes sense in the light of modern science and of our contemporary crisis.

So, we need a fourth way of reading the Bible that avoids the pitfalls of these three traditional ways of reading it. This approach regards the Bible as "ancient science." I use these two words intentionally and carefully. We need to employ the word "science" for the Bible, to signal several important things about its aims and the nature of its texts. First, biblical authors were intensely interested in the world of nature that represents the domain of scientific inquiry today. The physical world was not a concern peripheral to their theological interests, as the theological camp claims. Rather, nature was the foundational context within which they did their theologizing, and its origins and orders were crucial to their construction of reality. Second, biblical texts reflect key aspects of the modern scientific method: close observation of natural facts, careful classification of details observed, and the construction of theories to explain these facts and their relationships. To be sure, the explanatory theory of divine causation held by all ancients, including biblical writers, is different from the materialistic theories of causation in modern science, but this should not blind us to the many ways in which biblical writers worked with aims and methods not unlike those of modern science. Biblical thought is not the different, irrational, mythic mindset that is often subsumed under the term "mythopoeic thought"; it is rational and logical and shares many of the aims and methods of the contemporary scientist.

In the designation "ancient science," I use the word *ancient* to convey the idea that the *scientific* perspectives in biblical texts are not the perspectives of contemporary science. They are, rather, a part of the history of science. They represent an early attempt at the observation and classification of natural facts and at explanations for them. Thus, we cannot oppose biblical science to modern science, as do the creationists, or try to make it fit with modern science, as do the accommodationists. We cannot demand that the Bible's science provide the same knowledge of nature that scientists have accumulated since. In fact, the Bible's cosmology with its geocentric universe is a cosmology that no modern person would accept. We can, however, appreciate this ancient science as a reasonable attempt to make sense of the universe in its time. In most respects, this early science provided an adequate explanation for the world as the biblical writers observed it in the first millennium B.C.E. As a matter of fact, these ancient scientists saw certain things about the natural world that still ring true in the context of contemporary scientific discoveries.

This fourth way of reading the Bible has not been very well articulated to a broad audience—I seldom encounter it in churches—yet it is the way biblical scholars tend to speak of the Bible. Julius Wellhausen, the 19th-century scholar who laid the foundations for the modern understanding of the authors of Genesis, thought that Gen 1 provides us with "the first beginnings of sober reflection about nature":

> The aim of the narrator is not mainly a religious one. Had he only meant to say that God made the world out of nothing, and made it good, he could have said so in simpler words, and at the same time more distinctly. There is no doubt that he meant to describe the actual course of the genesis of the world, and to be true to nature in doing so; he means to give a cosmogonic theory.[12]

E. A. Speiser, stressing the Mesopotamian backgrounds of the Bible's origin stories, is in substantial agreement with Wellhausen, believing that the Bible incorporated insights from "a society which was a pioneer in the gradual advance of science." For Speiser, the Bible "reflected the best that was available in contemporary scientific thinking."[13] More recently, Terence Fretheim has claimed that biblical writers were interested in what we today call scientific matters, and he refers to creation accounts as prescientific: "These chapters

---

12. Julius Wellhausen, *Prolegomena to the History of Ancient Israel* (New York: Meridian, 1957) 298, 304; repr. of *Prolegomena to the History of Israel* (trans. J. Sutherland Black and Allan Menzies; with preface by W. Robertson Smith; Edinburgh: Black, 1885); trans. of *Prolegomena zur Geschichte Israels* (2nd ed.; Berlin: Reimer, 1883).

13. E. A. Speiser, *Genesis* (New York: Doubleday, 1962) lv.

are prescientific in the sense that they predate modern science, but not in the sense of having no interest in those types of questions."[14]

Before turning to Gen 1 to explore this fourth approach to the Bible, we must recognize one additional factor that differentiates the ancient science in biblical texts from modern science. In biblical texts, scientific interests are combined with other interests, the kinds of intellectual pursuits we would now assign to discrete fields of study such as, for example, anthropology, sociology, history, and theology. Thus, biological science was not pursued by biblical writers as a quest in and of itself, as it is pursued today, but it was integrated into a larger project embracing all of the humanities, including religion. This was, of course, a different context for doing science than in the contemporary world, and it affected the way ancient science was done. To speak about the ancient science of the Bible we must differentiate its scientific aspects from the other interests with which it is combined.

This integrative approach to origins in the Bible does not nullify the authenticity of the scientific aims and elements in biblical texts. In fact, it represents an ancient version of a quest in which E. O. Wilson himself is involved today, the ultimate integration of all forms of knowledge. In another of his books, *Consilience*, E. O. Wilson sets out this integrative enterprise as his central aim: "The greatest enterprise of the mind has always been and always will be the attempted linkage of the sciences and the humanities."[15] Biblical authors worked, within the terms and constraints of their own culture, to construct an inclusive explanation of the world and of reality in which all aspects of the world and of human endeavor played an important part. With this comprehensive approach to the world and its beginnings, biblical writers provide us with an integrative model for thinking about science and theology today. We cannot copy their solution, but we can use their aims and intentions as a motivation to develop our own integrative world view.

With this understanding of the Bible as an integrative explanation of origins, including ancient scientific elements, we are now in a position to turn to the Bible itself and to begin a more substantive conversation with E. O. Wilson about biodiversity and about biblical warrants for taking it seriously. Genesis 1 is an excellent context for taking up this conversation because it is the primary arena in which debates about science and the Bible have been waged. Indeed, E. O. Wilson quotes Gen 1 at the beginning of his appeal and alludes to it throughout.[16] To illustrate the perspective on biodiversity in Gen 1, I wish to

---

14. Terence E. Fretheim, "Genesis," *NIB* 1.337.
15. E. O. Wilson, *Consilience* (New York: Knopf, 1998) 8.
16. Idem, *Creation*, 10.

focus on one key episode: the emergence of the first forms of life on the third day of creation (1:11–13). By doing so, I want to show that the Bible actually provides two kinds of warrants for taking biodiversity seriously: a scientific warrant not unlike the one E. O. Wilson uses as the basis for his appeal, together with a theological warrant that provides the basis for a religious response.

Let us first take up the Bible's scientific warrant for taking biodiversity seriously. To fully appreciate the scientific elements in the description of the first forms of life, the plant kingdom created on the third day, we need a precise translation of the Hebrew text. The actual description of plants in Gen 1:11–13 has been masked by commentators' and translators' overly general treatments of some of this text's Hebrew terminology. Here is a more precise translation that we can use as the basis for our analysis:

> The earth germinated plants (*deše'*): grasses (*ʿēśeb*) producing seed (*zeraʿ*), each according to its species (*mîn*), and trees producing fruit (*pěrî*) with its seed (*zeraʿ*) in it, each according to its species (*mîn*), and God considered it good. (Gen 1:12, my translation)

The first term for 'plant life', *deše'*, is now well understood. Most translators and commentators have moved beyond the old King James translation of the Hebrew term *deše'* as 'grass' and have recognized that this term signifies the entire world of plants (NRSV, NJPSV: 'vegetation'). By beginning with *deše'*, the author begins by referring to the entire plant kingdom, as the modern scientist would call it.

In the brief taxonomy that follows, the plant kingdom (*deše'*) is divided into two branches, grasses and fruits, branches that in modern scientific taxonomies would be identified as families. The branch of this taxonomy that commentators and translators have consistently misunderstood is the first division of plants: *ʿēśeb* 'grasses'. This term is universally interpreted and translated simply as 'plants' (e.g., NRSV, NJPSV, NIV), a general translation that hides the careful classification system employed here. In fact, the term *ʿēśeb* is used precisely by the authors of Genesis for grasses, primarily the cereals, wheat and barley, which were the basis of ancient Israel's grain-based agricultural economy.[17] At the end of Gen 1, grasses are identified as the primary food for humans (v. 29) and animals (v. 30). In this taxonomy, grasses and fruits are further subdivided into distinct species (*mîn*), and these species are identified with their seeds, which encode their unique traits.

---

17. Theodore Hiebert, *The Yahwist's Landscape: Nature and Religion in Ancient Israel* (New York: Oxford, 1996) 37.

This classification of the plant world is ancient rather than modern. It is, by comparison with modern scientific taxonomy, incomplete in several ways. First, out of the seven major ranks used by modern scientists to classify plants, it employs only three: kingdom, family, and species. Furthermore, its division of plants into two families is an oversimplification: although grasses do, in fact, represent a distinct family in modern scientific taxonomy, fruits are members of many different families. Finally, grasses and fruits do not come close to describing the vast panoply of plants that filled the Mediterranean world in which this author lived. Moreover, this ancient taxonomy is not based on observation alone but is influenced by its author's specific cultural context. It is based primarily on the two kinds of domesticated plants, grains and fruits, that were the basis of ancient Israel's agricultural economy. These were the foods on which the author's own survival depended.

Having identified these ancient aspects of the plant taxonomy in Gen 1, which would no longer be considered an adequate system of classification (even for the author's own ancient Mediterranean landscape), we can still appreciate its genuine scientific elements. First, it is based on careful observation—plants with seeds visible on their stalks (i.e., grasses) are separated from plants the seeds of which are hidden in their fruits. Second, this system of classification depends on grouping plants according to shared physical characteristics, the same principle used by modern scientists. By this process, the author of Genesis was able to separate grasses into a distinct family, a classification still present in modern taxonomies. Within the families of grasses and fruits, the author recognizes the existence of different species, the distinctions of which are encoded in their seeds: "producing seed, each according to its species."[18] This is much like the contemporary definition of species that E. O. Wilson presents to us: "genetically distinct populations that in many, but far from all, kinds of organisms are separated by their inability to crossbreed in natural environments."[19]

We have, therefore, in the description of plant life in Gen 1 a recognition of the diversity of life, which, with allowances for its ancient limitations and social influences, contains an appreciation for biodiversity not unlike the appreciation that E. O. Wilson himself forged out of careful attention to and study of the natural phenomena of life. Furthermore, the author of Gen 1 recognizes, as does Wilson, that "nature is not only an objective entity but vital to our physical and spiritual well-being."[20] Genesis 1 is not an otherworldly text,

---

18. Ellen Bernstein, *The Splendor of Creation* (Cleveland: Pilgrim, 2005) 37–38.
19. Wilson, *Creation*, 108.
20. Ibid., 26.

enticing its readers away from this planet, but a text describing human life embedded in this world. The Bible is an Iron Age text—as Wilson has described it—limited by its age, but it contains the kind of detailed information of the natural world common to traditional cultures, which Wilson himself recognizes as "in a real sense scientific knowledge."[21] The Bible's recognition of and respect for diversity is, therefore, at its most basic level a scientific insight that shares the same enthusiasm for biodiversity that E. O. Wilson hopes to communicate, as a modern biologist, in *The Creation*.

Having seen in these verses of Gen 1 the Bible's scientific warrants for recognizing and respecting the diversity of life on earth, we are now in a position to turn to its moral warrants. At the center of the Bible's perspective on biodiversity is the claim in Gen 1 that God brought all life into being; as a consequence, all of the earth's life in all of its forms is a part of God's design for the world. This theological claim contains strong ethical implications. If biodiversity is a part of the divine plan for the earth, then placing it under threat, as we humans are now doing, can only be seen as an act against God. Thus, for the heirs of Scripture, the diversity of life is not just a natural wonder on which our health depends, as scientists such as Wilson urge us to recognize, but it is a part of the earth as God intended it. To take God seriously is to take biodiversity seriously. To live religiously is to respect and preserve the world God made.

The claim that biodiversity is God's design for the world is only strengthened by God's repeated affirmation in Gen 1 that "it was good." This phrase is used for each of the forms of life—plants, sea animals, flying animals, and land animals—as they are created (1:12, 21, 25). There is no more powerful statement of the integrity of all of creation—including the entire diversity of its life—in the entire Bible. By making the diversity of life God's plan for the world and by describing God's valuation of it as good, the author of Gen 1 has granted ultimate value to all forms of life. Those who consider themselves heirs of this biblical tradition must take this divine valuation of the diversity of life as the starting point for any contemporary human ethic. To violate life, to contribute to the extinction of any of the species God has created and pronounced good is an act against God and against God's designs for the world. The Bible contains no more powerful warrant for taking E. O. Wilson's appeal to save life on earth seriously and for acting to protect it.

Although this biblical mandate, given the decimation of species in our generation, has escaped the attention of most modern Christians, the Bible's best interpreters have recognized and remarked on it. Rabbi Judah, the great

---

21. Idem, *The Diversity of Life* (New York: Norton, 1999), 42–44; and idem, *Creation*, 139.

2nd-century scholar and editor of the Mishnah, said: "Of all that the Holy One created in His world, He did not create a single thing that is useless." Early rabbinic exegesis took the summary of creation in Gen 2:1, "The heaven and the earth were completed and all that populated them," as an affirmation of all of life: "Even those creatures that you may look upon as superfluous in the world, such as flies, fleas, or gnats—they too are part of the entirety of creation. The Holy One effects His purpose through all creatures, even through a frog or a flea" (*Gen. Rab.* 10:7).[22] Augustine understood creation's diversity in Gen 1 in this way: "All nature's substances are good, because they exist and therefore have their own mode and kind of being, and, in their fashion, a peace and harmony among themselves. . . . it is the nature of things considered in itself, without regard to our convenience or inconvenience, that gives glory to the Creator."[23]

As an ancient scientist, theologian, and ethicist, the author of Gen 1 is acutely aware of the diversity of life and respects its inherent value in the world God created. He recognizes its role as the fundamental context for human life or, as E. O. Wilson puts it, "the cradle of humanity."[24] The entire world of life is created as the environment for humanity to inhabit. Yet it is just here, with the creation of humanity, that the biblical perspective on creation has come under its most withering criticism by contemporary environmentalists and ethicists. This is so, of course, because God creates humanity in God's image and commands humans to have dominion over the animal kingdom and to subdue the earth (1:28). I, too, have been critical of the value of this image for contemporary environmental ethics, and I have argued that the alternative image—the human as creation's *servant* in the Bible's second creation account in Gen 2–3—is a more constructive way of viewing the human place in nature today.[25] E. O. Wilson does not take on the biblical problem of human dominion, but we must consider it briefly in order to determine whether it undermines in any way the strong respect for life in all of its forms in Gen 1.

The Priestly image of humanity in Gen 1 is an image of power tempered by restraint (1:26–28). The biblical terms for having 'dominion' (*rādâ*) over the

---

22. Hayim Nahman Bialik and Yehoshua Hana Ravnitzky, eds., *The Book of Legends: Sefer Ha-Aggadah* (New York: Schocken, 1992) 12.

23. Augustine, *The City of God*, book 12, chaps. 4–5.

24. Wilson, *Creation*, 9.

25. Hiebert, *The Yahwist's Landscape*, 140–62; idem, "The Human Vocation: Origins and Transformations in Christian Traditions," in *Christianity and Ecology* (ed. Dieter T. Hessel and Rosemary Radford Ruether; Cambridge: Harvard University Press, 2000) 135–54; and idem, "Rethinking Dominion Theology," *Direction* 25/2 (1996) 16–25.

animals and 'subduing' (*kābaš*) the earth are very powerful terms, used elsewhere in the Bible to depict the power of kings over their subjects and masters over their servants. They cannot be interpreted as benign words in and of themselves, as some biblical scholars have tried to do. At the same time, by creating humanity in God's image, God puts restraints on the power inherent in these terms. The phrase "the image of [personal name]" is most commonly used in the ancient Near East for kings' statues, the function of which is to *represent* the presence and policies of the king to his subjects. This means that humans—the image of God—are given their power over life only as the representatives of God who created that life. In all of God's creation, humans stand for God's presence, policies, and power—the same power that created biodiversity as the divine design for the world and that pronounced it good. Thus, dominion must be employed to respect the inherent value created within every species of the world's diverse life and to ensure that it flourishes as God intended.

This Priestly image of humanity in Gen 1 is the source of the most common term used for our role in nature in all of environmental literature: *steward*. E. O. Wilson himself uses this term with echoes of Gen 1 when he says, "ecosystems and species can be saved only by understanding the unique value of each species in turn, and by persuading the people who have dominion over them to serve as their stewards."[26] At the conclusion of his appeal, he takes this image as the starting point for the alliance between science and religion: "In order to solve these problems, I've argued, it will be necessary to find common ground on which the powerful forces of religion and science can be joined. The best place to start is the stewardship of life."[27]

While the word *steward* is not actually used in Gen 1, it identifies accurately the conception of humans there: namely, the beings responsible for representing God's intentions in the world. As God's stewards, humans have great power but also great responsibility to use this power to make the earth's life flourish, just as God, their own master, intended it to flourish. With the power of humanity more evident than ever in our age, and given that the need to use this power with wisdom and benevolence is more urgent than ever, the image of humanity in Gen 1 indeed provides a powerful warrant for religious people to respond to the appeal that E. O. Wilson has extended to them.

---

26. Wilson, *Creation*, 92.
27. Ibid., 165.

All Creatures Great and Small: Recovering a Deuteronomic Theology of Animals

DANIEL I. BLOCK
Guenther H. Knoedler Professor of Old Testament
Wheaton College
Wheaton, Illinois

On January 17, 2007, a group of leading evangelicals announced the establishment of the Evangelical Climate Initiative and issued a manifesto called "Climate Change: An Evangelical Call to Action."[1] In recent years, several significant publications written by philosophers and ethicists have appeared appealing for a distinctly Christian response to critical environmental issues.[2] Although biblical scholars are beginning to work out an authentic biblical theology addressing these matters,[3] there are reasons why evangelicals are hesitant

---

Author's note: Combining a remarkable skill in extracting the theology from biblical texts with a passion not only to integrate this theology into one's belief system but also to translate it into everyday life, Prof. Elmer Martens has modeled God's design for a Christian scholar. See E. A. Martens, "Accessing Theological Readings of a Biblical Book," *AUSS* 34 (1996) 223–37. The goal of this investigation is to expand his legacy into an area where few evangelicals have ventured.

1. The document may be downloaded from http://www.christiansandclimate.org/statement. A list of signatories appears at the end.

2. See especially L. Wilkinson, ed., *Earthkeeping in the Nineties: Stewardship of Creation* (3rd ed.; Eugene, OR: Wipf & Stock, 2003); Fred Van Dyke, ed., *Redeeming Creation: The Biblical Basis for Environmental Stewardship* (Downers Grove, IL: InterVarsity, 1996); R. J. Berry, *The Care of Creation: Focusing Concern and Action* (Downers Grove, IL: InterVarsity, 2000); idem, ed., *Environmental Stewardship: Critical Perspectives—Past and Present* (New York: Continuum, 2006); and S. Bouma-Prediger, *For the Beauty of the Earth: A Christian Vision for Creation Care* (Grand Rapids: Baker, 2001).

3. Under the leadership of Norman C. Habel of Flinders University, the number of scholars concerned with the ecological and ecotheological messages of the OT is growing. Many of the articles in the journal *Ecotheology: The Journal of Religion, Nature and the Environment*, established in 1996 are devoted to OT texts and themes. The same is true of the papers presented at the annual meeting of the SBL, which recently established a special Ecological Hermeneutics Consultation.

to join these discussions; the philosophers and ethicists tend to be broadly ecumenical, often considering Buddhist, Hindu, Daoist, and other perspectives on a par with perspectives derived from the Hebrew Bible or the NT.[4] However, this is scarcely an excuse for silence on the wasteful, oppressive, and exploitative ways that we treat God's good earth.

Douglas Moo's recent appeal for a more thoughtful response in a mainstream evangelical journal[5] offers hope for a long overdue shift in thinking about the environment. With his massive bibliography and his erudite discussion of the theological issues involved in an evangelical ecotheology, Moo has established a firm basis for all of us to be engaged in environmental issues from the perspective of NT theology.

For cultural and theological reasons,[6] the OT often plays only a minimal role in the theological and ethical commitments of evangelicals. In ecotheological discussions, when appeal is made to the OT, it is natural to refer to the Genesis account of creation and affirm our obligations to the welfare of the world by virtue of our status as images of God. But having done so, we search for a biblical understanding by leapfrogging over the rest of the Torah to Ps 8 and then over the poetic and prophetic writings to Rom 8 and NT portrayals of new creation. I do not wish to denigrate these efforts—any serious exploration of Scripture for the purpose of establishing theological truth and practical sanctified living is to be welcomed. I simply lament the fact that with this hop-skip-and-jump approach we have overlooked many rich seams of ore to be mined in the constitutional, historical, cultic, wisdom, and prophetic writings of the OT. The time has come for a detailed and systematic analysis of the data provided by each of the books of the OT. Only when we have done this will we be able to develop a full-blown biblical zootheology.

The goal of this essay is to consider the theology of animals as it is presented in the book of Deuteronomy.[7] Analogous to the book of Romans in the NT, the book of Deuteronomy provides the most systematic presentation of the-

---

4. For an eloquent call to responsible treatment of environmental issues from a more general religious perspective, see R. S. Gottlieb, *A Greener Faith: Religious Environmentalism and Our Planet's Future* (Oxford: Oxford University Press, 2006).

5. Douglas J. Moo, "Nature in the New Creation: New Testament Eschatology and the Environment," *JETS* 49 (2006) 449–88.

6. Though they do so for different reasons, the emphasis on the discontinuities between the testaments among Lutherans, Anabaptists, and dispensationalists has resulted in a widespread and persistent denigration of the Hebrew Bible (OT) as a source and guide for Christian behavior.

7. In so doing, this essay seeks to buttress the discussion of the philosopher Robert N. Wennberg in his book *God, Humans, and Animals: An Invitation to Enlarge Our Moral Universe* (Grand Rapids: Eerdmans, 2003) 289–95.

ology that is found in the entire OT. Contrary to prevailing opinion, this book comes to us not as legislation but as a collection of final pastoral addresses by Moses to his people before he passes on and before they cross over the Jordan into the Promised Land. In reflecting on the theological and ethical implications of the glorious gospel embodied in Yahweh's love for the ancestors, his gracious election of Israel as his chosen people, his deliverance from the slavery of Egypt, his covenantal relationship established with his people, and his gracious revelation of his will, Moses, the pastor, touches on a wide range of subjects, from the conduct of Israel's rulers to the way in which ordinary citizens present their offerings to Yahweh.[8]

As biblical theologians have done with a wide range of topics, our investigation of the theology of animals in Deuteronomy involves collecting, studying, and applying the passages in the book that relate to this theme.[9] I propose to address the subject under two main headings: (1) The deuteronomic ontology of animals: what is an animal, and what dimensions of animal life does the book recognize? (2) The deuteronomic view of humankind's relationship to animals. This will be broken down into several subcategories. The primary goal of this essay is to collect and organize the evidence. Limitations of space will prevent full discussion of the theological and practical implications of our findings, a matter to which I will return in the future.[10]

The Definition and Classification of Animals

The distinction between plant and animal life is clear in the account of creation found in Gen 1, where God calls on the earth to yield its plants, but he creates all the animals by fiat proclamation. Here the general expression for animal, *nepeš ḥayyâ* 'living creature', occurs three times (Gen 1:20, 24, 30), but it will return in 2:19 and again in chap. 9 (vv. 12, 15, 16; see also Ezek 47:19). In Gen 2:7 the same phrase is used of the first man. Remarkably, this generic designation for animals never occurs in Deuteronomy.

---

8. The role of Moses in the composition is hotly disputed. Critical scholarship generally treats the book as a pseudepigraph, derived from a much later time, with Moses' name being attached to lend authority to the composition. For an alternative interpretation, see my "Recovering the Voice of Moses: The Genesis of Deuteronomy," *JETS* 44 (2001) 385–408. Whether Deuteronomy is historical or pseudepigraphic, because most of the book is presented as quoted speech, I will identify citations according to the purported speaker rather than the final author/editor of the book.

9. For a methodological summary of biblical theology, see Z. Zevit, "Jewish Biblical Theology: Whence? Why? And Whither?" *HUCA* 76 (2005) 305–6.

10. For a beginning, see my "Biological Diversity within the Created Order: Toward a Biblical Theology of Non-Human Life," in *Keeping God's Earth: Creation Care and the Global Environment* (ed. D. I. Block and N. J. Toly; Downers Grove, IL: InterVarsity, forthcoming).

The way Gen 1 presents the creation of the animals reflects a clear taxonomy of animal species divided into four categories: fish of the sea (*děgat ḥayyām*), birds of the sky (*ʿôp haššāmayim*), high-carriage land animals (*běhēmâ*), and "crawlies" that crawl on the ground (here *remeś hārōmēś ʿal hāʾāreṣ*, v. 26).[11] The same fourfold division of the animal kingdom is reflected in Deut 4:17–18, which forbids the manufacture of images of any creature for the purposes of worship: (1) 'any animal that is on the earth' (*kol běhēmat ʾăšer bāʾāreṣ*); (2) 'any bird of wing that flies in the sky' (*kol ṣippôr kānāp ʾăšer tāʿûp baššāmayim*); (3) 'any creeper on the ground' (*kol rōmēś bāʾădāmâ*); and (4) 'any fish that is in the water' (*kol dāgâ ʾăšer bammayim*).[12] Further information on ancient Israel's taxonomy of creaturely life is found in the dietary instructions of Lev 11:2–23, 29–31 and Deut 14:4–20. Although Lev 11:29–31 adds the class of low-carriage land animals that 'swarm on the ground' (*šereṣ haššōrēṣ ʿal hāʾāreṣ*). Both lists of clean and unclean animals follow the traditional taxonomy (see fig. 1). Specifically, Deut 14:4–20 recognizes four broad categories of animals: 'high-carriage land animals' (*běhēmâ*, vv. 4–8), 'sea creatures' (*dāgâ*, vv. 9–10), 'birds' (*ṣippôr*, vv. 11–18),[13] and insects, which are divided into 'unclean insects' (*šereṣ haʿôp* 'swarmers of fliers', v. 19)[14] and 'edible (clean) insects' (*ʿôp ṭāhôr*, v. 20).[15] The relationship between the categories in Deut 14 and modern designations may be compared by isolating the gazelle and juxtaposing the classifications as in fig. 2 (see p. 288). Whereas high-carriage animals are divided on the basis of their hooves and ruminant stomachs, the two primary classes of sea creatures are those that have fins and scales and those that do not. Apparently, the unclean animals would include sea mammals such as dolphins

---

11. For a discussion of these and other taxonomies, see R. Whitekettle, "Where the Wild Things Are: Primary Level Taxa in Israelite Zoological Thought," *JSOT* 93 (2001) 17–37.

12. Akkadian expressions for wild animals include *būl ṣēri* and *umām ṣēri* 'animals of the steppe'. For discussions of ancient Mesopotamian distinctions between the domestic and the wild, see B. R. Foster, "Animals in Mesopotamian Literature," in *A History of the Animal World in the Ancient Near East* (ed. B. J. Collins; Handbook of Oriental Studies: Section 1, The Near and Middle East 64; Leiden: Brill, 2002) 272–74; and C. E. Watanabe, *Animal Symbolism in Mesopotamia: A Contextual Approach* (Wiener Offene Orientalistik 1; Vienna: Institute für Orientalistik, University of Vienna, 2002) 147–50.

13. See Deut 4:17, where the expression is expanded to *ṣippôr kānap* 'bird of wing'. Leviticus 11:13 introduces the birds with *ʿôp*, on which see further below.

14. Though the expressions exhibit some overlap, elsewhere *šrṣ* 'swarmer' identifies primarily swarming insects and aquatic creatures, while *remeś* 'creeping thing' identifies low-carriage mammals and small reptiles. See A. E. Hill, "*remeś*," *NIDOTTE* 3.1127–28.

15. Hebrew *ʿôp* derives from *ʿûp* 'to fly'. In 28:26, the full expression, *ʿôp haššāmayim*, refers to 'birds of the sky', which occurs frequently elsewhere in the OT (Gen 1:30 + 17×; Gen 1:21 refers to birds as *ʿôp kānāp* 'bird of wing'). That 14:20 intends *ʿôp* to be interpreted as flying insects rather than birds is confirmed by Lev 11:20–23, where the general designation *šereṣ hāʿôp* 'swarmers of fliers' is followed by a list of edible locusts.

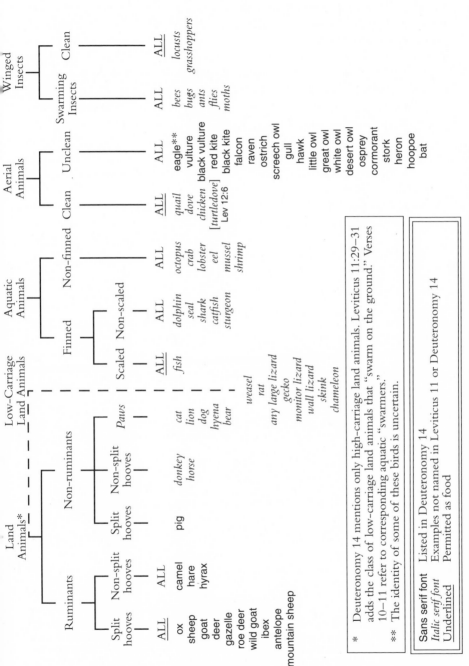

Fig. 1. *Clean and unclean animals according to Leviticus 11 and Deuteronomy 14.*

Category	Scientific Name	Hebrew Designation
Kingdom	Animalia	ḥayyâ 'animal'
Phylum	Chordata	
Class	Mammalia	bĕhēmâ 'land animal'
Order	Artiodactyla	mapreset parsâ wĕšōsaʿat šesaʿ šĕtê pĕrāsôt 'divided and cleft of hoof'
Family	Bovidae	maʿălat gērâ 'chews the cud, ruminant'
Subfamily	Antilopinae	
Genus	Gazella	
Species	G. arabica [a]	ṣĕbî 'gazelle'

a. The exact identity of ṣĕbî is uncertain. G. arabica is a good guess, but other possibilities include G. gazella, G. dorcas, and G. subgutturosa. See Oded Borowski, *Every Living Thing: Daily Use of Animals in Ancient Israel* (Walnut Creek, CA: AltaMira, 1998) 187. G. arabica is extinct, the only surviving specimen being on display in the Berlin Museum. For further information, see http://www.iucnredlist.org/search/details.php/8981/al.

Fig. 2. Comparing modern and Hebrew animal categories.

and whales, as well as octopus, catfish, and shrimp. Birds ("sky fliers") seem to be divided generally on the basis of their eating habits: that is, carnivorous birds (whether they kill their own prey or eat carrion, including bats) on the one hand, and those that eat grains on the other. This text seems to exclude all winged insects (šereṣ hāʿôp 'swarmers that fly'), though Lev 11:20–23 distinguishes between winged insects with four feet (despite the fact that insects have six!) and winged, hopping insects with jointed legs, which are edible—insects such as crickets, locusts, and grasshoppers.

Modern scientific approaches to biological taxonomies base their classifications on careful analysis and comparison of anatomical features, behaviors, breeding patterns, not to mention DNA testing.[16] These biblical classifications are obviously not based on scientific analysis but on phenomenological observations. To the ancient Hebrews, creaturely spheres of existence and the animals' diet were more significant markers than the boundaries we recognize between cold and warm-blooded animals or feathered and furry coverings. We will return to a consideration of the dietary significance of this taxonomy for Israel later.

16. DNA testing also occurs in our classifications, especially in the Latin names ascribed to creatures. For example, *Ailuropoda melanoleuca* 'black and white bear' is the scientific name of the giant panda, even though some biologists wondered whether the creature belonged to the raccoon or the bear family. Recent DNA tests have confirmed that, despite its exclusively herbivorous habits, the giant panda is indeed a bear, whereas the red panda belongs to the family that includes raccoons and skunks.

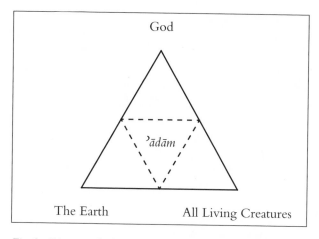

Fig. 3. Diagram of relationship among Creator, the earth, and its animal population.

The Relationship between Human Beings and Animals

Based on Gen 1–2, the renewal of the Adamic mandate to Noah in Gen 9 and Ps 8 as the image of God, humankind was assigned the honorific but responsible role of governing the world on God's behalf. The role of human beings in the maintenance of the relationship between Creator, the earth, and its animal population may be portrayed diagrammatically as in fig. 3.

The earth is the realm that human beings are charged to govern on God's behalf, and all living creatures are the subjects to be governed as God would, were he physically present. Proverbs 12:10 characterizes persons who show regard for the life of their animals as 'righteous' (*ṣaddîq*), that is, individuals who live according to covenantal standards. This accords not only with the deuteronomic paradigm of kingship in Deut 17:14–20,[17] but also with the trajectory of the deuteronomic instructions on the Israelites' treatment of creatures, both domestic and wild. The fundamental principle governing all of life is declared in 16:20: "Righteousness, righteousness you shall pursue, that you may live and possess the land that Yahweh your God is giving you."[18] Every subunit in

---

17. On which, see my "Burden of Leadership: The Mosaic Paradigm of Kingship (Deut 17:14–20)," *BSac* 162 (2005) 259–28.

18. Most translations render *ṣedeq ṣedeq* something like 'justice, and justice alone', but then the Hebrew should read *mišpāṭ mišpāṭ*. Furthermore, the issues dealt with in the following chapters are not limited to social justice issues but involve the full range of human behaviors, including dietary regulations, prohibitions on idolatry, and so on.

the second half of the second address (Deut 12:1–26:19)[19] should be interpreted as contributing to this agenda. Whereas Gen 1–2 bases human responsibility toward all living things on humanity's status as bearing the image of
God—that is, as God's representative and deputy—according to Deuteronomy, the human disposition toward and treatment of animals is a matter of
covenant righteousness.

In surveying the attention that Deuteronomy gives to animals, we quickly
see that human beings relate to animals at four levels: (1) some animals are wild
and live independent of and in opposition to human beings; (2) some animals
are domesticated and work for human beings; (3) some animals are used by
human beings as sacrificial offerings to the deity; and (4) some animals provide
food for human beings. We shall explore each of these in turn.

Animals as Wild and Independent of Human Beings

The most common generic epithet for wild animals, *ḥayyat haśśādeh* 'beasts
of the field', occurs only in Deut 7:22: "Yahweh your God will clear away
these nations before you little by little. You may not make an end of them at
once, lest the wild beasts multiply against you."[20] As in Exod 23:29, the idiom
rabbâ ʿālêkā 'to multiply against' portrays wild animals as antagonists and a threat
to human well-being. This threat is expressed explicitly in the covenant curse
of Lev 26:22, where Yahweh warns that he will dispatch wild animals against
his own people as agents of punishment for persistent rebellion against him.
This threat finds no counterpart in the deuteronomic version of the curses
(chap. 28), though earlier, Moses had spoken of Yahweh's sending 'hornets'
(*ṣirʿâ*) ahead of the Israelites to clear away the enemy,[21] and later in 28:26, he
refers to *běhēmat hāʾāreṣ* eating the carcasses of human victims of war.[22] In
Moses' final benediction of the tribes, several times he alludes metaphorically
to the threat that wild animals pose to human beings: "his [Joseph's] horns are
the horns of a wild ox;[23] with them he shall gore the peoples, all of them, to
the ends of the earth" (Deut 33:17).

---

19. The second address concludes with the blessings and curses of Deut 28. Chapter 27 seems
to have been secondarily inserted.

20. For discussion of wild animals in the OT and in the ancient Near East, see O. Borowski,
Every Living Thing: Daily Use of Animals in Ancient Israel (Walnut Creek, CA: AltaMira, 1998)
185–209.

21. The meaning of the term is uncertain. Many translate 'pestilence'. See NJPSV, NRSV.

22. See Jer 15:3: "I will appoint over them four kinds of destroyers—the declaration of
Yahweh—the sword to kill, the dogs to tear, and the birds of the air and the beasts of the earth
[*běhēmat hāʾāreṣ*] to devour and destroy." This expression occurs elsewhere in 1 Sam 17:44;
Isa 18:6; Jer 7:33; 16:4; 19:7; 34:20.

23. The expression *rěʾēm* occurs elsewhere only in the poetry of Balaam's oracles (Num 23:22
and 24:8), Pss 22:22[21]; 29:6; 92:11; Job 39:9, 10.

Because wild animals are sanctioned for human consumption as food (12:15, 22; 14:5–6; 15:22), human beings obviously pose a threat to wild animals as well. Although Deuteronomy intentionally reins in the abuse of power at every level, the book has remarkably little to say on the potential abuse of wild animals by human beings.[24] In fact, the deuteronomic policy on the sabbatical year of release (15:1–18) drops any hint of the concern for wild animals found in the Book of the Covenant: "The seventh year you shall let it [the land] rest and lie fallow, that the poor of your people may eat; and what they leave the beasts of the field [*hayyat hassadeh*] may eat. You shall do likewise with your vineyard, and with your olive orchard" (Exod 23:11). This does not mean that concern for wild animals is lacking. On the contrary, in Deut 22:6–7 Moses encourages a tender and sympathetic disposition toward wild birds:

> If you come across a bird's nest, in any tree or on the ground, with fledglings or eggs, with the mother sitting on the fledglings or on the eggs, you shall not take the mother with the young. Let the mother go; take only the young for yourself, that it may go well with you and you may live long.

In many respects this injunction is a riddle. What use is to be made of the young,[25] which finders may take for themselves? The eggs of poultry and game fowl were valued as food, but what about the eggs of other birds and, even more seriously, the fledglings? Unless these have some use, this text seems to authorize their wanton slaughter. At the same time, if the passage had allowed the mother to be taken but the young spared, the effect would be the same as if the life of both were taken, for unhatched eggs and fledgling birds are dependent on the continued care of the mother. But if the mother is released, she may nest again, incubate another batch of eggs, and see the new brood to maturity. The Israelites were neither to kill for killing's sake nor to exploit natural resources without concern for conservation.[26]

But this reasoning is speculative. In fact, the text expresses no explicit concern for the birds. Instead, it appears to ground the instructions in human self-interest: if the Israelites will treat birds' nests this way, it will go well with them and they will enjoy long life on the land. The addition of the motive clause promising well-being and long life for human beings not only highlights the covenantal significance of this injunction but also places it in the same class of weighty commandments as the general commands to obey the statutes and

---

24. Though Deut 20:19–20 expressly prohibits the Israelites from denuding the landscape of its trees when engaging enemy cities in battle.

25. Hebrew *bānîm* functions as shorthand for *'eprōhim* 'fledglings' and *bēṣîm* 'eggs'.

26. See Borowski, *Every Living Thing*, 152.

commandments that he has given the Israelites elsewhere in his three addresses (4:40; 5:29; 6:18; 12:28). Furthermore, it links them with other weighty pre-conditions to longevity (4:40; 5:33; 11:9; see also 30:18).[27]

This motive clause is grounded on an assumption of the triangular relationship that exists between God, the earth, and its animal inhabitants and of humankind's responsibility as the divine image, not only to subdue the earth and restrain evil, but to manage it in the interests of all the parties to this covenant. In the end, the Israelites' well-being was dependent on their righteousness, demonstrated in respect for the life of helpless creatures.

Animals as Domestic and Dependent on Human Beings

The counterpart to the designation for wild animals, *ḥayyat haśśādeh* 'beast of the field', should be *ḥayyat habbayit* 'beast of the house/household'. However, this expression never occurs in the OT. Instead, *běhēmâ*, which serves as a designation for high-carriage animals in general in Gen 1 and Deut 4:17, functions as the most common general designation for household animals that included sheep, goats, cattle, and donkeys.[28] The first two were valued primarily for their meat, their milk, and their wool and hair, respectively, for the manufacture of cloth and clothing. Cattle were valued for their milk and their meat but especially for their strength as draft animals, to transport goods and pull agricultural implements. Donkeys served primarily as pack animals, though they were also harnessed to pull carts and small plows.

Deuteronomy 22:1–4 seeks to secure the well-being of oxen, sheep, and donkeys by charging the Israelites to care for straying animals. The first response to finding a stray was to return it to its owner. However, if the owner lived some distance away or the identity of the owner was unknown, the finder was to bring[29] it home to his own house for safe-keeping. When the owner came to claim the animal, it had to be returned to him. The declaration "You are not allowed to hide yourself from them" (*hiʿallēm* 'ignore them')

---

27. Robert M. Johnson ("'The Least of the Commandments': Deuteronomy 22:6–7 in Rabbinic Judaism and Early Christianity," *AUSS* 20 [1982] 205–15) argues that the present instructions are included in "the least of these commandments" in Matt 5:19. According to Johnson, based on the hermeneutical principle of *qal we-ḥomer* 'light and heavy', in rabbinic tradition this commandment was interpreted to mean that, if God is so concerned about birds and their nests, how much more important to him are human beings! For a helpful study of the interpretation of vv. 6–7 in Rabbinic Judaism, see Eliezer Segal, "Justice, Mercy and a Bird's Nest," *JJS* 42 (1991) 176–95.

28. For a detailed study, see Borowski, *Every Living Thing*. See also P. J. King and L. E. Stager, *Life in Biblical Israel* (Library of Ancient Israel; Louisville: Westminster/John Knox, 2001) 112–22. Because horses were used primarily in military contexts, they are excluded from this list.

29. The verb *ʾāsap* 'to collect' may suggest a collective sense for the three types of animals referred to by singular nouns.

places the plight of the straying animals in the same category as the man who was attacked by thieves, ignored by the priest and the Levite, but ultimately rescued by the Samaritan (Luke 10:30–35).

However, Deuteronomy seems to assume that the threat of abusive masters was greater than the dangers of going astray. This issue is addressed by deliberately modifying the Sabbath command in a direction that establishes the profoundly humanitarian trajectory of the whole book (Deut 5:6–21).[30] By basing the observance of the seventh day as a day of rest on Israel's experience of slavery in Egypt rather than the pattern of divine activity in the creation of the cosmos (5:12–15), this command provides the Israelites with a constant reminder of their own abuse at the hands of brutal taskmasters.[31] Moses hereby acknowledges that, beyond patterning human creative work after the creative work of God, the Creator of heaven and earth, on the Sabbath heads of households are to allow all who work in the domestic economic unit—including the animals—to refresh themselves. In so doing, this command reins in potential abuse of power over livestock by the head of the household.

The problem of abuse of power is highlighted even more dramatically in 22:4: "You shall not see your brother's donkey or his ox fallen down by the way and ignore them. You shall help him to lift them up again." Here the attention shifts from an animal that has strayed (22:1–3) to an animal that is abused. Although the entire passage assumes that the treatment of the animals will be motivated by a sense of community with their owners, it also calls for sensitivity/compassion toward their livestock. Domestic animals played a vital role in securing the economic well-being of the people, but ownership and control could easily degenerate into harsh and abusive treatment.

The instruction in 25:4 is even more concrete: "You shall not muzzle an ox when it is treading out the grain." On the surface, this fragment of apodictic instruction seems unrelated to the preceding. However, because draft animals were often prodded with switches and rods, some suggest the references to flogging in vv. 2–3 may have triggered this insertion.[32] But if this had been the case, we would expect the present statement to curb excessive beating of one's animal. Instead, it displays a remarkable humanitarianism in a completely different form: oxen used for threshing grain were not to be muzzled.[33] The

---

30. See my essay "'You shall not covet your neighbor's wife': A Study in Deuteronomic Domestic Ideology" (paper presented to the Evangelical Theological Society, Washington, DC, Nov. 18, 2006).

31. In his second address, Moses will repeatedly buttress his ethical and spiritual appeals with reminders of the Israelites' experience as slaves in Egypt. See Deut 15:15; 16:12; and 24:18, 22.

32. Thus Tigay, *Deuteronomy*, 458.

33. On this passage, see J. T. Noonan Jr., "The Muzzled Ox," *JQR* 70 (1980) 172–75.

ordinance derives from the ancient practice of threshing grain by having oxen or donkeys trample the stalks or pull rock studded sledges over the stalks spread out on the threshing floor.[34] It so happens that what is a staple of life for human beings is also food for animals. Out of greed, a farmer might muzzle his ox or donkey to prevent it from slowing down and eating instead of working or simply to prevent it from eating what he hoped to harvest for his own consumption (see Prov 14:4). This text forbids Israelites to treat their animals this way.

The concern expressed here coheres with Deuteronomy's general concern to protect those vulnerable to exploitation, including widows, orphans, aliens, Levites, and now domestic animals. The heads of households are to safeguard the right to humane treatment of all under their roof. In this way they are to show the same regard for the life of the creatures as God himself does, as is reflected in several nature psalms (104:10–14; 145:16; 147:9). In 1 Cor 9:9 and 1 Tim 5:18, Paul applies the present ordinance to the right of apostles to derive their living from the work they do in spreading the gospel. Some would argue that his rhetorical question, "God is not concerned about oxen, is he?" which assumes a negative answer, is possible only if *šôr* 'ox' is interpreted as being figurative for human beings.[35] However, this is not necessary, if one interprets Deut 25:4 within the context of the entire chapter. Like Paul's statement, these instructions are addressed to human beings, not to animals. Throughout Deut 25, the concern has been to develop in the Israelites, the people of God, a sensitive and considerate disposition, especially toward the vulnerable. Moses' statement about the ox fits this agenda perfectly, extending even to animals the theological principle that in God's economy all workers, be they human or animal, deserve humane treatment and reward for their labor.[36]

---

34. The *Temple Scroll* of Qumran (11Q19 52:12) modifies the consonantal reading of the last word of MT *bdyšw* (which most interpret as a Qal infinitive: 'while it is treading'), to *ʾl dyšw* (which involves a noun: 'on its threshing floor'). This reading suggests a prohibition against muzzling an animal whenever food is present. For discussion, see E. Qimron, "The Biblical Lexicon in the Light of the Dead Sea Scrolls," *DSD* 2 (1995) 296–98; L. H. Schiffman, "Some Laws Pertaining to Animals in Temple Scroll Column 52," in *Legal Texts and Legal Issues: Proceedings of the Second Meeting of the International Organization for Qumran Studies Cambridge 1995: Published in Honour of Joseph M. Baumgarten* (ed. M. Bernstein; STDJ 23; Leiden: Brill, 1997) 173–74.

35. See F. W. Grosheide, *Commentary on the First Epistle to the Corinthians* (NICNT; Grand Rapids: Eerdmans, 1953) 205.

36. For a helpful discussion of the hermeneutical issues involved, see W. C. Kaiser Jr., "The Current Crisis in Exegesis and the Apostolic Use of Deuteronomy 25:4 in 1 Corinthians 9:8–10," *JETS* 21 (1978) 3–18, esp. pp. 11–16. For a discussion of the ethical implications of Paul's adaptation of this command to an entirely new situation, see Wennberg, *God, Humans, and Animals*, 297–98.

The present ordinance may help explain the enigmatic prohibition of boiling a kid in its mother's milk in 14:21. It is difficult to know whether this command is primarily about dietary issues (meat cooked in milk) or a humanitarian concern for creatures.[37] Whatever its original intent, the prohibition underlies the orthodox Jewish dietary law of *kashrut* that prohibits mixing milk and meat in a meal. This strange ordinance occurs in identical form in two other contexts, the Book of the Covenant (Exod 23:19) and the so-called Dodecalogue (Exod 34:26). In both of these instances, this command is linked with the annual pilgrimage festivals, which may suggest a cultic concern. If this interpretation is correct, the location of the command at the end of dietary instructions in Deut 14 would reinforce our linkage of the foods permitted on the Israelites' table with the sacrifices offered to Yahweh.

Animals as "Food" for Yahweh

According to the biblical narratives, the use of animals for sacrificial purposes is almost as old as the human race. Genesis 4:4 reports Abel presenting a firstling of the flock as an 'offering' (*minḥâ*) to Yahweh. This picture was developed in great detail in the priestly legislation of Exodus and Leviticus. The slaughter of the Passover lamb was a critical part of this festival to Yahweh (Exod 12:14), but there is no hint that this lamb was perceived as food to be eaten by Yahweh; on the contrary, the psalmist declares: "I will not accept a bull from your house or goats from your folds. . . . If I were hungry, I would not tell you, for the world and its fullness are mine. Do I eat the flesh of bulls or drink the blood of goats? Offer to God a sacrifice of thanksgiving, and perform your vows to the Most High" (Ps 50:9–14).

In contrast to the cultures around, where through ritual offerings people perceived themselves and their priests to be caring for and feeding the gods, in Israel this notion is thoroughly demythologized. Even though sacrifices often involved animals,[38] in many instances the meat was actually consumed by the

---

37. The literature on this enigmatic proscription is vast. See O. Keel, *Das Böcklein in der Milch seiner Mutter und Verwandtes im Lichte eines altorientalischen Bildmotivs* (OBO 33; Freiburg: Universitätsverlag / Göttingen: Vandenhoeck & Ruprecht, 1980); R. Ratner and B. Zuckerman, "A Kid in Milk?" *HUCA* 57 (1986) 15–60; M. Haran, "Seething a Kid in Its Mother's Milk," *JJS* 30 (1979) 23–35; C. J. Labuschagne, " 'You Shall Not Boil a Kid in Its Mother's Milk': A New Proposal for the Origin of the Prohibition," in *The Scriptures and the Scrolls* (ed. F. García Martínez, A. Hilhorst, and C. J. Labuschagne; VTSup 49; Leiden: Brill, 1992) 6–17; W. H. C. Propp, *Exodus 19–40: A New Translation with Introduction and Commentary* (AB 2A; New York: Doubleday, 2006) 286; and D. K. Stuart, *Exodus* (NAC 2; Nashville: Broadman & Holman, 2006) 539–40.

38. 'The Passover' (*pesaḥ*; a one-year-old lamb or kid without blemish; Exod 12:5); 'the whole burnt offering' (*ʿōlâ*; a bull or sheep or goat; Lev 1:1–17); 'the sacrificial meal' and 'the

worshiper in the presence of Yahweh. Deuteronomy 15:19–23 specifies that
the unblemished firstborn of the herds and flocks that the Israelites consecrate
to Yahweh may be eaten in his presence in the central sanctuary. Similarly the
Passover was to be eaten in the presence of Yahweh (Deut 16:1–8). Neither in
Deuteronomy nor elsewhere in the OT does Yahweh ever eat of the sacrifices
presented to him. The closest we get is metaphorical statements suggesting that
the sacrifices of God's people are a pleasing/soothing aroma to him.[39]

If Yahweh does not eat the animal sacrifices presented to him, then who
does? With reference to the ʿôlâ, the answer is no one; this offering is burned
up entirely on the altar.[40] As for the rest, Deut 18:1–8 provides a partial answer.
The Levitical priests, indeed any from the entire tribe of Levi—whether they
reside at the place of the central sanctuary or in the towns scattered throughout the land, those who are called to serve the nation spiritually in the name
of Yahweh—are entitled to portions of the animals offered as sacrifices by the
people, specifically, the shoulder, the jowls, and the stomach. However, a fuller
answer is provided by a half dozen verses scattered throughout the second half
of Moses' second address: "And you shall sacrifice peace offerings and shall eat
there, and you shall rejoice before Yahweh your God" (Deut 27:7; see also
12:7, 18; 14:23, 26; 15:20).

These texts portray Yahweh as a divine host, receiving the offerings of his
people and then turning around and spreading the meat of the offerings before
them, inviting them thereby to celebrate the privilege of relationship with
him. As sacrifices, the animals provided not only food for the people but also
a means whereby their relationship with Yahweh may be celebrated and
cemented. A more noble role for the creatures may scarcely be imagined.

Animals as Food for Human Beings in Everyday Life

The use of animals as food in cultic contexts leads naturally to a final issue:
the use of animals as food in everyday life. Our discussion must consider two

---

peace offering' (*zebaḥ* and *šĕlāmîm*; a bull or lamb or goat; Lev 3:1–17); 'the reparation offerings'
(*ʾāšām*; a ram without blemish; Lev 6:1–6); 'the purification offering' (*ḥaṭṭāʾt*; bulls, male or
female goats, lambs, turtledoves; Lev 4:1–21). On ancient Mesopotamian sacrifices as food for
the gods, see JoAnn Scurlock, "Animal Sacrifice in Ancient Mesopotamian Religion," in *History
of the Animal World in the Ancient Near East* (ed. B. J. Collins; Leiden: Brill, 2002) 389–97. On
ancient Israelite use of animals as sacrifices, see Borowski, *Every Living Thing,* 214–18.

39. The Hebrew expression *rêaḥ hannîḥôaḥ* 'the soothing aroma' occurs only in Gen 8:21,
but the idiom without the article occurs frequently: Exod 29:18; Lev 1:9, 13, 17; 2:2, 9; 3:5; 6:8,
14; 23:13, 18; Num 15:3, 7, 10, 13, 14; 28:8, 13, 24; 29:8, 13, 36; and Ezek 6:13. Although the
OT never includes wild ungulates in lists of sacrifices, the remains of wild ruminants have been
found in cult places (Borowski, *Every Living Thing,* 218). It is difficult to imagine how a wild
animal could be caught without causing some blemish, which would disqualify it from cultic use.

40. See R. E. Averbeck, "ʿôlâ," *NIDOTTE* 3.407.

issues: (1) What kinds of animals were permitted as food for Israel? (2) How was the flesh of the animal to be prepared? Although the descendants of Adam undoubtedly ate the flesh of animals, divine authorization for this custom is recorded for the first time in Gen 9:3, where Noah and his descendants are granted permission to eat the flesh of 'every moving thing that lives' (*kol remeś ʾăśer hûʾ ḥay*). Leviticus 11 and Deut 14 rein in this comprehensive authorization for the Israelites by establishing boundaries between clean and unclean food, with only the former being permitted in their diet.[41] Deuteronomy 14:1–21 is generally characterized as a collection of dietary laws. However, both the framework and the tone of the text suggest that this passage should instead be interpreted as an invitation to a family feast hosted by Yahweh himself.

The opening verses (vv. 1–2) and the concluding statement (v. 21) highlight Israel's special status before Yahweh and in the midst of all the nations of the earth. In the former, the people that make up this nation are identified as "the sons of Yahweh your God," "a holy people belonging to Yahweh your God," and Yahweh's 'special treasure' (*sĕgullâ*) chosen out of all the nations of the earth. Verse 21 distinguishes the Israelites from 'resident aliens' (*haggēr*) and 'strangers' (*hannokrî*). The significance of the instructions for Israel as Yahweh's covenantal people is reinforced by the fourfold repetition of "It is unclean for you" (vv. 7, 8, 10, 19).

According to Gen 9:3, after the great flood, God authorized Noah and his descendants to eat the meat of all living animals indiscriminately, though with the proviso that the blood, representing the life, be drained from the carcass. Based on the legislation in Lev 11, now Deuteronomy reins in this freedom for Israel. Because they are the holy people of Yahweh, the meat in their diet, whether from domesticated animals raised at home or animals that they hunt, must be like the food that God "eats" (in the sacrifices offered to him).[42] Indeed, if Deut 12:1–14 represented an invitation to worship Yahweh at the place he would choose, and 12:15–28 granted authorization to eat meat away from the central sanctuary, then the dietary instructions in chap. 14 suggest that every meal is a sacred moment, and every animal slaughtered for consumption is a sacrifice. Through their diet the Israelites were to declare to one another and to outsiders their unprecedented and unparalleled proximity to

---

41. For a detailed study of these texts, see J. Moskala, *The Laws of Clean and Unclean Animals in Leviticus 11: Their Nature, Theology, and Rationale (An Intertextual Study)* (Adventist Theological Society Dissertation Series; Berrien Springs, MI: Adventist Theological Society, 2000).

42. This is the reverse of the ancient Mesopotamian practice because "draft animals were not generally eaten by ancient Mesopotamians and, since gods usually share the tastes of their worshipers, horses or donkeys were not offered as food for the divine table" (Scurlock, "Animal Sacrifice," 392). Pigs represented an exception; they were generally eaten, but evidence for their use as offerings to divinities is scarce.

their God.[43] These dietary boundaries did not apply to people outside the covenant, as v. 21 will reiterate (the flesh of an animal that has died of natural causes may be given or sold to an outsider). Adapting a comment of Mary Douglas, we conclude that by rules of avoidance [Israel's] sanctified status as the covenant people of Yahweh "was given a physical expression in every encounter with the animal kingdom and at every meal."[44] Accordingly, the dietary instructions inserted between these frames are best considered an invitation to feast at the table of Yahweh, a conclusion reinforced by the singular designation of the guests as the "sons of Yahweh your God" in 14:1.[45]

The apodictic command in v. 3 functions as a thematic introduction to the material between the two frames, with vv. 4–20 fleshing out what is meant by the prohibited 'abominable food' (*tô*ʿ*ēbâ*). These 17 verses have the appearance of a self-contained literary unit, stylistically distinguished from the surrounding frame, not only by its lists of various kinds of land animals (10 kosher species, vv. 4–6; 4 prohibited species, vv. 7–8) and species of inedible fowl (21 species, vv. 12–18), but also by its relative secularity. Verses 4–20 represent the second-longest continuous text in Deuteronomy without any reference to the name of Yahweh.[46] Not that this material is lacking in theological significance; the fourfold reference to 'uncleanness' (*ṭmʾ*, vv. 7, 8, 10, 19) confirms that the concern here goes far beyond the mere listing of clean and unclean foods and diet.

A detailed comparison of the links between this passage and Lev 11 is beyond the scope of this study. But the net effect of the adaptations of material from Lev 11 in Deut 14 is to transform a legal document (concerned with precise definitions of the boundaries between clean and unclean and revolving around the technical understanding of defilement) into a moral document seeking to declare how Israel's status as 'Yahweh's holy people' (ʿ*am qādôš layhwh*) is to be demonstrated in all of life. In keeping with the pastoral concern of the present text, the tone of Deut 14:4–20 is much more positive than Lev 11:3–21; it seems more interested in affirming what the Israelites may do than in prohibiting what they may not do. This would account for the affirmations brought forward in the present context: the listing of the names of ten edible animals in vv. 4–5, as well as the direct confirmation that the Israelites may eat all clean fowl (v. 11) and all clean insects (v. 20).

---

43. Similarly E. Firmage, "Biblical Dietary Laws and the Concept of Holiness," in *Studies in the Pentateuch* (VTSup 41; ed. J. A. Emerton; Leiden: Brill, 1990) 196–97.

44. Mary Douglas, *Purity and Danger: An Analysis of the Concepts of Pollution and Taboo* (New York: Ark, 1984) 57.

45. Compare the fatherly similes in 1:31 and 8:5.

46. Only 21:11–22 is longer by word count.

But it would also account for some absences: the deletion of repetitive explanations as to why the camel and the hare are excluded (v. 7), the reduction of the extended presentation of clean and unclean aquatic creatures (as in Lev 11:9–12) to two simple statements affirming finned and scaled creatures as kosher food and excluding non-finned and non-scaled creatures (vv. 9–10)[47] and the elimination of the descriptions of edible insects (as in Lev 11:21–22). The net effect is one of psychologically "opening the door," rather than closing it. This impression is reinforced by opening the entire chapter of Deut 14 with "you are the sons of Yahweh your God" (v. 1a) and framing vv. 2–20 with statements that are profoundly ethical. Both vv. 1b–3 and v. 21 highlight the distinction between Israelites and outsiders, and both refer to Israel's status as Yahweh's holy people.

Having appealed to Israel to avoid food considered by Yahweh to be abominable, it was natural for Moses to remind the present generation of the established boundaries between kosher[48] and prohibited food. While all cultures appear to have their own sets of rules defining boundaries between the clean and unclean, especially in relationship to food, the rationale for the boundaries is not clearly understood. The same applies to Israel's understanding of dietary cleanness and uncleanness. Scholars have proposed a variety of theories for the prohibition on certain kinds of food as outlined in Lev 11 and Deut 14: cultic (because they are associated with Canaanite religious practices), aesthetic (because they are loathsome or repulsive), hygienic (because they cause illness), sociological (because they have an ambiguous form and lack physical integrity), and didactic (because they illustrate/teach wrongful behavior).[49] Both Lev 11 and Deut 14 link Israel's dietary laws with its status as a holy people. Deuteronomy in particular is concerned to celebrate Israel's status as a single people under the one God Yahweh. Even as the dietary instructions serve to unite the people around the table, they also function as boundary markers between Israel and all other nations.[50]

---

47. Where Lev 11:9–12 has 53 words, Deut 14:9–10 has only 22.

48. The Yiddish term *kosher* derives from an apparently common West Semitic root *kāšar* 'to be appropriate, deemed fit'. For the Hebrew, see *HALOT* 2.503; for Aramaic and Palmyrene, see *DNWSI* 1.539–40. For the Mishnaic Hebrew usage, see M. Jastrow, *A Dictionary of the Targumim, the Talmud Babli and Yerushalmi, and the Midrashic Literature* (New York: Pardes, 1950) 677–78.

49. For discussion of each of these and other explanations, see W. Houston, *Purity and Monotheism: Clean and Unclean Animals in Biblical Law* (JSOTSup 140; Sheffield: Sheffield Academic Press, 1993) 68–123. For an Asian perspective on the dietary laws, see Kim-Kwong Chan, "You Shall Not Eat These Abominable Things: An Examination of Different Interpretations on Deuteronomy 14:3–20," *East Asia Journal of Theology* 3 (1985) 95–104.

50. See Houston, *Purity and Monotheism*, 225–28.

Although both texts link the lists of clean and unclean animals with Israel's holiness, neither spells out what it is about the clean animals that coheres with the biblical notion of holiness or explains the features of unclean animals that violate those notions.[51] However, given the emphasis on the defiling effect of contact with the carcasses of dead animals in Lev 11:24–40[52] and the framing of the dietary regulations in Deut 14 with references to ritual practices related to the cult of the dead (v. 1), on the one hand, and brief regulations on the treatment of animals that have died a natural death, on the other (v. 21), the most likely hypothesis suggests that the forbidden animals are rejected because of their association with death.[53] Most are carnivores and/or scavengers that feed on carrion. Many of the rest are ground creatures that constantly come in contact with unclean matter.[54]

While this explanation is the most attractive, in the end we must admit that the OT fails to spell out the reasons for the boundaries it defines, and ultimately the only certain conclusion is that the boundaries are as they are because Yahweh, the God of Israel, declared them to be so. To modern readers they may seem arbitrary, but Yahweh's covenant with Israel is a suzerainty covenant—the terms are not negotiated and need not even make sense to the vassal. They are to be accepted simply because they represent the will of the divine suzerain. But this does not mean that they represented burdensome demands. On the contrary, both texts provide the Israelites with ample incentive to accept these dietary boundaries. In Lev 11:45, Yahweh reminds the Israelites that they are the objects of his gracious redemption; our text reminds them that they are the objects of his election and his exceptional favor. Accordingly, obedience to these regulations should have been a delight—a thankful response for unmerited kindness.

Furthermore, this chapter should be interpreted against the backdrop of the broader ancient Near Eastern cultural and religious climate from which it

---

51. See the discussion by Moskala, *Laws of Clean and Unclean Animals*, 315–48.

52. This section interrupts the catalog of clean and unclean animals that begins in Lev 11:2b–23 and is later resumed in vv. 41–43.

53. See Isa 65:2–7, which associates nocturnal and necromantic activity with eating swine's flesh (see also 66:17). R. Bulmer follows Douglas in arguing that animals are prohibited because they deviate from the norm applying to their respective species ("The Uncleanness of the Birds of Leviticus and Deuteronomy," *Man* 24 [1989] 304–21).

54. Leviticus 11:21–22 forbids winged insects that walk on all fours but permits locusts and grasshoppers that jump. It is probably not coincidental that these creatures are obvious vegetarians as well. Some of the animals are associated with ruins and the barren desert, concerned by many to be the abode of demons (W. Kornfeld, "Reine und unreine Tiere im Alten Testament," *Kairos* 7 [1965] 134–47, esp. pp. 146–47). For further discussion, see J. E. Hartley, *Leviticus* (WBC 4; Dallas: Word, 1992) 141–47; and J. E. Hartley, "Clean and Unclean," *ISBE* 1.718–23.

derives and to which it responds. As already noted, it is generally recognized that all cultures have their own taboos, particularly relating to edible and inedible food.[55] This was true also of the ancient Near Easterners in general.[56]

With all this attention to the boundaries between edible and inedible food, it is easy to overlook another vital element in the dietary implications of Israel's status as a holy people—the manner in which meat is prepared. Deuteronomy does not actually have much to say on the matter. The verb *biššēl* occurs in 14:21 and 16:7. In the former, *baḥălēb ʾimmô* 'in its mother's milk' suggests boiling, though *ḥālāb* may admittedly be used of milk products such as yoghurt as well.[57] However, elsewhere the verb *biššēl* is used of baking cakes (2 Sam 13:8), preparing manna (Num 11:8), and cooking meat for offerings (Ezek 46:20). Neither 14:21 nor 16:7 is concerned with the process by which food is prepared. For the people of Yahweh, the way an animal is slaughtered is of much greater consequence than the manner in which it is cooked. After freely permitting the consumption of meat, including domestic and wild animals, within the Israelites' own towns away from the central sanctuary, Deut 12:16 and 23–25 provide some explicit guidelines for the slaughter of animals:

> However, you shall not eat the blood; you shall pour it out on the earth like water. (v. 16)

> Only be sure that you do not eat the blood, for the blood is the life, and you shall not eat the life with the flesh. You shall not eat it; you shall pour it out on the earth like water. You shall not eat it, that all may go well with you and with your children after you, when you do what is right in the sight of Yahweh. (vv. 23–25)

This identification of the blood with life[58] derives from the common observance of the life of an animal or person ebbing away with the loss of blood.[59] Because the blood is identified with the life, the consumption of blood was viewed as the consumption of life itself, which explains the added comment in v. 23: "You may not eat the life with the meat." Although the blood of an animal slaughtered for its meat did not require satisfaction, in a sense all

---

55. See the discussion by Douglas, *Purity and Danger*, 41–57.

56. This passage should be interpreted in the light of texts such as the Sumerian "Prayer to Every God" that was discovered among the thousands of texts in the library of Ashurbanipal (668–633 B.C.). With telling frankness, the petitioner pleads with the god/goddess for some account of the dietary taboo. See *ANET* 391.

57. As reflected in the Jewish prohibition not to eat meat and dairy products together.

58. Whereas in vv. 15 and 20–22 *nepeš* had referred to the seat of desire, now the word denotes 'life, the vital self'. See *DCH* 5.728.

59. See Homer's reference to "life running out" (*Iliad* 14.518).

slaughter is sacrificial and substitutionary: a life for a life. Accordingly, the slaughter of animals may be profane (dissociated from the cult), but it is never secular.[60] The taboo on the consumption of blood provides a perpetual reminder that life is sacred, and life itself is a gift of God.

The prohibition on eating the meat of any animal that had died a natural death in 14:21 appears on the surface to arise out of a concern to protect Israel's status as the holy people of Yahweh. Here Moses authorizes the Israelites to sell this meat to a foreigner or give it to an alien living among them, but the members of the covenant community may not eat it. The present taboo may suggest that only Israelites are to guard the sanctity of life this way. However, the reason for the taboo probably lies elsewhere, presumably in the defiling effects that contact with this carcass had on the Israelites. In any case, this taboo on eating the blood goes back to the fountainhead of humanity (Gen 9:4), where God forbids the consumption of blood by any of Noah's descendants. The permanence and supra-Israelite validity of the ban on blood was recognized in the decision of the Council of Jerusalem to bind Gentile Christians to this ordinance in Acts 15:20.[61] The principle of the sanctity of all life transcends the Torah of Deuteronomy.

In the original ordinance (Lev 17:10–14), Yahweh had emphasized the importance of the taboo on the blood of slaughtered animals by threatening those who refused to comply with personal hostility and cutting them off from their people. In the present context (14:25), when Moses seeks to impress upon his audience the importance of this principle, he takes a more positive and pastoral approach; this is the precondition to well-being for them and their children, and it is guaranteed to win the approval of Yahweh. After all, they will be doing what is right in the eyes of Yahweh. The clause, *ta'ăśeh hayyāšār bĕ'ênê yhwh* answers directly to v. 8, where he had called upon the people to stop doing 'what was right in their own eyes' (*hayyāšār bĕ'ênāyw*). When people eat meat in their own towns, they may not be "before Yahweh" in the same sense as when they are at the central sanctuary, but they are still under his watchful care and supervision.

---

60. Contra M. Weinfeld, who in defense of a secularizing tendency in Deuteronomy argues that "pouring the blood out like water" means "the blood has no more a sacral value than water has" (*Deuteronomy and the Deuteronomic School* [Oxford: Oxford University Press, 1972; repr. Winona Lake, IN: Eisenbrauns, 1992] 214). The comparison with water relates to its liquid constitution rather than its religious significance.

61. For an excellent discussion of the relationship of these apostolic injunctions to and their grounding in Lev 17–18, see R. Davidson, "Which Torah Laws Should Gentile Christians Obey? The Relationship between Leviticus 17–18 and Acts 15" (paper presented to the Evangelical Theological Society, San Diego, Nov. 15, 2007).

Conclusion

With this observation we have reached the end of the presentation of the data. But this raises the question of the significance of this biblical information for us? The following represent preliminary conclusions on the relevance of Deuteronomy's theology of animals for evangelical Christians at the beginning of the 21st century.

First, if the heavens declare the glory of God and gazing at the sky inspires awe, this is no less true of the earth and its creatures, which are also the works of his hands. The creatures are all special to God simply because they are the work of his hands (Jonah 4:11). Furthermore, with all its variety and with its consistency, the animal world testifies both to the divine imagination and to the beauty of order. As in Gen 1, the zoological diversity recognized by Deuteronomy invites the reader to acknowledge in the animals the handiwork of God.

Second, the divine mission of Israel was to embody in microcosm the design of God for the cosmos. Just as humanity was created in the image of God and endowed with glory and majesty to govern the world for him (Ps 8), Israel's mission in the context of a fallen world was to declare to the world Yahweh's glory and grace by being redeemed, entering the land, and prospering in it (Deut 26:16–19). But this prosperity depended upon their fulfillment of covenant righteousness, the scope of which involved exclusive devotion to Yahweh and compassionate concern for the welfare of not only one's fellow Israelites and the marginalized[62] but also of the creaturely world. The humane treatment of animals is fundamental to covenant righteousness.

Third, while Christians are no longer bound by the dietary boundaries that marked the Israelites as the people of God (Acts 15:20),[63] the early disciples at the Council of Jerusalem reaffirmed the prohibitions on 'idolatry' (*eidōlothutos*) and 'sexual immorality' (*porneia*), as well as the prohibitions on the consumption of 'blood' (*haima*) and of meat from animals 'not properly slaughtered'

---

62. Note the emphasis on securing the well-being of the fatherless, widow, and sojourner in Deut 10:18; 14:29; 16:11, 14; 24:19–21; 26:12–13; and 27:19.

63. In the end, the significance of these dietary prescriptions may be linked to the sacrificial system of the old covenant. If indeed Deut 14 involves Yahweh's invitation to eat of the food in which he himself takes delight in the form of sacrifices, then with the termination of all sacrifices in Christ, these food regulations also become *passé*. Because we no longer provide God with these offerings but celebrate the sacrificial work of Jesus Christ, then whenever we partake of the Lord's table, that is the bread and the wine of communion, we participate in the feast to which the Lord has graciously invited us.

(*pniktos*).[64] The latter proscriptions recognize the sanctity of all life. In a sense, every meal, especially meals involving the meat of animals, is a sacrifice—an animal has given its life for our sakes. Neither the OT nor the NT calls for a vegetarian diet; on the contrary, they authorize the consumption of animals, provided the consumer continues to respect the sanctity of the life of the animal. Rightly understood, "humans do not live to eat, but they eat to live."[65] According to the Talmud, "A man's table is like an altar."[66] Moskala rightly declares that "both sacrifice and food should be taken with or as an expression of gratitude and thankfulness."[67] But this thankfulness is not only expressed in explicit declarations to God for his gracious provision of food but is also felt toward the animal world that has provided both pleasure and nourishment to God's vice-regent.

Fourth, Deut 22:6–7 reminded ancient Israelites and continues to remind modern readers of humanity's responsibility for the care of creation, even of the wild creatures. This notion is reflected in Gen 2:15, which explicitly declares humanity's mandate to be 'serving' (*ʿābad*) and 'preserving' (*šāmar*) the garden of Eden. The common translation of the former expression as 'to till' assumes an inordinate focus on the ground. Adam is commanded to care for the garden. But gardens are more than soil. This is the original *Tierpark*,[68] made up of soil, vegetation, and animals, the service of which involves much more than cultivating the soil. Like Yahweh himself in Jonah 4:11, God's vice-regents are to display compassion to all creatures. In securing the well-being of individual creatures and individual species, people secure the well-being of humanity and open themselves and the cosmos to the blessing of God.

Underlying Deuteronomy's portrayal of the Israelites' relationship to animals is a profound theology of privilege and holiness, the relevance of which transcends the old covenantal order. Like the Israelites, the people of God in every age should treasure the special status that has been afforded them by virtue of Yahweh's gracious election and his claims upon them as his holy people. Living as the holy people of God is not to be relegated to the days or

---

64. Note that the prohibitions are the same as those applied to 'native Israelites' (*ʾezraḥ*) and 'aliens' (*gēr*), who by faith had attached themselves to Israel as the holy community of faith (Davidson, "Which Torah Laws Should Gentiles Obey?"). The term *nokrî* 'stranger' in Deut 14:21 represents an ethnic and spiritual outsider to the covenant and is to be distinguished from the *gēr* of Lev 17–18.

65. Moskala, *Laws of Clean and Unclean Animals*, 106.

66. B. *Ḥagigah* 27a.

67. Moskala, *Laws of Clean and Unclean Animals*, 106.

68. For a comparison of the garden of Eden with Neo-Assyrian royal parks, see M. Hutter, "Adam als Gärtner und König (Gen 2:8, 15)," *BZ* 30 (1986) 258–62.

contexts of formal cultic service but is to be expressed in all areas of life. Like the ancient Israelites, we need to realize that everything about us, even the food we eat, should be governed by order, a respect for life, and a concern to represent Yahweh well before a watching world.[69]

---

69. I am grateful to my colleague Richard Schultz for his helpful responses to an earlier draft of this paper. Of course, any deficiencies in interpretation and style are my own.

The Word Made Bitter:
At the Table with Joshua, Buber, and Bakhtin

GORDON H. MATTIES
Associate Professor of Biblical Studies and Theology
Canadian Mennonite University
Winnipeg, Manitoba

The word of God sometimes tastes bitter. When Jeremiah "found" God's words and "ate them," they "became to me a joy" and "the delight of my heart" (Jer 15:16).[1] Unfortunately for Jeremiah, those words also filled him with such pain that he called God a "deceitful brook" (15:18). Ezekiel also ate God's scroll, which was filled with "words of lamentation and mourning and woe" (Ezek 2:10). At first the scroll was "sweet as honey" (3:3). He undertook his mission, however, compelled by the spirit, "in bitterness in the heat of my spirit" (3:14). Having arrived among the exiles, he sat for seven days among them, "stunned" (3:15). The book of Revelation takes up the same imagery when the voice from heaven tells John to eat a scroll, about which John says, "It was sweet as honey in my mouth, but when I had eaten it, my stomach was made bitter" (10:10). This same sort of bitterness has resulted in a spate of publications decrying the violence of monotheism or questioning the Bible's implicit religious sanction of ethnic violence and genocide.[2] Eating

---

Author's note: This essay is a prolegomenon to my forthcoming commentary on the book of Joshua. Prof. Elmer Martens, then OT editor for the Believers Church Bible Commentary (Herald Press), was instrumental in inviting my participation in that project.

1. All biblical citations are from the New Revised Standard Version.

2. Regina M. Schwartz sets up the case against Joshua well:

> Should we hold it culpable for emblazoning this desire for land acquisition on its readers, inscribing deep into our culture the primordial myth of an exodus that justifies conquest? From one perspective—that of the history of the text—the conquest narrative is only a wild fantasy written by a powerless dispossessed people who dream of wondrous victories over their enemies, of living in a land where milk and honey flow, and of entering that land with the blessing and support of an Almighty Deity. But from another perspective—that of the text's political afterlife—there is another story that is less appealing and considerably less innocent, telling of creating a people through the massive displacement

the scroll has resulted in a stomachache that leaves readers never wanting to return to the book that caused the pain. Of all books in the Bible, Joshua has created the greatest pain, offering a bitterness better avoided than consumed one more time.

Eugene Peterson makes much of the metaphor of eating the scroll to emphasize the "personal and participatory" dimensions of Bible reading.[3] In fact, when we read Scripture to be formed by and into its grand story of God's purposes for all of creation, we are not invited to "Live up to this" or to "Think like this." Rather, suggests Peterson, "The biblical way is to tell a story and in the telling invite: 'Live *into* this.'"[4] Just how, we might ask, does that happen when the words, the scroll, or the book, become bitter to the taste or make one sick to the stomach? Peterson himself asks, "Isn't there danger that this old, old book will impose a way of life on us that we will experience as alien and coercive?"[5] The problem, as Peterson acknowledges, is that some biblical texts and aspects of the biblical world view have become objectionable to contemporary readers. The book of Joshua, for example, seems hardly able, at first sight, to fulfill Peterson's hope for readers: "We are personally commanded

---

and destruction of other peoples, of laying claim to a land that had belonged to others, and of conducting this bloody conquest under the banner of divine will. (*The Curse of Cain: The Violent Legacy of Monotheism* [Chicago: University of Chicago Press, 1997] 57)

The conversation about the relationship of violence and the divine ranges widely; see, for example, John J. Collins, "The Zeal of Phineas: The Bible and the Legitimation of Violence," *JBL* 122 (2003) 3–21; Karen Armstrong, *Holy War: The Crusades and Their Impact on Today's World* (New York: Random House, 1988, 1991, 2001); René Girard, *Violence and the Sacred* (trans. Patrick Gregory; Baltimore: Johns Hopkins University Press, 1977); Gil Bailie, *Violence Unveiled: Humanity at the Crossroads* (New York: Crossroad, 1995); Marc H. Ellis, *Unholy Alliance: Religion and Atrocity in Our Time* (Minneapolis: Fortress, 1997); Oliver McTernan, *Violence in God's Name: Religion in an Age of Conflict* (Maryknoll, NY: Orbis, 2003); Mark Juergensmeyer, *Terror in the Name of God: The Global Rise of Religious Violence* (3rd ed.; Berkeley: University of California Press, 2003); Lloyd Steffen, *The Demonic Turn: The Power of Religion to Inspire and Restrain Violence* (Cleveland: Pilgrim, 2003); J. P. Larsson, *Understanding Religious Violence: Thinking Outside the Box on Terrorism* (Burlington, VT: Ashgate, 2004); Kenneth R. Chase and Alan Jacobs, eds., *Must Christianity Be Violent? Reflections on History, Practice, and Theology* (Grand Rapids: Brazos, 2003); Lee Griffith, *The War on Terrorism and the Terror of God* (Grand Rapids: Eerdmans, 2002); and Meic Pearse, *The Gods of War: Is Religion the Primary Cause of Violent Conflict?* (Downers Grove, IL: InterVarsity, 2008).

3. Eugene Peterson, *Eat This Book: A Conversation in the Art of Spiritual Reading* (Grand Rapids: Eerdmans, 2006) 38. Reading the Bible "invites our participation" (p. 40), drawing us into a narrative that "takes place under the broad skies of God's purposes" (p. 41). See also Gerard Loughlin, *Telling God's Story* (Cambridge: Cambridge University Press, 1996); especially part 1, "Consuming Text," and chap. 8, "Eating the Word."

4. Peterson, *Eat This Book*, 43.

5. Ibid., 44.

and blessed, rebuked and comforted, warned and guided."[6] In short, Peterson strives for a practical theology of Scripture, the most serious test of which, I suggest, is a reading of the book of Joshua.

Eschewing the extraction of "truths" or "principles" or the "moral" of the story, Peterson offers "entering the story, taking our place in the plot, and following Jesus."[7] He acknowledges that this alternative will take significant exegetical discipline, which requires "paying attention to the details."[8] Moreover, good exegesis submits to the texts; "it enters the world of the text and lets the text 'read' us."[9] But what if we do not feel particularly good about submitting to the book of Joshua? What if the details make us sick? What if we cannot readily take "our place in the plot," even if we are serious about "following Jesus"? In this essay I will explore this tension in three steps. First, I will bring Peterson's suggestions about "spiritual reading" into conversation with the metaphors of "performing" or "improvising" Scripture. Second, I will complement these metaphors with the dialogical hermeneutics of Martin Buber and Mikhail Bakhtin. And third, I will bring the hermeneutical insights of this conversation to a reading of the book of Joshua. Along the way I hope to contribute to a practical theology of Scripture that has the potential both of forming lives and of coming to terms with texts that make us sick. Although it may sound awkward to put it this way, I do so because I have heard from many people who, because of books like Joshua, no longer bother with the Bible. I have no intention of solving their problem by absolving the book of Joshua. I wish, rather, to offer some pointers toward reading the whole of Scripture in a way that enables us to understand more clearly that the sweet and the bitter both have their place in the "economy of salvation."[10]

From Puzzle to Performance

Practical creatures that we are, we want to solve problems. Peterson suggests that the "stomachache" comes from digesting an "uncongenial Bible" in which "not everything is to our liking in this book."[11] Many of us will readily

---

6. Ibid., 46. Peterson echoes here the longstanding appeal to 2 Tim 3:16 with its assumption that Scripture has a functional authority insofar as it is "useful for teaching, for reproof, for correction, and for training in righteousness, so that everyone who belongs to God may be proficient, equipped for every good work" (NRSV).

7. Ibid., 48.

8. Ibid., 50.

9. Ibid., 57.

10. I use the expression from Telford Work, *Living and Active: Scripture in the Economy of Salvation* (Grand Rapids: Eerdmans, 2002).

11. Peterson, *Eat This Book*, 63–64.

acknowledge that Joshua is among the most uncongenial of biblical books and that divinely sanctioned violence is the most distasteful of notions. Warfare carried out at God's command is especially odious because even now, in the early years of the 21st century, the sanction and blessing of the gods continues to motivate and justify communal violence and ethnic cleansing. It will not do to resort to problem-solving techniques. As Stephen Fowl puts it, "Interpretation as the reduction of puzzlement is measured in a punctilious way, in terms of problems encountered and solved. Interpretation ceases when there are no more puzzles."[12] The most puzzling of all, the all-out destruction of all living things (the *ḥērem*) can be explained away by resorting to a problem-solving interpretive strategy.[13] This approach accounts well for the recent book *Show them No Mercy: Four Views on God and Canaanite Genocide*, in which four authors present their solutions and comment on each other's positions.[14] I admit that it is not possible entirely to escape the puzzle-interpretation paradigm. The point, however, is that puzzle-solving most often ends with fixed solutions, or positions, which one must either defend or reject. And once one has a position, the biblical text is no longer needed. As Peterson puts it, those who resort to "some scheme or other that summarizes 'what the Bible teaches'" no longer need to read the Bible.[15]

But what happens when we are willing to give up on positions and solutions and "enter the story," as Peterson asks us to do? He suggests that we learn to listen to "the living voice," which is different from "reading a written word."[16] Because his point could be misunderstood, it is important to note his explanation:

> But it is not only the timbre and tone and rhythm of the personal speaking voice that disappears in the act of writing, it is also the entire complex

---

12. Stephen Fowl, *Engaging Scripture: A Model for Theological Interpretation* (Oxford: Blackwell, 1998) 161.

13. K. Lawson Younger Jr., "Warfare in Ancient Israel: A Descriptive Outline of Present Research Discussions and Developments" (paper presented at the annual meeting of the SBL, San Antonio, Nov. 20–23, 2004). Younger summarizes prevailing "solutions" to the problem of the *ḥērem*, the devotion to destruction sanctioned by God. Younger describes five approaches that work with the premise that *ḥērem* is a "problem" to be solved: a philological problem, a literary problem, a historical problem, a comparative problem, and an ethical problem (*In Search of Philip R. Davies: Whose Festschrift Is It Anyway?* [ed. Duncan Burns and John W. Rogerson; London: T. & T. Clark, forthcoming]).

14. C. S. Cowles et al., *Show Them No Mercy: Four Views on God and Canaanite Genocide* (Grand Rapids: Zondervan, 2003).

15. Peterson, *Eat This Book*, 66. Or, as William Stacy Johnson puts it, "on modernist grounds, once we arrive at an authoritative interpretation, we can file the text away and move on to something else" ("Reading the Scriptures Faithfully in a Postmodern Age," in *The Art of Reading Scripture* [ed. Ellen Davis and Richard B. Hays; Grand Rapids: Eerdmans, 2003] 118).

16. Peterson, *Eat This Book*, 85.

intricacy of other voices buzzing in the background, children interrupting with demands and questions, thrushes singing, the sound of rain on the roof, the fragrance of juniper burning in the fireplace, the bouquet of the wine and texture of the bread that accompanies conversation at the table.[17]

Words are not "artifacts" or "specimens," Peterson continues, but parts of a conversation. The point at which Peterson's affirmation about listening runs the risk of going off the rails, however, is where he drives a wedge between the spoken and the written word. For Peterson, spoken words belong to a conversation, whereas written words are derivative and all too easily managed. In order "to get the full force of the word, God's word, we need to recover its atmosphere of spokenness."[18] The way to this recovery, then, is an immersion in conversation with the text—in *lectio divina*—so that listening (true reading) and responding (prayer) takes place. "The text assumes," writes Peterson, "that we are participants in what is written. . . . By its very nature language connects; it is dialogic; it creates conversation."[19] In this way, "We *pray* what we read, working our lives into active participation in what God reveals in the word." Not only this, but

> God doesn't make us do any of this: God's word is personal address, inviting, commanding, challenging, rebuking, judging, comforting, directing. But not forcing. Not coercing. We are given space and freedom to answer, to enter into the conversation. From beginning to end, the word of God is a dialogical word, a word that invites participation. Prayer is our participation in the creation, salvation, and community that God reveals to us in Holy Scripture.[20]

This extended reflection on Peterson's *Eat This Book* sets the stage for an exploration of what kind of participation this "dialogical word" invites. I suggest that drawing on Martin Buber and Mikhail Bakhtin will fill the apparent gap between the written and the spoken. Moreover, it will help to clarify how listening to the text and "praying back" is only part of a larger conversation that informs our engagement with Scripture. But before drawing Buber and Bakhtin into this matter, we will detour into other articulations of the notion of "performing" or "embodying" Scripture and will further set the stage for engagement with the book of Joshua.

Nicholas Lash suggests that appropriate participation with Scripture is a kind of dramatic "performance" of the text, which is not the part-time activity

---

17. Ibid., 86.
18. Ibid., 87.
19. Ibid., 107.
20. Ibid., 109.

of expert interpreters but the full-time activity of the church.[21] Nevertheless, the church as interpreter must take responsibility for a variety of choices made in the process of performing the text. One of these choices concerns the relationship between genre and reader interests and responsibilities. As Lash puts it:

> What it means to read or interpret a text depends in part . . . on the kind of text that is being used. Different kinds of text call for different kinds of reading. And the reader must take responsibility for the reading, for deciding what kind of text it is with which he or she is dealing. This does not mean that it is simply "up to me" arbitrarily to decide what to do with a text. (It would be silly to sing railway timetables, rather than use them to catch trains.) What it does mean is that it is the *reading* of the text, rather than merely the text itself, the material object, the black marks on white paper, which embodies decisions as to what kinds of reading are appropriate. And the richer the text, the more complex its relationship to the culture which reads and remembers it, the more varied the range of more or less appropriate readings which it evokes.[22]

This sort of responsible reading, suggests Rowan Williams, is more than "a process of learning to perceive" through an uninformed synchronic reading of the Bible. Rather, "'dramatic' reading" will be thoroughly conscious of "the tensions realised and worked through in the time of the text" and will be interested in "resisting the premature unities and harmonies" of a reading only concerned with what the text might be saying to me.[23] Christian reading of Scripture

> resists the notion that the understanding of faith can be only a *moment* of interpretive perception with its own synchronic integrity of completeness, as opposed to a process with strong elements of risk and provisionality. Consequently, Christian interpretation is unavoidably engaged in "dramatic" modes of reading: we are invited to identify ourselves in the story being contemplated, to reappropriate who we are now, and who we shall or can be, in terms of the story. *Its* movements, transactions, transformations, become *ours*, we take responsibility for this or that position within the narrative."[24]

---

21. Nicholas Lash, "Performing the Scriptures," *Theology on the Way to Emmaus* (London: SCM, 1986) 37–46. Frances M. Young takes up the metaphor in her book *Virtuoso Theology: The Bible and Interpretation* (Cleveland: Pilgrim, 1993). For a summary and programmatic essay on this subject, see Stephen C. Barton, "New Testament Interpretation as Performance," *SJT* 52 (1999) 179–208. In this article, Barton interacts with the work of Nicholas Lash, Rowan Williams, and Frances Young.

22. Nicholas Lash, *Theology on the Way to Emmaus*, 38.

23. Rowan Williams, "The Literal Sense of Scripture," *Modern Theology* 7 (1991) 123, 125.

24. Ibid., 125.

Of special interest for this essay is Williams's notion of "taking responsibility." The idea complements Peterson's suggestion (above) that "God doesn't make us do anything." Integral to the process of entering the text (Peterson's emphasis) is the reciprocality of the conversation (which Peterson names prayer).

Frances Young, building on Lash's suggestions, writes that the biblical canon is like a musical or dramatic repertoire that has stood the test of time. The canon includes a variety of genres, each of which will need to be performed differently. Moreover, Young suggests that the biblical texts, as performed by its "orchestra," the "community of the faithful," require an improvisation (like the cadenzas in a concerto).[25]

Improvisation is implied in Stephen Barton's reflections on the performance metaphor, when he suggests that Scripture is an "'open text' that invites completion in the lives of its readers and looks forward to a future beyond its own time and place."[26] A similar and more extended analogy has been offered by N. T. Wright, who suggests that Christian readers may be likened to a troupe of actors who have been commissioned to improvise on a newly discovered but unfinished Shakespeare play. Four acts have been found, but the fifth is incomplete. Only the first scene has been written (the New Testament). The actors' job is to immerse themselves in the first four-plus acts (which he names creation, fall, Israel, Jesus) so as to discern a *telos* or goal toward which the narrative as a whole is striving.[27] Their task, as actors, is to improvise toward that end, the clues for which have been discerned in the first four acts, and live (improvise) in anticipation of the play's resolution.[28] Although the "New Testament offers us glimpses of where the story is to end," it is "our task to discover, through the Spirit and prayer, the appropriate ways of improvising the script between the foundation events and charter, on the one hand, and the complete coming of the Kingdom on the other."[29] Authentic "improvising" will depend, suggests Wright, on "a disciplined and careful listening to all

---

25. Young, *Virtuoso Theology*, 160–62.

26. Barton, "New Testament Interpretation," 195.

27. Samuel Wells has carefully adapted Wright's "acts" so that the five acts are creation, Israel, Jesus, church, and eschaton (*Improvisation: The Drama of Christian Ethics* [Grand Rapids: Brazos, 2004] 53–57).

28. N. T. Wright, *The New Testament and the People of God, Volume One: Christian Origins and the Question of God* (Minneapolis: Fortress, 1992) chap. 5. And in Wells's reiteration, the church lives in the fourth act, improvising in the light of the first three acts and in anticipation of the fifth. The outcome of the drama is not the church's to produce, which sets the church free from the compulsion either to do everything right the first time (as though imagining it is living in or must reiterate one of the first three acts) or to think that it is bringing about the consummation of the fifth act on its own terms and by its own performance (*Improvisation*, 55–57).

29. N. T. Wright, *The Last Word: Beyond the Bible Wars to a New Understanding of the Authority of Scripture* (San Francisco: HarperSanFrancisco, 2005) 126.

the other voices around us, and a constant attention to the themes, rhythms and harmonies of the complete performance so far, the performance which we are now called to continue."[30]

Wright's analogy works well as an alternative to the common practices of finding "timeless truths" or as "fuel for devotion."[31] To improvise while being grounded in authentic loyalty to the first four acts, however, is to acknowledge that: "Those who live in this fifth act have an ambiguous relationship with the four previous acts, not because they are being disloyal to them but precisely because they are being loyal to them as part of the story."[32] Wright recognizes that this sort of improvisation "will be in direct continuity with the previous acts (we are not free to jump suddenly to another narrative, a different play altogether), but such continuity also implies discontinuity, a moment where genuinely new things can and do happen. We must be ferociously loyal to what has gone before and cheerfully open about what must come next."[33] But his primary loyalty is clearly to the incomplete fifth act (the post–Easter Church). Perhaps this must be so. But the model does not create a real space for the impact of the first four acts except as resource for "themes, rhythms and harmonies of the complete performance so far." The new trumps the old, although vestiges of the old remain. The "genuinely new" is most important.

What, then, of difficult texts such as the book of Joshua? Although the performance metaphor is evocative, it is incomplete because it does not fully comprehend the complexity of the script(ure) on which the performance or improvisation is based. For one thing, performance ends up only distantly connected to the interpretive process of working with particular biblical texts. Wright's improvisation, for example, claims to stand in continuity with bib-

---

30. Ibid., 126. Wright extends his metaphor by suggesting that paying attention will lead us to "being fully obedient to the music so far." Although "obedience" (Wright) and "submission" (Peterson) are appropriate responses, they do not adequately capture the dialogical dimension of the way the improvisation actually works. Walter Brueggemann has made a similar suggestion that the church live "inside the counterdrama" of the Bible. "The Bible provides a script (not the only script available) for a lived drama that contains all the ingredients for a whole life" (*Texts under Negotiation: The Bible and Postmodern Imagination* [Fortress: Minneapolis, 1993] 67). As we live that counterdrama, "we stand before the text, no longer as its master but as its advocate" (p. 11). Robert W. Jenson draws on the same metaphor to suggest that Scripture is not "about some entity *outside* its story"; rather, "we and Scripture and what Scripture talks about are not external to one another, since Scripture tells a story about God and us that we are even now living" ("Scripture's Authority in the Church," in *The Art of Reading Scripture* [ed. E. Davis and R. B. Hays; Grand Rapids: Eerdmans, 2003] 30).
31. Wright, *The Last Word*, 122. Peterson also has little use for such limited or reductionistic modes of appropriating Scripture (*Eat This Book*, 41).
32. Wright, *The Last Word*, 122.
33. Ibid., 123.

lical books such as Joshua. But ultimately this book is not required for Christian improvisation within his "fifth act." It is enough to know that this book
was part of Act 3 (or Wells's Act 2) and not really integral to the current performance. If Wright does not mean to imply this, then we will need to explore
how a biblical book such as Joshua might contribute to the performance. It
could be that Joshua can be subordinated to thematic summaries such as
Mic 6:8 or the "great commandment."[34] Perhaps its conquest narratives both
inform and are transformed by the Gospels.[35] Or its dominant warfare motif
is transposed into "spiritual warfare" (Eph 6). In any case, even these transpositions into NT contexts end up leaving the book of Joshua behind.[36]
There is no conversation with Joshua left to be had.[37]

---

34. See the very helpful article by Moshe Greenberg, "On the Political Use of the Bible in
Modern Israel: An Engaged Critique," in *Pomegranates and Golden Bells: Studies in Biblical, Jewish,
and Near Eastern Ritual, Law, and Literature in Honor of Jacob Milgrom* (ed. David P. Wright, David
Noel Freedman, and Avi Hurvitz; Winona Lake, IN: Eisenbrauns, 1995) 461–71.

35. See Willard Swartley's comprehensive review in "The Formative Influence of the Old
Testament Way-Conquest (and Exodus) Traditions on the Synoptic Journey Narrative," in *Israel's
Scripture Traditions and the Synoptic Gospels: Story Shaping Story* (Peabody, MA: Hendrickson, 1994)
95–153.

36. Wells suggests two common interpretive mistakes. One is to think that Scripture is really
"a one-act play rather than a five-act play" that ends in the eschaton (*Improvisation*, 55). If God's
eschatological work is the fifth act of a drama in which we live in the fourth act, then Christians
are freed from the assumption that human performance will bring about the ultimate transformation of all things. The role of the church "is principally to keep the story going, rather
than assume it must make the story come out right" (p. 152). A second mistake, and one that
impinges on the reading of Joshua "is to get the wrong act" or to imagine one is living in a different act from Act 4, which is the life of the church (p. 55). The mistake of living in Act 2,
Israel, and, let's say, the narrative of the book of Joshua "is to behave as though the Messiah had
not yet come." Instead of living inside Israel's narrative, it is now possible to "concentrate on the
abundance we can share rather than the scarcity that will be fought over—this fact tends to be
ignored. These are the assumptions of Act Two" (p. 56). This sort of stereotyping of Act 2,
although helpfully acknowledging the possibilities inherent in the messianic transformation of
the story line, risks marginalizing narratives within Act 2 without attending carefully enough to
their voices.

37. For a helpful sketch of the challenges and prospects of the performance metaphor and of
improvisation as the church's way of engaging Scripture, see Wells, *Improvisation*, 62–70. Kevin
J. Vanhoozer challenges Wells's apparent minimizing of the Bible as "a script that needs performing" (Wells, *Improvisation*, 69) and presents a comprehensive engagement with the metaphor
of dramatic performance of Scripture as script "that calls for faithful yet creative performance.
Scripture is the norm . . . only when Scripture is conceived as more than a handbook of propo-
sitional truths" (*The Drama of Doctrine: A Canonical Linguistic Approach to Christian Theology*
[Louisville: Westminster/John Knox, 2005] 22). Wells's and Vanhoozer's works require a more
sustained engagement than I am able to offer here. Their differences on the role of Scripture
highlight the main reason why "performance" requires nuancing by the dialogic models of Buber
and Bakhtin.

In what follows, I will build on the discussion so far by suggesting that performing the Scriptures in life, which is the goal of ecclesial interpretation of Scripture,[38] requires a dynamic participation in a conversation during which the interpretive community sorts out (but not in a final way) how improvisation or performance ought to move forward. The metaphor of performance or improvisation requires a filling out of the *kind* of engagement that will empower the performance. In other words, the performance, if it is to bear the weight of authenticity and integrity, must be grounded in a vigorous and open-ended conversation that elicits an open-ended performance.

The metaphor of performance assumes a multiplicity of performances. Unlike the metaphor of interpretation as puzzle-solving, interpretation that leads to authentic embodiment in life "often involves the taking up of previous debates, discussions, and decisions and carrying them on in specific contexts. In this light, it is to be expected that such interpretations will generate and result in further debate, discussion, and disagreement."[39] Building on the work of Alisdair MacIntyre, Fowl suggests, "If a tradition is to live and carry on into the future, it must be able to sustain a certain amount of debate, argument, and disagreement about how to carry on the tradition in the present in ways continuous with the past."[40] But this debate within the tradition(s) of Christian interpretation must, as in the NT era, be shaped by the movement of the Spirit in the ongoing life of the community. Yet even the Spirit is not self-interpreting; Spirit and Scripture together confirm and sustain the direction of the debate.[41]

However, words such as *debate, discussion, argument*, and *disagreement* imply some sort of conversation. Fowl's exploration of Acts 10–15 assumes that all of these words would have applied to the earliest community of Christians as they wrestled with their appropriation and transformation of the biblical tradition. Reflecting on Paul's reading of the Abraham story (in Galatians), Fowl suggests that apparently novel readings such as Paul proposes are a result of an "interpretive struggle" that strives toward a "*counter*-conventional" reading of the story.[42] Struggle of this sort is born in attending to the voice of both text and Spirit as communities "read the scriptures under the guidance of the Spirit in the light of the life, death, and resurrection of Jesus." There is no "autono-

---

38. See, for example, Stephen E. Fowl and L. Gregory Jones, *Reading in Communion: Scripture and Ethics in Christian Life* (Grand Rapids: Eerdmans, 1991).
39. Fowl, *Engaging Scripture*, 161.
40. Ibid., 162.
41. Ibid., 114.
42. Ibid., 135.

mous voice of the Old Testament" over against which stands an "autonomous voice of the New Testament."[43] As René Girard puts it, Scripture is a "text in travail." Scripture is not simply a record of a developing theme or process but "a struggle that advances and retreats."[44]

Might it be possible, then, to enter the story (Peterson), thereby performing the text (Lash, Williams, Young, Loughlin, Wright, Wells, and Vanhoozer) so as to offer a counterconventional reading of Joshua that is born out of authentic dialogue? The problem with this prospect, of course, is that Joshua, a text about Israel's engagement with Canaanite enemies, has become our enemy. Many would rather not bother with Joshua at all. Let us say, however, for the sake of this conversation that the book of Joshua stands against everything we consider to be good and right and true as discerned by the community of readers under the guidance of the Spirit and in light of Jesus' life, death, and resurrection. With our heightened awareness of the history of genocide and of violent appropriation of the Bible's warfare texts, we do well to talk to the enemy.[45] The conversation must not forget these performances.

Of course it may be easier to ignore the text and the dreadful performances of the past, as we sometimes do with a person who has offended us. Or we could pretend that the relationship is not actually strained, as we sometimes do, hoping that what has come between us will go away on its own. How can we best imagine a healthy conversation, especially when so many of us would rather avoid difficult conversations? The authors of the book *Difficult Conversations* assume that neither avoidance nor pretense will bring healing to a relationship. Sometimes a "difficult conversation" is necessary—a conversation that gets beyond blame, unexpressed feelings, and perceived threats to authentic self-identity. The authors invite individuals who are struggling with challenging relationships "to turn the damaging battle of warring messages into the more constructive approach we call a learning conversation."[46]

For a learning conversation to take place, however, we need to return to the text not simply to listen and to submit, but to work diligently at restoring

---

43. Ibid., 131.

44. René Girard, *Violent Origins* (Stanford: Stanford University Press, 1987) 141.

45. Many have chronicled the use of the conquest texts in medieval crusades and modern colonial contexts. See, for example, Roland Bainton, *Christian Attitudes toward War and Peace: A Historical Survey and Critical Re-evaluation* (Abingdon: Nashville, 1960) 164–70; John H. Lynch, "The First Crusade: Some Theological and Historical Context," in *Must Christianity Be Violent?* (ed. K. R. Chase and A. Jacobs; Grand Rapids: Brazos, 2003) 23–36; and Michael Prior, *The Bible and Colonialism: A Moral Critique* (Biblical Seminar 48; Sheffield: Sheffield Academic Press, 1997).

46. Douglas Stone, Bruce Patton, and Sheila Heen, *Difficult Conversations: How to Discuss What Matters Most* (New York: Penguin, 1999) xviii.

the relationship, even while we continue to disagree.[47] Often restorative work will require argument, debate, and disagreement. But above all it will require hospitality. The difficult conversation encompasses all participants in the conversation through a hospitable attention to each other's stories; through being honest and truthful about the emotional and intellectual effects of and responses to those stories; and through acknowledging how textual and readerly identity shapes perception of the conflict among the parties. Truthful attention to the other will require self-giving hospitality, a true welcome of the stranger, even when the stranger is an enemy.

Performance as Hospitable Dialogue

In what follows I will describe a stance of hermeneutical hospitality that creates space for authentic dialogue with the text, including its history and its effects both past and present.[48] It will require mutuality, reciprocity, generosity, relinquishment of control, and even the expectation of what one might receive in the engagement.[49] Within this hospitable encounter, which seeks reconciliation with the other, dialogue is the primary activity by which to nurture reconciliation. The first of the insights I wish to bring to bear on conversation with the book of Joshua is Martin Buber's notion of "I-Thou" relations between people, works of art, and texts. The second concerns Mikhail Bakhtin's notion of dialogism, by which he means that utterances (including texts) are themselves part of a large conversation to which the text is responding and within which readers and communities participate through time.

In his famous *I and Thou*, along with other writings on dialogue, Buber articulated the conviction, "All actual life is encounter."[50] Moreover, in the next paragraph Buber qualifies this encounter by highlighting its nonutilitarian character:

> The relation to the You is unmediated. Nothing conceptual intervenes between I and You, no prior knowledge and no imagination; and memory itself is changed as it plunges from particularity into wholeness. No purpose intervenes between I and You, no greed and no anticipation; and longing itself is changed as it plunges from the dream into appearance. Every means is an obstacle. Only where all means have disintegrated encounters occur.[51]

---

47. This could be one way of applying Peterson's notion of praying back the text.

48. As suggested by Barton, "New Testament Interpretation as Performance," 206–7.

49. These terms describe the hospitable engagement by John B. Bennett, "The Academy and Hospitality," *Cross Currents* (Spring/Summer, 2000). Available online at http://www.crosscurrents.org/Bennett.htm (accessed January 25, 2008).

50. Martin Buber, *I and Thou* (trans. Walter Kaufmann; New York: Scribner, 1970) 62.

51. Ibid., 62–63.

For Buber not only is God the "eternal You,"[52] but works of art and even the text of Scripture become a Thou that invites response through dialogue. As Steven Kepnes puts it, "Art calls out to the interpreter. It beckons the interpreter to respond. When an interpreter responds the work takes on life, it becomes a Thou and a dialogue is initiated."[53] This understanding permeated Buber's own translation of the Bible, which he declared was a "'voice' and not a book."[54] Thus, the Bible is a record of "Israel touched in all its generations by the shuddering awe of a history experienced as dialogue."[55] For individuals who read the Bible throughout time, reading requires coming "before the biblical Word in order to hearken to or to take offense at it . . . [to] confront . . . his life with the Word."[56] For Buber, this confrontation takes place in the hope that "the torn bond" between God and humankind "shall once more be made whole."[57] Thus, it may be, as I have noted slightly differently above, not only has the text become enemy but God as well. The God depicted in Joshua, who commands the extermination of the Canaanites, seems hardly likely to be one with whom one might wish a reconciliation. Yet it is precisely this challenge that a dialogical hermeneutics of hospitality, with its transformation of the enemy relationship, invites with the text in and through time.

Mikhail Bakhtin's notion of dialogism expands and embodies the possibilities of this sort of vigorous and transformative conversation.[58] Dialogism helps us to come to terms with reading a difficult text such as Joshua because it overcomes the fragmentation and isolation of voices in the interpretive

---

52. Ibid., 123.

53. Steven Kepnes, *The Text as Thou: Martin Buber's Dialogical Hermeneutics and Narrative Theology* (Bloomington: Indiana University Press, 1992) 26. For the following insights, I depend on Kepnes's analysis of Buber's hermeneutics.

54. Ibid., 45.

55. Martin Buber, *Kingship of God* (trans. R. Scheimann; New York: Harper & Row, 1967) 67; cited in Kepnes, *The Text as Thou*, 50.

56. Buber, "The Man of Today," in *On the Bible* (ed. N. Glatzer; New York: Schocken, 1982) 4; cited in Kepnes, *The Text as Thou*, 57.

57. Buber, "The Man of Today," in *On the Bible*, 1; cited in Kepnes, *The Text as Thou*, 129. For an explanation of Buber's notion of "distance" and "relation," see ibid., 131–33.

58. Bakhtin's writings include *Problems of Dostoevsky's Poetics* (ed. and trans. Caryl Emerson; Theory and History of Literature 8; Minneapolis: University of Minneapolis Press, 1984); *Speech Genres and Other Late Essays* (ed. Caryl Emerson and Michael Holquist; trans. Vern W. McGee; Austin: University of Texas Press, 1986); and *The Dialogic Imagination: Four Essays by M. M. Bakhtin* (ed. Michael Holquist; trans. Caryl Emerson and Michael Holquist; University of Texas Press Slavic Series 1; Austin: University of Texas Press, 1981). For a bibliography of Bakhtin's work and of authors who write about him, see the online bibliography on the web site of the Bakhtin Group of the AAR and SBL at http://home.nwciowa.edu/wacome/ Bakhtinbib.htm (accessed January 25, 2008).

process.[59] Instead of focusing on one dimension of analysis—the author (history), the text (literary), or the reader (audience)—dialogism assumes that this understanding occurs, to use Buber's term, in active response to a Thou, and, in the light of Bakhtin, in a community of Thous. Bakhtin's notion of dialogism provides the mediate context for approaches to Scripture text as site of the church's performance that is missing from models of Scripture that highlight performance or improvisation.[60] Dialogism is the dynamic interactivity that creates hospitable space for the ongoing conversation required in the process of performing the text. In fact, the dialogue, if conceived as embodied word, is the performance. As he notes in his reflections on Dostoevsky, referring not only to the novel but to life itself: "Dialogic relationships . . . are a much broader phenomenon than mere rejoinders in a dialogue, laid out compositionally in the text; they are an almost universal phenomenon, permeating all human speech and all relationships and manifestations of human life—in general, everything that has meaning and significance."[61] In other words, texts participate in a larger human conversation and do not in and of themselves have something to say or to teach without participating in a conversation in which their "say" participates in the interplay of voices, including author, textual voices past and present, and readers. Six aspects of dialogism deserve to be highlighted before we draw out a trajectory for the conversation in which the book of Joshua participates.[62]

---

59. Bakhtin's work has been appropriated in biblical studies in various ways. See, for example, Walter L. Reed, *Dialogues of the Word: The Bible as Literature according to Bakhtin* (New York: Oxford University Press, 1993); Barbara Green, *Mikhail Bakhtin and Biblical Scholarship: An Introduction* (SemeiaSt 38; Atlanta: Society of Biblical Literature, 2000); Roland Boer, ed., *Bakhtin and Genre Theory in Biblical Studies* (SemeiaSt 63; Atlanta: Society of Biblical Literature, 2007); Carol Newsom, "Bakhtin, the Bible, and Dialogic Truth," *JR* 76 (1996) 290–306; idem, "Bakhtin," in *Handbook of Postmodern Biblical Interpretation* (ed. A. K. M. Adam; St. Louis: Chalice, 2000) 20–27; Robert Polzin, *Moses and the Deuteronomist: A Literary Study of the Deuteronomistic History, Part One: Deuteronomy, Joshua, Judges* (New York: Seabury, 1990); Gerhard Hauch, *Text and Contexts: A Literary Reading of the Conquest Narrative (Joshua 1–11)* (Ph.D. diss., Princeton Theological Seminary, 1991); Dennis T. Olson, "Biblical Theology as Provisional Monologization: A Dialogue with Childs, Brueggemann and Bakhtin," *BibInt* 6 (1998) 162–80; and L. Juliana M. Claassens, "Biblical Theology as Dialogue: Continuing the Conversation on Mikhail Bakhtin and Biblical Theology," *JBL* 122 (2003) 127–44. See also the papers presented since 2001 by the Bakhtin Group at the annual meeting of the AAR and the SBL, available online at http://home.nwciowa.edu/wacome/bakhtinsbl.html.

60. Vanhoozer begins to address this concern in *The Drama of Doctrine*, 290–91 and in other places throughout his book.

61. Bakhtin, *Problems of Dostoevsky's Poetics*, 40. For a concise definition of dialogism, see the glossary in idem, *Dialogic Imagination*, 426.

62. To elaborate in detail about Bakhtin's understanding of communication as dialogism is more than can be done here. I shall outline several dimensions of Bakhtin's understanding of dialogism in order to illustrate how the book of Joshua might be drawn into the larger discussion of Joshua's contribution within the biblical canon.

First, the utterance, that which is spoken among speaking and responding subjects is the basic unit of speech communication.[63] And every utterance is a response to or an invitation for other utterances. As Bakhtin writes:

> Any concrete utterance is a link in the chain of speech communication of a particular sphere. The very boundaries of the utterance are determined by a change of speech subjects. Utterances are not indifferent to one another, and are not self-sufficient; they are aware of and mutually reflect one another. . . . Therefore, each kind of utterance is filled with various kinds of responsive reactions to other utterances of the given sphere of speech communication.[64]

Thus, Bakhtin continues, every utterance is "in some measure a response to what has already been said about the given topic, on the given issue, even though this responsiveness may not have assumed a clear-cut external expression. . . . After all, our thought itself—philosophical, scientific, artistic— is born and shaped in the process of interaction and struggle with others' thought."[65] Having said this, however, does not mean that one can "understand dialogic relations simplistically or unilaterally, reducing them to contradiction, conflict, polemics, or disagreement."[66]

Second, speech genres, including textual genres, are not simply literary forms but ways of seeing. As Barbara Green puts it, Bakhtin "anthropomorphically but powerfully spoke of genres as having eyes and ears and memories. By such language he conveyed the sense that genres help us visualize and utilize things to which we may have limited insight." Thus, states Green, "Genre is the overall shape of the utterance, the form it has taken to accomplish its purposes."[67] In this way, genres generate and articulate world views, which may also be in conversation with one other. It should also be said that, like a novel or the book of Joshua, secondary speech genres "absorb and digest various primary (simple) genres that have taken form in unmediated speech communion. These primary genres are altered and assume a special character when they enter into complex ones. They lose their immediate relation to actual reality and to the real utterances of others."[68] Furthermore, genre preserves

> undying elements of the *archaic*. . . . [which] are preserved in it only thanks to their constant *renewal*, which is to say, their contemporization. A genre is

---

63. Bakhtin, *Speech Genres*, 71.
64. Ibid., 91.
65. Ibid., 92.
66. Ibid., 125.
67. Green, *Mikhail Bakhtin and Biblical Scholarship*, 55.
68. Bakhtin, *Speech Genres*, 62. Bakhtin provides the example of "everyday dialogue or letters found in a novel. . . . enter into actual reality only via the novel as a whole, that is, as a literary-artistic event and not as everyday life" (ibid.).

always the same and yet not the same, always old and new simultaneously. Genre is reborn and renewed at every new stage in the development of literature and in every individual work of a given genre. This constitutes the life of the genre. Therefore even the archaic elements preserved in a genre are not dead but eternally alive; that is, archaic elements are capable of renewing themselves. A genre lives in the present, but always *remembers* its past, its beginning. Genre is a representative of creative memory in the process of literary development.[69]

Third, "dialogic relations" are not limited to "dialogic speech" strictly defined. Therefore even "monologic speech works" embody "dialogic relations."[70] For this reason, Bakhtin can say, "I hear *voices* in everything and dialogic relations among them."[71] Thus, a work such as a novel may contain a variety of voices: "Authorial speech, the speech of narrators, inserted genres, the speech of characters are merely those fundamental compositional unities with whose help heteroglossia [*raznorečie*] can enter the novel." By these means the text as a whole is characterized by a "dispersion into the rivulets and droplets of social heteroglossia."[72] Through arcane expression such as this, Bakhtin expresses the notion that texts "speak" but not with one voice. Voices inhabit narratives insofar as they answer other voices and elicit yet others.

Fourth, all utterances assume responsivity and answerability. "Any understanding is imbued with response and necessarily elicits it in one form or another: the listener becomes the speaker. . . . Of course, an utterance is not always followed immediately by an articulated response. . . . Sooner or later what is heard and actively understood will find its response in the subsequent speech or behavior of the listener."[73] Thus, "the speaker talks with an expectation of a response, agreement, sympathy, objection, execution, and so forth."[74] It must be noted, also, that even the speaker is also a respondent, since the speaker, or text, is "a link in a very complexly organized chain of other utterances."[75]

Fifth, every utterance has an addressee, "whose responsive understanding the author of the speech work seeks and surpasses," and, at the same time, "the author of the utterance, with a greater or lesser awareness, presupposes a

---

69. Idem, *Problems of Dostoevsky's Poetics*, 106. Bakhtin concludes by noting: "For the correct understanding of a genre, therefore, it is necessary to return to its sources" (ibid.).

70. Idem, *Speech Genres*, 125.

71. Ibid., 169.

72. Idem, *The Dialogic Imagination*, 263. Italicization by the translator.

73. Idem, *Speech Genres*, 68–69.

74. Ibid., 69.

75. Ibid.

higher *superaddressee* . . . , whose absolutely just responsive understanding is presumed, either in some metaphysical distance or in distant historical time." Depending on time, context, and world view, this superaddressee may "assume various ideological expressions (God, absolute truth, the court of dispassionate human conscience, the people, the court of history, science, and so forth)."[76] This

> invisibly present third party . . . is a constitutive aspect of the whole utterance, who, under deeper analysis, can be revealed in it. . . . For the word (and, consequently, for a human being) there is nothing more terrible than a lack of response. Even a word that is known to be false is not absolutely false, and always presupposes an instance that will understand and justify it . . . [Thus,] the word moves ever forward in search of responsive understanding.[77]

Bakhtin's "outsider," who is able to stand outside the debate is able to comprehend what those inside the conversation do not perceive.[78] Readers, therefore, may find themselves at times addressed inside the narrative, and at other times as outsiders coming to understand from a distance. Fluidity of this sort never finalizes the position of the addressee as though he or she stands as mere recipient of a monologic discourse. Rather, the addressee takes on, identifies with, speaks back to, or comprehends from a distance.

Sixth, dialogism assumes an openendedness to the future in order for transformation through dialogical understanding to foster the performance of this understanding in life. As Bakhtin puts it:

> The single adequate form for *verbally expressing* authentic human existence is the *open-ended dialogue*. Life by its very nature is dialogic. To live means to participate in dialogue: to ask questions, to heed, to respond, to agree, and so forth. In this dialogue a person participates wholly and throughout his whole life: with his eyes, lips, hands, soul, spirit, with his whole body and deeds. He invests his entire self in discourse, and this discourse enters into the dialogic fabric of human life, into the world symposium.[79]

It is as though understanding is kinesthetic in such a way that the body remembers its past, honors it, confesses it, and works in the dialogue at healing the relationship between the text, its author, all within the purview of the Spirit (the superaddressee). With this sort of ongoing dialogue in mind when reading the book of Joshua, we may well be able to say with Bakhtin that:

---

76. Ibid., 126.
77. Ibid., 126–27.
78. Ibid., 6–7.
79. Idem, *Problems of Dostoevsky's Poetics*, 293.

There is neither a first nor a last word and there are no limits to the dialogic context (it extends into the boundless past and the boundless future). Even past meanings, that is, those born in the dialogue of the past centuries, can never be stable (finalized, ended once and for all)—they will always change (be renewed) in the process of subsequent, future development of the dialogue. . . . Nothing is absolutely dead: every meaning will have its homecoming festival. The problem of *great time*.[80]

Difficult Conversations with Joshua

I shall now offer six corresponding theses for practicing dialogic relations in conversation with the book of Joshua.[81] Assuming an I-Thou relationship among dialogue partners places readers in a position not simply to submit to the text, or to obey the text, but to wrestle with it and even to advocate for it as one might do in a difficult conversation, in which broken relationships call out for mending.[82] Although it may be difficult, "interpretive charity" will evoke "generosity and patience toward the text"[83] and toward the interpretive traditions that have sometimes exercised abusive power over others because of their reading of the texts.

First, the book of Joshua participates in a larger dialogue. Although this conversation extends across the biblical canon, it begins within the book itself and reverberates outward both backward and forward (although not simply chronologically). Joshua shares in Bakhtin's "great time," which is the "infinite and unfinalized dialogue in which no meaning dies."[84] As such, the book of Joshua reaches beyond itself in space and time, by which it becomes both less and more than it was originally: "in the process of their posthumous life they are enriched with new meanings, new significance: it is as though these works outgrow what they were in the epoch of their creation."[85] The conversation ranges widely, including Joshua's appropriation of ancient Near Eastern con-

---

80. Idem, *Speech Genres*, 170.

81. Each of these points could be developed in more detail. Along the way I will suggest how these dialogical practices are already being engaged, or where they might more fruitfully be practiced so as to attend to the hospitality of dialogical hermeneutics.

82. This is the stance of Ellen F. Davis, who suggests that we, like the biblical writers themselves, practice "the artful negotiation of difficulty" ("Critical Traditioning: Seeking an Inner Biblical Hermeneutic," *AThR* 82 [2000] 736; reprinted in *The Art of Reading Scripture* [ed. E. Davis and R. B. Hays; Grand Rapids: Eerdmans, 2003] 163–80). Earlier in the article, she suggests that "no biblical text may be safely repudiated as a potential source of edification for the Church" (p. 734).

83. Ibid., 749.

84. Bakhtin, *Speech Genres*, 169.

85. Ibid., 4.

quest accounts,[86] innerbiblical interpretation,[87] and the history of the text's reception and interpretation.[88] This all-encompassing dialogue reflects what was going on within ancient Israel itself, where, as Ellen Davis puts it, a "critical traditioning" process was at work that came to terms with difficult texts. This innerbiblical dialogue does not eliminate the conquest tradition but submits it to critique[89] or draws it into a figural network or transposes it into another key.[90] In other words, no epoch has either the first word or the last word on the book of Joshua. Because the book of Joshua is already a response to previous (or other) utterances, it also anticipates responses that may offer insights that Joshua itself is not able to provide.[91] For this insight we turn to Bakhtin's notion of genres as ways of seeing.

Second, because the book of Joshua is a "secondary genre," it absorbs archaic as well as other genres so as to generate something new. As Newsom

86. K. Lawson Younger Jr., *Ancient Conquest Accounts: A Study in Ancient Near Eastern and Biblical History Writing* (JSOTSup 98; Sheffield: Sheffield Academic Press, 1990).

87. Michael Fishbane, *Biblical Interpretation in Ancient Israel* (Oxford: Clarendon, 1985); and Polzin, *Moses and the Deuteronomist*.

88. From the early church fathers to John Calvin to global and postcolonial perspectives, the book of Joshua has always been a site of contested readings. See, for example, John R. Franke, ed., *Joshua, Judges, Ruth, 1–2 Samuel* (ACCS 4; Downers Grove, IL: InterVarsity, 2005); and Ronald Goetz, "Joshua, Calvin, and Genocide," *ThTo* 32 (1975) 263–74. The recent book by Cowles, Merrill, Gard, and Longman, *Show Them No Mercy: Four Views on God and Canaanite Genocide*, also belongs to the conversation, as does the "global" commentary of Dora Mbuwayesango ("Joshua," in *Global Bible Commentary* [ed. Daniel Patte; Nashville: Abingdon, 2004]) and the critical reflections of Robert Allen Warrior, "A Native American Perspective: Canaanites, Cowboys, and Indians," in *Voices from the Margin: Interpreting the Bible in the Third World* (ed. R. S. Sugirtharajah; 2nd ed.; Maryknoll, NY: Orbis, 1991) 277–85.

89. Davis, "Critical Traditioning," 739. Davis continues:

> A living tradition is a potentially courageous form of shared consciousness, because a tradition, in contrast to an ideology, preserves (in some form) our mistakes, our atrocities, as well as our insights and moral victories. Moreover, with its habit of retention, a tradition preserves side by side the disagreements that are still unresolved in the present. So the price that must be paid by those who are (from a biblical perspective) privileged to live within a tradition, is accepting a high degree of inherent tension. The possibility open to them, which is not open to committed ideologues, is repentance . . . *metanoia*, literally "a change of mind." (pp. 739–40)

90. On the richness of the dialogue through time, see Martin Jan Mulder, ed., *Mikra: Text, Translation, Reading and Interpretation of the Hebrew Bible in Ancient Judaism and Early Christianity* (Philadelphia: Fortress, 1988). On figural reading, see John David Dawson, *Christian Figural Reading and the Fashioning of Identity* (Berkeley: University of California Press, 2002); and Frances M. Young, *Biblical Exegesis and the Formation of Christian Culture* (Cambridge: Cambridge University Press, 1997).

91. James Sanders's writings reflect a similar understanding. See especially his overview in "Canon as Dialogue," in *The Bible at Qumran: Text, Shape, and Interpretation* (ed. Peter W. Flint; Grand Rapids: Eerdmans, 2001) 7–26.

puts it, "every instance of a genre can be understood as a reply to other instances of that genre and as a reply to other genres, whether or not self-
consciously conceived of as such. The dialogical relationship carries forward
the ever changing configuration of the genre."[92] Although many primary
genres have been incorporated into the book of Joshua, I will illustrate my
point by referring to Joshua's incorporation of conquest accounts.[93] As Lawson
Younger has demonstrated, Joshua's conquest accounts share in all of the
generic conventions of ancient Near Eastern conquest accounts. For example,
Joshua's conquest accounts share with the Mesha Inscription both theological
assumptions about the relationship among deity, people, and land and warfare
world view and practices (e.g., *ḥērem*).[94] As it does so, Joshua also incorporates
conventional conquest narratives in conversation with other genres within the
book itself.

Understood as participating in a conversation that includes ancient Near
Eastern conquest accounts, the book of Joshua is not simply an Israelite creation that stands in contrast to a text such as the Moabite Mesha Inscription.
The contexts within which both "texts" derive are not alien to one another.
They are neighbors. They share essentially the same language. Mark S. Smith
even suggests that the ancient texts are not mere foils to the Bible. Rather, the
world view of those texts are Israelite world views in the process of (trans)-
formation. "This polytheistic context was Israel's own, not simply one it was
combating because of other peoples and their deities. Israel's own production
of what came to be viewed as revelation involved a process of dialogue and
debate with many currents within its own culture and beyond."[95]

This conversation generates questions about the warfare world view implied
by the conquest account genre. In other words, one cannot read the conquest
accounts in Joshua at face value as though they convey some abstract truth

---

92. Carol Newsom, "Spying out the Land: A Report from Genology," in *Bakhtin and Genre Theory in Biblical Studies* (ed. Roland Boer; SemeiaSt 63; Atlanta: SBL, 2007) 28.

93. Joshua incorporates dialogues, short stories, ethnographic and geographic lists, sermonic covenant speeches, death notices, and so on.

94. Younger, *Ancient Conquest Accounts*. See also Lori Rowlett, *Joshua and the Rhetoric of Vio-lence: A New Historicist Analysis* (JSOTSup 226; Sheffield: Sheffield Academic Press, 1996); John Van Seters, "Joshua's Campaign of Canaan and Near Eastern Historiography," *SJOT* 2 (1990) 1–12; Jeffrey J. Niehaus, "Joshua and Ancient Near Eastern Warfare," *JETS* 31 (1988) 37–50.

95. Mark S. Smith, *The Memoirs of God: History, Memory, and the Experience of the Divine in Ancient Israel* (Minneapolis: Fortress, 2004) 169. Smith even suggests that ancient Near Eastern texts function as "the Old Testament of the Old Testament" (borrowing from the title of a book by R. W. L. Moberly). Smith continues as though he were borrowing from Bakhtin: "Such interaction involves adoption from others and conflict with others, as well as various sorts of engagement in between" (p. 169).

about God or warfare. These accounts have been drawn into a conversation within a longer narrative, in which other topics are actually more significant than the conquest world view itself (e.g., faithfulness to *torah*, obedience to the words/voice of the Lord, covenanting with a Canaanite woman and Gibeonite strangers, celebrating Passover, crossing the Jordan River as the previous generation had crossed the Red Sea, trust in Yahweh, and so on). The conquest accounts, although rife with distasteful rhetoric and offensive theological assumptions, do not have either the first or the last word in the book of Joshua. In fact, the whole book of Joshua subordinates the conquest accounts to other voices, a topic to which we turn next.[96]

Third, the voices reflected in the book of Joshua encompass the genres as well as the characters, the narrator, and the perspectives and echoes of voices from outside the text. Much of the book reflects a conversation with the book of Deuteronomy.[97] Tensions inherent within the book of Joshua, for example, between assertions of complete and incomplete conquest also reflect voices in a dialogical engagement. In other words, the book of Joshua is not a monological text.[98] Voices within Joshua are reflected in an innerbiblical conversation

---

96. Many of the motifs I have mentioned have been explored in depth, particularly by Polzin, *Moses and the Deuteronomist*; Gordon Mitchell, *Together in the Land: A Reading of the Book of Joshua* (JSOTSup 134; Sheffield: Sheffield Academic Press, 1993); Lawson G. Stone, "Ethical and Apologetic Tendencies in the Redaction of the Book of Joshua," *CBQ* 53 (1991) 25–36; and Daniel L. Hawk, *Every Promise Fulfilled: Contesting Plots in Joshua* (Literary Currents in Biblical Interpretation; Louisville: Westminster/John Knox, 1991).

97. Robert Polzin's *Moses and the Deuteronomist* assumes two voices in Joshua—that of Moses, which he calls "authoritative dogmatism," and that of the narrator, or "critical traditionalism." Although these two voices serve to highlight the tensions between Deuteronomy and Joshua, more could be said about how other voices, both within and outside Joshua, reverberate through the conversation elicited within the book. The stories in the book of Joshua highlight the reversal of expectations about Canaanites (Rahab and the Gibeonites) and Israelites (the two and a half Transjordanian tribes and Achan). According to Polzin, "exceptional outsiders" destabilize the assumption about who constitutes "Israel" and serve to question both ethnic and geographical boundaries. Moreover, the book of Joshua presents a narrative that runs counter to the exclusive voice of Deuteronomy except on one point—exclusive allegiance to Yahweh.

98. Mitchell (*Together in the Land*) explores the tension between the extermination of the Canaanites and the fact that many remain in the land. Hawk (*Every Promise Fulfilled*) develops the notion of "contesting plots" in Joshua. Hauch (*Text and Contexts*) develops a rich analysis of the "apparent" story of the progress of law and the "submerged" story that "'covertly' questions it" (p. 75). Hauch explains that

the dialogic between the apparent and the submerged stories, between the point and the counterpoint, is one that reassesses the law, not only in terms of the promise, but also in terms of the original blessing and the curse, the condition of the human heart and the contingencies of historical existence. In the process another fuller dialogue is generated between justice and mercy, blessing and curse, memory and desire, and yes, between promise and law. (pp. 76–77)

that ranges widely throughout the OT.[99] These echoes imply Bakhtin's notion of "great time," during which many voices take up responses to the enigma that "the secret things belong to the LORD our God," yet even the "revealed things," life under divine instruction (*torah*), may not be as straightforward as one might imagine (Deut 29:29). The discernment of those secret things is the task of the community in exile and the community in the many contexts where the conversation embraces the painful questions and elusive answers elicited by the text.[100] Of course all of these are innerbiblical voices and voices of implied readers. The conversation continues in the dialogue with interpreters through time.

Fourth, all utterances assume responsivity and answerability. The internal structure of the book of Joshua assumes responsivity. God's address to Joshua invites his (and our) response because we, like Solomon after him, continue to be addressed by this word—a word that the two and a half tribes are invited to "remember" (1:13) and to which they respond with words of commitment. Joshua 1 not only begins a dialogical narrative that embraces voices within but also evokes voices outside the text. Throughout the narrative from this point on we are drawn into responses that invite our attention and our own answers. This give and take within the dialogue of and with the text is not transparent

---

99. A few examples will have to suffice. (1) The death reports of Joseph and Joshua frame the exodus-conquest narrative (Gen 50:24–26; Josh 24:29; Judg 2:8). Both are 110 years old at death (the only such notices in the OT). And the narratives that follow both death reports tell of "the forgetfulness of those who arose afterward" (Hauch, *Text and Context*, 64–65). (2) The conversation between Joshua and the man with the drawn sword (5:13–15) echoes the incident at the burning bush (Exod 3:5–6) but with a twist. As Moses wishes to know the name of God, Joshua wishes confirmation of the battle's outcome. The "no" of the commander allows for no unambiguous answer. (3) The fact that Joshua and Josiah are "twins" and that Joshua "succeeds" whereas Josiah "fails" suggests that the larger narrative of Israel's entry into and exile from the land must be mapped by a complex dialogue of divine word and human response that is not simply summed up by the correlation of obedience to success. (4) The Lord's commission to Joshua in chap. 1 is taken up in Joshua's charge to the people in 23:6 and again only by David in 2 Kgs 2:2–4, a narrative that goes on to present both Solomon's success (based on the gift of wisdom) and the failure of Solomon to heed the gift of torah (see Deut 17:14–20; 1 Kgs 4:22–28; 10:26–29; 11:4–8). This conversation continues on in Mic 4:1–5, where the torah-shaped life brings a restful life under vine and fig tree that stands in ironic tension with the same effects brought about by Solomon's militaristic enterprise (see Walter Brueggemann, "Vine and Fig Tree: A Case Study in Imagination and Criticism," *CBQ* 43 [1981] 188–204. (5) Joshua's warning that the people could "perish from this good land" (23:13) echoes the implied ending of the narrative of 2 Kings, which had been more or less predicted in Moses' speeches in Deuteronomy (4:26–30; 29:28). (6) The poetic critique of warfare offers a counterimaginative voice that speaks even about Yahweh's character as warrior and at the same time as one who brings wars to a final end (e.g., Ps 46:8–11; Isa 2:2–4; Hos 2:18).

100. See the list of questions evoked in the exilic context of reading by Terence E. Fretheim in his *Deuteronomic History* (Nashville: Abingdon, 1983) 46–47.

with regard to its *telos* or goal. The commander of the army of the LORD says "no" to Joshua's either/or (5:13–15). Rahab and Achan are "twins" in the conversation about inside and outside, confession and complicity. The Gibeonites employ comic deception and the Israelites discern badly, yet the bumbling conversation problematizes the law of total extermination. The altar-building incident at the border provides a splendid example of talking past one another. Who knows what misunderstandings saved Israel that day (22:31)? Both Joshua's assertion "You cannot serve the LORD" (24:19) and Israel's vigorous reply (24:21) echo a hope hardly discernible that wonders who really knows whether they will all "perish from this good land" or not (23:13). Although responsivity and answerability begin within the text and reverberate outward, backward, and forward through the grand narrative, later generations of readers end up finding themselves written into that same dynamic and evocative interactivity.

Fifth, this reciprocity both assumes an addressee and imagines a super-addressee. Whether the two and a half tribes or Rahab, whether Achan or the Gibeonites, whether Joshua himself or all Israel, the reader and overhearer stand responsive or with hardened heart. The site of address, be it Adam and Eve in the garden or Joshua and Israel in the land may also become Adam and Eve outside the garden and Israel in exile. And if God is, at times, a character whose voice is heard inside the story, God may also be an addressee—one who comprehends the whole—who responds to the people who remember the voice that said "you will not live long on it but will be utterly destroyed" (Deut 4:26) with the contervoice, "he will neither abandon you nor destroy you" (Deut 4:31). The addressee who hears the possibility of "perishing" (Josh 23:13) and of being "destroyed" (23:15) may well discover in Babylonian Exile that even the confessions and commitments and good will of the "we will serve the LORD" (Josh 24:21) or the good efforts of Josiah to imitate Joshua may not be able fully to comprehend an adequate response except to listen to the one who promises, even then, not to abandon. The "rest" partially received as gift and lost remains elusively present to those who remain attentive to the word spoken and received and who, with the One who comprehends all but who cannot be comprehended, remain fiercely loyal even when obedience and disobedience do not guarantee an outcome beyond anticipation of the gift and longing for its arrival.

Sixth, dialogism as hospitable hermeneutical practice means that there is no first and last word. Interpretation of Scripture's difficult texts cannot wrest meaning apart from the dialogue, as though extracting something external to the dialogue can itself change reality or fully comprehend God's ways. Can God command genocide? Is history the site of divine justice? Do human actions count for anything at all? Is the gift dependent on the Othering of the non-elect and the elimination of the anti-elect?[101] Or is the innerbiblical conversation about divine sanction of genocide a conversation about coming to terms with historic evil in the world—evil that refuses to be conceptualized but that must be named with real names and real people? Is the conversation unending and unfinalizable because this coming to terms is in so many ways beyond the human capacity either to grasp or to do anything about it? Joshua's genocide is not a "primitive holdover" but a current reality that turns both ways: either to take matters in one's own hands in killing the dangerous other in God's name or "to yearn for God's justice to prevail over evils so irrational that they seem demonic" or even divine.[102]

This dangerous appropriation juxtaposed with or identified with holy longing has characterized the history of interpretation of the conquest narratives and the land acquisition narrative of the book of Joshua.[103] Because this kind of monologization of the book of Joshua—assuming it speaks with one prescriptive voice—has been common, it behooves all readers to confess the same proclivity in us. We do well to remember, however, that the history of engagement with the land acquisition and conquest narratives has not unilaterally assumed a violent appropriation. Those transpositions have assumed that the biblical canon is itself hospitable to reimagination and counterimagination. Voices negotiate and reconcile, even when at the beginning of the conversation positions seemed hardened.[104] Especially because canon itself is dia-

    101. For an in-depth reflection on the distinction among elect, non-elect and anti-elect, see Joel Kaminsky, *Yet I Loved Jacob: Reclaiming the Biblical Concept of Election* (Nashville: Abingdon, 2007), especially chap. 7, "The Anti-elect in the Hebrew Bible."
    102. Ibid., 116.
    103. Bainton, *Christian Attitudes toward War and Peace*, 165–70; Michael Prior, *The Bible and Colonialism: A Moral Critique* (The Biblical Seminar 48; Sheffield: Sheffield Academic Press, 1997); Donald Hartman Akenson, *God's Peoples: Covenant and Land in South Africa, Israel, and Ulster* (Ithaca, NY: Cornell University Press, 1992); R. Douglas Francis and Chris Kitzan, eds., *The Prairie West as Promised Land* (Calgary: University of Calgary Press, 2007); and Nur Masalha, *The Bible and Zionism: Invented Traditions, Archaeology and Post-Colonialism in Israel-Palestine* (New York: Zed, 2007).
    104. Even the war texts from Qumran do not assume a monologized conquest tradition. See Jean Duhaime, *The War Texts: 1QM and Related Manuscripts* (Companion to the Qumran Scrolls 6; London: T. & T. Clark, 2004). Postbiblical Jewish literature "rewrites" and thereby offers a counter-voice to a monological reading of violence. See Betsy Halpern-Amaru, *Rewriting the Bible: Land and Covenant in Postbiblical Jewish Literature* (Valley Forge, PA: Trinity Press International, 1994). This sort of reimagining of alternative voices in the conversation is reflected in the "spiritual conflict" tradition within both Jewish and Christian (including NT) theological reflection. See, for example, Tom Yoder Neufeld, *'Put on the Armour of God': The Divine Warrior from Isaiah to Ephesians* (JSNTSup 140; Sheffield: Sheffield Academic Press, 1997); Gordon M.

logical, hearing multiple voices becomes paradigmatic for continuing rather than closing down the conversation, even when tempted by the compulsion to fix God's character *either* as warrior or as peacemaker. The biblical canon does not conceal its voices, and in not doing so, voices are elicited and evoked, drawn out and provoked. By embracing the opportunity of dialogue, we set ourselves free from the danger of word-idolatry in order to attend to the Word that cannot be fixed by words themselves but must, rather, be eaten and performed.

The warfare paradigm is not taken up unchanged in Scripture, nor does it offer a pattern for practice. Because Scripture participates in an unending dialogue that anticipates the end of all violence in the love of God, I have not attempted in this essay to solve the puzzle of the conquest narratives in the book of Joshua. I have suggested, with Bakhtin, that texts and readers are conversation partners in a hospitable dialogical space, an unfinished story, a striving in, with, against, and for an ending that is a "rest" not yet achieved. There is no idea, no message, no principle, and no moral of the story apart from the conversation with the text in which everything we tend to reduce to one thing must be rejected in favor of the hope that, although we may well perish, the Voice who continues to beckon us forward will never let us go (Deut 4:31). In other words, Scripture participates in a divine condescension, a *kenosis*.[105] It offers us utterances that call out for response and counterimagination. Even particular divine words do not say anything without the dialogue in which they are embedded. Fragments cannot tell the truth. Only the entirety can reveal the truth, which according to Bakhtin and the Bible is unfinalizable because the divine purpose strives within us for an end beyond naming. Even the warfare texts have a place at the table, but only as we also participate in the reciprocal hospitality and confess our own complicity in violent appropriation. We live in hope, not because the book of Joshua has the answer, but because in its own ambiguity it demonstrates openness to the questions.

Zerbe, *Non-retaliation in Early Jewish and New Testament Texts: Ethical Themes in Social Contexts* (JSPSup 13; Sheffield: Sheffield Academic Press, 1993); and Gregory A. Boyd, *God at War: The Bible and Spiritual Conflict* (Downers Grove, IL: InterVarsity, 1997).

105. "Scripture is God accountable," writes Telford Work. "The Bible is part of our voyage home, a point of departure for idolaters and a means of sustenance for weary pilgrims. And that must mean that in delivering it to the world, God makes his words vulnerable, for a time, to abuse" (*Living and Active: Scripture in the Economy of Salvation* [Grand Rapids: Eerdmans, 2002] 64). Throughout the book, Work develops a theology of a vulnerable text in which a vulnerable God, in Christ, transforms even the violence of the "oppressive history" (pp. 209–10). I would add, however, that Jesus is the embodiment of the Word that was already in conversation, striving to transform swords into plowshares.

Scripture does not unambiguously reveal God. Like Moses on the mountain, we are shielded from full revelation. We catch only glimpses of God's back side. Rather, Scripture invites us into a conversation, an argument, a give and take in which we are honored as partners in God's great hope that all will one day be restored to its rightful wholeness. In the meantime, we, like Abraham and Moses, continue to argue with God when Scripture's articulation of God's ways remains hidden by a text in travail. When we engage the dialogue in humility and hospitality, our lives become "congruent with the text"[106] because the text itself is dialogue. We have eaten the book. We have entered the drama.

---

106. Peterson, *Eat This Book*, 28.

Index of Authors

Index of Scripture

New Testament

green press
INITIATIVE

Bench 12" ~~long~~ high
26" long

rouse drums $7"